GW01464170

Laudate

a hymn book for the liturgy

P RAISE GOD IN HIS HOLY PLACE,
  SING praise in the mighty heavens.
  SING praise for God's powerful deeds,
praise God's surpassing greatness.

SING praise with sound of trumpet,
SING praise with lute and harp.
SING praise with timbrel and dance,
SING praise with strings and pipes.

SING praise with resounding cymbals,
SING praise with clashing of cymbals.
LET everything that lives and that breathes
give praise to the LORD. Alleluia!

Psalm 150

Decani Music

Decani Music, Oak House, 70 High Street, Brandon, Suffolk IP27 0AU

First published in 1999 by Decani Music. 5th reprint with corrections April 2004

ISBN   1 900 314 05 3 Paperback edition
              1 900 31406 1 PVC covered edition

Compilation and editorial content © 1999 Decani Music.

Edited by Stephen Dean. Editorial Advisers: Jennifer Burridge Susan Dean, Ellen Flynn, Martin Foster, Peter Gallacher, Philip Jakob, Paul Kenny, Julie McCann, Peter McGrail

With grateful thanks to Ed Harris and John Limb

Printed by the Bath Press, Lower Bristol Road, Bath BA2 3BL

Thanks are given to copyright holders who have granted permission for their work to be used in this book. Every effort has been made to contact copyright holders. If there any errors or omissions we apologise, and will rectify them in future editions.

Addresses of main copyright holders

See page 399 on for full copyright details

Ateliers et Presses de Taizé: administered in UK and Ireland by Calamus

Benedictine Foundation of the State of Vermont, via Calamus

Boosey & Hawkes Ltd. 295 Regent Street, London W1R 8JH

Bishops' Conference of England and Wales: contact The Liturgy Office, 39 Eccleston Square, London SW1V 1PL

Burns & Oates Ltd: part of Continnum

Cassell plc, part of Continnum

Christian Conference of Asia, Pak Tin Village, Mei Tin Road, Shatin, N.T., Hong Kong

Church Hymnal Corporation, 800 Second Avenue at 42nd Street, New York NY10017

The Continuum International Publishing Group Ltd,, The Tower Buiding, 11 York Road, London SE1 7NX

CopyCare, P.O. Box 77, Hailsham, East Sussex, BN27 3EF

Dean, Stephen via Calamus

G.I.A. Publications Inc. administered in UK and Ireland by Calamus

Grail (England), The: administered by A.P. Watt Ltd, 20 John Street, London WC1N 2DR,

Hope Publishing Co. via Copycare

Hymns Ancient & Modern. St Mary's Works, St Mary''s Plain, Norwich NR3 3BH

International Committee on English in the Liturgy (ICEL) Inc., 1522 K Street, N.W. Suite 1000, Washington D.C. 20005-1202 USA. For non-commercial reprint requests apply to The Liturgy Office, 39 Eccleston Square, London SW1V 1PL

Josef Weinberger Ltd, 12-14 Mortimer St London W1N 7RD

Kevin Mayhew Ltd., Buxhall, Stowmarket, Suffolk IP14 3DJ

Kingsway's Thankyou Music, Lottbridge Drove, Eastbourne, E.Sussex BN23 6NT

Jubilate Hymns, 13 Stoddart Avenue, Southampton SO19 4ED

McCrimmon Publishing Co. Ltd, 10-12 High Street, Great Wakering, Essex, SS3 0EQ

National Council of Churches of Christ, Division of Christian Education, 475 Riverside Drive, New York NY10027

Novello & Co Ltd (also J. Curwen & Sons) 8/9 Frith Street, London W1V 5TZ

OCP Publications: administered in UK and Ireland by Calamus

Oxford University Press, Hymn Copyright Department, Great Clarendon Street, Oxford OX2 6DP

Sisters of St Mary of Namur, 909 West Shaw, Fort Worth, Texas 76110 USA

Stainer & Bell Ltd. PO Box 110 Victoria House, 23 Gruneisen Road, London N3 1DZ

Stanbrook Abbey (Liturgical Secretary), Callow End, Worcester WR2 4TD

Wild Goose Resource Group, Iona Community, 4th Floor, Savoy House, 140 Sauciehall Street, Glasgow G2 3DH

Timothy Dudley-Smith, 9 Ashlands, Ford, Salisbury SP4 6DY (no telephone calls please)

World Library Publications, Inc., 3825 N. Willow Road, Schiller Park. Il 60176-9936. In UK: via Calamus A.P.Watt Ltd, 20 John Street, London WC1N 2DR

Asking permission to reproduce

You must *always* obtain permission to reproduce copyright music or words. It is possible, though, to obtain an annual Copyright Licence which removes the necessity of applying for every item separately. All but a few of the items in this book are covered by one of two schemes, the Christian Copyright Licence (CCLI) and Calamus. The Calamus licence allows reproduction of words and melody line and covers mainly G.I.A., OCP, (and New Dawn), Taizé, McCrimmon, Weston Priory, World Libraryand many individual composers. CCLI has two licences: one which allows reproduction of words only, and an add-on licence which allows the limited use of music as well. It covers Mayhew, OUP, Stainer & Bell, Kingsway's Thankyou, Copycare, Jubilate and many others not in this book. For fuller details apply to:

CALAMUS, Oak House, 70 High Street, Brandon, Suffolk IP27 0AU. Phone 01842 819830, fax 01842 819832

CHRISTIAN COPYRIGHT LICENSING INTERNA-TIONAL, 26 Gildredge Road, Eastbourne, East Sussex BN21 4SA. Phone 01323 417711, fax 01323 417722

Contents

LAUDATE is arranged by category. Some hymns however are suitable for use in more than one category, and occasionally a 'See also..' cross-reference line will be found. This should help plan music for any liturgical occasion. There are also some planning guidelines on pp. 405-9.

LITURGY OF THE HOURS

'Public and common prayer by the people of God is rightly considered to be among the primary duties of the Church.' (*General Instruction on the Liturgy of the Hours, §1.*) This prayer which we learn from Christ's example and bidding, has, since the earliest days of the Church, taken the form of prayer at set times of day. This section provides a means of such prayer. Based on the *Liturgy of the Hours,* it may be used in conjunction with it or on its own. The Liturgy of the Hours is a prayer of *praise and petition*, with psalmody and intercession as its main elements.

MORNING PRAYER

1   Introduction

All make the sign of the cross on their lips

O Lord,   o-pen our   lips,   and we   shall praise your   name.

Alternative introduction: O Lord come to our help (no 11)

2   Morning Hymn I

1 Now that the daylight fills the sky,
we lift our hearts to God on high,
that God in all we do and say
would keep us free from harm today.

2 O Lord, restrain our tongues from strife,
from wrath and anger shield our life;
and guard with watchful care our eyes
that we will choose from all that's wise.

3 O may our inmost hearts be pure,
from thoughts of folly be secure,
and all our pow'rs devoted be
to deeds of love, that keep us free.

4 So we, when this day's work is o'er,
and shades of night return once more,
our path of trial safely trod,
shall give the glory to our God.

5 All praise to God the Father be,
and praise the Son eternally,
whom with the Spirit we adore,
One God alone, for evermore.
Latin, 8th C; tr. J.M. Neale (1818-66), alt

3   Morning Hymn II

1 To God with gladness sing
your Rock and Saviour bless
within your temple bring
your songs of thankfulness!
O God of might, to you we sing,
enthroned as King on heaven's height!

2 He cradles in his hand
the heights and depths of earth;
he made the sea and land
he brought the world to birth!
O God most high, we are your sheep,
on us you keep your shepherd's eye.

3 Your heav'nly Father praise,
acclaim his only Son,
your voice in homage raise
to him who makes all one!
O dove of peace, on us descend
that strife may end and joy increase!

Psalm 95, versified by James Quinn, S.J.

Other morning hymns: 668-673

Morning Thanksgiving (optional)
The leader may give thanks for the day.

Psalmody

*One or more psalms are now sung, taken from the Office of the Day, or selections
from the Psalter. (See Psalm Index on p. 409). A suggested weekly cycle is:*

Sunday: 63, Daniel 3, or 148
Monday: Psalm 5, 28 or 96
Tuesday: Psalm 24, 65 or 144
Wednesday: Psalm 47, 92 or 97

Thursday: Psalm 57, 147a
Friday: Psalm 51 ,100
Saturday: Psalm 8, or 150

4   Psalm 63:2-9

Antiphon I

At dawn I look— to you, my God, to be— my strength this day.

Antiphon 2

My soul is— thirsting for you, O— Lord,— thir-sting for you, my God.—

Psalm tone

omit for last stanza

Gelineau tone

omit for last stanza

2 O Gód, you are my Gód, for you I lóng;
   for yóu my sóul is thírsting.
   My bódy pínes for yóu
   like a drý, weary lánd without wáter.
3 So I gáze on yóu in the sánctuary
   to sée your stréngth and your glóry.

4 For your lóve is bétter than lífe,
   my líps will spéak your práise.
5 So I will bléss you all my lífe,
   in your náme I will líft up my hánds.
6 My sóul shall be fílled as with a bánquet,
   my móuth shall práise you with jóy.

Antiphon 2 & Psalmtone by Stephen Dean. Antiphon 2 by Richard Proulx. Psalmtone 2 by Joseph Gelineau, S.J. Text: The Grail

⁷ On my béd I remémber yóu.
On yóu I múse through the níght
⁸ for yóu have béen my hélp;
in the shádow of your wíngs I rejóice.
⁹ My sóul clíngs to yóu;
your ríght hand hólds me fást.

Give práise to the Fáther Almíghty,
to his Són, Jesus Chríst the Lórd;
to the Spírit who dwélls in our héarts
both nów and for éver, Amén..

Other settings of Psalm 62 (63): My soul is
thirsting (49), Your love is finer than life (213).

Psalm Prayer

(optional)   After each psalm there may be a prayer, read by the leader, to which all answer Amen.

5   **Psalm 150** *(psalmtone version)*

Let ev' - ry-thing that lives   praise   the   Lord.

Psalm tone

Gelineau tone

¹ Praise Gód in his hóly pláce,
Sing práise in the míghty héavens.
² Sing práise for God's pówerful déeds,
práise God's surpássing gréatness.

³ Sing práise with sóund of trúmpet,
Sing práise with lúte and hárp.
⁴ Sing práise with tímbrel and dánce,
Sing práise with stríngs and pípes.

⁵ Sing práise with resóunding cymbals,
Sing práise with cláshing of cymbals.
⁶ Let éverything that líves and that bréathes
give práise to the Lórd. Amén.

Give práise to the Fáther Almíghty,
to his Són, Jesus Chríst the Lórd;
to the Spírit who dwélls in our héarts
both nów and for éver, Amén..

Antiphon by A. Gregory Murray, O.S.B..Psalmtone 1: Laurence Bévenot, O.S.B. Psalmtone 2: J.Gelineau, S.J.. Text: The Grail

6   **Psalm 150** *(metrical version)*

1 Blest be the Lord our God!
with joy let heaven ring;
Before his presence let all the earth
its songs of homage bring!
His mighty deeds be told;
his majesty be praised;
to God enthroned in heavenly light
let every voice be raised.

2 All that has life and breath
give thanks with heartfelt songs
to him let all creation sing
to whom all praise belongs!
Acclaim the Father's love,
who gave us Christ his Son;
praise too, the Spirit giv'n by both,
with both forever one.

Psalm 150, versified by James Quinn S.J.

The Word of God

A short scripture passage is read, taken from the Office of the Day or another source.

7 Gospel Canticle: The Benedictus Luke 1:68-75 *(chant version)*

Vi - sit us, O Lord, like the dawn from on high;
guide us, guide us in - to the way of peace.

Blessed be the Lord, the God of Israel!
Omit B & C
He has visited his people and redeemed
them.

He has raised up for us a mighty saviour
in the house of David his servant,
as he promised by the lips of holy men,
those who were his prophets from of old.

A saviour who would free us from our foes,
from the hands of all who hate us.
So his love for our fathers is fulfilled
and his holy covenant remembered.

He swore to Abraham our father to grant us,
that free from fear, and saved from the
hands of our foes,
we might serve him in holiness and justice
all the days of our life in his presence.

As for you, little child,
you shall be called a prophet of God, the
Most High.
You shall go ahead of the Lord
to prepare his ways before him.

To make known to his people their salvation
through forgiveness of all their sins,
the loving-kindness of the heart of our God
who visits us like the dawn from on high.

He will give light to those in darkness,
those who dwell in the shadow of death,
omit C
and guide us into the way of peace.

Glory be to the Father, and to the Son,
and to the Holy Spirit,
as it was in the beginning, is now and ever
shall be,
world without end. Amen.

Music by Stephen Dean. Text: The Grail

8 The Benedictus *(metrical version)*

1 Now bless the God of Israel,
who comes in love and power,
who raises from the royal house
deliv'rance in this hour.
Through holy prophets God has sworn
to free us from alarm,
to save us from the heavy hand
of all who wish us harm.

2 Remembering the covenant
God rescues us from fear,
that we might serve in holiness
and peace from year to year:
and you, my child, shall go before
to preach, to prophesy,
that all may know the tender love,
the grace of God most high.

3 In tender mercy, God will send
   the dayspring from on high,
   our rising sun, the light of life
   for those who sit and sigh.

God comes to guide our way to peace,
that death shall reign no more,
sing praises to the Holy One!
O worship and adore.

Versified by Ruth Duck

A further version: Blest be the Lord, the God of Israel (83)

Intercessions

The leader now introduces the Intercessions, and all make the response.

9 **Response to the Intercessions**

Fa - ther, may your king-dom come!

Intercessions (and responses) may be taken from the Office for the Day or another source (see 26-29, 73 (Advent), 221, 547-552, 740, 928-9)

The Leader collects all the petitions in the Our Father which may be said or sung.

10 **Lord's Prayer** (modern text)

Our Fa-ther in hea - ven, hal - lowed be your name, your king - dom come,

your will be done, on earth as in hea - ven. Give us to -

day our dai-ly bread. For-give us our sins as we for-give those who sin___ a -

gainst__ us. Save us from the time of trial and de - li - ver us from e - vil.

Other versions: 30, 587-88

Concluding Prayer

The prayer is taken from the Office of the Day or another source. All respond **Amen.**

Blessing

When a priest or deacon presides at Morning Prayer, a blessing is given. When a lay person presides, the conclusion is as follows:

The Lord bless us, and keep us from all evil, and bring us to everlasting life.
Amen.

Evening Prayer

Evening Prayer may begin with the Introduction or with a Service of Light as at no. 13 on.

11 Introduction

Leader:

O God, come to our aid.

All:

O Lord, make haste to help us. Glory be to the Father, the Son and the Holy Spirit, as it was in the beginning, is

( ) *Omitted during Lent*

now and ev-er shall be, world with-out end, A-men. [Alle-lu - ia].

12 Evening Hymn

Philip Gaisford, O.S.B.

1. In the qui-et of the eve-ning, now the work of day is done, turn our thoughts, most lo-ving Fa-ther to the work of Christ, your Son.

2 In our wandering we have travelled
far from you throughout the day,
yet forgiving all, you sent us
Christ to lead us, Christ the way.

3 When our ignorance is danger,
or we credit worldly lies,
then, with timely care, you give us
Christ the truth to make us wise.

4 As the light of day is fading,
Father, keep us in your sight;
pierce the dark of sin with splendour
shining out from Christ the light.

5 Glory be to God the Father,
glory be to God the Son,
glory be to God the Spirit,
glory to the Three in One.

Patrick Lee

Other hymns for evening, 674-682

Continue with Psalmody, no. 17 on

Service of Light (Lucernarium)

13 Greeting

Je - sus Christ is the light of the world!
A light the dark - ness can - not o - ver - power!

14 Hymn to Christ the Light (1st version)

1 O gracious Light, Lord Jesus Christ,
in you the Father's glory shone.
Immortal, holy, blest is he,
and blest are you, his only Son.

2 Now sunset comes, but light shines forth,
the lamps are lit to pierce the night.
Praise Father, Son and Spirit: God
who dwells in the eternal light.

3 Worthy are you of endless praise,
O Son of God, Life-giving Lord:
wherefore you are through all the earth
and in the highest heaven adored.

Greek, 3rd Century, tr. F. Bland Tucker (1895-1984)

15 Hymn to Christ the Light (2nd version)

1. Light of glad - ness, shi - ning ra - diance of the heav'n - ly Fa - ther's face:

Je - sus Christ, we greet you, bless you, ho - ly Lord of sa - ving grace.

2 As the day draws near its ending
sunlight dims with fading rays;
to the Father, Son and Spirit
now we sing our song of praise.

3 Son of God, the world's redeemer,
endless praises are your due;
Lord of life, may all creation
bring its joyful thanks to you.

See also O Gladsome Light (677)

Greek, 3rd Century, tr. Paul Inwood

16 Evening Thanksgiving

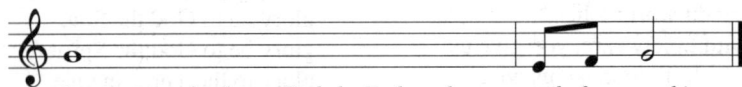

Let us give thanks to God the Father always and for everything.
In the name of our Lord Je - sus Christ.

The leader makes the thanksgiving to which all respond: **Amen.**

Evening Prayer continues with Psalmody (opposite.)

Psalmody

*Psalms are found in the Psalter (39-63) The Psalm and Canticle given here may
be sung as a simple Evening Prayer on any day.*

17 Psalm 140 (141) 1st Setting   *Incense may be burnt during the singing of this psalm.*

1 I have called to you, Lord; hasten to help
me.
Hear my voice when I cry to you.

2 Let my prayer arise before you like
incense,
the raising of my hands like an evening
oblation.

3 Set, O Lord, a guard over my mouth;
keep watch, O Lord, at the door of my lips.

4 Do not turn my heart to things that are
wrong,
to evil deeds with those who are sinners.

Never allow me to share in their feasting.

5 If the upright strike or reprove me it is
kindness;
but let the oil of the wicked not anoint
my head.
Let my prayer be ever against their malice.

8 To you, Lord God, my eyes are turned;
in you I take refuge; spare my soul!

9 From the trap they have laid for me
keep me safe;
keep me from the snares of those who
do evil.

Give praise to the Father Almighty,
to his Son, Jesus Christ, the Lord.
To the Spirit who dwells in our hearts
both now and for ever. Amen.

*Music:
Stephen Dean*

18   Psalm 140 (141): 2nd Setting   *Michael Joncas*

Hurry, Lord! I call and call!
Listen! I plead with you.
Let my prayer rise like incense,
my upraised hands, like an evening sacrifice.

Lord, guard my lips,
watch my every word.
Let me never speak evil
    or consider hateful deeds,
let me never join the wicked
    to eat their lavish meals.

If the just correct me,
I take their rebuke as kindness,
but the unction of the wicked
    will never touch my head.
I pray and pray
    against their hateful ways.

Let them be thrown
against a rock of judgment,
then they will know
I spoke the truth.
Then they will say,
'Our bones lie broken upon the ground,
scattered at the grave's edge.'

Lord my God, I turn to you,
in you I find safety.
Do not strip me of life.
Do not spring on me
the traps of the wicked.
Let evildoers get tangled
in their own nets,
but let me escape.

Psalm Prayer　　*The leader reads the prayer and all answer* **Amen.**

19　Canticle of the Lamb (Rev. 19: 1,2,5-7)　*outside Lent*　Stephen Dean

Antiphon Sundays 1 & 3

The Lord is King, our God, the Al-migh-ty, al - le - lu - ia!___

Sundays 2 & 4

Praise God, all you his ser-vants, both_ small and great, al-le-lu - ia, al-le-lu - ia!

Verses

Cantor　　　　　　　　　　　　　　　　*All*

1. Salvation and glory　and power be - long　to　our　God.　**Al - le - lu - ia!**
2. Praise our　　　God,　　all　you　his　　servants.
3. The　Lord our　God, the　al - mighty　　reigns.
4. The　mar - riage feast　of　the　Lamb has　　come.

Cantor　　　　　　　　　　　　　　　　*All*

1. His　judgements　are　true · and　just.　**Al-le-lu - ia,　al-le-lu - ia!**
2. You who　fear　him,　　small　and　great.
3. Let　us　rejoice, and exult, and give　him the　glory.
4. And his　bride has　　made　herself　ready.

Repeat Antiphon
after verse 2 & 4

Revelations 15: 3-4

Antiphon

Great and wonder-ful are your deeds, O Lord God the al-migh-ty.

Verses

1. Just and true are your ways, O King of the a-ges. ℟.

2. Who shall not fear and glo - ri-fy your

name, O Lord, for you a-lone are ho - ly. ℟.

3. All na - tions shall come and wor-ship you, for your

judge-ments have been re - vealed. ℟.

4. Praise the Fa - ther the Son and the Ho - ly

Spi - rit, both now and for - e - ver, A - men. ℟.

Alternative Canticle: Every knee shall bow (755)

21 Lent Canticle (I Pet 2:21-24) 1st Setting

Martin Foster

By his wounds we have been healed.

Christ suffered for you, leaving you an example,
that you should follow in his steps.
He committed no sin; no guile was found on his lips.
When he was reviled, he did not revile in return.

When he suffered, he did not threaten;
but trusted to him who judges justly.
He himself bore our sins in his body on the tree,
that we might die to sin and live to righteousness.

I Pet 2:21-24

22 Lent Canticle (I Pet 2:21-24) 2nd Setting

Stephen Dean

Ours were the griefs he bore, ours were the pains he car-ried,

ours were the sins he took on him: and by— his wounds we are healed.

The verses may be read or sung.

1. Christ suffered for you,
   leaving you an example
   that you should follow in his steps.
   He committed no sin,
   no guile was found on his lips.
   When he was reviled,
   he did not revile in return.

2. When he suffered, He did not threaten;
   but he trusted to him who judges justly.
   He himself bore our sins
   in his body on the tree,
   that we might die to sin
   and live to righteousness.

   I Pet 2:21-24

Another setting: As prophets foretold (235)

The Word of God

A short scripture passage is read, taken from the Office of the Day or another source.

23 **Gospel Canticle: The Magnificat** (Luke 1:46-55) Grail version Ist setting

Joseph Gelineau, S.J.

The Lord has done mar - vels for me: ho - ly___ is his name.

1		My soul			glorifies		the	Lord,
2		He looks	on his	servant		in	her	lowliness;
9		the mercy			promised		to our	fathers,
10	Praise the Father,		the	Son	and	Holy		Spirit,

	my spirit	re - joices	in	God	my	Saviour.
	hence- forth	all ages	will	call	me	blessed.
	for Abra -	ham	and	his	children for	ever.
	both now	and for ever,		world	without	end.

3 The Al-mighty works marvels for me. Holy his name!
5 He puts forth his arm in strength, and scatters the proud-hearted.
7 He fills the starving with good things, sends the rich away empty.

4 His mercy is from age to age, on those who fear him.
6 He casts the mighty from their thrones and raises the lowly.
8 He pro-tects Israel his servant, re - membering his mercy.

24

2nd Setting

Laurence Bévenot, O.S.B. (1901-91)

My soul glorifies the Lord,
my spirit rejoices in God my Saviour.
He looks on his servant in her lowliness;
henceforth all ages will call me blessed.

The Almighty works marvels for me.
Holy his name!
His mercy is from age to age,
on those who fear him.

He puts forth his arm in strength,
and scatters the proudhearted.

He fills the starving with good things,
sends the rich away empty.

He protects Israel his servant,
remembering his mercy,
the mercy promised to our fathers,
for Abraham and his children for ever.

Give praise to the Father Almighty,
to his Son Jesus Christ, the Lord,
to the Spirit who dwells in our hearts,
both now and for ever. Amen.

25

1. Great is the Lord my soul— pro-claims, in him my
2. A - ges to come shall know— that I am blessed and

spi - rit sings— for joy; for he who saves has looked on
fa - voured by— the Lord: his name is ho - ly, migh - ty

me with bound - less love— to raise— me high.
God; his wond - rous power— on me— is poured.

3 All those who fear him find his love,
   in every age, in every land.
   His strong right arm puts down the proud,
   disperses them like grains of sand.

4 Down from their thrones he casts the strong,
   and raises up the meek of heart.
   He gives the hungry choicest food;
   in emptiness the rich depart.

5 Israel his servant knows his help,
   in keeping with the promise sworn
   to Abraham and all his race:
   God's love will never be withdrawn.

6 Glory to God: the Father, Son,
   and Spirit – Trinity sublime.
   All honour, thanks and praise be theirs
   across the spans of endless time.

Luke 1:46-55, versified by Paul Inwood.

Other settings of the Magnificat: nos. 335-340

Intercessions

The leader now introduces the Intercessions, and all make the response. Intercessions may be taken from the Office for the Day or another source, Suggested responses are given below.
Prayers should be made for:

    the church throughout the world   *justice and peace*
    our own community   *the harvest*
    governments and others in authority   *the sick and dying*
    (in Lent) those preparing for baptism, and   *the faithful departed.*
    (In Eastertide) the newly baptized

26   **Response to the Intercessions: Advent & Christmastide**

Come and de - li - ver us, come and de - li - ver us, come and de - li - ver us, Lord.

➤ See also no. 70

27 Response to the Intercessions: Lent

Lord, have mer - cy, Lord, have mer - cy, Lord, have mer - cy on your peo ple.

28 Response to the Intercessions: Eastertide

O Christ, Vic - tor o - ver death, have mer - cy on us and hear our prayer.

29 Response to the Intercessions: Ordinary Time

Lord, in your mer - cy hear our prayer.

➤ See also nos. 9, 73 (Advent), 221, 547-552, 740, 928-9

The Leader collects all the petitions in the Our Father *which may be said or sung:*

30 Lord's Prayer

Philip Duffy

Our Fa-ther, who art in heav'n, hal-lowed be thy name; thy king-dom come,

thy will be done on earth as it is in heav'n. Give us this day our dai - ly bread,

and for-give us our tres-passes, as we for-give those who tres - pass ag-ainst us.

And lead us not in-to temp-ta-tion, but de - li - ver us from e - vil.

Other versions: 10 (modern text) 587-88

Concluding Prayer
The prayer is taken from the Office of the Day or another source. All respond **Amen.**

Blessing
When a priest or deacon presides at Morning Prayer, a blessing is given. When a lay person presides, the conclusion is as follows:

The Lord bless us, and keep us from all evil, and bring us to everlasting life. **Amen.**

Night Prayer

31 Introduction

Leader:

O God, come to our aid.

All:

O Lord, make haste to— help us. Glo - ry be to the Fa- ther, the Son and the Ho - ly Spi- rit, as it was in the be - gin- ning, is now and ev - er shall be, world with-out end, A - men. [Al le - lu - ia].

(Omitted during Lent)

Examination of Conscience

An examination of conscience is recommended. This may be included in a penitential act using the formulas given in the Missal.

32 Hymn

1 We praise you, Father, for your gift
of dusk and nightfall over earth,
foreshadowing the mystery
of death that leads to endless birth.

2 Within your hands we rest secure;
in quiet sleep our strength renew
yet give your people hearts that wake
in love to you, unsleeping Lord.

3 Your glory may we ever seek
in rest as in activity,
until its fullness is revealed,
O source of life, O Trinity

The Benedictine Nuns of West Malling

1. We praise you, Fa - ther, for your gift of dusk and night- fall o- ver earth, fore sha-dow- ing the myste- ry— of death that leads to end-less birth.

Other suitable hymns: nos. 674-682

Psalmody

Other psalms may be chosen from the Psalm section (39-63)

33 Psalm 90 (91)

Ant. He will con-ceal you with his wings; you will not fear the ter-ror of the night.

1 Those who dwell in the shelter of the
   Most High
   and abide in the shade of the Almighty
2 say to the Lord: 'My refuge,
   my stronghold, my God in whom I trust!'

3 It is God who will free you from the snare
   of the fowler who seeks to destroy you;
4 God will conceal you with his pinions,
   and under his wings you will find refuge.

5 You will not fear the terror of the night
   nor the arrow that flies by day,
6 nor the plague that prowls in the darkness
   nor the scourge that lays waste at noon.

7 A thousand may fall at your side,
   ten thousand fall at your right,
   you, it will never approach;
4c God's faithfulness is buckler and shield.

8 Your eyes have only to look
   to see how the wicked are repaid,
9 you who have said: 'Lord, my refuge!'
   and have made the Most High your
      dwelling.

10 Upon you no evil shall fall,
   no plague approach where you dwell.
11 For you God has commanded the angels,
   to keep you in all your ways.

12 They shall bear you upon their hands
   lest you strike your foot against a stone.
13 On the lion and the viper you will tread
   and trample the young lion and the
   dragon.

14 You set your love on me so I will save you,
   protect you for you know my name.
15 When you call I shall answer: 'I am
      with you,'
   I will save you in distress and give you
      glory.

16 With length of days I will content you;
   I shall let you see my saving power.

   Give praise to the Father Almighty,
   to his Son, Jesus Christ, the Lord,
   to the Spirit who dwells in our hearts,
   both now and for ever. Amen.

Music: Margaret Daly-Denton. Text: The Grail

34
Psalm 4

Lord,_____ have mer - cy and hear me.

2 When I call, answer me, O God of justice;
from anguish you released me, have mercy and hear me!

3 You rebels, how long will your hearts be closed,
will you love what is futile and seek what is false?

4 It is the Lord who grants favours to those who are merciful;
the Lord hears me whenever I call.

5 Tremble; do not sin: ponder on your bed and be still.

6 Make justice your sacrifice and trust in the Lord.

7 'What can bring us happiness?' many say.
Lift up the light of your face on us, O Lord.

8 You have put into my heart a greater joy than they have from abundance of corn and new wine.

9 I will lie down in peace and sleep comes at once
for you alone, Lord, make me dwell in safety.

Give praise to the Father, the Son and Holy Spirit
both now and for ages unending. Amen.

35
Psalm 134 *Simple setting*

Bless___ the Lord, bless__ the Lord through_____ the night.

1 O come, bless the Lord,
all you who serve the Lord,
who stand in the house of the Lord,
in the courts of the house of our God.

2 Lift up your hands to the holy place
and bless the Lord through the night.

3 May the Lord bless you from Zion,
God who made both heaven and earth.

Give glory to the Father Almighty
to his Son, Jesus Christ our Lord;
To the Spirit who dwells in our hearts
both now and for ever. Amen.

Melodic setting: no 36

Music: Psalm 4, Margaret Daly-Denton; Psalm 134, Stephen Dean

36

Ant. *mp*

O come, bless— the Lord, all you who serve the Lord,——— who stand in the house of the Lord, in the courts of the house of our God.———

Verses

1. Lift up your hands to the ho - ly place,— and bless the Lord through the night.—

May the Lord bless you from Zi - on, he who made both hea - ven and earth. *R/.*

2. Glo - ry be to the Fa - ther, the Son and the Spi - rit,

as it was, is now,— and for e - ver shall be. A - men. *R/.*

The Word of God

Hear, O Israel: the Lord our God is one Lord; and you shall love the Lord your God with all your heart, and with all your soul, and with all your might. And these words which I command you this day shall be upon your heart; and you shall teach them diligently to your children, and shall talk of them when you sit in your house, and when you walk by the way, and when you lie down, and when you rise.

(Deuteronomy 6:4-7: Reading for Sunday)

37 **Response to the Word**

Response *Omit in Lent*

In - to your hands, O Lord, I com-mend my Spi-rit. [Al- le- lu- ia, al- le- lu - ia.]
All: Into your hands..

v.1 You have re - deemed us, Lord God of truth. *All: Into your hands..*

v.2 Glo-ry be to the Fa- ther, and to the Son, and— to the Ho- ly Spi- rit.

Antiphon

Save us, O Lord, while we are a-wake, pro-tect us while— we sleep, that we may keep watch with Christ, and rest here in peace.

Verses

1. At last, all-powerful Master, you give leave to your servant to go in peace, ac-cording to your pro-mise.

2. For my eyes have seen your sal-
3. the light to en-ligh-ten the
4. Give praise to the Father al-
5. To the Spirit who dwells in our

vation which you have pre-pared for all— na-tions,
Gentiles, and give glo-ry to Is-ra-el your peo-ple.
mighty, to his Son, Je-sus Christ,— the— Lord,—
hearts both now and for e-ver. A-men.—

Another setting of the Nunc Dimittis: no 176

Concluding Prayer

Visit this house, we pray you, Lord:
drive far away from it all the snares of the enemy.
May your holy angels stay here and guard us in peace,
Through Christ our Lord.
Amen.

(Prayer for Sunday)

Blessing

The Lord grant us a quiet night and a perfect end. **Amen.**

Anthem to Our Lady

Salve Regina, no 367. During Eastertide: *Regina Caeli, no.368*

The Psalter

Psalm 5: *Lord, as I wake I turn to you (672)*

Psalm 8

39

Antiphon

How great is your name, O Lord our God,____ through all the earth!

Verses

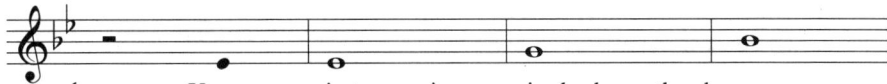

1. Your majesty is praised above the heavens;
2. When I see the heavens, the work of your hands,
3. Yet you have made us little less than gods;
4. All of them, sheep and cattle,
   Give glory to the Father Al - mighty,

on the lips of children and of babes
the moon and the stars which you ar - ranged,
and crowned us with glory and honour,
yes, even the savage beasts,
to his son, Jesus Christ, the Lord,

you have found praise to foil your enemy,
what are we that you should keep us in mind,
you gave us power over the work of your hands,
birds of the air,/ and fish
to the Spirit who dwells in our hearts

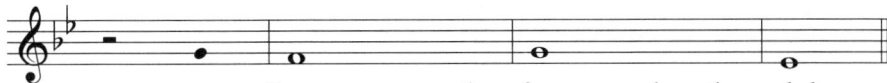

to silence the foe and the rebel.
mere mortals that you care for us?
put all things under our feet.
that make their way through the waters.
both now and for ever. A - men.

Text: The Grail. Antiphon by A.Gregory Murray, O.S.B. Psalm tone by Joseph Gelineau, S.J.

Preserve me, God, I take refuge in you.(†)
²ᵃ I say to you Lord: 'You are my God.
²ᵇ My happiness lies in you alone.' *omit B & C*

3   You have put into my heart a marvellous love
for the faithful ones who dwell in your land.

4   Those who choose other gods increase their
      sorrows. (†)
Never will I offer their offerings of blood.
Never will I take their name upon my lips.

5   O Lord, it is you who are my portion and cup,
it is you yourself who are my prize.

6   The lot marked out for me is my delight,
welcome indeed the heritage that falls to me!

7   I will bless you, Lord, you give me counsel,
and even at night direct my heart.

8   I keep you, Lord, ever in my sight,
since you are at my right hand, I shall stand
      firm.

9   And so my heart rejoices, my soul is glad;
even my body shall rest in safety.

10   For you will not leave my soul among the
      dead,
nor let your beloved know decay.

11   You will show me the path of life,
the fullness of joy in your presence,   *omit C*
at your right hand happiness for ever.

Give praise to the Father, the Son and Holy
     Spirit,   *omit B & C*
both now and for ages unending. Amen.

Response 1

Show us, Lord, the path of— life.

Response 2

O— Lord, it is you who are my por - tion and cup.

Response 3

Show us, Lord, the path of life, di - rect our hearts, and guide our foot-steps; keep us e - ver in your sight, for with you at our right hand, you at our right hand, what can we fear?

Psalm tone

Responses 1 & psalm tone by Fintan O'Carroll. Responses 2 & 3 by Stephen Dean. Response 4 by Paul Inwood.

Response 4

Keep me safe, O God, I take re-fuge in you.—

Keep me safe, O God, I take re-fuge in you.—

See the music editions for the setting of the verses accompanying this response.

• **Another setting of Psalm 16:** *Centre of my life (423)*

Psalm 18(19):8-15   41

THE LAW OF THE LORD IS PERFECT,
it revives the soul.
  The rule of the Lord is to be trusted,
  it gives wisdom tò the simple.

9 The precepts of the Lord are right,
  they gladden the heart.
  The command of the Lord is clear,
  it gives light tò the eyes.

10 The fear of the Lord is holy,
  abiding for ever.
  The decrees of the Lord are truth
  and all òf them just.

11 They are more to be desired than gold,
  than the purest of gold
  and sweeter are they than honey,
  than honey fròm the comb.

12 So in them your servant finds instruction;
  great reward is in their keeping.

13 But can we discern all our errors?
  From hidden faults àcquit us.

14 From presumption restrain your servant
  and let it not rule me.
  Then shall I be blameless,
  clean fròm grave sin.

15 May the spoken words of my mouth,
  the thoughts of my heart,
  win favour in your sight, O Lord,
  my rescuèr, my rock!

*Praise the Fáther, the Són, and Holy Spírit,
both nów and for éver,
The God who ís, who wás, and who wíll be,
wórld without énd.*

Response 1

The pre-cepts of the Lord glad-den the heart.

Psalm tone

May be sung by two alternating groups.

Response 2

You, Lord, have the mes-sage of e-ter-nal life.

Response 1 & psalm tone by Stephen Dean. Response 2 by Paul Inwood.

Psalm 22 (23)

1. Lord, you are my shepherd;
2. You guide me a - long the right path;
3. You have pre - pared a banquet for me
4. Surely goodness and kindness shall follow me
5. To the Father and Son give glory,

1. there is nothing I shall want.
2. You are true to your name.
3. in the sight of my foes.
4. all the days of my life.
5. give glory to the Spirit.

1. Fresh and green are the pastures
2. If I should walk in the valley of darkness
3. My head you have a - nointed with oil;
4. In the Lord's own house shall I dwell
5. To God who is, who was and who will be

1. where you give me re - pose. Near restful
2. no evil would I fear. You are there with your
3.
4.
5.

1. waters you lead me, to re - vive my droop-ing spi - rit.
2. crook and your staff; with these you give me com - fort.
3. my cup is o - ver-flow - ing.
4. for e - ver and e - ver.
5. for e - ver and e - ver.

Resp. 1

The— Lord is my— shep-herd; there is no-thing I shall— want.

Resp. 2

My shep-herd is the Lord; no - thing in - deed shall I want.

Text: The Grail. Psalmtone and Response 2 by Joseph Gelineau, S.J. Response 1 by Fintan O'Carroll

Other settings of Psalm 22(23) *Because the Lord is my shepherd (948); God alone may lead (949); Shepherd me, O God (951); The King of love (804); The living God (805); The Lord's my shepherd (806)*

Psalm 23(24) *Fling wide the gates (104)*

Psalm 24 (25)

43

To you, O Lord, I lift up my soul. (†)
² My God, I trust you, let me not be
disappointed;
do not let my enemies triumph.
³ Those who hope in you shall not be
disappointed
but only those who wantonly break faith.

⁴ Lord, make me know your ways.
Lord, teach me your paths.
⁵ Make me walk in your truth, and teach me,
for you are God my saviour.

In you I hope all the day long (†)
⁷ because of your goodness, O Lord.
⁶ Remember your mercy, Lord, (†)
and the love you have shown from of old.
⁷ Do not remember the sins of my youth.
In your love remember me.

⁸ The Lord is good and upright.
showing the path to those who stray,
⁹ guiding the humble in the right path,
and teaching the way to the poor.

¹⁰ God's ways are steadfastness and truth
for those faithful to the covenant decrees.

¹¹ Lord, for the sake of your name
forgive my guilt, for it is great.
¹² Those who revere the Lord (†)
will be shown the path they should choose.
¹³ Their souls will live in happiness (†)
and their children shall possess the land.
¹⁴ The Lord's friendship is for the God-fearing;
and the covenant is revealed to them.
¹⁵ My eyes are always on the Lord,
who will rescue my feet from the snare.
¹⁶ Turn to me and have mercy
for I am lonely and poor.
¹⁷ Relieve the anguish of my heart
and set me free from my distress.
¹⁸ See my affliction and my toil
and take all my sins away.
¹⁹ See how many are my foes, (†)
how violent their hatred for me.
²⁰ Preserve my life and rescue me. (†)
Do not disappoint me, you are my refuge.
²¹ May innocence and uprightness protect me
for my hope is in you, O Lord.
²² (D) Redeem Israel, O God, from all its distress.

Glory be: see after Ps 33 (34), p.30

Resp. 1

To you, O Lord, I lift up my soul.

Psalmtone

Resp. 2 *See the music editions for the setting of the verses accompanying this response.*

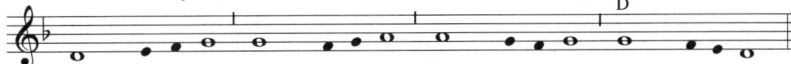

Lord, your ways are faith- ful- ness and love, for those who keep your co- ve- nant.

Text by The Grail (England). Response 1 by Stephen Dean..Psalmtone by Laurence Bévenot, O.S.B. Response 2 by Peter Jones

Another setting of Psalm 24(25):   *Remember, remember your mercy Lord (843)*

THE LORD IS MY LIGHT AND MY HELP;
whom shall I fear?
The Lord is the stronghold of my life;
before whom shall I shrink?

2 When evildoers draw near
to devour my flesh,
it is they, my enemies and foes,
who stumble and fall.

3 Though an army encamp against me
my heart would not fear.
Though war break out against me
even then would I trust.

4 There is one thing I ask of the Lord,
for this I long,
to live in the house of the Lord,
all the days of my life,
to savour the sweetness of the Lord,
to behold his temple.

5 For God makes me safe in his tent
in the day of evil.
God hides me in the shelter of his tent,
on a rock I am secure.

6 And now my head shall be raised
above my foes who surround me
and I shall offer within God's tent
a sacrifice of joy.

(A) I will sing and make music for the Lord.

7 O Lord, hear my voice when I call;
have mercy and answer.

8 Of you my heart has spoken:
'Seek God's face.'

It is your face, O Lord, that I seek;
9 hide not your face.
Dismiss not your servant in anger;
you have been my help.

Do not abandon or forsake me,
O God my help!
10 Though father and mother forsake me,
the Lord will receive me.

11 Instruct me, Lord, in your way;
on an even path lead me.
When they lie in ambush 12 protect me
from my enemies' greed.
False witnesses rise against me,
breathing out fury.

13 I am sure I shall see the Lord's goodness
in the land of the living.
14 In the Lord, hold firm and take heart.
Hope in the Lord!

*Praise the Fáther, the Són, and Holy Spírit,
both nów and for éver,
The God who ís, who wás, and who wíll be,
wórld without énd.*

Response

The Lord is my light and my help.

Psalmtone

Verses 4, 11

Other settings of Psalm 26 (27)   *Awake from your sleep* (403); *May the choirs of angels* (443);
One thing I ask of the Lord (990); *Those who seek your face* (393)

Text: The Grail,. Response and Psalmtone by Stephen Dean

Ring out your joy to the Lord, O you just
for praise is fitting for loyal hearts. (A & D)

2 Give thanks to the Lord upon the harp
with a ten-stringed lute play your songs.
3 Sing to the Lord a song that is new,
play loudly, with all your skill.

4 For the word of the Lord is faithful
and all his works done in truth.
5 The Lord loves justice and right
and fills the earth with love.

6 By God's word the heavens were made,
by the breath of his mouth all the stars.
7 God collects the waves of the ocean;
and stores up the depths of the sea.

8 Let all the earth fear the Lord,
all who live in the world stand in awe.
9 For God spoke; it came to be.
God commanded, it sprang into being.

10 The Lord foils the designs of the nations,
and defeats the plans of the peoples.
11 The counsel of the Lord stands forever,
the plans of God's heart from age to age.

12 They are happy, whose God is the Lord,
the people who are chosen as his own.
13 From the heavens the Lord looks forth
and sees all the peoples of the earth.

14 From the heavenly dwelling God gazes
on all the dwellers on the earth;
15 God who shapes the hearts of them all
and considers all their deeds.

16 A king is not saved by his army,
nor a warrior preserved by his strength.
17 A vain hope for safety is the horse;
despite its power it cannot save.

18 The Lord looks on those who fear him,
on those who hope in his love,
19 to rescue their souls from death,
to keep them alive in famine.

20 Our soul is waiting for the Lord.
The Lord is our help and our shield.
21 Our hearts find joy in the Lord.
We trust in God's holy name.

22 May your love be upon us, O Lord,
as we place all our hope in you. (A & D)

R. 1

Glory be: see after Ps 33 (34)

May your love be u-pon us, O Lord, as we place all our hope in you.

Psalmtone

R..2

The Lord fills the earth with his love, his love, the

Lord fills the earth with his love.

See the music editions for the full setting of the verses accompanying response 2.

Another setting of Psalm 32(33): *Happy the people the Lord has chosen (no 394)*

Response 1 by Anne Ward. REsponse 2 by Paul Inwood. Psalmtone by Stephen Dean.

I WILL BLESS THE LORD AT ALL TIMES,
God's praise always on my lips;
3 in the Lord my soul shall make its boast.
The humble shall hear and be glad.

4 Glorify the Lord with me.
Together let us praise God's name.
5 I sought the Lord and was heard;
from all my terrors set free.

6 Look towards God and be radiant;
let your faces not be abashed.
7 When the poor cry out the Lord hears them
and rescues them from all their distress.

8 The angel of the Lord is encamped
around those who fear God, to rescue them.
9 Taste and see that the Lord is good.
They are happy who seek refuge in God.

10 Revere the Lord, you saints.
They lack nothing, who revere the Lord.
11 Strong lions suffer want and go hungry
but those who seek the Lord lack no blessing.

12 Come, children, and hear me
that I may teach you the fear of the Lord.

13 Who are those who long for life
and many days, to enjoy their prosperity?

14 Then keep your tongue from evil
and your lips from speaking deceit.
15 Turn aside from evil and do good;
seek and strive after peace.

16 The eyes of the Lord are toward the just
and his ears toward their appeal.
17 The face of the Lord rebuffs the wicked
to destroy their remembrance from the earth.

18 They call and the Lord hears
and rescues them in all their distress.
19 The Lord is close to the brokenhearted;
those whose spirit is crushed God will save.

20 Many are the trials of the upright
but the Lord will come to rescue them,
21 keeping guard over all their bones,
not one of their bones shall be broken.

22 Evil brings death to the wicked;
those who hate the good are doomed.
23 The Lord ransoms the souls of the faithful.
None who trust in God shall be condemned.

*Give práise to the Fáther Almíghty,
to his Són, Jesus Chríst, the Lórd,
to the Spírit who dwélls in our héarts
both nów and for éver. Amén.*

Response

Taste and see that the Lord is good.

Psalmtone

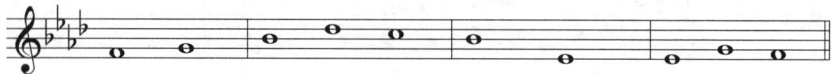

Response by Francis Duffy. Psalmtone by Stephen Dean.

Other settings of Psalm 33 (34) *Taste and see (617 & 618), The cry of the poor (892)*

L IKE THE DÉER THAT YÉARNS
for rúnning stréams,
só my sóul is yéarning
for yóu, my Gód.

3 My sóul is thírsting for Gód
the Gód of my lífe;
whén can I énter and sée
the fáce of Gód?

4 My téars have becóme my bréad
by níght, by dáy,
as I héar it said áll the day lóng:
'Whére is your Gód?'

5 Thése things will Í remémber (†)
as I póur out my sóul:
how I would léad the rejóicing crówd (†)
into the hóuse of Gód,
amid críes of gládness and thanksgíving,
the thróng wild with jóy.

6 Why are you cast dówn, my sóul,
why gróan withín me?
Hope in Gód; I will práise yet agáin,
my sáviour and my Gód.

42 (43):3-5

O SÉND FORTH YOUR LÍGHT AND YOUR TRÚTH;
let thése be my gúide.
Let them bríng me to your hóly móuntain,
to the pláce where you dwéll.

4 And I will cóme to your áltar, O Gód,
the Gód of my jóy.
My redéemer, I will thánk you on the hárp,
O Gód, my Gód.

5 Whý are you cast dówn, my sóul,
why gróan withín me?
Hope in Gód; I will práise yet agáin,
my sáviour and my Gód.

Glory be: as after Ps 26 (27)

Response 1

Like the deer that yearns for___ run-ning streams,
so my soul is year-ning for you, my___ God.

Psalmtone

Use underlinings in text.

Response 2

My soul is thirst-ing for the Lord; when shall I see him face to face?___

Psalmtone

Use accents in text.

Other settings of these psalms
As longs the deer (450); As the deer longs (214); Like as the deer (219); The thirsty deer (215)

Text: The Grail. Response 1 and psalmtone by Fintan O'Carroll. Response 2 and psalmtone by Joseph Gelineau, S. J.

HAVE MÉRCY ON ME, GÓD, IN YOUR KÍNDNESS.
In your compássion blot óut my offénce.
⁴ O wásh me more and móre from my gúilt
and cléanse me fróm my sín.

⁵ My offénces trúly I knów them;
my sín is álways befóre me.
⁶ Against yóu, you alóne, have I sínned;
what is évil in your síght I have dóne.

That you may be jústified whén you
give séntence
and bé without repróach when you júdge,
⁷ O sée, in gúilt I was bórn,
a sínner was Í concéived.

⁸ Indéed you love trúth in the héart,
then in the sécret of my héart teach me
wísdom.
⁹ O púrify me, thén I shall be cléan;
O wásh me, I shall be whíter than snów.

¹⁰ Make me héar rejóicing and gládness
that the bónes you have crúshed may
revíve.
¹¹ From my síns turn awáy your fáce
and blót out áll my gúilt.

¹² A púre heart creáte for me, O Gód,
put a stéadfast spírit withín me.
¹³ Do not cást me awáy from your présence,
nor depríve me of your hóly spírit.

¹⁴ Give me agáin the jóy of your hélp;
with a spírit of férvour sustáin me,
¹⁵ that I may téach transgréssors your wáys
and sínners may retúrn to yóu.

¹⁶ O réscue me, Gód, my hélper,
and my tóngue shall ríng out your góodness.
¹⁷ O Lórd, ópen my líps
and my móuth shall decláre your práise.

¹⁸ For in sácrifice you táke no delíght,
burnt óffering from mé you would refúse;
¹⁹ my sácrifice, a cóntrite spírit,
a húmbled, contrite héart you will not spúrn.

²⁰ In your góodness, show fávour to Zíon;
rebúild the wálls of Jerúsalem.
²¹ Thén you will be pléased with lawful
sácrifice,†
(burnt ófferings whólly consúmed),
then you will be óffered young búlls on
your áltar.

*Give práise to the Fáther Almíghty,
to his Són, Jesus Chríst, the Lórd,
to the Spírit who dwélls in our héarts
both nów and for éver. Amén.*

Response 1 A— pure heart cre-ate for me, O God.—

R. 2 Have mer-cy on us, O Lord, for we— have sinned.

Psaomtone

Follow accents in the text. Underlinings are for use with a psalmtone such as that on p.27

Text: The Grail (Enghland) Responses 1 & 2 by Stephen Dean. Psalmtone by Joseph Gelineau, S.J.

Other settings of Psalm 50 (51) *Come back to the Lord (194); Give me a new heart (195)*

Psalm 62 (63)   49

My soul is thir- sting, my soul is thir- sting, my soul is thir- sting for
you, O Lord my God.

1. O God, you are my God whom I seek:
   O God. you are my God whom I seek:
   for you my flesh pines. my soul thirsts
   like the earth,
   parched, lifeless, without water.

2. Thus have I gazed toward you in your
   holy place
   to see your power and your glory.
   Your kindness is a greater good than life
   itself;
   my lips will glorify you.

3. Thus will I bless you while I live;
   lifting up my hands I will call upon
   your name.
   As with a banquet shall my soul be
   satisfied;
   with exultant lips my mouth shall praise
   you.

4. For you have been my help, you have
   been my help;
   in thc shadow of your wings I shout for
   joy.
   My soul clings fast to you: your right
   hand holds me firm:
   in the shadow of your wings I sing for joy

Text: Ps 63: 2.3-4.5-6.8-9. & Music: Michael Joncas

Other settings of Psalm 62 (63):   *O God, you are my God (4); Your love is finer than life (213).*

Psalm 83(84):   *O how holy (454); O how lovely is your dwelling place (457)*

Psalm 84(85): 9-14   50

I WILL HEAR WHAT THE LORD HAS TO SAY,
   a voice that speaks of peace,
peace for his people and friends
   and those who turn to God in their hearts.
10 Salvation is near for thè God-fearing,
   and his glory will dwell in our land.

11 Mercy and faithfulness have met;
   justice and peace have embraced.
12 Faithfulness shall spring fròm the earth, and
   justice look down from heaven.
13 The Lord will make us prosper
   and our earth shall yield its fruit.
14 Justice shall march in the forefront,
   and peace shall follow the way.

Let us see, O Lord, your mer- cy and_ give us your sa- ving help.

Text: The Grail. Music by Alan Smith

T̲hose who dwéll in the shélter of the̲
    Most Hígh
  and abíde in the sháde of the̲ Almíghty
2 sáy to the Ló̲rd: 'My réfuge,
  my strónghold, my Gód in who̲m I trúst!'

3 It is Gód who will frée you fro̲m the snáre
  of the fówler who séeks to̲ destróy you;
4 Gód will concéal you wi̲th his pínions,
  and únder his wíngs you wi̲ll find réfuge.

5 You will not féar the térror o̲f the níght
  nor the árrow that flí̲es by dáy,
6 nor the plágue that prówls i̲n the dárkness
  nor the scóurge that lays wá̲ste at nóon.

7 A thóusand may fáll a̲t your síde,
  ten thóusand fáll a̲t your ríght,
  yóu, it will néve̲r appróach;
4c God's fáithfulness is búckle̲r and shíeld.

8 Your éyes have ónl̲y to lóok
  to sée how the wícked a̲re repáid,

9 yóu who have sáid: 'Lo̲rd, my réfuge!'
  and have máde the Most Hí̲gh your dwélling.

10 Upon yóu no évi̲l shall fáll,
  no plágue appróach whe̲re you dwéll.
11 For yóu God has commánde̲d the ángels,
  to kéep you in á̲ll your wáys.

12 They shall béar you upó̲n their hánds
  lest you stríke your fóot aga̲inst a stóne.
13 On the líon and the víper yo̲u will tréad
  and trámple the young líon a̲nd the drágon.

14 You sét your love on mé so I̲ will sáve you,
  protéct you for you knó̲w my náme.
15 When you cáll I shall ánswer: 'I̲ am wíth you,'
  I will sáve you in distréss and gi̲ve you glóry.

16 With léngth of dáys I wi̲ll contént you;
  I shall lét you sée my sa̲ving pówer.

Give práise to the Fáther Almíghty,
to his Són, Jesus Chríst, the Lórd,
to the Spírit who dwélls in our héarts
both nów and for éver. Amén.

Response 1

Psalmtone

Be with me, O Lord,   in   my   dis - tress.

Accents in the text are for use with this psalmtone, underlinings with the tone below

R.esponse 2

My— re-fuge, my— strong-hold,   my— God   in   whom   I   trust.

Psalm-tone

A   B   C   D

Other settings of Psalm 90 (91):
Night Prayer (31), On eagle's wings (952); Safe in the shadow of the Lord (953)

Text: The Grail. Response 1 & Psalmtone: Bill Tamblyn. Response 2 & Psalmtone: Stephen Dean.

Psalm 94 (95)   52

COME, RÍNG OUT OUR JÓY TO THE LÓRD;
háil the róck who sáves us.
2 Let us cóme before Gód, giving thánks,
with sóngs let us háil the Lórd.

3 A míghty Gód is the Lórd, †
a gréat king abóve all góds,
4 in whose hánds are the dépths of the éarth;†
the héights of the móuntains as wéll.
5 The séa belongs to Gód, who máde it
and the drý land sháped by his hánds.

6 Come ín; let us bów and bend lów;
let us knéel before the Gód who máde us
7 for thís is our Gód and wé †

the péople who belóng to his pásture,
the flóck that is léd by his hánd.

O that todáy you would lísten to God's vóice!
8 Hárden not your héarts as at Meríbah,†
as on that dáy at Mássah in the désert
9 when your áncestors pút me to the tést;
when they tríed me, though they sáw
my work.

10 For forty yéars I was wéaried of these péople
and I sáid: "Their héarts are astráy, †
these péople do not knów my wáys."
11 Thén I took an óath in my ánger:
Néver shall they énter my rést.'"

R. 1

O that to-day you would lis-ten to his voice! Har-den not your hearts.

Psalmtone

R. 2

A migh-ty God is the Lord, come, let us a - dore him!

Psalmtone 2
omit for 4-line stanza

omit for 5-line st.

Other settings of Psalm 94 (95) *To God with gladness sing (3)* **Psalms 96-98:** *see overleaf*
Response 1 & psalmtone by Fintan O'Carroll.. Response 2 by Stephen Dean. Psalmtone by Joseph Gelineau, S.J.

Psalm 99 (100)   53

CRY OUT WITH JÓY TO THE LÓRD, ALL THE ÉARTH.
Sérve the Lórd with gládness.
Come befóre God, sínging for jóy.

3 Knów that the Lórd is Gód,
Our Máker, to whóm we belóng.
We are God's péople, shéep of the flóck.

4 Énter the gátes with thanksgíving,
God's cóurts with sóngs of práise.
Give thánks to God and bléss his náme.

5 Indéed, how góod is the Lórd,
whose mérciful lóve is etérnal;
whose fáithfulness lásts foréver.

We are his peo-ple, the sheep of his flock; his peo-ple, the sheep of his flock.

Text: The Grail. Music by Stephen Dean

Psalm 95 (96) *All the ends of the earth (121); praise the Lord, all you nations (461)*

Psalm 97 (98) *Go into the world (424), Sing a new song (Schutte) (697)*

Other settings of Psalm 99 (100)   *All people that on earth do dwell (466); All the earth proclaim the Lord (460); Jubilate Deo (691); Jubilate, everybody (472); Sing all creation (467)*

Psalm 102 (103)   54

M Y SOUL, GIVE THANKS TO THE LORD,
   all my being, bless God's holy name.
2   My soul, give thanks to the Lord
    and never forget all God's blessings.

3   It is God who forgives all your guilt, †
    who heals every one of your ills,
4   who redeems your life from the grave, †
    who crowns you with love and compassion,
5   who fills your life with good things,
    renewing your youth like an eagle's.

6   The Lord does deeds of justice,
    gives judgement for all who are oppressed.
7   The Lord's ways were made known to Moses
    the Lord's deeds to Israel's children.

8   The Lord is compassion and love, †
    slow to anger and rich in mercy.
9   The Lord will not always chide, †
    will not be angry forever.
10 God does not treat us according to our sins
    nor repay us according to our faults.

11 For as the heavens are high above the earth
    so strong is God's love for the God-fearing,
12 As far as the east is from the west
    so far does he remove our sins.

13 As parents have compassion on their children,
    the Lord has pity on those who are
        God-fearing
14 for he knows of what we are made,
    and remembers that we are dust.

15 As for us, our days are like grass;
    we flower like the flower of the field;
16 the wind blows and we are gone
    and our place never sees us again.

17 But the love of the Lord is everlasting
    upon those who fear the Lord.
    God's justice reaches out to children's
        children †
18   when they keep his covenant in truth,
    when they keep his will in their mind.

19 The Lord has set his throne in heaven †
    and his kingdom rules over all.
20 Give thanks to the Lord, all you angels,
    mighty in power, fulfilling God's word,
    who heed the voice of that word.

21 Give thanks to the Lord, all you hosts,
    you servants who do God's will.
22 Give thanks to the Lord, all his works, †
    in every place where God rules.
    My soul, give thanks to the Lord!

Glory be: see after Ps 90 (91)

The— Lord is com-pas - sion and— love, slow to an-ger and rich in mer - cy.

Text: The Grail. Music by Fintan O'Carroll

Psalm 114-5 (116)

(114)

A*LLELUIA!*
I love the Lord, for the Lord has heard
the cry of my appeal.
2 The Lord was attentive to me
in the day when I called.

3 They surrounded me, the snares of death,
with the anguish of the tomb;
they caught me, sorrow and distress.
4 I called on the Lord's name. †

O Lord, my God, deliver me!

5 How gracious is the Lord, and just;
our God has compassion.
6 The Lord protects the simple hearts;
I was helpless so God saved me.

7 Turn back, my soul, to your rest
for the Lord has been good,
8 and has kept my soul from death, †
(my eyes from tears,)
my feet from stumbling.

8 I will walk in the presence of the Lord
in the land of the living.   *(omit B, C)*

(115)   **55**

10 I trusted, even when I said:
'I am sorely afflicted,'
11 and when I said in my alarm:
'There is no one I can trust.'

12 How can I repay the Lord
for his goodness to me?
13 The cup of salvation I will raise;
I will call on the Lord's name.

14 My vows to the Lord I will fulfill
before all the people.
15 O precious in the eyes of the Lord
is the death of the faithful.

16 Your servant, Lord, your servant am I;
you have loosened my bonds.
17 A thanksgiving sacrifice I make;
I will call on the Lord's name.

18 My vows to the Lord I will fulfill
before all the people,
19 in the courts of the house of the Lord,
in your midst, O Jerusalem.

Praise the Fáther, the Són, and Holy Spírit,
both nów and for éver,
The God who ís, who wás, and who wíll be,
wórld without énd.

R. 1

I will walk in the pre sence of the Lord___ in the land of the li-ving.

Psalmtone

Setting 2

Our___ bles- sing cup___ is a com - mu- nion with the blood of Christ;___

and the bread we break,___ it is a   sha - ring___ in the bo- dy of the Lord.___

Text: The Grail. Response 1 and psalmtone by Stephen Dean. Setting 2 by Bob Hurd.   *See music editions for verses*

Other settings of Ps 116: *God, our fountain of salvation (459); How can I repay (619); Lord, how*
can I repay (620)

Psalm 116 (117)   *Come praise the Lord (700); Praise the Lord (461); Holy is God (699)*

Psalm 117 (118)   *The stone which the builders (258); This is the day (257)*

Psalm 121 (122)   56

I REJOICED WHEN I HEARD THEM SAY:
'Let us go to God's house.'
2 And now our feet are standing
within your gates, O Jerusalem.

3 Jerusalem is built as a city
strongly compact.
4 It is there that the tribes go up,
the tribes of the Lord.

For Israel's law it is,
there to praise the Lord's name.
5 There were set the thrones of judgement
of the house of David.

6 For the peace of Jerusalem pray:
'Peace be to your homes!
7 May peace reign in your walls,
in your palaces, peace.'

8 For love of my family and friends
I say, 'Peace upon you.'
9 For love of the house of the Lord
I will ask for your good.

Praise the Fáther, the Són, and Holy Spírit,
both nów and for éver,
The God who ís, who wás, and who wíll be,
wórld without énd.

I re-joiced when I heard___ them say: 'Let us go to God's house.'

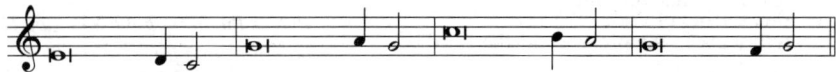

Other settings of Psalm 121 (122):   *I rejoiced (992)*   Text: The Grail. Music by Finatan O'Carroll

Psalm 125 (126)   57

W HEN THE LÓRD DELIVERED ZÍON from
bóndage,
it séemed like a dréam.
2 Thén was our móuth filled with láughter,
on our líps there were sóngs.

The héathens themsélves said: what márvels
the Lórd worked for thém!'
3 What márvels the Lórd worked for ús!
Indéed we were glád.

4 Delíver us, O Lórd, from our bóndage
as stréams in dry lánd.
6 Thóse who are sówing in téars
will síng when they réap.

6 They go óut, they go óut, full of téars,
carrying séed for the sówing;
they come báck, they come báck, full of sóng,
cárrying their shéaves.

Glory be: see after previous psalm

Psalmtone   A   B   C   D

(response on next page)

What mar - vels the Lord worked for us!___ In - deed___ we were glad.
⁷ Those who are so - wing in tears___ will sing___ when they reap.

Psalm 127 (128)

58

O BLESSED ARE YOU WHO FEAR THE LORD
and walk in God's ways!

2 By the labour of your hands you shall eat.
You will be happy and prosper;

3 your wife like a fruitful vine
in the heart of your house;
your children like shoots of the olive,
around your table.

4 Indeed thus shall be blessed
those who fear the Lord.

5 May the Lord bless you from Zion
5c all the days of your life!

6 May you see your children's children
5b in a happy Jerusalem!

On Israel, peace!

O blessed are those who fear the Lord, and walk in his ways,

O blessed are those who fear the Lord, and walk in his ways.

Text: The Grail. Music by Paul Inwood.

Another setting of Psalm 127 (128): *Blessed are those who love you (409)*

Psalm 129 (130) FIRST SETTING

59

O UT OF THE DEPTHS I CRY TO YOU, O LORD,
2 Lord, hear my voice!
O let your ears be attentive
to the voice of my pleading.

3 If you, O Lord, should mark our guilt,
Lord, who would survive?

4 But with you is found forgiveness:
for this we revere you.

5 My soul is waiting for the Lord.
I count on God's word.

6 My soul is longing for the Lord
more than those who watch for daybreak.
(Let the watchers count on daybreak
7 and Israel on the Lord.)

(repeat C+D)

Because with the Lord there is mercy
and fullness of redemption,

8 Israel indeed God will redeem
from all its iniquity.

With the Lord there is mer - cy and ful-ness of re-demp-tion.

A   B   C   D

Text: The Grail. Music by Fintan O'Carroll.

Other settings: *Overleaf and: Out of the depths (452); Out of the direst depths (207);*
Grant them eternal rest (439) (v.1)

Psalm 129 (130) *second setting* 60

R.

I place all my trust in you, my God, all my hope is in your sa- ving word.

Verses

1. Out of the depths I cry to you, O Lord,
2. If you, O Lord, should mark our guilt,
3. My soul is wai-ting for the Lord.
4. Be - cause with the Lord there is mercy
   To the Fa - ther Al - mighty give glory,

Lord, hear my voice! O let your
Lord, who would sur - vive? But with you is
I count on God's word. My soul is
and fullness of re-demption, Israel in -
give glo - ry to his Son, to the Spirit most

ears be at-tentive to the voice of my plea - ding.
found for - giveness: for this we re - vere you.
long-ing for the Lord more than watch - man for day - break.
deed God will re - deem from all its i - ni - quity.
Holy give praise, whose reign is for e - ver.

Text: The Grail. Music by Joseph Gelineau, S.J.

Psalm 131 (132) *Like a child rests (453), My soul is longing (950)*

Psalm 132 (133) *O come, bless the Lord (35, 36)*

Psalm 135 (136) 61

1. O give thanks to the LORD who is good,
2. Who a - lone has wrought mar - vel - lous works,
3. It was God who made the great lights,
4. The first - born of the E - gyp - tians God smote,
5. God di - vided the Red Sea in two,
6. God led the people through the desert,
7. God let Israel in - he - rit their land,
8. And God snatched us a - way from our foes,

Great is God's love, love with - out end;

Give thanks to the God _____ of gods,
whose wisdom it was made the skies,
the sun to rule in the day,
and brought Israel out from their midst,
and made Israel pass through the midst,
Nations in their great - ness God struck,
the heritage of Is - rael, God's servant;
God gives food to all li - ving things,

Great is God's love, love with - out end;

Give thanks to the Lord _____ of lords,
who fixed the earth firmly on the seas,
the moon and stars in the night,
arm out-stretched, with po - wer - ful hand,
Who flung Pharoah and his force in the sea,
Kings in their splen - dour God slew,
God re - mem - bered us in our dis - tress,
to the God of hea - ven give thanks.

Great is God's love, love with - out end.

Psalm 136 (137) v.1 *By the waters (216)*

Text: The Grail. Music: Joseph Gelineau, S.J.

Psalm 137 (138) **62**

I Lord, may our prayer__ rise like in-cense in your sight, may this
II In the__ pre-sence of the an - gels, O Lord, may we
III Lord, on the day__ that I called__ out for help, you__

place be__ filled with the fra-grance of Christ.
praise your__ name, may we praise__ your name.
an - swered me, you__ an - swered me.

1 I will thank you, Lord, with all of my heart,
   you have heard the words of my mouth.
   In the presence of the angels I will bless you,
   I will adore before your holy temple.

2 I will thank you, Lord,
   for your faithfulness and love
   beyond all my hopes and dreams.

On the day that I called you answered;
you gave life to the strength of my soul.

3 All who live on earth shall give you thanks
   when they hear the words of your voice.
   And all shall sing of your ways:
   'How great is the glory of God!'
   Psalm 138:1-5, David Haas

Psalm 138 (139) *O God, you search me (779); Yahweh, I know you are near (777); You know me, Lord (778)*

Psalm 140 (141) *Let my prayer rise (17, 18)*

Psalm 144 (145) 63

I WILL GIVE YOU GLÓRY, O GÓD MY KÍNG,
I will bléss your náme for éver. *(omit B, C)*

2 I will bléss you dáy after dáy
and práise your náme for éver.

3 You are gréat, Lord, híghly to be práised,
your gréatness cánnot be méasured.

4 Age to áge shall procláim your wórks,
shall decláre your míghty déeds,

5 shall spéak of your spléndour and glóry,
tell the tále of your wónderful wórks.

6 They will spéak of your térrible déeds,
recóunt your gréatness and míght.

7 They will recáll your abúndant góodness;
age to áge shall ríng out your jústice.

8 You are kínd and fúll of compássion,
slow to ánger, abóunding in lóve.

9 How góod you are, Lórd, to áll,
compássionate to áll your créatures.

10 All your créatures shall thánk you, O Lórd,
and your friénds shall repéat their bléssing.

11 They shall spéak of the glóry of your réign
and decláre your míght, O Gód,

12 to make knówn to áll your mighty déeds
and the glórious spléndour of your réign.

13 Yóurs is an éverlasting kíngdom;
your rúle lasts from áge to áge.

You are fáithful in áll your wórds
and lóving in áll your déeds.

14 You suppórt all thóse who are fálling
and ráise up áll who are bowed dówn.

15 The éyes of all créatures look to yóu
and you gíve them their fóod in due séason.

16 You ópen wíde your hánd,
grant the desíres of áll who líve.

17 You are júst in áll your wáys
and lóving in áll your déeds.

18 You are clóse to áll who cáll you,
who cáll on yóu from their héarts.

19 You gránt the desíres of those who féar you,
you héar their cry´ and you sáve them.

20 Lórd, you protéct all who lóve you;
but the wícked you will útterly destróy.

21 Let me spéak your práise, O Lórd,
let all péoples bléss your holy náme
for éver, for áges unénding. *(omit C)*

Glory be: see after Ps 90 (91), p.34

R. 1 I will bless your name for e - ver, O God my King.

Psalmtone
(underlinings in text) A B C D

R. 2 I will bless your name for e - ver, O God my King.

Psaomtone
(accents in text)

Text: The Grail. Response 1 and psalmtone by A. Gregory Murray, O.S.B. Response 2 and psalmtone by Stephen Dean

Ps145 (146) God my King (702); *Ps 147* Fill you hearts (703); *Ps 148* O praise ye (406);
Pss 149-50 Bring to the Lord (705); *Ps 150* see nos 5-6

The Seasons: Advent

64 Litany of the Word

Bernadette Farrell

1. Word of jus-tice, Al-le-lu - ia, Come to dwell here. Ma-ra-na-tha!

2 Word of mercy, ...
　　live among us, ...
3 Word of power, ...
　　live within us, ...
4 Word of freedom, ...
　　save your people.
5 Word of healing, ...
　　heal our sorrow.
6 Word of comfort, ...
　　bring us hope now, ...
7 Word of gladness, ...
　　fill our hearts now, ...
8 Word of wisdom, ...
　　Come renew us, ...
9 Word we long for, ...
　　word we thirst for, ...

10 Key of David, ...
　　Son of Mary, ...
11 Promised Saviour, ...
　　True Messiah, ...
12 Cry of prophets, ...
　　hope of ages, ...
13 Light of nations, ...
　　light in darkness, ...
14 Risen Saviour, ...
　　Lord of glory, ...
15 You we long for, ...
　　you we thirst for, ...
16 Here among us, ...
　　living in us, ...

Bernadette Farrell

65 Advent Wreath Service

John Schiavone

The priest gives the greeting in the usual manner, and then reads an introduction to the Sunday. He or another minister lights one candle on the Wreath while the cantor or choir sing the first invocation, ending with:

1st: Cantor. 2nd: All

Ky - ri - e　e - lei - son.
(Lord,＿＿ have mer - cy.)

After the second invocation:

1st: Cantor. 2nd: All

Chris - te　e - lei - son.
(Christ,＿＿ have mer - cy).

After the third invocation Lord have mercy *is sung, as above. Then the priest says:*
May Almighty God have mercy on us, forgive us our sins,
and bring us to everlasting life. **Amen.**

66 Advent Kyrie 2

Missa Emmanuel:Plainsong, arr. Richard Proulx

Each phrase: first time Cantor, repeated by all.

Lord, ___ have ___ mer- cy. Christ, ___ have ___ mer - cy. ___
Lord, ___ have ___ mer- cy. Christ, ___ have ___ mer - cy. ___

Repeat: Lord have mercy....

See also: *Kyrie Orbis Factor (501)*

67 Advent Kyrie 3

Short Mass for Advent & Lent, Stephen Dean

Cantor sings, all repeat

Ky - ri - e e - le - i - son. Chris - te e - le - i - son.
Ky - ri - e e - le - i - son. Chris - te e - le - i - son.

Repeat: Kyrie eleison

May almighty God have mercy on us, forgive us our sins, and bring us to everlasting life:

All (or Cantor, then All)

A - men.

Common Responsorial Psalms: *Psalm 24(25) no.43 ; psalm 84 (85), no. 50*

68 Gospel Acclamation 1 for Advent

Ken Simmons

Refrain

Je- sus is Lord, al - le - lu - ia! Je - sus shall come, Al - le - lu - ia!

Verses Cantor   ALL

Pre - pare a way for the Lord. Je - sus shall come, Al - le - lu - ia!

Cantor   ALL

Make straight the path for him. Je - sus shall come, Al - le - lu - ia!

Repeat Refrain

69 Gospel Acclamation 2 for Advent

Michael Joncas

Hal - le - lu - ia, hal - le - lu - ia, hal - le - lu - ia, hal - le - lu - ia.

70 Gospel Acclamation 3 for Advent

Stephen Dean

Cantor then All:

Al - le - lu - ia, al - le - lu - ia, Al - le - lu - ia, ma - ra - na - tha;

Al - le - lu - ia, al - le - lu - ia, Al - le - lu, al - le - lu - ia.

Cantor sings verse, then all repeat

Longer Ending: after the cantor's verse the music continues:

Cantor   **ALL**   *Cantor*   **ALL**

Al - le - lu - ia, al - le - lu - ia, Al - le - lu - ia, al - le lu - ia,

The refrain is then sung by all, as above, followed by the conclusion:

Cantor   **ALL**   *Cantor*   **ALL**

Al - le - lu - ia, al - le - lu - ia, Al - le - lu - ia, al - le - lu - ia.

71 Gospel Acclamation 4 for Advent

Christopher Walker

Cantor   **All**   *Cantor*   **All**

Al - le - lu - ia, al - le - lu - ia, Al - le - lu - ia, al - le - lu - ia.

72 Advent Gospel Acclamation for younger people

Christopher Walker

1. Stay a - wake, be— rea - dy, you do not know the hour when the

Lord is co ming. Stay a - wake, be— rea - dy, the Lord is coming soon!

Al - le - lu - ia, al-le - lu - ia, the Lord is co-ming___ soon.

2a/b, 3c   Change your lives, he's coming,
the one who will baptise with the Holy Spirit.
Change your lives, he's coming,
the Lord is coming soon!
Alleluia, alleluia the Lord is coming soon.

2c. Prepare! He's coming!
The one who will give peace to the world is coming.
Prepare! He's coming!
The reign of God is near.
Alleluia, alleluia! 'The reign of God is near.'

3a. Go back, tell John
all that you have heard and seen me doing.
Go back, tell John
the wonders that you see!
Alleluia, alleluia! 'The wonders that you see.'

3b. Change your lives, he's coming,
the one who is the light of the world is coming.
Change your lives, he's coming,
the Lord is coming soon!
Alleluia, alleluia! 'The Lord is coming soon.'

4a/b. By the pow'r of the Spirit,
Mary will give birth to a son called Jesus.
By the pow'r of the Spirit,
Emmanuel is near.
Alleluia, alleluia! 'Emmanuel is near.'

4c. You are blessed among women.
Mary you are blessed, you believe God's promise.
You are blessed among women,
the mother of my Lord.
Alleluia, alleluia! 'The Mother of my Lord.'

73 General Intercessions Response for Advent

We pray to the Lord. Come, Lord Je - sus, ma - ra - na-tha!___

➤ see also no 26

74 Eucharistic Acclamations: Sanctus

First time Cantor, second time All.   *Missa Emmanuel, Richard Proulx*

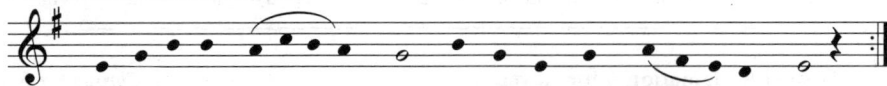

Ho- ly, ho- ly, ho - ly Lord, God of pow'r and God___ of might.
Ho- ly, ho- ly, ho - ly Lord, God of pow'r and God___ of might.

Cantor only.

Hea - ven and earth___ are full___ of your glo - ry.

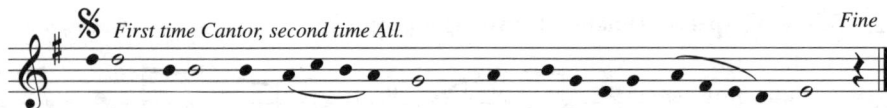

First time Cantor, second time All.   *Fine*

Ho-san - na in the high - est, ho - sanna in the high - est.
Ho-san - na in the high - est, ho - sanna in the high - est.

D.S. al Fine

Cantor only.

Bles - sed is he who comes in the name___ of___ the Lord. Hosanna...

75/6 Memorial Acclamation & Amen

Missa Emmanuel, Richard Proulx

May be sung first by cantor and repeated by All.

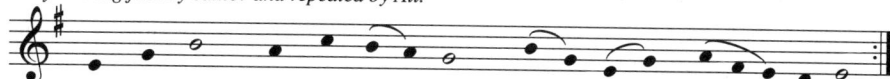

Christ has died, Christ is ri - sen, Christ will come a- gain.
A - men, a - men, a - men, a - men.

77 Agnus Dei

Missa Emmanuel, Richard Proulx

Cantor:

1. Je - sus, wis - dom and migh - ty Lord, you take a-way the
2. Je - sus, true branch of Jes - se's tree:
3. Key of Da - vid and Day- spring from on high:
4. De - sire of na - tions, our Em - ma - nu - el:

1, 2, 3.

4.

sins of the world, have mer - cy on us, grant us— peace,
All: Have mer - cy on us. *All:* Grant us— peace.

78 Advent Communion Song 1

Bernadette Farrell

Refrain

Bread of life, hope of the world, Je - sus Christ, our bro - ther:

feed us now, give us life, lead us to one a - no- ther.

Verses

1. Be with your peo - ple, Lord, send us your sa - ving Word;
2. Bring to our world of fear the truth we long to hear;

Je- sus Christ, light of glad - ness, come a- mong us now.
Je- sus Christ, hope of a - ges, come to save us now.

Christmas words

1 A child is born for us,
   a son is given to us,
   in our midst, Christ, our Lord
      and God
   comes as one who serves.

2 With our own eyes we see,
   with our own ears we hear
   the salvation of all the world,
   God's incarnate Word.

3 You are the hope of all,
   our promise and our call,
   radiant light in our darkness,
   truth to set us free.

Lent words

1 Our hunger for your Word,
   our thirsting for your truth,
   are the sign of your life in us
   till we rest in you.

2 To those whose eyes
      are blind
   you give a light to see;
   dawn of hope in the
      midst of pain,
   love which sets us free.

General words overleaf.

General words

Bread of life, hope of the world,
Jesus Christ, our brother:
feed us now, give us life,
lead us to one another.

1 As we proclaim your death,
   as we recall your life,
   we remember your promise
   to return again.

2 The bread we break and share
   was scattered once as grain;
   just as now it is gathered,
   make your people one.

3 We eat this living bread,
   we drink this saving cup:
   sign of hope in our broken world,
   source of lasting love.

4 Hold us in unity,
   in love for all to see;
   that the world may believe in you,
   God of all who live.

5 You are the bread of peace,
   you are the wine of joy,
   broken now for your people,
   poured in endless love.
   Bernadette Farrell

79 Advent Communion Song 2

Stephen Dean

Come, O come, Lord Je-sus;— come, O come, Lord Je-sus;—
come, O come, Lord Je-sus;— Come, Lord Je-sus, quick-ly come.

Repeat as required

Verses are sung above the chorus.

1 You, Lord, have spread a banquet for us,
   you, Lord, have spread a banquet for us,
   you, Lord, have spread a banquet for us,
   Come, Lord Jesus, quickly come.

2 You, Lord, have showered gifts upon us...

3 Your day will dawn in peace and justice...

4 Your day will see all sorrow banished...

5 Darkness will flee away for ever...

6 Come, Lord, into our hearts and heal us...

7 Join us in hope and love together...

80 Advent Communion Song 3

Marty Haugen

God of our jour-neys, day-break to night; lead us to
jus-tice and light. Grant us com-pass-ion,
strength for the day, wis-dom to walk in your way.

➤ *Verses: see Now in this banquet (623). Aother refrain: Lord, you can open (192)*

81

Come to set us free, come to make us your own.__ Come to show the

way to your peo-ple, your cho - sen.__ O - pen our lives__ to the light_

of your pro - mise.__ Come to our hearts_ with hea - ling,

come to our minds with po-wer, come to us and bring us your life.__

Verse

1 You are light which shines in dark-ness, Mor-ning Star which ne - ver sets.

O-pen our eyes which on - ly dim-ly see the truth which sets us free.

2 You are hope which brings us courage,
 you are strength which never fails.
 Open our minds to ways we do not know,
 but where your Spirit grows.

3 You are promise of salvation,
 you are God in human form.
 Bring to our world of emptiness and fear
 the Word we long to hear.

Bernadette Farrell

82

Verses 1 Bright and clear, as a trum-pet blast, a her - ald shout goes out:
 2 Take your stand on a lof - ty place, Mes–sen - ger of God.

drive a path through the wil - der-ness, a high-way for our God;
Shout, O shout with a voice of joy, cast all fear a - side.

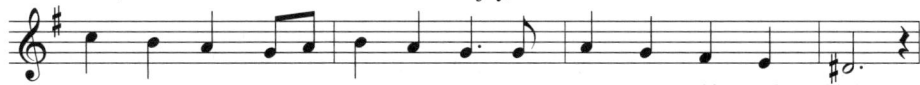

hills and moun-tains to be laid low, the val - leys lif - ted high,
Say to all in Je - ru - sa - lem, the ci - ty of the Lord:

ev' - ry na - tion and land shall see the glo - ry of our God.
'Look a - round you, the hour has come: see, here is your God.'

Refrain overleaf

Come, Lord, to a world of lon-ging, lis-ten to cre-a-tion's cry;

An-swer na-ture's dee-pest year-ning; ma-ni-fest God's reign.

Come, Lord, shi-ning star of mor-ning, rise up, scat-ter death's dark shade.

Come, Lord, migh-ty King E-ter-nal! Je-sus, Em-ma-nu-el!

3   See, he comes in pow'r and might, Master of all things.
See, the Lord of Victories, he the King of Kings.
Shepherd-like he will feed his flock and take them to his arms,
leading them to a place of rest, Saviour, King and God.

Peter McGrail

83

1 Blest be the Lord, the God of Israel,
who brings the dawn and darkest night dispels,
who raises up a mighty saviour from the earth,
of David's line, a son of royal birth.

2 The prophets tell a story just begun
of vanquished foe and glorious vict'ry won,
of promise made to all who keep the law
    as guide:
God's faithful love and mercy will abide.

3 This is the oath once sworn to Abraham:
all shall be free to dwell upon the land,
free now to praise, unharmed by the
    oppressor's rod,
holy and righteous in the sight of God.

4 And you, my child, this day you shall be called
the promised one, the prophet of our God,
for you will go before the Lord to clear the way,
and shepherd all into the light of day.

5 The tender love God promised from our birth
is soon to dawn upon this shadowed earth,
to shine on those whose sorrows seem to
    never cease,
to guide our feet into the path of peace.

The Benedictus (Luke 1:68-79), Owen Alstott

84

1 Like a sea without a shore
love divine is boundless.
Time is now and evermore
and his love surrounds us.
Maranatha! Maranatha!
Maranatha!
Come, Lord Jesus, come!

2 So that we could all be free
he appeared among us,
blest are those who have not seen,
yet believe his promise.

3 All our visions, all our dreams,
are but ghostly shadows
of the radiant clarity
waiting at life's close.

4 Death where is your victory?
Death where is your sting?
Closer than the air we breathe
is our risen King.

Estelle White

➤ Melody for no 83: see no 338

85

1 Before the earth had yet begun
her journey round the burning sun,
before a seed of life had stirred,
there sounded God's creating word.

2 In that bright dawning of the world,
ere ocean surged or wind unfurled,
the vaults of heaven with praises rang,
the morning stars together sang.

3 Thus when creation's Lord did take
the clay of earth our form to make,
God willed that to our race belong
the gifts of music, word, and song.

4 For us who would this God attend,
no earthly mind can comprehend
Eternal glory; praise alone
is our companion by that throne.
Herbert O'Driscoll

86

1 God is working his purpose out
as year succeeds to year,
God is working his purpose out
and the time is drawing near;
nearer and nearer draws the time,
the time that shall surely be,
when the earth shall be filled with the
glory of God
as the waters cover the sea.

2 From utmost east to utmost west
where human foot hath trod,
by the mouth of many messengers
goes forth the voice of God.
'Give ear to me, ye continents,
ye isles give ear to me,
that the earth may be filled with the
glory of God
as the waters cover the sea.'

3 What can we do to work God's work,
to prosper and increase
the friendship of all humankind,
the reign of the Prince of Peace?
What can we do to hasten the time,
the time that shall surely be,
when the earth shall be filled with the
glory of God
as the waters cover the sea?

4 March we forth in the strength of God
with the banner of Christ unfurled,
that the light of the glorious Gospel of
truth may shine throughout the world.
Fight we the fight with sorrow and sin,
to set their captives free,
that the earth may be filled with the
glory of God
as the waters cover the sea.

5 All we can do is nothing worth
unless God blesses the deed;
vainly we hope for the harvest–tide
till God gives life to the seed;
yet nearer and nearer draws the time,
the time that shall surely be,
when the earth shall be filled with the
glory of God
as the waters cover the sea.
A. C. Ainger (1841–1919)

87

1 Creator of the stars of night
the people's everlasting light,
Redeemer, Saviour of us all
O hear your servants when they call.

2 As once through Mary's flesh you came
to save us from our sin and shame,
so now, Redeemer, by your grace,
come heal again our fallen race.

3 And when on that last judgment day
we rise to glory from decay,
then come again, O Saviour blest,
and bring us to eternal rest.

4 To God the Father, God the Son,
and God the Spirit, three in one,
Praise, honour, might and glory be
from age to age eternally.
Irwin Udulutsch, OFM Cap, from
Conditor alme siderum (9th C.)

Wait for the Lord, whose day is near. Wait for the Lord, keep watch, take heart.

89

1 The day of the Lord shall come
as prophets have told,
when Christ shall make all things new,
no matter how old;
and some at the stars may gaze,
and some at God's word,
in vain to predict the time,
the Day of the Lord.

The desert shall spring to life
the hills shall rejoice;
the lame of the earth shall leap,
the dumb shall find voice;
the lamb with the lion shall lie,
and the last shall be first;
and nations for war no more
shall study or thirst.

2 The Day of the Lord shall come:
a thief in the night,
a curse to those in the wrong
who think themselves right,
a pleasure for those in pain
or with death at the door,
a true liberation for
the prisoners and poor.

3 The Day of the Lord shall come
and judgement be known,
and nations, like sheep and goats,
come close to the throne.
Then Christ shall himself reveal
asking all to draw near,
and see in his face all faces
once ignored here.

4 The Day of the Lord shall come,
but now is the time
To subvert earth's wisdom
with Christ's folly sublime,
by loving the loveless,
turning the tide and the cheek,
by walking beneath the cross
in step with the weak.
John Bell & Graham Maule

90

1 When the King shall come again
all his power revealing,
splendour shall announce his reign,
life and joy and healing:
earth no longer in decay,
hope no more frustrated;
this is God's redemption day
longingly awaited.

2 In the desert trees take root
fresh from his creation;
plants and flowers and sweetest fruit
join the celebration:
rivers spring up from the earth,
barren lands adorning;
valleys, this is your new birth,
mountains, greet the morning!

3 Strengthen feeble hands and knees,
fainting hearts, be cheerful!
God who comes for such as these
seeks and saves the fearful:
now the deaf can hear the dumb
sing away their weeping;
blind eyes see the injured come
walking, running, leaping.

4 There God's highway shall be seen
   where no roaring lion,
   nothing evil or unclean
   walks the road to Zion:
   ransomed people homeward bound
   all your praises voicing,
   see your Lord with glory crowned,
   share in his rejoicing!
Christopher Idle

91

1 Wake, awake! For night is dying,'
   the watchmen on the heights are crying,
   'Awake, Jerusalem, at last!'
   Midnight hears the welcome voices,
   and at the thrilling cry rejoices:
   'Come forth, you virgins, night is past;
   the bridegroom comes; awake,
   your lamps with gladness take, alleluia!
   And for his marriage feast prepare,
   for you must go to meet him there.'

2 Sion hears the watchmen singing,
   and all her heart with joy is springing;
   she wakes, she rises from her gloom:
   for her Lord comes down all-glorious,
   the strong in grace, in truth victorious;
   her star is risen, her light is come.
   Now come, O blessed one,
   God's own beloved Son; alleluia!
   We follow to the festal hall
   to feast with you, the Lord of all.

3 Now let earth and heaven adore you,
   as men and angels sing before you
   with harp and cymbal's joyful tone;
   of one pearl each shining portal,
   where we join with the choirs immortal
   of angels round your dazzling throne.
   No eye has seen, nor ear
   is yet attuned to hear,
   such great glory;
   alleluia, as here we sing
   our praise to you, eternal King!
Philipp Nicolai (1556-1608),
tr. Catherine Winkworth (1827-78) , alt.

92

1 Hark! a herald voice is calling;
   'Christ is nigh!' it seems to say;
   'Cast away the dreams of darkness,
   waken, children of the day!'

2 Startled at the solemn warning,
   let the earth–bound soul arise;
   Christ her Sun, all sloth dispelling,
   shines upon the morning skies.

3 Lo! the Lamb so long expected,
   comes with pardon down from heaven;
   let us meet him with repentance,
   pray that we may be forgiven.

4 So when next he comes with glory,
   wrapping all the earth in fear,
   may he then as our Defender
   on the clouds of heav'n appear.

5 Honour, glory, praise and blessing,
   to the Father and the Son,
   with the everlasting Spirit,
   while unending ages run.
6th C, tr. E.Caswall (1814–78), alt.

93

Christmas is coming,
the Church is glad to sing,
and let the Advent candles
brightly burn in a ring.

1 The first is for God's promise
   to put the wrong things right,
   and bring to earth's darkness
   the hope of love and light.

2 The second for the prophets,
   who said that Christ would come
   with good news for many
   and angry words for some.

3 The third is for the Baptist,
   who cried, 'Prepare the way.
   Be ready for Jesus,
   both this and every day.'

➤ *See also The Lord's coming (982-989); I rejoiced (992)*

4 The fourth is for the Virgin,
who mothered God's own son
and sang how God's justice
was meant for everyone.

5 At last we light the candle
kept new for Christmas day,
This shines bright for Jesus,
new-born, and here to stay.

Christ is among us.
The candles in the ring
remind us that our Saviour
will light up everything.
John L. Bell

94

1 On Jordan's bank the Baptist's cry
announces that the Lord is nigh;
come then and hearken, for he brings
glad tidings from the King of kings.

2 Then cleansed be every Christian breast,
and furnished for so great a guest!
Yea, let us each our heart prepare,
for Christ to come and enter there.

3 For thou art our salvation, Lord,
our refuge and our great reward;
without thy grace our souls must fade,
and wither like a flower decayed.

4 Stretch forth thy hand to heal our sore,
and make us rise, to fall no more;
once more upon thy people shine,
and fill the world with love divine.

5 All praise, eternal Son, to thee
whose advent sets thy people free,
whom, with the Father, we adore,
and Holy Ghost, for evermore.
C. Coffin (1676–1749), tr. J. Chandler (1808–76)

95

Come Sa - viour, come like dew on the grass;⸺ break
Ro - ra - te cae - li de - su - per⸺ et

through the clouds⸺ like gen - tle rain.
nu - bes plu - ant jus - tum.

1 Be angry, Lord, no more with us;
remember no longer our transgression.
See the city of God laid waste and desolate:
Zion is turned to wilderness,
Jerusalem, ravaged and ruined,
your dwelling place and the Holy of holies,
the house of your glory;
silent are those voices now
that once proclaimed your praise.

2 We have gone astray;
in the multitude of our sins
we have been made unclean,
fallen, fallen,
stricken as the leaves of autumn.
The stormwind carries us away,
the tempest of our evil deeds;

you have turned away from us
the face of your mercy,
and our iniquity has crushed us
like a potter's vessel.

3 O Lord our God, look upon your people
in their affliction:
be mindful of your promises.
Send us the Lamb who will
set up his dominion
from the Rock of the Wilderness to Zion
throned on her mountain.
There is no other whose power
can break our chains and set us free.

4 Be comforted, be comforted,
take heart, my people:
you shall quickly see your salvation.

Why do you waste yourself with grief,
though you have walked so long
    with sorrow?
I am your Saviour, be afraid no more.

For am I not God,
the Lord your God whom you worship,
the Holy One of Israel,
come to redeem you?

Latin, 10th C., tr. Luke Connaughten (1919-76)

96

1 Console my people, the ones dear to me;
    speak to the heart of Jerusalem:
    the time of your mourning is ended now,
    the Lord of life will come.

*Michael Joncas, based on
Isaiah 40:1-11*

A voice cries out in the wil - der - ness: Pre - pare a way for the Lord!___

A voice cries out in the wil - der - ness: Make straight a high-way for God!___

2 Ev'ry valley is made a plain,
    ev'ry mountain is levelled;
    the glory of God shall then be revealed,
    and the nations will sing in praise.

3 A voice shouts: 'Cry!' O what shall I cry?
    All flesh is like grass and its flowers;
    the grass may wither, the flowers may fade,
    but the Word of the Lord is forever.

4 Zion, shout from the mountain-top,
    lift up your voice, O Jerusalem,
    and say to the people of God's own land,
    'Behold, behold your God!'

5 The Lord will appear as a shepherd,
    holding his lambs in his arms,
    keeping his flock so close to his heart,
    leading them all, old and young.

97

1 Comfort, comfort, now my people,
    Speak of peace- so says your God;
    comfort all who sit in darkness,
    burdened by a heavy load.
    To Jerusalem proclaim:
    God will take away your shame.
    Now get ready to recover,
    guilt and suffering are over.

2 Hear the herald's proclamation
    in the desert far and near,
    calling all to true repentance,
    telling that the Lord is near.

Oh, that warning cry obey!
For your God prepare a way.
Let the valleys rise to greet him
and the hills bow down to meet him.

3 Straighten out what has been crooked,
    make the roughest places plain;
    Let your hearts be true and humble,
    as befits God's holy reign.
    Soon the glory of the Lord
    shall on earth be shed abroad;
    Human flesh shall surely see it;
    God is ready to decree it.

*Is 40:1-8; J. Olearius (1611-84); tr. Catherine
Winkworth (1827-78), alt. by John L. Bell*

98

Be-hold the Lamb of God,— who comes to take our sins— a-way, to bind the bro-ken heart,— and set the captives free:— his king-dom will not end,— his. mer-cy will not fal - ter. He comes, the hope of a - ges, the joy of all the world.

Stephen Dean

1 Hear ye the voice:
   'Prepare a way for one who comes!'
   Make straight his paths,
   the Saviour comes with power to heal.

2 Speak to my flock:
   'Your time of woe is ended.'

   Shout from the heights,
   'Jerusalem, your God is near!'

3 See from the heavens,
   the Spirit comes to rest on him.
   God's voice resounds:
   'Behold my well-beloved Son.'

99

1 O comfort my people and calm all their fear,
   and tell them the time of salvation draws near.
   O tell them I come to remove all their shame.
   Then they will forever give praise to my name.

2 Proclaim to the cities of Juda my word:
   that gentle yet strong is the hand of the Lord.
   I rescue the captives, my people defend
   and bring them to justice and joy without end.

3 All mountains and hills shall become as a plain
   for vanished are mourning and hunger and pain.
   And never again shall these war against you.
   Behold I come quickly to make all things new.
   Chrysogonus Waddell, OCSO, from Isaiah 40:1-2.4.9

100

1 Come, thou long–expected Jesus,
   born to set thy people free,
   from our fears and sins release us,
   let us find our rest in thee.

2 Israel's strength and consolation,
   hope of all the earth thou art;
   dear desire of every nation,
   joy of every longing heart.

3 Born thy people to deliver,
   born a child and yet a king,
   born to reign in us for ever,
   now thy gracious kingdom bring.

4 By thine own eternal Spirit
   rule in all our hearts alone;
   by thine all–sufficient merit
   raise us to thy glorious throne.
   Charles Wesley (1707–88)

101

1 Now watch for God's coming, be
   patient till then;
   like sunshine he'll brighten all women
   and men;
   who hope in the Lord will possess
   fertile land;
   the poor he will welcome and grasp
   by the hand.

2 Our steps are directed, God watches
   our path;
   he guides us and holds us and saves us
   from wrath,
   and though we may fall we will not go
   headlong,
   for God gives sound footing and keeps
   us from wrong.

3 So wait for his coming, be patient
   till then;
   the wicked are armed and would kill
   honest men.
   Their arms shall be broken, no refuge
   they'll see,
   but saved are the needy by God's
   own decree.

4 Now those who do evil will wither
   like grass,
   like green of the springtime they fade
   and they pass,
   so trust in the Lord and to him give
   your life,
   he'll bring heart's desires and peace in
   our strife.
   Willard F. Jabusch

102

1 Hail to the Lord's anointed!
   Great David's greater son!
   Hail, in the time appointed,
   his reign on earth begun!
   He comes to break oppression,
   to set the captive free;
   to take away transgression,
   and rule in equity.

2 He shall come down like showers
   upon the fruitful earth,
   and love, joy, hope, like flowers,
   spring in his path to birth:
   before him on the mountains
   shall peace the herald go;
   and righteousness in fountains
   from hill to valley flow.

3 Kings shall fall down before him,
   and gold and incense bring;
   all nations shall adore him,
   his praise all people sing;
   to him shall prayer unceasing
   and daily vows ascend;
   his kingdom still increasing
   a kingdom without end.

4 O'er every foe victorious,
   he on his throne shall rest,
   from age to age more glorious,
   all–blessing and all–blest;
   the tide of time shall never
   his covenant remove;
   his name shall stand for ever;
   that name to us is love.
   James Montgomery (1771–1854)

103

1 Promised Lord, and Christ is he,
   may we soon his kingdom see.
   Come, O Lord, speedily;
   come in glory, come in glory,
   come in glory, speedily.

2 Teaching, healing once was he,
   may we soon his kingdom see.

3 Dead and buried once was he,
   may we soon his kingdom see.

4 Risen from the dead is he,
   may we soon his kingdom see.

5 Soon to come again is he,
   may we soon his kingdom see.
   Come, O Lord, speedily,
   in our lifetime, in our lifetime,
   in our lifetime may it be.
   Roger Ruston, based on a Passover song

104

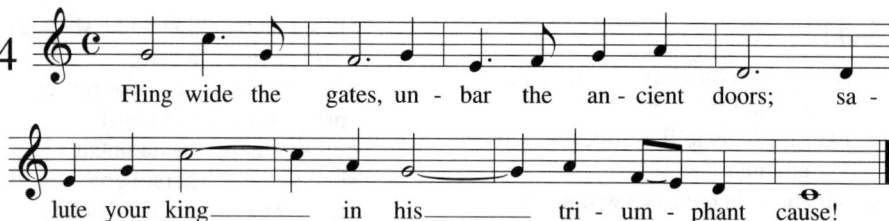

Fling wide the gates, un-bar the an-cient doors; sa-lute your king____ in his____ tri-um-phant cause!

1 Now all the world belongs to Christ our Lord:
let all creation greet the living Word!

2 Who has the right to worship him today?
All those who gladly serve him and obey.

3 He comes to save all those who trust his name,
and will declare them free from guilt and shame.

4 Who is the victor glorious from the fight?
He is our King, our life, our Lord, our right!

Michael Perry (1942-96) from Psalm 24

105

1 Lift up your heads, you mighty gates;
behold the King of glory waits!
The King of kings is drawing near;
the Saviour of the world is here.

2 O blest the land, the city blest,
where Christ the ruler is confessed!
O happy hearts and happy homes
to whom this King of triumph comes!

3 Fling wide the portals of your heart;
make it a temple, set apart
from earthly use for heav'n's employ,
adorned with prayer and love and joy.

4 So come, my Sovereign, enter in!
Let new and nobler life begin;
your Holy Spirit guide us on,
until the glorious crown be won.
George Weissel (1590-1635), tr.
Catherine Winkworth (1827–1878), alt

106

1 The King shall come when morning dawns
and light triumphant breaks,
when beauty gilds the eastern hills
and life to joy awakes.

2 Not as of old a little child,
to bear and fight and die,
but crowned with glory like the sun
that lights the morning sky.

3 O brighter than the rising morn
when he, victorious, rose,
and left the lonesome place of death,
despite the rage of foes.

4 O brighter than the glorious morn
shall this fair morning be,
when Christ our King in beauty comes,
and we his face shall see!

5 The King shall come when morning dawns
and light and beauty brings;
'Hail, Christ the Lord!' your people pray,
'Come quickly, King of kings!'
John Brownlie (1859–1925)

107

The King of glory comes, the nation rejoices,
open the gates before him, lift up your voices.

1 Who is the King of glory
how shall we call him?
He is Emmanuel,
the promised of ages.

2 In all of Galilee,
in city and village,
he goes among his people,
curing their illness.

3 Sing then of David's Son,
our Saviour and brother;
in all of Galilee
was never another.

4 He gave his life for us,
the pledge of salvation.
He took upon himself
the sins of the nation.

5 He conquered sin and death;
he truly has risen.
And he will share with us
his heavenly vision.
Willard F. Jabusch

108

1 The voice of God goes out to all the
world:
his glory speaks across the universe.
The Great King's herald cries from star
to star;
*with power, with justice, he will walk
his way.*

2 Give glory to the mystery revealed,
the voice of God, his image and his Word:
his word of peace, the image of his grace:

3 The Lord has said: Receive my messenger,
my promise to the world, my pledge
made flesh,
a lamp to every nation, light from light:

4 The broken reed he will not trample down,
nor set his heel upon the dying flame.
He binds the wounds, and health is in
his hand:

5 Anointed with the Spirit and with power,
he comes to crown with comfort all the
weak,
to show the face of justice to the poor:

6 His touch will bless the eyes that
darkness held,
the lame shall run, the halting tongue
shall sing,
and prisoners laugh in light and liberty:
Luke Connaughton (1919–79)

109

1 Lo, he comes with clouds descending,
once for favour'd sinners slain;
thousand thousand saints attending
swell the triumph of his train:
Alleluia! Alleluia! Alleluia!
God appears on earth to reign.

2 Every eye shall now behold him
robed in glorious majesty;
those who set at naught and sold him,
pierced and nailed him to the tree,
deeply wailing,
shall the true Messiah see.

3 Those dear tokens of his passion
still his dazzling body bears,
cause of endless exultation
to his ransomed worshippers:
with what rapture
gaze we on those glorious scars.

4 Yea, Amen, let all adore thee,
high on thine eternal throne;
Saviour, take the power and glory,
claim the kingdom for thine own:
Come, Lord Jesus!
Everlasting God, come down!
Charles Wesley (1707–1788)

110

1 The coming of our God
our thoughts must now employ;
then let us meet him on the road
with songs of holy joy.

2 The everlasting Son,
was born to set us free;
and he a servant's form put on,
to gain our liberty.

3 Daughter of Sion, rise
to greet your infant King,
nor let your stubborn heart despise
the pardon he doth bring.

4 In glory from his throne
again will Christ descend,
and summon all that are his own
to joys that never end.

5 Let deeds of darkness fly
before the approaching morn,
for unto sin 'tis ours to die,
and serve the virgin–born.

6 Our joyful praises sing
to Christ, that set us free;
like tribute to the Father bring,
and, Holy Ghost, to thee.

Charles Coffin (1676–1749), tr. R.
Campbell (1814–68), alt.

111

For you, O Lord, my soul in still-ness waits; tru-ly my hope is in you.

1. O Lord of Light, our on - ly hope of glo - ry, your ra - diance shines in all who look to you, come, light the hearts of all in dark and sha-dow.
2. O Spring of Joy, rain down up - on our spi - rits, our thir - sty hearts are year-ning for your Word, come, make us whole, be com - fort to our hearts.
3. O Root of Life, im - plant your seed with - in us, and in your ad - vent, draw us all to you, our hope re - born in dy - ing and in ri- sing.
4. O Key of Know - ledge, guide us in our pil-gri-mage, we ev - er seek, yet un - ful- filled re - main, o - pen to us the path-way of your peace.

5 Come, let us bow before the God who made us,
let ev'ry heart be opened to the Lord,
for we are all the people of his hand.

6 Here we shall meet the Maker of the heavens,
Creator of the mountains and the seas,
Lord of the stars, and present to us now.

Marty Haugen

112

1 O come, O come, Emmanuel,
and ransom captive Israel,
that mourns in lonely exile here
until the Son of God appear:
Rejoice, rejoice! Emmanuel
shall come to thee, O Israel.

2 O come, thou wisdom from on high,
and order all things mightily;
to us the path of knowledge show,
and teach us in her ways to go.

3 O come, O come, thou Lord of might,
who to thy tribes, on Sinai's height
in ancient times, didst give the law
in cloud and majesty and awe:

4 O come, thou Rod of Jesse, free
thine own from Satan's tyranny;
from depths of hell thy people save,
and give them vict'ry o'er the grave:

5 O come, thou key of David, come
and open wide our heavenly home;
make safe the way that leads on high,
and close the path to misery.

6 O come, thou dayspring, come and cheer
our spirits by thine advent here;
disperse the gloomy clouds of night,
and death's dark shadows put to flight:

7 O come, desire of nations, bind
in one the hearts of humankind;
bid every sad division cease,
and be thyself our Prince of peace.

> *From the 'Great O Antiphons' (12th–13th*
> *C.), tr. J.M. Neale (1818–66) (vv1,3,5,6);*
> *composite (others)*

113

1 The angel Gabriel from heaven came,
his wings as drifted snow, his eyes as flame;
'All hail,' said he, thou lowly maiden
    Mary,
most highly favoured lady.' Gloria!

2 For known a blessed Mother thou shalt be,
all generations laud and honour thee,
thy Son shall be Emmanuel, by seers
    foretold;
most highly favoured lady.' Gloria!

3 Then gentle Mary meekly bowed her head,
To me be as it pleaseth God,' she said.
'My soul shall laud and magnify his
    holy name.'
Most highly favoured lady. Gloria!

4 Of her, Emmanuel, the Christ was born
in Bethlehem, all on a Christmas morn,
and Christian folk throughout the world
    will ever say
'most highly favoured lady.' Gloria!
> *Basque carol, paraphrased by*
> *Sabine Baring–Gould (1834–1924)*

114

1 When the Angel came to Mary,
he said 'Be at peace'
for the Lord God shall be with you,
his love will not cease.'
And Mary bore Jesus Christ,
our Saviour for to be:
and the first and the last and
the greatest is he, is he, is he;
and the first and the last and
the greatest is he.

2 When the Angel came to Mary,
he said 'Do not fear.
for his power shall be upon you,
a child you will bear.'

3 When the Angel came to Mary,
he said 'Hear his name,
for his title shall be Jesus
of kingly acclaim.'

4 When the Angel came to Mary,
she said 'Be it so:
for the Lord God is my master,
his will I must do.'
> *Michael Perry (1942-96)*

➤ *See also Our Lady (Annunciation, 330-4;*
Magnificat: 23-25, 335-340, 880)

115

1 Praise we the Lord this day,
this day so long foretold,
whose promise shone with cheering ray
on waiting saints of old.

2 The prophet gave the sign
for faithful men to read;
a virgin, born of David's line,
shall bear the promised seed.

3 Ask not how this should be,
but worship and adore;
like her, whom heaven's majesty
came down to shadow o'er.

4 Meekly she bowed her head
to hear the gracious word,
Mary, the pure and lowly maid,
the favoured of the Lord.

5 Blessèd shall be her name
in all the Church on earth,
through whom that wondrous mercy came,
the incarnate Saviour's birth.

6 Jesus, the virgin's son,
we praise thee and adore,
who art with God the Father One
and spirit evermore.

Anonymous

116

1 Long ago, prophets knew
Christ would come, born a Jew,
come to make all things new,
bear his people's burden,
freely love and pardon.
  Ring, bells, ring, ring, ring!
  Sing, choirs, sing, sing, sing!
  When he comes,
  when he comes,
  who will make him welcome?

2 God in time, God in man,
this is God's timeless plan:
he will come, as a man,
born himself of woman,
God divinely human:

3 Mary, hail! Though afraid,
she believed, she obeyed.
In her womb God is laid,
till the time expected,
nurtured and protected:

4 Journey ends: where afar
Bethlem shines, like a star,
stable door stands ajar.
Unborn Son of Mary,
Saviour, do not tarry.
  Ring, bells, ring, ring, ring!
  Sing, choirs, sing, sing, sing!
  Jesus comes,
  Jesus comes:
  we will make him welcome.

F. Pratt Green

117

1 O come, divine Messiah!
The world in silence waits the day
when hope shall sing its triumph,
and sadness flee away.

Dear Saviour, haste; come, come to earth:
dispel the night, and show your face,
and bid us hail the dawn of grace.
O come, divine Messiah!
The world in silence waits the day
when hope shall sing its triumph,
and sadness flee away.

2 O come, desired of nations,
whom priests and prophets long foretold,
will break the captive fetters,
redeem the long–lost fold.

3 O come in peace and meekness,
for lowly will your cradle be:
all clothed in human weakness
shall we your Godhead see.

Abbé Simon-Joseph Pellegrin (1663-
1745); tr. Sr Mary of St Philip, 1877, alt

118   Christmas Gathering Song

Piae Cantiones, 1582

Gau-de - te, gau de - te, Chris-tus est na-tus ex Ma - ri - a vir- gi-ne. Gau-de-te.

Verses

Na - ture mar - vels at the sight, an - gels sing the glo - ry:
Hail___ Ma - ry, ev - er blest, Moth - er of the prom - ise.
With the wise men from the east, with the stars of heav - en,
Now is born Em - ma - nu - el, now is come sal - va - tion.

God be - comes a lit - tle child, shep-herds tell the sto - ry.
By your word the Word - made - flesh came to dwell a - mong us.
with the shep - herd and the sheep, come, let us a - dore him.
Sing we all no - el, no - el! Sing in ex - ul - ta - tion!

119   Christmastide Gloria 1

Missa Ubi Caritas, Bob Hurd

Glo-ri - a in ex - cel - sis De - o, et in ter- ra pax ho-mi-ni-bus

bo - nae vo - lun - ta- tis.

After last refrain   *Fine*

A - men.   A - men.

120   Christmastide Gloria 2

1 Joyful news to you I bring:
Christ the Lord is here on earth,
our Redeemer and our King:
sing with gladness at his birth.
Gloria in excelsis Deo!

2 Joyful news to you I bring:
Jesus Christ is born tonight,
Now let all the heavens ring:
praises to the Lord of light.

3 Joyful news to you I bring:
Jesus Christ, a living sign,
for our human ransoming
comes to us through love divine.

4 Joyful news we sing today:
incarnation, living bread,
passion, taking sin away,
resurrection from the dead.

Paul Inwood

121 Psalm for Christmastide (Ps 97(98)) 1-6

David Haas & Marty Haugen

Responses 1 & 2

R.1 All the ends of the earth have seen the pow-er of God;
R.2 Sing to the Lord a new song, for God has done won-der-ful deeds.

all the ends of the earth have seen the po-wer of God.
Sing to the Lord a new song, for God has done won-der-ful deeds.

Response 3

The Lord comes to the earth to rule the earth with

Lord comes to the earth to rule the earth with jus-tice.

1. Sing to the Lord a new song,
for God has done wondrous deeds;
whose right hand has won the vict'ry for us,
God's holy arm.

2. The Lord has made salvation known,
and justice revealed to all.
Remembering kindness and faithfulness
to Israel.

3. All of the ends of earth have seen
salvation by our God.
Joyfully sing out all you lands,
break forth in song.

4. Sing to the Lord with harp and song,
with trumpet and with horn.
Sing in your joy before the king,
the king, our Lord.

122 Gospel Acclamation for Christmastide

Stephen Dean

Al-le-lu - ia, al-le-lu - ia, al-le-lu - ia.

Midnight Mass verse
I bring you tidings of great joy:
Today a Saviour has been born to us,
he is Christ the Lord.

Christmas Day verse
A hallowed day has dawned upon us.
O come you nations, worship the Lord,
for today a great light has shone down upon the
earth.

Holy Family verse
May the peace of Christ reign in your hearts.
May the message of Christ
find a home with you, alleluia.

Second Sunday of Christmas verse
Glory to you, Lord Jesus Christ,
proclaimed to the nations,
preached to the pagans, believed by the world

Epiphany verse
We saw his star as it rose,
and we we have come to give him homage,
alleluia.

123 Communion Song for Christmas

➢ *See no. 78, Bread of life*

➢ *Lamb of God with seasonal verses: no. 593*

124

John L.Bell

He became poor that we may be rich, lo-ving the world and lea-ving his throne;

King of all kings, and Lord of all lords, flesh of our flesh and bone — of our bone.

125

1. A child is born in Beth - le - hem, al - le - lu - ia:
2. Through Ga - bri - el the Word has come, al - le - lu - ia:
3. With - in a man - ger now he lies, al - le - lu - ia:
4. The shep-herds hear the an - gel's word, al - le - lu - ia:

so leap with joy Je - ru - sa - lem, al - le - lu - ia, al - le - lu - ia.
the Vir - gin will con - ceive a son, al - le - lu - ia, al - le - lu - ia.
who reigns on high be - yond the skies, al - le - lu - ia, al - le - lu - ia.
this child is tru - ly Christ the Lord, al - le - lu - ia, al - le - lu - ia.

Refrain

A new song let us sing: for Christ is born, let us a-dore and let our glad-ness ring.

5 From Saba, from the rising sun, *alleluia:*
with incense, gold, and myrrh they come,
alleluia, alleluia.

6 Till with their gifts they enter in,
and kings adore the new–born King,

7 From virgin's womb this child is born,
the Light from Light who brings the dawn,

8 He comes to free us from our strife,
and share with us the Father's life,

9 At this the coming of the Word,
O come, let us adore the Lord,

10 To Father, Son, and Spirit praise,
from all his creatures all their days,

Latin, 14th C., tr. Ralph Wright, O.S.B.

126

1 A noble flow'r of Juda
from tender roots has sprung,
a rose from stem of Jesse,
as prophets long had sung;
a blossom fair and bright,
that in the midst of winter
will change to dawn our night.

2 The rose of grace and beauty
of which Isaiah sings
is Mary, virgin mother,
and Christ the flow'r she brings.
By God's divine decree
she bore our loving Saviour
who died to set us free.

3 To Mary, dearest mother,
with fervent hearts we pray:
grant that your tender infant
will cast our sins away,
and guide us with his love
that we shall ever serve him
and live with him above.

German, 15th century, tr. Anthony G Petti

127

1 O little town of Bethlehem,
how still we see thee lie!
Above thy deep and dreamless sleep
the silent stars go by.
Yet, in thy dark streets shineth
the everlasting light;
the hopes and fears of all the years
are met in thee tonight.

2 O morning stars, together
proclaim the holy birth,
and praises sing to God the King,
and peace to men on earth;
for Christ is born of Mary;
and, gathered all above,
while mortals sleep, the angels keep
their watch of wondering love.

3 How silently, how silently,
the wondrous gift is given!
So God imparts to human hearts
the blessings of his heaven.
No ear may hear his coming;
but in this world of sin,
where meek souls will receive him, still
the dear Christ enters in.

4 O holy child of Bethlehem,
descend to us, we pray;
cast out our sin, and enter in,
be born in us today.
We hear the Christmas angels
the great glad tidings tell:
O come to us, abide with us,
our Lord Emmanuel.

Phillips Brooks (1835–93)

128

1 Once in royal David's city
stood a lowly cattle shed,
where a mother laid her baby
in a manger for his bed;
Mary was that Mother mild,
Jesus Christ her little child.

2 He came down to earth from heaven,
who is God and Lord of all,
and his shelter was a stable
and his cradle was a stall;
with the poor, and mean, and lowly,
lived on earth our Saviour holy.

3 And through all his wondrous childhood
he would honour and obey,
love, and watch the lowly maiden
in whose gentle arms he lay;
Christian children all must be
mild, obedient, good as he.

4 For he is our childhood's pattern,
day by day like us he grew;
he was little, weak and helpless,
tears and smiles like us he knew;
and he feeleth for our sadness,
and he shareth in our gladness.

5 And our eyes at last shall see him
through his own redeeming love,
for that child so dear and gentle
is our Lord in heaven above;
and he leads his children on
to the place where he is gone.

6 Not in that poor lowly stable,
with the oxen standing by,
we shall see him; but in heaven,
set at God's right hand on high;
when like stars his children crowned
all in white shall wait around.

Mrs C.F. Alexander (1818-1895)

129

1 God rest you merry, gentlemen,
let nothing you dismay,
for Jesus Christ our Saviour
was born on Christmas Day,

to save us all from Satan's pow'r
when we were gone astray;
O tidings of comfort and joy,
comfort and joy,
O tidings of comfort and joy.

2 In Bethlehem, in Judah,
this blessed Babe was born,
and laid within a manger,
upon this blessed morn;
the which his Mother Mary,
did nothing take in scorn.

3 From God our heavenly Father,
a blessed angel came;
and unto certain shepherds
brought tidings of the same;
how that in Bethlehem was born
the Son of God by name:

4 'Fear not', then said the angel,
'Let nothing you affright,
this day is born a Saviour
of a pure virgin bright,
to free all those who trust in him
from Satan's power and might.'

5 The shepherds at those tidings
rejoicèd much in mind,
and left their flocks a-feeding,
in tempest, storm and wind;
and went to Bethlehem straightway,
this blessed Babe to find.

6 And when to Bethlehem they came
whereat this infant lay,
they found him in a manger,
where oxen feed on hay;
his mother Mary kneeling,
unto the Lord did pray.

7 Now to the Lord sing praises,
all you within this place,
and with true love and fellowship
each other now embrace;
this holy tide of Christmas
all others doth deface.
English Traditional Carol (18th cent.)

130

1 Angels we have heard in heaven
sweetly singing o'er our plains,
and the mountain tops in answer
echoing their joyous strains.
Gloria in excelsis Deo.
Gloria in excelsis Deo.

2 Shepherds, why this exultation?
Why your rapturous strain prolong?
Tell us of the gladsome tidings,
which inspire your joyous song.

3 Come to Bethlehem, and see him
o'er whose birth the angels sing,
come, adore, devoutly kneeling,
Christ the Lord, the new–born king.

4 See him in a manger lying
whom the choir of angels praise!
Mary, Joseph, come to aid us
while our hearts in love we raise.
James Chadwick (1813–82)

131

1 Angels from the realms of glory,
wing your flight o'er all the earth;
you who sang creation's story,
now proclaim Messiah's birth:
Come and worship,
come and worship,
worship Christ, the new-born King.

2 Shepherds, in the fields abiding,
watching o'er your flocks by night,
God on earth is now residing,
yonder shines the infant light:

3 Sages, leave your contemplations,
brighter visions beam afar;
seek the great Desire of nations,
you have seen his morning star:

4 Though an infant now we view him,
he shall fill his heav'nly throne,
gather all the nations to him;
every knee shall then bow down.
Vv.1-3, James Montgomery (1771-1854);
v4 from 'Christmas Box', 1825

132

1. Twas in the moon of win-ter-time, when all the birds had fled,
that God the Lord of all the earth sent an-gel choirs in-stead;
Be-fore their light the stars grew dim, and wand'-ring hun-ters heard the hymn:
Je-sus your King is born, Je-sus is born, in ex-cel-sis glo-ri-a.

2 The earliest moon of wintertime
is not so round and fair
as was the ring of glory round
the helpless infant there.
The chiefs from far before him knelt
with gifts of fox and beaver pelt.
Jesus your king is born,..

3 Oh, children of the forest free,
the angel song is true:
the holy child of earth and sky
is born this day for you;
come kneel before the radiant boy,
who brings you beauty, peace and joy.
Jesus your king is born ...

Jean de Bréboeuf (1593-1649), tr. Jesse E.
Middleton (1872-1960)

133

1 While shepherds watched their flocks
    by night,
all seated on the ground,
the angel of the Lord came down,
and glory shone around.

2 'Fear not,' said he, (for mighty dread
had seized their troubled mind)
'Glad tidings of great joy I bring
to all of humankind.'

3 'To you in David's town this day
is born of David's line
a Saviour, who is Christ the Lord;
and this shall be the sign:

4 'The heavenly Babe you there shall find
to human view displayed,
all meanly wrapped in swathing bands,
and in a manger laid.'

5 Thus spoke the Seraph; and forthwith
appeared a shining throng
of angels praising God, who thus
addressed their joyful song:

6 'All glory be to God on high,
and on the earth be peace,
goodwill henceforth from heaven to all
begin and never cease.'

Nahum Tate (1652–1715)

134

1 On Christmas night all Christians sing,
to hear the news the angels bring:
on Christmas night all Christians sing,
to hear the news the angels bring:
news of great joy, news of great mirth,
news of our merciful King's birth.

2 Then why should we on earth be so sad,
  since our Redeemer made us glad?
  Then why should we on earth be so sad,
  since our Redeemer made us glad?
  When from our sin he set us free,
  all for to gain our liberty?

3 When sin departs before his grace,
  then life and health come in its place;
  when sin departs before his grace,
  then life and health come in its place;
  angels and men with joy may sing,
  all for to see the new–born King.

4 All out of darkness we have light,
  which made the angels sing this night:
  all out of darkness we have light,
  which made the angels sing this night:
  'Glory to God and peace to men,
  now and for evermore. Amen.'
            The Sussex Carol. Traditional

135

1 It came upon the midnight clear,
  that glorious song of old,
  from angels bending near the earth
  to touch their harps of gold;
  'Peace on the earth, good will to all,
  from heaven's all gracious King!'
  The world in solemn stillness lay
  to hear the angels sing.

2 Yet with the woes of sin and strife
  the world has suffered long;
  beneath the angel–strain have rolled
  two thousand years of wrong;
  and man, at war with man, hears not
  the love song which they bring:
  O hush the noise, ye men of strife,
  and hear the angels sing!

3 For lo, the days are hastening on,
  by prophets seen of old,
  when with the ever–circling years
  shall come the time foretold,
  when the new heaven and earth shall own
  the Prince of Peace their king,
  and all the world repeat the song
  which now the angels sing.
            E. H. Sears (1810–76)

136

1 Silent night, holy night,
  all is calm, all is bright,
  round yon virgin mother and child;
  holy infant, so tender and mild:
  sleep in heavenly peace,
  sleep in heavenly peace.

2 Silent night, holy night.
  Shepherds quake at the sight,
  glories stream from heaven afar,
  heavenly hosts sing alleluia;
  Christ, the Saviour is born,
  Christ, the Saviour is born.

3 Silent night, holy night.
  Son of God, love's pure light
  radiant beams from thy holy face,
  with the dawn of redeeming grace:
  Jesus, Lord, at thy birth,
  Jesus, Lord, at thy birth.
            Joseph Mohr (1792–1848), tr. J. Young

137

1 Away in a manger, no crib for a bed,
  the little Lord Jesus laid down his sweet
      head,
  the stars in the bright sky looked down
      where he lay,
  the little Lord Jesus asleep on the hay.

2 The cattle are lowing, the baby awakes,
  but little Lord Jesus no crying he makes.
  I love thee, Lord Jesus! Look down from
      the sky,
  and stay by my side until morning is nigh.

3 Be near me, Lord Jesus; I ask thee to stay
  close by me for ever, and love me, I pray.
  Bless all the dear children in thy tender
      care,
  and fit us for heaven, to live with thee there.
            Vv. 1 & 2: Anon;
            v. 3 J.T. McFarland (1851–1913)

138

1 Infant holy, infant lowly,
for his bed a cattle stall;
oxen lowing, little knowing
Christ the babe is Lord of all.
Swift are winging angels singing,
nowells ringing, tidings bringing:
Christ the babe is Lord of all;
Christ the babe is Lord of all!

2 Flocks were sleeping, shepherds keeping
vigil till the morning new,
saw the glory, heard the story
tidings of a gospel true.
Thus rejoicing, free from sorrow,
praises voicing, greet the morrow:
Christ the babe was born for you;
Christ the babe was born for you!

From a Polish Carol,
tr. E. M. G. Reed (1885–1933)

139

Come, come, come to the manger,
children, come to the children's King:
sing, sing, chorus of Angels,
stars of morning o'er Bethlehem sing.

1 He lies 'mid the beasts of the stall,
who is Maker and Lord of us all;
the wintry wind blows cold and dreary,
see, he weeps, the world is weary;
Lord, have pity and mercy on me!

2 He leaves all his glory behind;
to be born and to die for mankind.
With grateful beasts his cradle chooses,
thankless man his love refuses;
Lord, have pity and mercy on me!

3 To the manger of Bethlehem come,
to the Saviour Emmanuel's home;
the heav'nly hosts above are singing,
set the Christmas bells a–ringing;
Lord, have pity and mercy on me!

19th C, Anonymous

140

1 Sleep, holy babe,
upon thy mother's breast;
great Lord of earth and sea and sky,
how sweet it is to see thee lie
in such a place of rest.

2 Sleep, holy babe;
thine angels watch around,
all bending low, with folded wings,
before th'incarnate King of kings,
in reverent awe profound.

3 Sleep, holy babe,
while I with Mary gaze
in joy upon that face awhile,
upon the loving infant smile,
which there divinely plays.

4 Sleep, holy babe,
ah, take thy brief repose,
too quickly will thy slumbers break,
and thou to lengthen'd pains awake,
that death alone shall close.

5 O lady blest,
sweet Virgin, hear my cry;
forgive the wrong that I have done
to thee, in causing thy dear Son
upon the cross to die.

Edward Caswall (1814–78)

141

1 Child in the manger, infant of Mary;
outcast and stranger, Lord of all;
child who inherits all our transgressions,
all our demerits on him fall.

2 Once the most holy child of salvation
gently and lowly lived below;
now as our glorious mighty Redeemer,
see him victorious o'er each foe.

3 Prophets foretold him, infant of wonder;
angels behold him on his throne:
worthy our Saviour of all their praises;
happy for ever are his own.

Mary Macdonald (1789–1872),
tr. Lachlan MacBean (1853–1931)

142

1 Jesus, Saviour, holy child, sleep tonight,
slumber deep till morning light.
Lullaby, our joy, our treasure,
all our hope and all our pleasure:
at the cradle where you lie
we will worship lullaby!

2 From your Father's home you come
    to this earth,
by your lowly manger birth:
Child of God, our nature sharing,
Son of Man, our sorrows bearing;
rich, yet here among the poor:
Christ the Lord, whom we adore!

3 Now to heaven's glory song we reply
with a Christmas lullaby.
Hush, the eternal Lord is sleeping
close in Mary's tender keeping:
babe on whom the angels smiled
Jesus, Saviour, holy child.
Michael Perry (1942-96)

143

1 Who is the baby an hour or two old,
looked for by shepherds far strayed from
    their fold,
lost in the world though more precious
    than gold?
This is God with us in Jesus.

2 Who is the woman with child at her breast,
giving her milk to earth's heavenly guest,
telling her mind to be calm and at rest?
Mary, the mother of Jesus.

3 Who is the man who looks on at the door,
welcoming strangers, some rich but
    most poor,
scanning the world as if somehow unsure?
Joseph, the father of Jesus.

4 Who are the people come in from the street,
some to bring presents and some just to meet,
joining their song to what angels repeat?
These are the new friends of Jesus.

5 Will you come with me, even though I
    feel shy,
come to his cradle and come to his cry,
give him your nod or your yes
    or your aye,
give what you can give to Jesus?
John Bell &Graham Maule

144

1 In the bleak midwinter,
frosty wind made moan,
earth stood hard as iron,
water like a stone;
snow had fallen, snow on snow,
snow on snow,
in the bleak midwinter
long ago.

2 Our God, heaven cannot hold him
nor earth sustain;
heaven and earth shall flee away,
when he comes to reign.
In the bleak midwinter
a stable–place sufficed
the Lord God Almighty,
Jesus Christ.

3 Enough for him, whom Cherubim
worship night and day,
a breastful of milk,
and a mangerful of hay:
enough for him, whom angels
fall down before,
the ox and ass and camel
which adore.

4 Angels and archangels
may have gathered there,
Cherubim and Seraphim
thronged the air –
but only his mother
in her maiden bliss
worshipped the beloved
with a kiss.

last verse overleaf

5 What can I give him,
  poor as I am?
  If I were a shepherd
  I would bring a lamb;
  if I were a wise man
  I would do my part;
  yet what I can I give him –
  give my heart.
Christina G. Rossetti (1830–94)

145

1 What child is this, who, laid to rest,
  on Mary's lap is sleeping?
  Whom angels greet with anthems sweet,
  while shepherds watch are keeping?
  This, this is Christ the King,
  whom shepherds guard and angels sing:
  come, greet the infant Lord,
  the Babe, the Son of Mary!

2 Why lies he in such mean estate,
  where ox and ass are feeding?
  Good Christian, fear: for sinners here
  the silent Word is pleading.
  Nails, spear, shall pierce him through,
  the cross be borne for me, for you:
  hail, hail the Word made flesh,
  the Babe, the Son of Mary!

3 So bring him incense, gold and myrrh,
  come peasant, king, to own him.
  The King of kings salvation brings,
  let loving hearts enthrone him.
  Raise, raise the song on high,
  the Virgin sings her lullaby:
  joy, joy for Christ is born,
  the Babe, the Son of Mary!
W. C. Dix (1837-1898)

146

1 Angel voices richly blending,
  shepherds to the manger sending,
  sing of peace from heav'n descending!
  Shepherds, greet your Shepherd King.

2 Lo! a star is brightly glowing!
  Eastern Kings their gifts are showing
  to the King whose gifts pass knowing!
  Gentiles, greet the Gentiles' King!

3 To the manger come adoring,
  hearts in thankfulness outpouring
  To the child, true peace restoring,
  Mary's Son, our God and King!
German, 15th C, tr. James Quinn, S.J.

147

1. What shall we give to the child in the man-ger? What shall we give him that he will en-joy? Milk and wild ho-ney for this lit-tle stran-ger, food to give strength to a new lit-tle boy.

2. What shall we give to the first-born of Ma-ry; things that will nou-rish a new life be-gun? Fruits of the for-est and figs from the fig-tree Nur-tured in so-il and ri-pened by sun.

*Catalan carol, adapted
by Stephen Dean*

3 This Child must grow to inherit a kingdom,
  blossom and ripen like fields of good corn,
  bearing a seed that will fall and lie buried,
  springing up new in the bright Easter morn.

4 What shall we give to the child in the manger?
  What shall we give him that he will enjoy?
  Give of the best to the one who will save us,
  food to give strength to this man still a boy.

148

1. Ho-ly Child with - in the man - ger, long a - go yet ev-er near;
come as friend to ev - 'ry stran - ger, come as hope for ev - 'ry fear.
As you lived to heal the bro - ken, greet the out - cast, free the bound, as you
taught us love un - spo - ken, teach us now where you are found.

2 Once again we tell the story -
how your love for us was shown,
when the image of your glory
wore an image like our own.
Come, enlighten with your wisdom,
come, and fill us with your grace,
may the fire of your compassion
kindle ev'ry land and race.

3 Holy Child within the manger,
lead us ever in your way,
so we see in ev'ry stranger
how you come to us today.
In our lives and in our living
give us strength to live as you,
that our hearts might be forgiving
and our spirits strong and true.

Marty Haugen

149

1 Let us bring to him the lonely,
let us bring to him the poor,
for salvation lies in a manger,
God's Son lies wrapped in straw.
Do you hear all the heavenly singing?
See the light in a Bethlehem cave?
For the light that shines in the darkness
is Christ the Lord who will save.

2 Let us bring to him the children,
let us bring to him the old,
for one look from him will bring comfort
and strength to brave the cold.
Do you hear ....

3 Let us bring the tired people
who have never time to pray.
for his love is stronger than sorrow
and freedom is his way.

4 Let us bring to him the suffering,
people sick in heart and mind,
for his touch is gentle and healing
their pain he can unbind.

5 Let us bring to him the hungry,
those who thirst, in prison dwell,
if we care for the least of his children
we care for him as well.

Christopher Walker

150

1 The first Nowell the angel did say
was to certain poor shepherds in fields
as they lay;
in fields where they lay keeping their sheep,
on a cold winter's night that was so deep.
Nowell, Nowell, Nowell, Nowell,
born is the King of Israel!

2 They lookèd up and saw a star,
  shining in the east, beyond them far,
  and to the earth it gave great light,
  and so it continued both day and night.

3 And by the light of that same star,
  three wise men came from country far.
  To seek for a king was their intent,
  and to follow the star wherever it went.

4 This star drew nigh to the north–west,
  o'er Bethlehem it took its rest,
  and there it did both stop and stay
  right over the place where Jesus lay.

5 Then entered in those wise men three,
  full reverently upon their knee,
  and offered there in his presence,
  their gold and myrrh and frankincense.

6 Then let us all with one accord
  sing praises to our heavenly Lord,
  that hath made heaven and earth of
      nought,
  and with his blood mankind hath bought.
  Traditional English carol

151

1 See, amid the winter's snow,
  born for us on earth below,
  see, the tender lamb appears,
  promised from eternal years.
  Hail, thou ever–blessèd morn,
  hail, redemption's happy dawn!
  Sing through all Jerusalem,
  Christ is born in Bethlehem.

2 Lo, within a manger lies
  he who built the starry skies;
  he who, throned in heights sublime,
  sits amid the cherubim.

3 Say, ye holy shepherds, say,
  what your joyful news today?
  Wherefore have ye left your sheep
  on the lonely mountain steep?

4 'As we watched at dead of night,
  lo, we saw a wondrous light;
  angels, singing peace on earth,
  told us of the Saviour's birth.'

5 Sacred infant, all divine,
  what a tender love was thine,
  thus to come from highest bliss,
  down to such a world as this!

6 Virgin mother, Mary blest,
  by the joys that fill thy breast,
  pray for us, that we may prove
  worthy of the Saviour's love.
  Edward Caswall (1814–78)

152

The last line of each verse is repeated

1 Unto us is born a Son,
  King of quires supernal;
  see on earth his life begun,
  of lords the Lord eternal.

2 Christ, from heav'n descending low,
  comes on earth a stranger:
  ox and ass their owner know
  becradled in a manger.

3 This did Herod sore affray,
  and grievously bewilder:
  so he gave the word to slay,
  and slew the little childer.

4 Of his love and mercy mild
  this the Christmas story,
  and O that Mary's gentle Child
  might lead us up to glory!

5 O and A and A and O
  cum cantibus in choro,
  let the merry organ go,
  Benedicamus Domino.
  15th C, tr. G.R. Woodward 1849-1934

153

1 Ding dong! merrily on high
  in heav'n the bells are ringing,
  ding dong! verily the sky
  is riv'n with angels singing.
  Gloria, hosanna in excelsis!

2 E'en so here below, below,
  let steeple bells be swungen,
  and io, io, io,
  by priest and people sungen.

3 Pray you, dutifully prime
your matin chime, ye ringers;
may you beautifully rime
your evetime song, ye singers.
G.R.Woodward (1848–1934)

154

1 Good Christians all, rejoice
with heart and soul and voice!
Give ye heed to what we say:
Jesus Christ is born today.
Ox and ass before him bow,
and he is in the manger now:
Christ is born today,
Christ is born today

2 Good Christians all, rejoice
with heart and soul and voice!
Now ye hear of endless bliss;
Jesus Christ was born for this.
He hath opened heaven's door,
and we are blessed for evermore:
Christ was born for this,
Christ was born for this.

3 Good Christians all, rejoice
with heart and soul and voice!
Now ye need not fear the grave;
Jesus Christ was born to save,
calls you one, and calls you all,
to gain his everlasting hall:
Christ was born to save,
Christ was born to save.
German, 14th C., tr.J. M. Neale (1818–66)

155

1 Hark! the herald angels sing,
glory to the new–born King;
peace on earth and mercy mild,
God and sinners reconciled:
joyful, all ye nations, rise,
join the triumph of the skies;
with the angelic host proclaim:
'Christ is born in Bethlehem'.
*Hark, the herald Angels sing,
glory to the new–born King.*

2 Christ, by highest heaven adored,
Christ, the everlasting Lord,
late in time behold him come,
offspring of a Virgin's womb.
Veiled in flesh the Godhead see!
Hail the incarnate Deity!
Pleased as man with man to dwell,
Jesus, our Emmanuel:

3 Hail the heaven–born Prince of Peace!
Hail the Sun of righteousness!
Light and life to all he brings,
risen with healing in his wings.
Mild he lays his glory by,
born that man no more may die,
born to raise the sons of earth,
born to give them second birth:
Charles Wesley (1707-88), alt.

156

1 Joy to the world, the Lord has come!
Let earth receive her King;
let every heart prepare Him room,
    and heaven and nature sing,
    and heaven and nature sing,
and heaven, and heaven and nature sing.

2 Joy to the earth, the Saviour reigns!
Let all their songs employ
while fields and floods, rocks, hills and
    plains
    repeat the sounding joy,
    repeat the sounding joy,
repeat, repeat the sounding joy.

3 No more let sin and sorrows grow,
nor thorns infest the ground;
he comes to make his blessings flow
    far as the curse is found,
    far as the curse is found,
far as, far as the curse is found.

4 He rules the world with truth and grace,
and makes the nations prove
the glories of his righteousness,
    the wonders of his love,
    the wonders of his love,
the wonders, wonders of his love.
Isaac Watts (1674–1748) based on Psalm 98

157

1 A-wake! a-wake, and greet the new morn, for an - gels he-rald its
2 To us, to all in sor-row and fear, Em - ma nu - el comes—a

dawning,_ sing out your joy, for now he is born, Be - hold! the Child of our
sing-ing,— his hum - ble song is qui - et and near, yet fills the earth with its

long-ing. Come as a ba - by weak and poor, to bring all hearts to - ge - ther, he
ring-ing; mu - sic to heal the bro - ken soul and hymns of lov - ing kind-ness, the

o - pens wide the heav - 'nly door and lives now in - side us for e - ver._
thun - der of his an - thems roll to shat - ter all ha - tred and blind-ness.__

3 In darkest night his coming shall be,
   when all the world is despairing,
   as morning light so quiet and free,
   so warm and gentle and caring.
   Then shall the mute break forth in song,
   the lame shall leap in wonder,
   the weak be raised above the strong,
   and weapons be broken asunder.

4 Rejoice, rejoice, take heart in the night,
   though dark the winter and cheerless,
   the rising sun shall crown you with light,
   be strong and loving and fearless;
   love be our song and love our prayer,
   and love, our endless story,
   may God fill every day we share,
   and bring us at last into glory.

Marty Haugen

158

1. In deepest night we hear the story:
   the morning star has risen plain:
   for us an infant has been born,
   'the Lord-shall-save-us' is his name.
   Open your hearts, believe your senses,
   and trust in what you plainly see;
   how God's own word from highest
      heaven
   is wrought in us so humanly.

2 To us no other sign is given,
   no other light comes breaking through:
   this man alone is our companion,
   a God who is our brother, too.
   Sing for your God who has unfolded
   in Jesus his great love for all.
   The world becomes a new creation,
   all flesh receives his saving call.

3 The way the sun comes up in glory,
   a bridegroom shedding light and fire,
   so comes the king of peace to join us,
   and, once for all, has come his hour.
   And joining ev'ryone together,
   his love doled out as nourishment,
   he gives his body to our keeping
   that we may live his covenant.

Huub Oosterhuis, tr. David Smith

159

1 O come, all ye faithful,
   joyful and triumphant.
   O come ye, O come ye to Bethlehem;
   come and behold him,
   born the king of angels:

O come, let us adore him,
O come, let us adore him,
O come, let us adore him,
Christ the Lord.

2 God of God,
light of light,
lo! he abhors not the virgin's womb;
very God, begotten not created:

3 Sing, choirs of angels,
sing in exultation,
sing all ye citizens of heaven above;
glory to God in the highest:

4 Yea, Lord, we greet thee,
born this happy morning,
Jesu, to thee be glory given;
word of the Father,
now in flesh appearing:
attributed to John F. Wade, c.1711-1786, tr.
Frederick Oakeley (1802–80) alt.

159a

1 Adeste fideles,
laeti triumphantes,
venite, venite in Bethlehem.
Natum videte regem angelorum.
Venite adoremus
venite adoremus,
venite adoremus Dominum.

2 Deum de Deo,
lumen de lumine
gestant puellae viscera.
Deum verum, genitum non factum.

3 Cantet nunc io,
chorus angelorum,
cantet nunc aula caelestium.
gloria in excelsis Deo.

4 Ergo qui natus
die hodierna
Jesu tibi sit gloria.
Patris aeternae
verbum caro factum
attributed to John F. Wade, c.1711-1786.

160

1 Of the Father's love begotten,
ere the worlds began to be,
he is Alpha and Omega,
he the source, the ending he,
of all things that are and have been
and that future years shall see:
Evermore and evermore.

2 By his word was all created;
he commanded, it was done:
heaven and earth and depth of ocean,
universe of three in one,
all that grows beneath the shining
of the light of moon and sun:
evermore and evermore.

3 Blessed was the day for ever
when the virgin, full of grace,
by the Holy Ghost conceiving,
bore the Saviour of our race,
and the child, the world's Redeemer,
first revealed his sacred face:
evermore and evermore.

4 O, ye heights of heaven, adore him,
angels and archangels sing!
Every creature bow before him
singing praise to God our King;
let no earthly tongue be silent,
all the world with homage ring:
evermore and evermore.

5 He, by prophets sung, is here now,
promised since the world began,
now on earth in flesh descended
to atone for sins of man.
All creation praise its Master,
see fulfilment of his plan:
evermore and evermore.

6 Glory be to God the Father,
glory be to God the Son,
glory to the Holy Spirit,
persons three, yet Godhead one.
Glory be from all creation
while eternal ages run:
evermore and evermore.
Aurelius Prudentius (348–c.413) tr. J.M. Neale
(1818–66), H.W. Baker (1823–77), and others

161

1 Jesus the Word has lived among us,
   sharing his fullness, truth and grace,
   God's only Son, the Father's loved one
   reveals him to the human race.
   Jesus the Word has lived among us
   sharing his fullness, truth and grace.

2 He was with God from the beginning
   and through him all things came to be.
   He lightens darkness, conquers evil,
   gives life for living, glad and free.
   He was with God from the beginning
   and through him all things came to be.

3 Sing praise to God who sent Christ Jesus
   to be his sign of endless love;
   sent him to live his life among us,
   lifting our hearts to things above.
   Sing praise to God who sent Christ Jesus
   to be his sign of endless love!
   John 1, par. by Keith D. Pearson

162

1 I wonder as I wander out under the sky,
   how Jesus the Saviour did come for
      to die
   for poor ord'n'ry people like you and
      like I.
   I wonder as I wander out under the sky.

2 When Mary birthed Jesus,'twas in a
      cow's stall
   with wise men and farmers and shepherds
      and all.
   But high from God's heaven a star's light
      did fall,
   and the promise of ages it did then recall.

3 If Jesus had wanted for any wee thing,
   a star in the sky, or a bird on the wing,
   or all of God's angels in heav'n for to
      sing,
   he surely could have it,'cause he was
      the king.
   J.J. Niles (1892-1980), possibly from an
   Appalachian carol

163

1 Behold a star shining
   upon a child's head,
   and low-bending shepherds
   by God's angels led;
   three kings all their treasures
   before him unfold;
   the fragrance of spices,
   frankincense and gold.

2 The incense his Godhead,
   God's kingship proclaims,
   the myrrh's bitter sweetness
   his cross and his pains;
   what have we to give thee
   but what thou first gave?
   Take, Jesus, our homage
   and all that we have.

3 Our Faith as the incense
   be pleasant to thee
   the myrrh speak our Hoping,
   the gold Charity;
   so Jesus and Mary
   and Joseph, fare well;
   may angels surround you
   and God keep you well.
   Brian Moore, S.J. (1931-97)

164

Go, tell it on the mountain,
over the hills and ev'rywhere.
Go, tell it on the mountain
that Jesus Christ is born.

1 While shepherds kept their watching
   o'er silent flocks by night,
   behold, throughout the heavens
   there shone a holy light.

2 The shepherds feared and trembled
   when lo! throughout the earth
   rang out the angel chorus
   that hailed our Saviour's birth.

3 And lo, when they had seen it,
they all bowed down and prayed,
they travelled on together
to where the Babe was laid.

4 Down in a lowly manger
the humble Christ was born
and God sent us salvation
that blessed Christmas morn.

Afro-American spiritual (19th C.) adapted by
John Wesley Work Jr (1872-1925)

New Year

165

1 The God of all eternity
unbound by space yet always near,
is present where his people meet
to celebrate the coming year.

2 What shall we offer God today -
our dreams of what we cannot see,
or, with eyes fastened to the past,
our dread of what is yet to be?

3 God does not share our doubts and fears,
nor shrinks from the unknown or strange:
the one who fashioned heaven and earth
makes all things new and ushers change.

4 Let faith or fortune rise or fall,
let dreams and dread both have their day;
those whom God loves walk unafraid
with Christ their guide and Christ their
way.

5 God grant that we, in this new year,
may show the world the Kingdom's face,
and let our work and worship thrive
as signs of hope and means of grace.
John Bell & Graham Maule

Epiphany

166

1 As with gladness men of old,
did the guiding star behold,
as with joy they hailed its light,
leading onward, beaming bright,
so, most gracious God, may we
evermore be led to thee.

2 As with joyful steps they sped,
to that lowly manger–bed,
there to bend the knee before
him whom heaven and earth adore,
so may we with willing feet
ever seek thy mercy–seat.

3 As they offered gifts most rare,
at that manger rude and bare,
so may we with holy joy,
pure, and free from sin's alloy,
all our costliest treasures bring,
Christ, to thee our heavenly King.

4 Holy Jesus, every day
keep us in the narrow way;
and, when earthly things are past,
bring our ransomed souls at last
where they need no star to guide,
where no clouds thy glory hide.

5 In the heavenly country bright
need they no created light,
thou its Light, its Joy, its Crown,
thou its Sun which goes not down;
there for ever may we sing
alleluias to our King.
W.C.Dix (1837–98)

167

1 Bethlehem! of noblest cities
none can once with thee compare;
thou alone the Lord from heaven
didst for us incarnate bear.

2 Fairer than the sun at morning
was the star that told his birth,
to the lands their God announcing,
hid beneath a form of earth.

3 By its shining beauty guided,
see the eastern kings appear;
see them bend, their gifts to offer –
gifts of incense, gold and myrrh.

4 Solemn things of mystic meaning!
Incense doth the God disclose;
gold a royal child proclaimeth;
Myrrh a future tomb foreshows.

5 Holy Jesu, in thy brightness
to the gentile world display'd,
with the Father and the Spirit,
endless praise to thee be paid.
Aurelius Prudentius (348–c. 413),
tr. E. Caswall (1814–78), alt.

168

1 The race that long in darkness pined
has seen a glorious light:
the people dwell in day, who dwelt
in death's surrounding night.

2 To hail thy rise, thou better sun,
the gathering nations come,
joyous as when the reapers bear
the harvest treasures home.

3 To us a child of hope is born,
to us a Son is given;
him shall the tribes of earth obey,
him all the hosts of heaven.

4 His name shall be the Prince of Peace
for evermore adored,
the Wonderful, the Counsellor
the great and mighty Lord.

5 His power increasing still shall spread,
his reign no end shall know;
justice shall guard his throne above,
and peace abound below.
John Morison (1749–98)

169

1 O worship the Lord in the beauty of
holiness!
Bow down before him, his glory proclaim;
with gold of obedience, and incense of
lowliness,
kneel and adore him, the Lord is his name!

2 Low at his feet lay thy burden of
carefulness,
high on his heart he will bear it for thee,
comfort thy sorrows, and answer thy
prayerfulness,
guiding thy steps as may best for thee be.

3 Fear not to enter his courts in the
slenderness
of the poor wealth thou wouldst reckon
as thine:
truth in its beauty, and love in its
tenderness,
these are the offerings to lay on his shrine.

4 These, though we bring them in
trembling and fearfulness,
he will accept for the name that is dear;
mornings of joy give for evenings of
tearfulness,
trust for our trembling and hope for our
fear.

5 O worship the Lord in the beauty of
holiness!
Bow down before him, his glory proclaim;
with gold of obedience, and incense of
lowliness,
kneel and adore him, the Lord is his name!
J.S. Monsell (1811–75)

170

1 We three Kings of Orient are;
bearing gifts we traverse afar,
field and fountain, moor and mountain,
following yonder star.
O Star of wonder, star of night,
star with royal beauty bright,
westward leading, still proceeding,
guide us to thy perfect light.

2 Born a King on Bethlehem plain,
  gold I bring, to crown him again,
  King for ever, ceasing never,
  over us all to reign.

3 Frankincense to offer have I,
  Incense owns a Deity nigh.
  Prayer and praising, all are raising,
  worship him, God most high.

➤ *See also Angel voices (146), The first
nowell (150)*

The Baptism of the Lord

171

1 When Jesus comes to be baptised,
  he leaves the hidden years behind,
  the years of safety and of peace,
  to bear the sins of all mankind.

2 The Spirit of the Lord comes down,
  anoints the Christ to suffering,
  to preach the word, to free the bound,
  and to the mourner, comfort bring.

3 He will not quench the dying flame,
  and what is bruised he will not break,
  but heal the wound injustice dealt,
  and out of death his triumph make.

4 Our everlasting Father, praise,
  with Christ, his well-beloved Son,
  who with the Spirit reigns serene,
  untroubled Trinity in One.

The Benedictines of Stanbrook

172

1 Songs of thankfulness and praise,
  Jesu, Lord to you we raise,
  manifested by the star
  to the sages from afar;
  branch of royal David's stem,
  in your birth at Bethlehem;
  Anthems be to you addressed,
  God in flesh made manifest.

4 Myrrh is mine, its bitter perfume
  breathes a life of gathering gloom;
  sorrowing, sighing, bleeding, dying,
  sealed in the stone–cold tomb.

5 Glorious now behold him arise,
  King and God and sacrifice.
  'Alleluia, alleluia!'
  earth to heaven replies.

John Henry Hopkins (1822–1900)

2 Manifest at Jordan's stream,
  prophet, Priest and King supreme;
  and at Cana wedding–guest,
  in your Godhead manifest;
  manifest in power divine,
  changing water into wine;
  anthems be to you addressed,
  God in flesh made manifest.

3 Manifest in making whole
  palsied limbs and fainting soul;
  manifest in valiant fight,
  quelling all the devil's might;
  manifest in gracious will,
  ever bringing good from ill;
  anthems be to you addressed,
  God in flesh made manifest.

4 Sun and moon shall darkened be,
  stars shall fall, the heavens shall flee;
  Christ will then like lightning shine,
  all will see his glorious sign;
  all will then the trumpet hear,
  all will see the judge appear;
  you by all will be confessed;
  God in flesh made manifest.

5 Grant us grace to see you, Lord,
  mirrored in your holy word;
  may we imitate you now,
  and on us your grace endow;
  that we like to you may be
  at your great Epiphany,
  and may praise you, ever blest,
  God in flesh made manifest.

Christopher Wordsworth (1807–85), alt.

173

1 When John baptised by Jordan's river
in faith and hope the people came,
that John and Jordan might deliver
their troubled souls from sin and shame.
They came to seek a new beginning,
the human spirit's ageless quest,
repentance, and an end of sinning,
renouncing every wrong confessed.

2 There as the Lord, baptised and praying,
rose from the stream, the sinless one,
a voice was heard from heaven saying,
'This is my own beloved Son.'

There as the Father's word was spoken,
not in the power of wind and flame,
but of his love and peace the token,
seen as a dove, the Spirit came.

3 O Son of Man, our nature sharing,
in whose obedience all are blest,
Saviour, our sins and sorrows bearing,
hear us and grant us this request:
Daily to grow, by grace defended,
filled with the Spirit from above;
in Christ baptised, beloved, befriended,
children of God in peace and love.
Timothy Dudley–Smith

➤ *See also The light of Christ (747);*
Advent hymns, e.g. 94-99

The Presentation of the Lord

174 Processional Antiphon

Christ is the light of the na-tions, and the glo-ry of Is-ra-el his peo-ple.

Original version

Verses of the Nunc Dimittis: no. 36

Lu-men ad re-ve-la-ti-o-nem gen-ti-um, et glo-ri-am ple-bis tu-ae Is-ra-el.

175

1 In his temple now behold him,
see the long-expected Lord;
ancient prophets had foretold him,
God has now fulfilled his word;
now to praise him, his redeemèd
shall break forth with one accord.

2 In the arms of her who bore him,
Virgin pure, behold him lie,
while his aged saints adore him
ere in faith and hope they die.
Alleluia! Alleluia!
See, th'incarnate God most high.

3 Jesus, by your presentation,
when they blessed you, weak and poor,
make us see our great salvation,
seal us with your promise sure,
and present us in your glory
to your Father, cleansed and pure.

4 Prince and author of salvation,
be your boundless love our theme!
Jesus, praise to you be given,
by the world you did redeem,
with the Father and the Spirit,
Lord of majesty supreme.
Vv. 1-3, Henry J. Pye (1825-1903); v.4,
William Cooke (1821-94)

176

A light, a light to the Gen-tiles and the glo-ry of Is-ra-el!

Lord, let your servant now die in peace,
for you kept your promise.
With my own eyes I see the salvation you
prepared for all peoples.

A light of revelation for the Gentiles and
glory to your people Israel.
Luke 2:22-28. Text: ICEL. Music by
Peter McGrail

177

1 Now let your servant go in peace;
for praise and blessing here increase;
for in our midst your word is done
and you have sent your Promised One.

2 Before the peoples you prepare
your way of life which all may share.
your saving power is now made known;
among the nations love is shown.

3 Child, you are chosen as a sign
to test the human heart and mind;
for secrets hidden in the night
shall be revealed in piercing light.

4 Now let us sing our Saviour's praise,
and tell God's goodness all our days,
while breath is ours, let praise be heard
for God's own faithful, saving word.
Luke 2:22-28; Ruth M. Duck

178 *Alleluia*

Hal-le, hal-le, hal-le-lu-jah! Hal-le, hal-le, hal-le-lu-jah! Hal-le, hal-le, hal-le-lu-jah! Hal-le-lu-jah! Hal-le-lu-jah!

Traditional Caribbean, arr. John Bell

Alleluia is not sung between Ash Wednesday and the Easter Vigil.

Lent

Seasonal Music: 179-193. Lent Hymns: 194-237

179 Call to Worship

James Chepponis

This is the time of ful - fil - ment! The reign of God is at hand.

180 Gathering Song 1

1 Led by the Spirit of our God,
we go to fast and pray
with Christ into the wilderness;
we join his paschal way.
'Rend not your garments, rend your hearts.
Turn back your lives to me.'
Thus says our kind and gracious God,
whose reign is liberty.

2 Led by the Spirit, we confront
temptation face to face,
and know full well we must rely
on God's redeeming grace.
on bread alone we cannot live,
but nourished by the Word
we seek the will of God to do:
this is our drink and food.

3 Led by the Spirit, now draw near
the waters of rebirth
with hearts that long to worship God
in spirit and in truth.
'Whoever drinks the drink I give
shall never thirst again.'
Thus says the Lord who died for us,
our Saviour, kin and friend.

4 Led by the Spirit, now sing praise
to God the Trinity:
the Source of Life, the living Word
made flesh to set us free,
the Spirit blowing where it will
to make us friends of God:
this myst'ry far beyond our reach,
yet near in healing love.

Bob Hurd

181 Lent Penitential Rite 1

Bob Hurd

1,3 Ky - ri - e e - le - i - son, ky - ri - e e - le - i - son.
2. Chris - te e - le - i - son, Chris - te e - le - i - son.

➤ *See also: Advent Kyrie 3 (67)*

182 Gathering Song 2

1 From ashes to the living font
your Church must journey, Lord;
baptised in grace, in grace renewed
by your most holy word.

2 Through fasting, prayer, and charity
your voice speaks deep within,
returning us to ways of truth
and turning us from sin.

3 *Sundays I & II*
From desert to the mountaintop
in Christ our way we see,
so, tempered by temptation's might
we might transfigured be.

3 *Sunday III*
For thirsting hearts let waters flow
our fainting souls revive;
and at the well your waters give
our everlasting life.

3 *Sunday IV*
We sit beside the road and plead,
'Come, save us, David's son!'
Now with your vision heal our eyes,
the world's true Light alone.

3 *Sunday V*
Our graves split open, bring us back,
your promise to proclaim:
to darkened tombs call out 'Arise!'
and glorify your name.

4. From ashes to the living font
your Church must journey still;
through cross and tomb to Easter joy,
in Spirit-fire fulfilled.
Alan J.Hommerding

183 Penitential Litany

Parce Domine, arr Gary Daigle

Introduction: Repeat after Cantor

Hold us in your mer - cy.   Hold us in your mer - cy.
Hold us in your mer - cy.   Hold us in your mer - cy.

Verses

1. Ma - ker's love poured out from hea - ven.   Hold us in your mer - cy.
2. Born as one of home - less pil - grims.
3. You who shared the sin - ner's ta - ble.

Mer - cy's word made flesh a - mong us.   Hold us in your mer - cy.
Sent to bring the poor good news.
You who cleansed the le - per's flesh.

4 You who shared our life and labour.
   You who chose to walk our roads.

5 You who silence raging demons.
   you who bid the storm be silent.

6 You whose cross has gone before us.
   you who bear our cross with us.

7 Innocent, you faced the guilty.
   one in death with us for ever.

8 Come and break the chains that bind us.
   Free us from addiction's prison.

9 Break the power of the darkness.
   Let us rise to life with you.

10 Kyrie eleison!
    Christe eleison!

11 Hold us in your mercy!
    Hold us in your mercy!
    repeat as required

Common Responsorial Psalms for Lent   *Pss 50(51), no.48; 90(91) no.51; no129(130) no. 59-60
- and see Psalm Index, p.409*

184 Gospel Acclamation 1 for Lent

James Walsh

Praise to you, O Christ, king of e - ter - nal glo-ry!
Glo - ry to you, O Christ, you are the Word of God!___

185 Gospel Acclamation 2 for Lent

Martin Foster

Praise_ to_ you, Lord Je - sus Christ, Word of the Fa - ther, Son of God.

186 Gospel Acclamation 3 for Lent

Chris O'Hara

Glo-ry and praise to you, Lord! You are the Word____ of Life.

187 Gospel Acclamation 4 for Lent

Stephen Dean

Glo-ry to you, O Christ;___ glo-ry to you, O Christ, you are the

word of God, the word of God: glo-ry to you, O Christ!

➤ SEE ALSO: *Word of God* (197); *Praise to you, O Christ* (200)

188

Gospel Responses for Sundays of Lent

Delores Dufner, O.S.B.

1st Sunday, A, B & C

O Spirit-filled Christ Jesus,
in fasting and in prayer
you went into the desert
and you were tempted there.

O Jesus, like us, tempted
to glory, wealth, and pow'r,
make us, like you, unyielding,
strong in temptation's hour.

2nd Sunday, A, B & C

O Christ who shares our nature,
in whom God found delight,
you stood in radiant glory,
transfigured by the light.

Resplendent in God's favour,
O Christ in beauty bright,
illumine all who seek you,
transform us by your light.

3rd Sunday, A

O source of living water
athirst at your own well,
You promised to the woman
a gift no tongue can tell.

Christ, lead us to the fountain,
that we may be immersed.
Give us the living water,
that we may never thirst.

4th Sunday, A

Christ, when you saw your brother,
you healed his blinded eyes.
from isolation's darkness
you summoned him to rise.

O Jesus, heal our blindness
with clarity of sight.
lead us from sin and evil
to walk the way of light.

5th Sunday, A

Christ, when you came in sorrow
to Lazarus, your friend,
you loosed the linen binding
and gave him life again.

Now see the chains that bind us
and all humanity.
from sin and every bondage
untie us, set us free!

Passion (Palm) Sunday, A, B & C

Christ, human in your weakness,
by nature yet divine,
your love is undefeated,
your death, its saving sign.

O Jesus, suff'ring servant,
your death has set us free.
may we who share your dying
share Easter's victory.

189 Gospel Responses for Year B

1st and 2nd Sunday, *as Year A*

3rd Sunday, B

Christ, when you saw the temple
with merchants everywhere,
you drove them out in anger:
this is a house of prayer!

Christ Jesus, see this temple,
keep it a holy place.
cleanse every heart of evil,
transform us by your grace.

4th Sunday, B

You came, the gift of God's love,
not to condemn but save.
to win our joy eternal,
your life you freely gave.

Your cross, O Christ, was lifted
for all who would believe.
Let us, with hearts of welcome,
your gift of life receive.

5th Sunday, B

Unless a grain of wheat dies,
a single seed remains,
but when for love surrendered,
that seed new life attains.

Christ, sow us in your wheat field
where, buried, we may root.
So will the seed, by dying,
bring forth abundant fruit.

Passion (Palm) Sunday *as Year A*

190 Gospel Responses for Year C

1st and 2nd Sunday, *as Year A*

3rd Sunday, C

The owner of the fig tree
had hoped its fruit to share,
he tasted not of harvest,
but disappointment there.

Have mercy, vineyard keeper,
on every barren tree,
till roots and branches tended
bear fruit abundantly.

4th Sunday, C

The spendthrift son, returning,
was pardoned all his wrong,
was welcomed home with feasting,
with ring and robe and song.

God, spendthrift in your mercy,
rejoicing our return,
guide all your children homeward,
your lavish love to learn.

5th Sunday, C

A woman stood before you
in silent shame, alone.
But you did not condemn her,
they dared not cast a stone.

Our sins accuse us, Jesus,
but hear our heartfelt plea:
toward weakness show compassion,
forgive us, set us free.

Passion (Palm) Sunday, *as Year A*

191 Lent Communion Song 1

Stephen Dean

Not on bread a-lone are we nou-rished, but on ev-ery word from the mouth of God.

192 Lent Communion Song 2

Marty Haugen

Lord, you can o-pen hearts that are stone; live in our flesh and our bone.

Lead us to won-der, mys-t'ry and grace, one in your lo-ving em-brace.

Lent Communion Song 3: *Bread of Life (78) with seasonal verses*

Verses: no. 623

Lent Hymns

193

Re - turn to God with all your heart, the source of grace and mer - cy; come seek the ten - der faith-ful-ness of God.

1 Now the time of grace has come,
   the day of salvation:
   come and learn now the way of our God.

2 I will take your heart of stone
   and place a heart within you,
   a heart of compassion and love.

3 If you break the chains of oppression,
   if you set the pris'ner free;
   if you share your bread with the hungry,
   give protection to the lost;
   give a shelter to the homeless,
   clothe the naked in your midst,
   then your light shall break forth like the dawn

Marty Haugen

194

Come back to the Lord with all your heart,
leave the past in as-hes; and turn to God with tears and
fas-ting, for God is slow to an-ger and rea-dy to for-give.

Verses

1. Have mér-cy on me, Gód, for your kínd-ness, in com-pás-sion, blot óut my offénce. O wásh me from áll my gúilt; make me cléan from áll my sín.

2 I know my sins, every one,
  they stand before me in reproach,
  It is you alone I have offended,
  I have done what is evil in your sight.

3 You are just, O God, when you speak,
  your judgments are true and upright.
  In guilt I have languished since my birth,
  a sinner, even in the womb.

4 Truth in the heart is what you seek,
  plant your wisdom deep within me,
  Purify me, Lord, make me clean;
  wash me from all my sin.

5 A pure heart create within me,
  put a spirit renewed in my breast,
  Cast me not away from your presence,
  nor withhold your Spirit from me.

6 Deliver me from death, O God,
  and my tongue shall sing of your goodness
  Open my lips, O Lord,
  and my mouth shall sing your praise.

7 Sacrifice gives you no delight,
  burnt-offerings from me you would spurn.
  The sacrifice I bring you is my spirit,
  a broken, contrite heart you will befriend.

Psalm 50 (51), versified by Stephen Dean

195

Give me a new heart, O God. Put your Spi-rit in me.
Keep me with you, give me joy. Give me a new heart, O God.

1 God in your love, have mercy on me.
  in your compassion cleanse me.
  All of my guilt, wash it away,
  Lord, make me clean from my sin.

2 All of my faults, I know them so well.
  All of my sins, I know them.
  For against you alone have I sinned,
  evil in your sight have I done.

3 Truth in the heart you love most of all,
   now fill my mind with wisdom.
   Wash me from sin and I shall be clean,
   I shall be pure as the snow.

   Give me a new heart, O God,
   put your Spirit in me.
   Keep me with you, give me joy,
   give me a new heart, O God.

4 Give me again the joy of your help.
   Put a new spirit in me,

   that I may teach sinners your ways,
   that they will turn back to you.

5 You do not want a sacrifice made.
   You would refuse burnt offerings.
   My spirit is humble, offered to you.
   You will not spurn my humble heart.

6 O spare my life and save me, O God.
   I will proclaim your goodness.
   Open my lips and help me to speak
   and I will praise you with joy.

   Psalm 50 (51), versified by Christopher Walker

196 Attende, Domine

Latin (10th C), tr. Ralph Wright, OSB

Refrain

Hear us, al-migh-ty Lord, show us your mer-cy, sin-ners we stand here be-fore— you.
At - ten- de Do - mi - ne   et   mi - se - re - re qui - a pec - ca - vi- mus ti - bi.

Verses

1 Je- sus our Sa- viour,— Lord of all the na - tions, Christ our Re - dee- mer,
2 Word of the Fa - ther,— key-stone of God's buil - ding, source of our glad-ness,

hear the prayers we of - fer, Spare us and save us, com-fort us in sor - row.
gate- way to the King- dom, free us in mer- cy from the sins that bind—us.

3 God of compassion, Lord of might and
      splendour,
   graciously listen, hear our cries of anguish,
   touch us and heal us where our sins have
      wounded.

4 Humbly confessing that we have offended,
   stripped of illusions, naked in our sorrow,

pardon, Lord Jesus, those your blood has
   ransomed.

5 Innocent captive, you were led to
      slaughter,
   sentenced by sinners when they
      brought false witness.
   Keep from damnation those your death
      has rescued.

197

Word of God, Je - sus our Lord!

O - pen our hearts to your Truth and Love.

Word of Peace, hope for our world, cas-ting a-side all
Word of Joy, Mes-sage of life, glad-den the wea-ry
Word of Hope, com-for in pain, light in the dar-kest
Word of God, Li-ving and True, pier-cing the stub-born

fear: Speak, and we shall live!
heart: Speak, and we shall live!
grief: Speak, and we shall live!
mind: Speak, and we shall live!

Peter McGrail

➤ SEE ALSO:*Lent Gospel Acclamations (184-7); Praise to you, O Christ (200)*

198

1. We rise a-gain from ash-es, from the good we've failed to
2. We of-fer you our fai-lures, we of-fer you at-
3. Then rise a-gain from ash-es, let hea-ling come to
4. Thanks be to the Fa-ther, who made us like him-

do. We rise a-gain from ash-es, to cre-ate our-selves a-
tempts, the gifts not ful-ly gi-ven, the dreams not ful-ly
pain, though spring has turned to win-ter, and sun-shine turned to
self. Thanks be to the Son, who saved us by his

new. If all our world is ash-es, then must our lives be
dreamt. Give our stum-bl-ings di-rec-tion, give our vi-sions wi-der
rain. The rain we'll use for grow-ing, and cre-ate the world a-
death. Thanks be to the Spi-rit, who cre-ates the world a-

true, an of-fer-ing of ash-es, an of-fer-ing to you.
view, an of-fer-ing of ash-es, an of-fer-ing to you.
new, from an of-fer-ing of ash-es, an of-fer-ing to you.
new, from an of-fer-ing of ash-es, an of-fer-ing to you.

Tom Conry

199

1 Again we keep this solemn fast,
a gift of faith from ages past,
this Lent which binds us lovingly
to faith and hope and charity.

2 The law and prophets from of old
in figured ways this Lent foretold,
which Christ, all ages' Lord and Guide,
in these last days has sanctified.

3 More sparing, therefore, let us make
the words we speak, the food we take,
our sleep, our laughter, every sense;
learn peace through holy penitence.

4 Let us avoid each harmful way
that lures the careless mind astray;

by watchful prayer our spirits free
from scheming of the Enemy.

5 We pray, O blessed Three in One,
our God while endless ages run,
that this, our Lent of forty days,
may bring us growth and give you praise.

Ascribed to St Gregory the Great, c.540-604; tr. Peter J. Scagnelli

200

Bernadette Farrell

Praise to you, O Christ our— Sa-viour, Word of the Fa-ther, cal-ling us to life;
Son of God who leads us to freedom: glo - ry to you, Lord Je-sus Christ.

Verses

1. You are the Word who calls us out of dark - ness, you are the
2. You are the one whom pro - phets hoped and longed for; you are the

Word who leads us in - to light; you are the Word who
one who speaks to us to - day; you are the one who

brings us through the de - sert: glo - ry to you, Lord Je - sus Christ!
leads us to our fu - ture: glo - ry to you, Lord Je - sus Christ!

3. You are the Word who calls us to be
servants;
you are the Word whose only law is love;
you are the Word-made-flesh who lives
among us:
glory to you, Lord Jesus Christ!

4 You are the Word who binds us and
unites us,
you are the Word who calls us to be one;
you are the Word who teaches us
forgiveness;
glory to you, Lord Jesus Christ!

Bernadette Farrell

➤ SEE ALSO: Lent Gospel Acclamations (184-7) Word of God (197)

201

1. When Sa - tan speaks____ in an - gel tones and
2. When stones to bread____ means more for us and
3. When clim - bing high____ at - tracts a crowd and

san - cti - fies	the	road	to	ru -	in;	if	on that path	we're
more	for	us	seems	most	al - lu -	ring;
cheap	ac - claim	per -	verts	our	cal -	ling,

asked to go, Oh Je - sus, give us then the cou - rage to say No.___

4 When bowing down to serve the worst
brings all we want but breaks our
    conscience
if on that path we're asked to go, Oh Jesus,
give us then the courage to say No.

5 When Satan speaks in angel tones
and sanctifies the road to ruin;
if on that path we're asked to go,
    Oh Jesus,
give us then the courage to say No.
John L.Bell

202

1 Lord Jesus, as we turn from sin
with strength and hope restored,
receive the homage that we bring
to you our risen Lord.

2 We call on you whose living word
has made the Father known,
O Shepherd, we have wandered far,
find us and lead us home.

3 Your glance at Peter helped him know
the love he had denied,
now gaze on us and heal us, Lord,
of selfishness and pride.

4 Reach out and touch with healing pow'r
the wounds we have received,
that in forgiveness we may love
and may no longer grieve.

5 Then stay with us when ev'ning comes
and darkness makes us blind,
O stay until the light of dawn
may fill both heart and mind.
Ralph Wright, O.S.B.

203

1 As earth that is dry and parched in the sun
lies waiting for rain,
my soul is a desert, arid and waste;
it longs for your Word, O Lord.

Come to the waters, all you who thirst;
come now, and eat my bread.

2 Though you have no money, come, buy
    my corn,
and drink my red wine.
Why spend precious gold on what will
    not last?
Hear me, and your soul will live.

3 As one on a journey strays from the road
    and falls in the dark,
my mind is a wanderer, choosing
    wrong paths
and longing to find a star.

4 The Lord is your light, the Lord is your
    strength;
turn back to him now.
For his ways are not the ways you
    would choose,
and his thoughts are always new.

5 As rain from the mountains falls
    on the land
and brings forth the seed,
the word of the Lord sinks deep in our
    hearts,
creating the flower of truth.
Anne Conway, from Isaiah 55:1, 2, 6, 9 & 12

204

1 Lord Jesus, think on me,
and purge away my sin;
from earthborn passions set me free,
and make me pure within.

2 Lord Jesus, think on me,
with care and woe oppressed;
let me thy loving servant be,
and taste thy promised rest.

3 Lord Jesus, think on me
amid the battle's strife;
in all my pain and misery
be thou my health and life.

4 Lord Jesus, think on me,
nor let me go astray;
through darkness and perplexity
point thou the heavenly way.

5 Lord Jesus, think on me,
when flows the tempest high:
when on doth rush the enemy,
O Saviour, be thou nigh.

6 Lord Jesus, think on me,
that, when the flood is past,
I may the eternal brightness see,
and share thy joy at last.
Synesius of Cyrene (c.375–430)
tr. A. W. Chatfield (1808–96)

205

1 Lord, who throughout these forty days
for us didst fast and pray,
teach us with thee to mourn our sins,
and close by thee to stay.

2 As thou with Satan didst contend,
and didst the victory win,
O give us strength in thee to fight,
in thee to conquer sin.

3 As thirst and hunger thou didst bear,
so teach us, gracious Lord,
to die to self, and daily live
by thy most holy word.

4 And through these days of penitence,
and through thy Passiontide,
yea, evermore, in life and death,
Lord Christ, with us abide.
Claudia F. Hernaman (1838–98)

206

1 Forty days and forty nights
thou wast fasting in the wild;
forty days and forty nights
tempted still, yet unbeguiled:

2 Sunbeams scorching all the day,
chilly dew–drops nightly shed,
prowling beasts about thy way,
stones thy pillow, earth thy bed.

3 Let us thy endurance share
and from earthly greed abstain
with thee watching unto prayer,
with thee strong to suffer pain.

4 Then if evil on us press,
flesh or spirit to assail,
victor in the wilderness,
help us not to swerve or fail!

5 So shall peace divine be ours;
holier gladness ours shall be,
come to us angelic powers,
such as ministered to thee.

6 Keep, O keep us, Saviour dear,
ever constant by thy side,
that with thee we may appear
at the eternal Eastertide.
G.H. Smyttan (1822–70)
& Francis Pott (1832–1909)

207

1 Out of the direst depths
I make my deepest plea.
O graciously bow down your ear
and listen, Lord, for me.

2 If you kept note of sins,
before you who could stand?
But since forgiveness is your right,
our reverence you command.

3 My soul longs for the Lord,
and hopes to hear God's word.
More keenly than some watch for dawn,
I wait and watch for God.

4 Yes, with the Lord is grace
and power to free and save.
Redemption from their every sin
God's people yet shall have.
Psalm 130, versified by John L. Bell

Transfiguration (cf 2 Sunday of Lent)

208

1 O raise your eyes on high and see
there stands our sovereign Lord,
his glory is this day revealed,
his Word a two–edged sword.

2 We glimpse the splendour and the power
of him who conquered death,
the Christ in whom the universe
knows God's creating breath.

3 Of every creed and nation King
in him all strife is stilled;
the promise made to Abraham
in him has been fulfilled.

4 The prophets stand and with great joy
give witness as they gaze;
the Father with a sign has sealed
our trust, our hope, our praise.

5 This glory that today our eyes
have glimpsed of God's own Son
will help us ever sing with love
of Three who are but One.
Ralph Wright, OSB

209

1 How good, Lord, to be here!
Your glory fills the night;
your face and garments, like the sun,
shine with unborrowed light.

2 How good, Lord, to be here,
your beauty to behold,
where Moses and Elijah stand,
your messengers of old.

3 Fulfiller of the past,
promise of things to be:
we hail your body glorified,
and our redemption see.

4 Before we taste of death,
we see your kingdom come;
we still would hold the vision bright,
and make this hill our home.

5 How good, Lord, to be here!
Yet we may not remain;
but since you bid us leave the mount,
come with us to the plain.
J. Armitage Robinson (1858-1933), alt.

210

*We behold the splendour of God
shining on the face of Jesus.
We behold the splendour of God
shining on the face of the Son.*

1 And oh, how his beauty transforms us,
the wonder of Presence abiding.
Transparent hearts give reflection
of Tabor's light within;
of Tabor's light within.

2 Jesus, Lord of Glory,
Jesus beloved Son.
Oh how good to be with you;
how good to share your light,
how good to share your light.
Carey Landry

211

1 Our Father, we have wandered
and hidden from your face,
in foolishness have squandered
your legacy of grace.
But now, in exile dwelling,
we rise with fear and shame,
as distant but compelling,
we hear you call our name.

2 And now at length discerning
the evil that we do,
behold us Lord, returning
with hope and trust to you.

In haste you come to meet us
and home rejoicing bring.
In gladness there to greet us
with calf and robe and ring.

3 O Lord of all the living,
both banished and restored,
compassionate, forgiving
and ever caring Lord,
grant now that our transgressing,
our faithlessness may cease.
Stretch out your hand in blessing
in pardon and in peace.

Kevin Nichols

212

1 All ye who seek a comfort sure
in trouble and distress,
whatever sorrow vex the mind,
or guilt the soul oppress:

2 Jesus, who gave himself for you
upon the cross to die,
opens to you his sacred heart,–
oh, to that heart draw nigh!

3 Ye hear how kindly he invites;
ye hear his words so blest:
'All ye that labour, come to me,
and I will give you rest.'

4 Jesus, thou joy of saints on high!
Thou hope of sinners here!
Attracted by those loving words,
to thee I lift my prayer.

5 Wash thou my wounds in that dear blood
which forth from thee doth flow;
new grace, new hope inspire; a new
and better heart bestow.

18th century, tr. Edward Caswall (1814–78)

213

Oh God, I seek you, my soul thirsts for
you, your love is fi-ner than life.

Verses

1. As a dry and wea - ry___ de - sert land, so my
2. I think of you when at night I rest, I re -
3. I will bless your name all the days I live, I will

soul is thirs - ting for my God, and my flesh is faint for the
flect u - pon your stead-fast love. I will cling to you, oh___
raise my hands and call on you. My joy - ful lips shall___

God I seek, for your love is more to me than life.___
Lord my God, in the sha - dow of your wings I sing.___
sing your praise, you a - lone have filled my hun - gry soul.___

Psalm 62 (63), adapted by Marty Haugen

214

Refrain

As the deer longs for run-ning streams, so I— long,
so I— long,—— so I— long for you.

Verses

1. A-thirst my soul— for you the God who is my life! When shall I see,
2. ' Ech-oes meet— as deep is cal-ling un-to deep, o-ver my head,
3. Con-ti-nual-ly— the foe de-lights in taun-ting me: 'Where is God,——
4. De-fend me, God,— send forth your light— and your truth, they will lead me
5. Then I shall go— un-to the al-tar of my God. Prai-sing you,——

when shall I— see,—— see the face of God?
all your migh-ty wa-ters, swee-ping o-ver me.
where is your— God?'—— Where, O where, are you?
to your ho-ly moun-tain, to your dwel-ling place.
O my joy and glad-ness, I shall praise your name.

Bob Hurd, based on Psalm 41 (42)

215

1. The thirs-ty deer will yearn and— dream to find the cool-ing,
2. My foes look on; they laugh at— me: 'Where is your God: yes
3. O Lord, my life is filled with woe; my heart is crushed, my

run-ning stream. So— too, my God you still come first; and
where is he?' Now— I re-call those times of prayer when
spir-it low. But— morn-ing, noon, and night I share your

like the deer, for you I thirst.
songs of joy would fill the air.
liv-ing pres-ence, found in prayer.

Refrain

Why should I be sad,——
trou-bled or in pain? My hope is in my God, my hope is not in vain.

Robert Brennan, based on Psalm 41 (42), Music by Robert LeBlanc

216

1. By___ the wa - ters, the wa - ters of Ba - by- lon,
2. On___ the wil - lows, the wil - lows of Ba - by- lon,
3. There___ our cap - tors, our cap - tors from Ba - by- lon,
4. Should___ I not___ re - mem - ber Je - ru - sa- lem.

we sat down and wept,___ and wept___ for thee, Zi - on;
we hung up our harps,___ our harps,___ for thee, Zi - on;
tried to make us sing,___ and sing,___ of thee Zi - on;
Let my right hand wi- ther, my tongue___ cleave to my mouth.

we re - mem- ber thee, re - mem- ber thee, re - mem- ber thee, Zi- on.
how___ can we sing,___ can we sing,___ sing of thee, Zi- on.
but___ we could not sing, we could not sing, we could not sing, Zi- on.
Should I prize not thee, I prize not thee, my joy, Je - ru - sa- lem.

Anon, based on Psalm 136 (137). V.4 editorial

217

1 Gift of love, dawning bright,
pierces through endless night:
God of life, sharing might,
all creation holding,
earth and sky enfolding.
   Gift of love, love, love,
   gift of love, love, love.
   Glory be, Lord to thee,
   God of our salvation.

2 Thus you spoke from on high:
choose to live or to die,
love to give or deny -
life and love now blending;
love is life unending.

3 Then you came on the earth,
gift of love from your birth;
shared our life, gave us worth;
to yourself inviting,
God with us uniting.

4 For our sake you were killed;
once foretold, now fulfilled;
love so great, be not stilled!
Beams of love you lifted,
and with life were gifted.
   Robert C. Trupia

218

Deep with - in___ I will plant my law,___ not on stone,___ but in your heart. Fol- low me,___ I will bring you back,— ___ you will be my own, and I will be your God.___

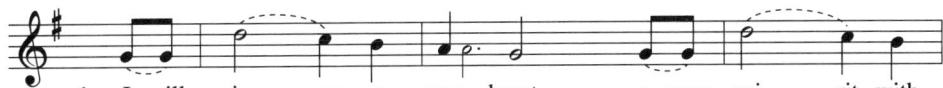

1. I will give you a new heart, a new spi - rit with -
2. { Seek_____ my face,____ and__ see____your
3. Re - turn_____ to me,____ with__ all____your

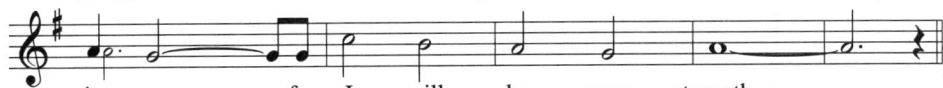

in you, for I will be your strength._____
God,_____ ⁊ for I will be your hope._____
heart,_____ ⁊ and I will bring you back._____

David Haas, from Jer 31:33, Ezekiel 36:26, Joel 2:12

219

Like as the deer that yearns for flowing wa - ters, so longs my

soul for God, the li - ving God.

3 These things will I remember
   as I pour out my soul:
   how I would lead the rejoicing crowd
   into the house of God.

1 Like the deer that yearns
   for flowing waters:
   so my soul is yearning
   for you, my God.

4 Send forth your light and truth,
   let these be my guide:
   let them bring me to your holy mountain,
   to the place where I dwell.

2 My soul is thirsting for God,
   the God of my life:
   when can I enter and see
   the face of God?

5 And I will come to the altar of God,
   the God of my joy!
   My redeemer, I will thank you on the harp,
   O God, my God.

Text: Psalm 41 (42), The Grail. Music from the abbey of Tamié

220

Grant to us, O Lord, a heart re - newed; re - cre - ate in us your own Spi - rit, Lord!

1 Behold, the days are coming,
   says the Lord our God,
   when I will make a new covenant
   with the house of Israel.

3. I will be their God,
    and they shall be my people.

2 Deep within their being
   I will implant my law;
   I will write it in their hearts.

4. And for all their faults
    I will grant forgiveness;
    never more will I remember their sins.

Lucien Deiss, from Jer 31:31-34

John L. Bell

221

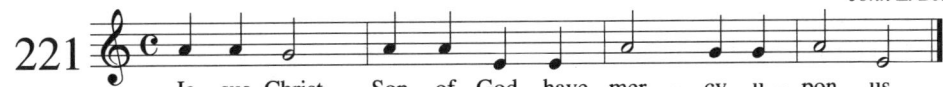

Je - sus Christ, Son of God, have mer - cy u - pon us.

222 Crucem tuam/O Lord, your cross

Cru-cem tu - am a - do - ra- mus Do-mi - ne, re- sur-rec-ti- o-nem
O Lord, your cross we a - dore and glo- ri - fy, for your ho- ly re- sur-

tu - am lau - da - mus Do - mi - ne. Lau - da - mus et glo - ri - fi - ca-mus.
rec- tion we praise you Lord of life. We praise you and we glo- ri-fy you.

Re - sur - rec - ti - o - nem tu - am lau - da - mus Do - mi - ne.
For your ho - ly re - sur - rec - tion we praise you, Lord of life.

Taizé chant by Jacques Berthier

223

1 At the cross her station keeping,
   stood the mournful mother weeping,
   close to Jesus to the last;

2 Through her heart his sorrow sharing,
   all his bitter anguish bearing,
   now at length the sword has pass'd.

3 Oh, how sad and sore distress'd
   was that mother highly blest,
   of the sole–begotten One.

4 Christ above in torment hangs;
   she beneath beholds the pangs
   of her dying glorious Son.

5 Is there one who would not weep,
   'whelm'd in miseries so deep,
   Christ's dear mother to behold?

6 Can the human heart refrain
   from partaking in her pain,
   in that mother's pain untold?

7 Bruised, derided, cursed, defiled,
   she beheld her tender child,
   all with bloody scourges rent;

8 For the sins of his own nation,
   saw him hang in desolation,
   till his spirit forth he sent.

9 O thou mother! Fount of love!
   Touch my spirit from above,
   make my heart with thine accord:

10 Make me feel as thou hast felt;
   make my soul to glow and melt
   with the love of Christ my Lord.

11 Holy Mother, pierce me through,
   in my heart each wound renew
   of my Saviour crucified.

12 Let me share with thee his pain
   who for all my sins was slain,
   who for me in torments died.

13 Let me mingle tears with thee,
   mourning him who mourn'd for me,
   all the days that I may live:

14 By the cross with thee to stay,
   there with thee to weep and pray,
   is all I ask of thee to give.

15 Virgin of all virgins best,
   listen to my fond request:
   let me share thy grief divine;

16 Let me, to my latest breath,
   in my body bear the death
   of that dying Son of thine.

17 Wounded with his every wound
    steep my soul till it hath swoon'd
    in his very blood away.

18 Be to me, O Virgin, nigh,
    lest in flames I burn and die,
    in his awful judgement day.

19 Christ, when thou shalt call me hence,
    be thy mother my defence,
    be thy cross my victory.

20 While my body here decays,
    may my soul thy goodness praise,
    safe in paradise with thee.

Ascribed to Jacopone da Todi (d 1306). tr. Edward Caswall (1814–78)

224

We a - dore you, O Je - sus Christ;

for by your cross you re - deemed the world.

Suzanne Toolan, RSM

225

1 Were you there when they crucified my
   Lord?
   Were you there when they crucified my
   Lord?
   Oh sometimes it causes me to tremble,
   tremble, tremble.
   Were you there when they crucified my
   Lord?

2 Were you there when they nailed him to
   a tree? …

3 Were you there when they pierced him
   in the side? …

4 Were you there when the sun refused to
   shine? …

5 Were you there when they laid him in
   the tomb? …

6 Were you there when they rolled the
   stone away?
   Afro–American Spiritual

226

1 O come and mourn with me awhile;
   see, Mary calls us to her side;
   O come and let us mourn with her;
   Jesus our love, Jesus our love
   is crucified.

2 Have we no tears to shed for him,
   while soldiers scoff and men deride?
   Ah! look how patiently he hangs;

3 How fast his feet and hands are nailed;
   his blessed tongue with thirst is tied;
   his failing eyes are blind with blood;

4 Seven times he spoke, seven words of
   love,
   and all three hours his silence cried
   for mercy on humanity;

5 O love of God! O human sin!
   In this dread act your strength is tried;
   and victory remains with love;
   F.W. Faber (1814–63), alt.

227 Hosanna

Taizé chant by Jacques Berthier

Canon

Ho - san - na, ho-san - na, ho-san - na in ex - cel - sis. Ho -

228

Sing ho - san - na, sing ho-san - na to the King, Son of Da - vid!

Here he comes! Fol - low the Mas - ter for he comes to save us all.

Bles sings on the King who comes in the name of the Lord!___

They came run-ning down the street so ex - ci - ted were the chil-dren as they came, (singing:)

The chil-dren came with ol - ive bran-ches. They tried to touch him as he came:

for they loved him, they be-lieved him, and they fol-lowed him to Je - ru - sa lem; (The)

Christopher Walker

229

All glory, laud and honour,
to thee, Redeemer King,
to whom the lips of children
made sweet hosannas ring.

1 Thou art the King of Israel,
thou David's royal Son,
who in the Lord's name comest,
the King and blessed one.

2 The company of angels
are praising thee on high,
and mortal folk, with all things
created, make reply.

3 The people of the Hebrews
with palms before thee went:
our praise and prayer and anthems
before thee we present.

4 To thee before thy passion
they sang their hymns of praise;
to thee now high exalted
our melody we raise.

5 Thou didst accept their praises,
accept the prayers we bring,
who in all good delightest,
thou good and gracious king.

St Theodulph of Orleans (d 821) tr. J.M. Neale (1818–66)

230

1 Ride on! Ride on in majesty!
Hark, all the tribes hosanna cry;
thy humble beast pursues his road
with palms and scattered garments strowed.

2 Ride on! Ride on in majesty!
In lowly pomp ride on to die;
O Christ, thy triumphs now begin
o'er captive death and conquered sin.

3 Ride on! Ride on in majesty!
The wingèd squadrons of the sky
look down with sad and wondering eyes,
to see the approaching sacrifice.

4 Ride on! Ride on in majesty!
Thy last and fiercest strife is nigh;
the Father, on his sapphire throne,
expects his own anointed Son.

5 Ride on! Ride on in majesty!
In lowly pomp ride on to die;
bow thy meek head to mortal pain,
then take, O God, thy power, and reign.

H. H. Milman (1791–1868)

232

1 Ah holy Jesus, how have you offended?
that man to judge you has in hate pretended?
by foes derided, by your own rejected,
O most afflicted!

2 Who was the guilty? Who brought this
        upon you?
It is my treason, Lord, that has undone you.
And I, O Jesus, I it was denied you,
I crucified you.

231

Come to Jerusalem, rejoicing before him
Greet him with loud hosannas,
bow down, adore him!

1 All peoples clap your hands,
cry out to your Maker!
God is the Lord of all,
O tremble and fear him!

2 God mounts the throne with joy,
  with blaring of trumpets!
Sing praise to God almighty,
king of all nations!

3 God is the king of all the nations,
  O praise him!
Praise him with all your skill,
enthroned in his temple!

4 Peoples and princes come
in homage to meet him.
God is the mighty one,
the world is his kingdom!

Stephen Dean, based on Psalm 46 (47)

---

3 See how the shepherd for the sheep is
    offered,
the slave has sinned and yet the son has
    suffered;
for our atonement hangs the Saviour
    bleeding,
God interceding.

4 For me, kind Jesus, was your incarnation,
your dying sorrow and your life's oblation;
your bitter passion and your desolation,
for my salvation.

5 O mighty Saviour, I cannot repay you;
I do adore you and will here obey you;
recall your mercy and your love unswerving,
    not my deserving.

Robert Bridges (1844-1930) after J. Heerman (1585-1647). Revised by Jubilate Hymns

233   **All you who pass this way**   *Taizé chant by Jacques Berthier*

All   you   who   pass   this   way,   look   and   see.

234

Fa - ther,—— if this cup may not pass me by—— but I must drink it; your will be done,—— your will be done.

Stephen Dean

235

Refrain

As pro - phets fore - told long a - go,—— God's ser - vant, the Christ, would suf - fer and die.— By his wounds we are healed.——

Verses

1. He com - mit - ted no sin, on his lips was no guile.—— When re -
2. Bo - dy bro - ken in pain, yet he ut - tered no threat,—— but
3. He him - self bore our sins in his pas - sion and pain,—— so that

viled and ab - used he was sil - ent,—— he was si - lent.——
trus - ted the judge-ment of God,—— and God's jus - tice.——
dy - ing to sin we might live,—— we might live.——

1 Pet 2:21-24. Peter Jones

236

1. See, Christ was wounded for our sake
   and bruised and beaten for our sin,
   so by his suff'rings we are healed,
   for God has laid our guilt on him.

2. Look on his face, come close to him
   - see, you will find no beauty there;
   despised, rejected, who can tell
   the grief and sorrow he must bear?

3. Like sheep that stray we leave God's path
   to choose our own and not his will,
   like lamb to slaughter he has gone,
   obedient to his Father's will.

4. Cast out to die by those he loved,
   reviled by those he died to save,
   see how sin's pride has sought his death,
   see how sin's hate has made his grave.

5. For on his shoulders God has laid
   the weight of sin that we should bear;
   so by his passion we have peace,
   through his obedience and his prayer.

Brian Foley

237

1 O sacred head ill-uséd,
   by reed and bramble scarred;
   that idle blows have bruiséd
   and mocking lips have marred:
   how dimmed that eye so tender,
   how wan those cheeks appear,
   how overcast the splendour
   that angel hosts revere!

2 What marvel if thou languish,
   vigour and virtue fled,
   wasted and spent with anguish
   and pale as are the dead?
   O by thy foes' derision,
   that death endured for me,
   grant that thy open vision
   a sinner's eyes may see.

3 Good Shepherded, spent with loving,
   look on me, who have strayed,
   oft by those lips unmoving
   with milk and honey stayed;
   spurn not a sinner's crying
   now from thy love out cast,
   but rest thy head in dying
   on these frail arms at last.

4 In this thy sacred Passion
   O, that some share had I!
   O, may thy Cross's fashion
   o'erlook me when I die!
   For these dear pains that rack thee
   a sinner's thanks receive;
   O, lest in death I lack thee,
   a sinner's care relieve.

5 Since death must be my ending,
   in that dread hour of need,
   my friendless cause befriending,
   Lord, to my rescue speed;
   thyself, dear Jesus, trace me
   that passage to the grave,
   and from thy Cross embrace me
   with arms outstretched to save.

P.Gerhardt (1607–76), tr. R.A Knox (1888-1957)

The Easter Triduum

238

1 The glory of the cross we sing
   the cross of Jesus Christ our Lord,
   who died and rose to set us free
   our way from death to life secured.

2 As once God's people rested safe,
   protected by a lamb's own blood,
   so we acclaim the sacrifice
   of Jesus Christ the Lamb of God.

3 As once the Chosen People passed
   from pain to freedom through the sea,
   so now baptismal water saves
   the chosen, called to liberty.

4 At passover before he died
   Christ Jesus took the bread and wine:
   'This is my body, this my blood,
   do this as my memorial sign.'

5 What once by Jesus was achieved
   we celebrate with heart and soul,
   recalling and effecting now
   the saving work that makes us whole.
   John Ainslie

239

1 The heav'nly Word, proceeding forth
   yet leaving not the Father's side,
   accomplishing his work on earth
   had reached at length life's eventide.

2 By false disciple to be giv'n
   to foemen for his life athirst,
   himself, the very bread of heav'n,
   he gave to his disciples first.

3 He gave himself in either kind,
   he gave his flesh, he gave his blood;
   in love's own fullness thus designed,
   to be, for humankind, the food.

4 O saving victim, opening wide
   the gate of heav'n to all below,
   our foes press on from every side;
   thine aid supply, thy strength bestow.

5   To thy great name be endless praise,
    Immortal Godhead, one in three:
    O grant us endless length of days
    in our true native land with thee.

St. Thomas Aquinas (1227–74),
tr. J. M. Neale (1818–66)

240   Reception of the Oils

1. Behold the oil of the sick, blessed by our Bishop,
   sent to us for the anointing of all who suffer illness *(Refrain A or B)*

Ref. A: Thanks be to God! Thanks be to God!
Ref. B: Bless'd be God for e - ver! Bless'd be God for e - ver!

2 Behold the oil of the catechumens, blessed by our Bishop
  send to us for the anointing of our catechumens
  in preparation for their baptism.

3 Behold the sacred chrism, oil mixed with sweet perfume,
  and consecrated by our Bishop, sent to us with the anointing
  of the baptized who are to be sealed with the Holy Spirit.

John Schiavone

241

Jesu, Jesu, fill us with your love,
show us how to serve
the neighbours we have from you.

1 Kneels at the feet of his friends,
  silently washes their feet,
  Master who pours out himself for them.

2 Neighbours are rich folk and poor,
  neighbours are black folk and white,
  neighbours are nearby and far away.

3 These are the ones we should serve,
  these are the ones we should love,
  all these are neighbours to us and you.

4 Kneel at the feet of our friends,
  silently washing their feet,
  this is the way we should live with you.

Ghana folk song, adapted by Tom Colvin

242

God is love, and where true love is
God himself is there.

1 Here in Christ we gather, love of Christ
    our calling.
  Christ, our love, is with us, gladness be
    his greeting.
  Let us love and serve him, God of all
    the ages.
  Let us love sincerely, seeing Christ in
    others.

2 When we Christians gather, members of
    one Body,
  Christ, our God, be present, loving and
    beloved.
  Let there be no discord, banished every
    quarrel.
  Let there be one Spirit, bond of peace
    among us.

3 Grant us love's fulfillment, joy with all the blessed,
  when we see your glory, risen Lord and Saviour
  bathe us in your splendour, Light of all creation,
  be our bliss forever as we sing your praises.

  Ubi Caritas, versified by James Quinn, SJ

243

1 Into one we all are gathered through the love of Christ.
  Let us then rejoice with gladness. In him we find love.
  Let us fear and love the living God,
  and love and cherish humankind.
  Where charity and love are, there is God.

2 Therefore, when we are together in the love of Christ,
  let our minds know no division, strife or bitterness,
  may the Christ our God be in our midst.
  Through Christ our Lord all love is found.

3 May we see your face in glory, Christ our loving God.
  With the blessed saints of heaven give us lasting joy.
  We will then possess true happiness,
  and love for all eternity.

  Ubi Caritas. versified by Michael Cockett

244

U- bi ca - ri - tas et a - mor,—— De-us i - bi est.
(est ve - ra)*——

*Either wording may be sung

1 Congregavit nos in unum Christi amor.
  Exsultemus et in ipso iucundemur.
  Timeamus et amemus Deum vivum.
  Et ex corde diligamus nos sincero.

2 Simul ergo cum in unum congregamur:
  ne nos mente dividamus, caveamus.
  Cessent iurgia maligna, cessent lites.
  Et in medio nostri sit Christus Deus.

3 Simul quoque cum beatis videamus
  glorianter vultum tuum, Christe Deus:
  gaudium quod est immensum, atque probum,
  saecula per infinita saeculorum.

  Latin, 9th Century

245 Ubi caritas

U - bi ca - ri - tas et a - mor,

U - bi ca - ri - tas De - us i - bi est.

Taizé chant by Jacques Berthier

246

1 Of the glorious body telling,
 O my tongue, its myst'ries sing,
 and the blood, all price excelling,
 which the world's eternal king,
 in a noble womb once dwelling,
 shed for this world's ransoming.

2 Giv'n for us, for us descending,
 of a virgin to proceed,
 man with man in converse blending,
 scattered he the gospel seed,
 'till his sojourn drew to ending,
 which he closed in wondrous deed.

3 At the last great supper lying,
 circled by his brethren's band,
 meekly with the law complying,
 first, he finished its command.
 Then, immortal food supplying,
 gave himself with his own hand.

4 Word made flesh, by word he maketh
 very bread his flesh to be;
 man in wine Christ's blood partaketh,
 and if senses fail to see,
 faith alone the true heart waketh,
 to behold the mystery.

5 Therefore, we before him bending,
 this great sacrament revere;
 types and shadows have their ending,
 for the newer rite is here;
 faith, our outward sense befriending,
 makes the inward vision clear.

6 Glory let us give, and blessing,
 to the Father and the Son;
 honour, might and praise addressing,
 while eternal ages run;
 ever too his love confessing,
 who from both, with both is one.

St. Thomas Aquinas (1227–74),
tr. J. M. Neale, (1818–66)
E. Caswall (1814–78), and others

247

1 Pange, lingua, gloriosi
 corporis mysterium,
 sanguinisque pretiosi,
 quem in mundi pretium
 fructus ventris generosi
 Rex effudit gentium.

2 Nobis datus, nobis natus
 ex intacta Virgine;
 et in mundo conversatus,
 sparso verbi semine,
 sui moras incolatus
 miro clausit ordine.

3 In supremae nocte coenae
 recumbens cum fratribus,
 observata lege plene
 cibis in legalibus:
 cibum turbae duodenae
 se dat suis manibus.

4 Verbum caro, panem verum
 Verbo carnem efficit:
 fitque sanguis Christi merum;
 et si sensus deficit,
 adfirmandum cor sincerum
 sola fides sufficit.

5 Tantum ergo Sacramentum
 veneremur cernui:
 et antiquum documentum
 novo cedat ritui:
 præstet fides supplementum
 sensuum defectui.

6 Genitori, genitoque
 laus, et jubilatio,
 salus, honor, virtus quoque
 sit et benedictio:
 procedenti ab utroque
 compar sit laudatio. Amen.

St Thomas Aquinas (1227–74)

248

1 An upper room did our Lord prepare
for those he loved until the end:
and his disciples still gather there,
to celebrate their Risen Friend.

2 A lasting gift Jesus gave his own:
to share his bread, his loving cup.
Whatever burdens may bow us down,
he by his cross shall lift us up.

3 And after Supper he washed their feet,
for service, too, is sacrament.
In him our joy shall be made complete –
sent out to serve, as he was sent.

4 No end there is! We depart in peace.
He loves beyond the uttermost:
in every room in our Father's house
he will be there, as Lord and Host.

F. Pratt Green

249 Stay with me

Taizé chant by Jacques Berthier

Stay with me,   re- main here with me,   watch__   and   pray,   watch and pray.__

250

1 Sing, my tongue, the song of triumph,
tell the story far and wide;
tell of dread and final battle,
sing of Saviour crucified;
how upon the cross a victim,
vanquishing in death he died.

2 God in pity saw us fallen,
shamed and sunk in misery,
when we fell on death by tasting
fruit of the forbidden tree;
then another tree was chosen
which the world from death should free.

3 Thirty years among us dwelling
his appointed time fulfilled,
born for this, he meets his Passion,
for that this he freely willed,
on the Cross the Lamb is lifted
where his life-blood shall be filled.

4 He endured the nails, the spitting,
vinegar, and spear, and reed;
from that holy body broken
blood and water forth proceed:
earth and stars, and sky, and ocean
by that flood from stain are freed.

5 Faithful cross! Above all other,
one and only noble tree!
None in foliage, none in blossom,
none in fruit your peer may be;
sweetest wood and sweetest iron!
Sweetest weight is hung on thee.

6 Bend your boughs, O tree of glory!
All your rigid branches, bend!
For a while the ancient temper
that your birth bestowed, suspend;
and the king of earth and heaven
gently on your bosom tend.

7 Praise and honour to the Father,
praise and honour to the Son,
praise and honour to the Spirit,
ever three and ever one,
one in might and one in glory,
while eternal ages run.

Venantius Fortunatus (530–609),
tr. J. M. Neale (1818–66), and others

251

Peter Jones, from the Reproaches

O— my peo-ple, what have I done to of-fend— you so? Tell me, give answer, tell me.

252

1 The royal banners forward go,
the cross shines forth in mystic glow,
where he in flesh, our flesh who made,
our sentence bore, our ransom paid.

2 There whilst he hung, his sacred side
by soldier's spear was open'd wide,
to cleanse us in the precious flood
of water mingled with his blood.

3 Fulfill'd is now what David told
in true prophetic song of old,
how God the heathen's king should be;
for God is reigning from the tree.

4 O tree of glory, tree most fair,
ordain'd those holy limbs to bear,
how bright in purple robe it stood,
the purple of a saviour's blood!

5 Upon its arms, like balance true,
he weigh'd the price for sinners due,
the price which none but he could pay:
and spoil'd the spoiler of his prey.

6 To thee, eternal Three in One,
let homage meet by all be done,
as by the cross thou dost restore,
so rule and guide us evermore. Amen.

Venantius Fortunatus (530–609), tr. J. M. Neale (1818–66), and others

253 Jesus, remember me

Taizé chant by Jacques Berthier

Je-sus, re-member me when you come in-to your King-dom.

Je-sus, re-member me when you come in-to your King-dom.

The Easter Vigil

Exodus 15. Stephen Dean

254

I will sing to the Lord, glor-ious his tri-umph,

glo-rious his tri-umph! I will sing to the Lord.

Easter

Seasonal Service Music 255-66; Hymns 267-88

Chorus

255

Hail, O fes-ti-val day! Blest day that is hal-lowed for e-ver;

day when our Lord a-rose, brea-king the king-dom of death.

Verses 1, 3, 5, 7

1. All the fair beau-ty of earth from the death of the win-ter a-ri-sing!
3. Dai-ly the love-li-ness grows, a-dorned with the glo-ry of blos-som;
5. God the Al-migh-ty, the Lord, the__ ru-ler of earth and the hea-vens,
7. Spi-rit of life and of power, now__ flow in us, fount of our be-ing,

To chorus

Ev'-ry good__ gift of the year__ now with its Ma-ster re-turns.
hea-ven her__ gates un-bars,__ fling-ing her in-crease of light:
guard us from__ harm with-out,__ cleanse us from e-vil with-in:
light that en-ligh-tens__ all,__ life that in all may a-bide:

Verses 2, 4, 6, 8

2. He who was nailed to the cross is__ Lord and the ru-ler of all things;
4. Rise from the grave now, O Lord, who art au-thor of life and cre-a-tion.
6. Je-sus the health of the world, en-ligh-ten our minds, great Re-dee-mer,
8. Praise to the Gi-ver of good! O__ Lo-ver and au-thor of con-cord,

To chorus

all things cre-a-ted on earth sing to the glo-ry of God:__
Trea-ding the path-way of death, new life you give to us all:__
Son of the Fa-ther su-preme, on-ly be-got-ten of God:__
pour out your balm on our souls, or-der our ways in your peace:__

Salve festa dies, Venantius Fortunatus (530-609). Tr. composite. Music by R. Vaughan Williams (1872-1958)

256 Blessing of Water

Stephen Dean

I saw streams of wa-ter flow-ing from the tem-ple's right side,
hea-ling pow'r and life be-stow-ing from the one who had died: Al-le-
lu - ia, al-le-lu - ia, from our Sa-viour glo-ri-fied.

1 Into day from deepest night,
out of darkness into light,
Christ our Saviour comes once more,
opens wide salvation's door!

2 He has healed us with his blood,
led us safe through Jordan's flood,

on the further bank we stand,
gazing on the promised land!

3. He has raised us from the grave,
from the Red Sea's mighty wave.
Dead to sin we rise with Christ,
paschal Lamb now sacrificed.

Stephen Dean

➤ *SEE ALSO: You have put on Christ (400)*

257 Psalm/Gathering Song (Ps 117 (118))

This is the day the Lord— has made, let us re-joice and be glad.—
This is the day the Lord— has made, let us re-joice and be glad.—

1 Give thanks to the Lord for he is good,
his mercy endures for ever;
let the house of Israel say:
'His mercy endures for ever.'

2 The Lord's right hand has struck with
pow'r,
the Lord's right hand is exalted;
I shall not die, but live
and declare the works of the Lord.

3 The stone which the builders rejected
has become the cornerstone.
By the Lord this has been done;
it is wonderful in our eyes!

Michael Joncas

Psalm 118: Response, ICEL; verses,
Confraternity of Christian Doctrine, alt.

258 Psalm/Gathering Song (Ps 117 (118)) — *Bernadette Farrell*

The stone which the buil-ders re-jec-ted has become the cor-ner-stone;___ al-le-lu-ia,___ al-le-lu-ia,___ has be-come the cor-ner-stone.___

1 Let the family of Israel say:
 'God's love has no end, God's love has no end.'
 Let the family of Aaron say:
 'God's love has no end, God's love has no end.'
 And let all who fear God, and let all who fear God
 say his love is without end.
 Alleluia, alleluia, say his love is without end.

2 I called to the Lord in my distress,
 he answered me and set me free.
 God is at my side, God is at my side,
 God is here to help me now.
 Alleluia, alleluia, God is here to help me now.

3 Open to me the gates of holiness;
 I will enter and give thanks.
 This is the Lord's own gate,
 the gate where the just may enter in.
 I will thank you, Lord, I will thank you, Lord.
 for you hear and answer me.
 Alleluia, alleluia, for you hear and answer me.

4 Go forward with branches, go forward processing,
 go to the altar of the Lord
 and give thanks to God,
 and give thanks to God
 for his love is without end.
 Alleluia, alleluia, for his love is without end.

259 Sequence: Victimae paschali laudes

(Original version overleaf)

1 O Flock of Christ, your homage bring
 to Christ the Lamb, your glorious King!
 His Easter praise in triumph sing!
 Alleluia, alleluia, alleluia!

2 Peace has come down from God on high!
 The King of peace in death did lie!
 To save the sheep the Lamb did die!

3 Never on earth was stranger sight:
 life fought with death in darkest night,
 yet lives to reign in endless light!

4 What saw you, Mary, on your way?
 'I saw the tomb where Life once lay,
 whose glory shone this Easter Day!

5 Angels their joyful tidings spread!
 Grave-clothes I saw where none lay dead,
 the cloth that once had veiled his head!

6 'Christ is my hope, who rose for me!
 Soon will you all his glory see!
 Christ bids you go to Galilee!'

7 Christ lives again, whose blood was shed,
 the Lord of life, our living Bread,
 the Firstborn risen from the dead!
 Alleluia, alleluia, alleluia!

*ascribed to Wipo of Burgundy, d.1048;
tr. James Quinn, S.J.*

➤ SEE ALSO Christ the Lord is risen today (273)

260 Sequence: Victimae paschali laudes (original version)

1. Vic - ti - mae pas - cha - li lau - des im - mo - lent Chri - sti - a - ni.
1. *Chris-tians, praise the pas - chal vic - tim! Of - fer thank - ful sa - cri-fice.*

2. Ag - nus re - de - mit o - ves, Chri - stus in - no-cens Pa - tri re - con-
3. Mors et vi - ta du - el - lo con - fli - xe - re mi - ran-do: dux vi -
2. *Christ the Lamb has saved the sheep, Christ the just one paid the price re - con-*
3. *Death and life fought bit - ter - ly for this won-drous vic - to - ry; the Lord*

ci - li - a - vit pec - ca - to - res. 4. Dic no - bis, Ma - ri - ia,___
tae mor - tu - us re - gnat vi - vus. 6. An - ge - li - cos tes - tes,___
ci-ling sin-ners to the Fa-ther. 4. O Ma - ry come and say___
of life who died reigns glo - ri-fied! 6. Bright an - gels tes - ti - fied,___

quid vi - dis - ti in vi - a? 5. Se - pul-chrum Chri - sti vi -
su - da - ri - um et ves - tes. 7. Sur - rex - it Chri - stus spes
what you saw at break of day. 5. 'The emp - ty tomb of my
shroud and grave - clothes side by side! 7. 'Yes, Christ my hope rose glo -

ven - tis, et glo - ri - am vi - di re - sur - gen - tis:
me - a: prae - ce - det su - os in Ga - li - lae - am.
li - ving Lord! I saw Christ Je - sus ri - sen and a - dored!
ri - ous - ly. He goes be - fore you in - to Ga - li - lee.'

8. Sci - mus Chri - stum sur - re - xis - se a mor - tu - is ve - re:
8. *Share the good news, sing joy - ful - ly: his death is vic - to - ry!*

tu no - bis, vic - tor Rex, mi - se - re - re. (A - men.___ Al-le-lu - ia.)
Lord Je - sus, vic - tor King, show us mer - cy.

ascribed to Wipo of Burgundy, d.1048; English tr. by Peter J. Scagnelli

Gospel Acclamations for Easter

Traditional melody

261

Al - le - lu - ia, al - le - lu - ia,— al - le - lu - ia.

Bernadette Farrell

262

Refrain

Al - le - lu - ia, al - le - lu - ia, Je - sus, ri - sen Lord of life!

Al - le - lu - ia, al - le - lu - ia, al - le - lu - ia!

Verses

1. Word of the Fa-ther: Je - sus Christ! Hope of the world: Je-sus Christ!
2. Light of the na-tions: Je - sus Christ! Way, truth and life: Je-sus Christ!
3. Li - ving a-mong us: Je - sus Christ! Word in our flesh: Je-sus Christ!

Bro-ken and bur-ied: Je - sus Christ! Ri - sen to life: Je-sus Christ!
Bea-ring our sor-row: Je - sus Christ! With us through time: Je-sus Christ!
Ser-vant of oth-ers: Je - sus Christ! Friend of the poor: Je-sus Christ!

Stephen Dean

263

Verses Cantor: *All:*

1. Did not our hearts burn with-in us, Al-le-lu - ia, al-le-lu - ia.
2. Come, ri - sen Lord, walk be - side us.
3. O - pen our hearts, ri - sen Je-sus.

Cantor: *All:*

As we heard the ri - sen Je - sus? Al - le - lu - ia.
May your gos - pel e - ver guide us.
May your Spi - rit ne - ver leave us.

Refrain *All:*

Al - le - lu - ia, praise the Lord, praise his Word!

Al - le - lu - ia, praise the ri - sen Lord!

264 Refrain *Traditional Melody*

Al - le - lu - ia,—— al - le - lu-ia, al-le-lu - ia!

Verses

1. O sons and daugh - ters, let—— us sing; the King of hea-ven, the
2. Glo - ry and praise—— to you,—— O Christ, who shed for us—— your

glo - rious King, this day from death— rose tri - um-phing: al-le-lu - ia!——
blood— un-priced, pass - o - ver Lamb— now sa - cri-ficed: Al-le-lu - ia!——

Processional Chants/Communion Songs

Taizé chants by Jacques Berthier

265 **Christus resurrexit**

Mmm....   Christus re-sur-re - xit, Chris-tus re-sur-re - xit,

Mmm....   al - le - lu - ia, al-le-lu - ia!

266 **Surrexit Christus**

A1   B

(hum)——————— Sur - re - xit Chris - tus, al - le - lu - ia!

A2   C

(hum)——————— Can-ta - te Do-mi-no, al - le - lu - ia!

267

1 Jesus Christ is ris'n today, alleluia!
   Our triumphant holy day, alleluia!
   Who did once, upon the cross, alleluia!
   Suffer to redeem our loss, alleluia!

2 Hymns of praise then let us sing, alleluia!
   Unto Christ, our heavenly king, alleluia!
   Who endured the cross and grave, alleluia!
   Sinners to redeem and save, alleluia!

3 But the pains that he endured, alleluia!
   Our salvation have procured; alleluia!
   Now above the sky he's king, alleluia!
   Where the angels ever sing, alleluia!

   Lyra Davidica (1708)

268

Alleluia, alleluia,
give thanks to the risen Lord.
Alleluia, alleluia,
give praise to his name.

1 Jesus is Lord of all the earth.
   He is the King of creation.

2 Spread the good news o'er all the earth.
   Jesus has died and has risen.

3 We have been crucified with Christ.
   Now we shall live for ever.

4 God has proclaimed the just reward.
   Life for us all, alleluia.

5 Come, let us praise the living God,
   joyfully sing to our Saviour.

   Don Fishel

269

1 At the Lamb's high feast we sing
   praise to our victorious king,
   who hath washed us in the tide
   flowing from his piercèd side.
   Praise we him whose love divine
   gives the guests his blood for wine,
   gives his body for the feast,
   love the victim, love the priest.

2 Where the paschal blood is poured,
   Death's dark angel sheathes his sword;
   Israel's hosts triumphant go
   through the wave that drowns the foe.
   Christ the Lamb, whose blood was shed.
   Paschal victim, paschal bread;
   with sincerity and love
   eat we manna from above.

3 Mighty victim from the sky,
   powers of hell beneath thee lie;
   death is conquered in the fight;
   thou has brought us life and light,
   now thy banner thou dost wave;
   vanquished Satan and the grave;
   angels join his praise to tell –
   see o'erthrown the prince of hell.

4 Paschal triumph, paschal joy,
   only sin can this destroy;
   from the death of sin set free
   souls re–born, dear Lord, in thee.
   Hymns of glory, songs of praise,
   Father, unto thee we raise.
   Risen Lord, all praise to thee,
   ever with the Spirit be.

   Anonymous, 7th century,
   tr. Robert Campbell (1814–68)

270

1 Christ is alive, with joy we sing;
   we celebrate our risen Lord,
   praising the glory of his name.
   Alleluia, alleluia, alleluia.

2 He is the grain of wheat that died;
   sown in distress and reaped in joy,
   yielding a harvest of new life.

3 He is the sun which brings the dawn:
   he is the light of all the world,
   setting us free from death and sin.

4 He is the vine set in the earth,
   sharing our life, becoming man,
   that we might share in God's own life.

5 Christ is alive, with joy we sing;
we celebrate our risen Lord,
praising the glory of his name.
Pamela Stotter

271

1 Battle is o'er, hell's armies flee:
raise we the cry of victory
with abounding joy resounding,
alleluia, alleluia.

2 Christ who endured the shameful tree,
o'er death triumphant welcome we,
our adoring praise outpouring,
alleluia, alleluia.

3 On the third morn from death rose he,
clothed with what light in heaven shall be,
our unswerving faith deserving,
alleluia, alleluia.

4 Hell's gloomy gates yield up their key,
paradise door thrown wide we see;
never–tiring be our choiring,
alleluia, alleluia.

5 Lord, by the stripes they laid on thee,
grant us to live from death set free,
this our greeting still repeating,
alleluia, alleluia.
Simphonia Sirenum (1695)
tr. R.A. Knox (1888–1957)

272

1 Christ is alive! Let Christians sing;
the cross stands empty to the sky:
let streets and homes with praises ring.
Love, drowned in death, shall never die.

2 Christ is alive! No longer bound
to distant years in Palestine,
but saving, healing, here and now,
and touching every place and time.

3 In every insult, rift and war,
where colour, scorn or wealth divide,
Christ suffers still, yet loves the more,
and lives, where even hope has died.

4 Women and men, in age and youth,
can feel the Spirit, hear the call,
and find the way, the life, the truth,
revealed in Jesus, freed for all.

5 Christ is alive, and comes to bring
good news to this and every age,
till earth and sky and ocean ring
with joy, with justice, love and praise.
Brian A. Wren

273

1 Christ the Lord is risen today!
Christians, haste your vows to pay,
offer ye your praises meet
at the paschal victim's feet;
for the sheep the Lamb hath bled,
sinless in the sinner's stead.
Christ the Lord is ris'n on high;
now he lives, no more to die.

2 Christ, the victim undefiled,
all to God hath reconciled
when in strange and awful strife
met together death and life;
Christians, on this happy day
haste with joy your vows to pay.
Christ the Lord is ris'n on high;
now he lives, no more to die.

3 Say, O wond'ring Mary, say
what thou sawest on thy way.
'I beheld, where Christ had lain,
empty tomb and angels twain,
I beheld the glory bright
of the rising Lord of light;
Christ my hope is ris'n again;
now he lives, and lives to reign.'

4 Christ, who once for sinners bled,
now the first–born from the dead,
throned in endless might and power,
lives and reigns for evermore.
Hail, eternal hope on high!
Hail, thou king of victory!
Hail, thou Prince of life adored!
Help and save us, gracious Lord.
Victimae paschali., *tr. Jane E. Leeson (1809–81)*

274

1. Dark - ness is gone,___ day - light has come: God's
2. See now the cross,___ see___ now the grave: they,

heir to heav'n and earth a - ri - ses___ with the dawn. Death
va - cant, ce - le - brate how God's foo-lish-ness can save. The

lo - ses its si - ni-ster sting, God's pro-mise to do a new thing is
cri-mi-nal nailed as a fraud is raised by the po-wer of God and

done, and Hal - le - lu - jah, earth joins heav'n to sing.___
lives. So Hal - le - lu - jah! Scat - ter the news a - broad.___

3 Greener the grass, brighter the sun,
   the God-loved world proclaims a new
        age has begun.
   Creation is decked for her guest
   who, free from his grave clothes is dressed
   in light and, Hallelujah!
   tells that the earth is blessed.

4 The needed trust, the longed-for peace
   are passed as hands from sword and
        shackle are released.
   The violence of hate reigns no more:
   the victory of love is the core
   of hope and, Hallelujah!
   Love means an open door.

5 'The kingdom comes!' the King proclaims:
   Justice and joy abound where Christ-
        filled faith pertains.
   Religion, remote and typecast,
   is gone, and the future is vast.
   New tongues sing 'Hallelujah!
   God is for us at last!'

6 Enrol the drum, enlist the gong
   to celebrate in sound that right has
        conquered wrong.
   Join hands with the neighbour unknown,
   unite through the love that is shown
   in Christ, for, Hallelujah!
   Christ is our Lord alone.
                    John Bell & Graham Maule

275

1 The strife is o'er, the battle done;
   the victory of life is won:
   the song of triumph has begun:
        Alleluia, alleluia, alleluia!

2 On the third morn he rose again
   glorious in majesty to reign;
   O let us swell the joyful strain:

3 He closed the yawning gates of hell,
   the bars from heav'ns high portals fell;
   let hymns of praise his triumphs tell:

4 Lord, by your death on Calvary,
   from death's dread sting your people
        free,
   that we may live eternally!
        17th C, tr Francis Pott (1832-1909) alt.

276

1 He is risen, tell the story
to the nations of the night;
from their sin and from their blindness,
let them walk in Easter light.
Now begins a new creation,
now has come our true salvation.
Jesus Christ, the Son of God!

2 Mary goes to tell the others
of the wonders she has seen;
John and Peter come a'running
what can all this truly mean?
O Rabboni, Master holy,
to appear to one so lowly!
Jesus Christ, the Son of God!

3 He has cut down death and evil,
he has conquered all despair;
he has lifted from our shoulders,
all the weight of anxious care.
Risen Brother, now before you,
we will worship and adore you.
Jesus Christ, the Son of God!

4 Now get busy, bring the message,
so that all may come to know
there is hope for saint and sinner,
for our God has loved us so.
Ev'ry church bell is a'ringing,
ev'ry Christian now is singing.
Jesus Christ, the Son of God!

Willard F. Jabusch

277

1. Easter glory fills the sky! *Alleluia!*
Christ now lives, no more to die! *Alleluia!*
Darkness has been put to flight! *Alleluia!*
By the living Lord of light! *Alleluia!*

2 See, the stone is rolled away
from the tomb where once he lay!
He has risen as he said,
glorious Firstborn from the dead!

3 Mary, Mother, greet your Son
radiant from his triumph won!
By his cross you shared his pain,
so for ever share his reign!

4 Magd'len, wipe away your tears!
He has come who calms your fears!
Hear the Master speak your name;
turn to him with heart aflame!

5 Shepherd, seek the sheep that strayed!
Come to contrite Peter's aid!
Strengthen him to be the rock;
make him shepherd of your flock!

6 Seek not life within the tomb;
Christ stands in the upper room!
Risen glory he conceals,
risen Body he reveals!

7 Though we see his face no more,
he is with us as before!
Glory veiled, he is our Priest,
his true flesh and blood our feast!

8 Christ, the Victor over death,
breathes on us the Spirit's breath!
Paradise is our reward,
endless Easter with our Lord!
James Quinn, S.J.

278

1 Now the green blade riseth from the
buried grain,
wheat that in the dark earth many days
has lain;
love lives again, that with the dead
has been:
love is come again like wheat that
springeth green.

2 In the grave they laid him, Love whom
men had slain,
thinking that never he would wake again,
laid in the earth like grain that sleeps
unseen:
love is come again like wheat that
springeth green.

3 Forth he came at Easter, like the risen
    grain,
  he that for three days in the grave had lain,
  quick from the dead my risen Lord is seen:
  love is come again like wheat that
    springeth green.

4 When our hearts are wintry, grieving or
    in pain,
  thy touch can call us back to life again,
  fields of our heart that dead and bare
    have been:
  love is come again like wheat that
    springeth green.
                        J. M. C. Crum (1872-1958)

279

1 Ye choirs of new Jerusalem,
  your sweetest notes employ,
  the Paschal victory to hymn
  in strains of holy joy.

2 How Judah's Lion burst his chains,
  and crushed the serpent's head;
  and brought with him, from death's
    domain,
  the long–imprisoned dead.

3 From hell's devouring jaws the prey
  alone our leader bore;
  his ransomed hosts pursue their way
  where he hath gone before.

4 Triumphant in his glory now
  his sceptre ruleth all:
  earth, heaven, and hell before him bow
  and at his footstool fall.

5 While joyful thus his praise we sing,
  his mercy we implore,
  into his palace bright to bring,
  and keep us evermore.

6 All glory to the Father be,
  all glory to the Son,
  all glory, Holy Ghost, to thee,
  while endless ages run.
              St. Fulbert of Chartres (c. 1000),
              tr. R. Campbell (1814–68)

280

Alleluia, alleluia, alleluia!

1 O sons and daughters, let us sing!
  the King of heav'n, the glorious King,
  o'er death today rose triumphing,
  Alleluia!

2 That Easter morn, at break of day,
  the faithful women went their way
  to seek the tomb where Jesus lay.

3 An angel clad in white they see,
  who sat, and spoke unto the three,
  'Your Lord has gone to Galilee.'

4 That night th'apostles met in fear
  amidst them came their Lord most dear
  and said, 'My peace be on all here.'

5 When Thomas first the tidings heard,
  how they had seen the risen Lord,
  he doubted the disciples' word.

6 'My wounded side, O Thomas, see;
  behold my hands, my feet', said he,
  and doubt not, but believe in me.'

7 When Thomas saw that wounded side,
  the truth no longer he denied:
  'You are my Lord and God!' he cried.

8 How blest are they who have not seen,
  and yet whose faith has constant been,
  for they eternal life shall win.

9 On this most holy day of days,
  to God your hearts and voices raise,
  in laud, and jubilee and praise.
        O filii et filiae, Jean Tisserand, d.1494,
        tr. J.M.Neale (1818–66), alt.

281

Alleluia, alleluia, alleluia!

1 Glory to God who does wondrous things,
  let all the people God's praises now sing,
  all of creation in splendour shall ring:
    Alleluia!

2 See how salvation for all has been won,
  up from the grave our new life has begun.
  Life now perfected in Jesus, the Son:

3 Now in our presence the Lord will appear,
shine in the faces of all of us here,
fill us with joy and cast out all our fear:

4 Call us, Good Shepherd, we listen for you,
wanting to see you in all that we do,
we would the gate of salvation pass
through:

5 Lord, we are open to all that you say,
ready to listen and follow your way,
you are the potter and we are the clay:

6 If we have love, than we dwell in the Lord,
God will protect us from fire and
sword,
fill us with love and the peace of his word:

Marty Haugen

282

Sing to the mountains, sing to the sea.
Raise your voices, lift your hearts.
This is the day the Lord has made.
Let all the earth rejoice.

1 I will give thanks to you, my Lord.
You have answered my plea.
You have saved my soul from death.
You are my strength and my song.

2 Holy, holy, holy Lord.
Heaven and earth are full of your glory.

3 This is the day that the Lord has made.
Let us be glad and rejoice.
He has turned all death to life.
Sing of the glory of God.

Robert J. Dufford, S.J.

283

1 The day of resurrection!
Earth, tell it out abroad;
the Passover of gladness
the Passover of God!
From death to life eternal,
from earth unto the sky,
our Christ hath brought us over
with hymns of victory.

2 Our hearts be pure from evil,
that we may see aright
the Lord in rays eternal
of resurrection–light;
and listening to his accents,
may hear so calm and plain
his own 'All hail' and, hearing,
may raise the victor strain.

3 Now let the heavens be joyful,
and earth her song begin,
the round world keep high triumph,
and all that is therein;
let all things seen and unseen
their notes of gladness blend,
for Christ the Lord hath risen,
our joy that hath no end.

St. John Damascene (c. 750),
tr. J. M. Neale (1818–66)

284

1. We walk by faith, and not by sight: no gracious words we hear of him who spoke as none e'er spoke, but we be-lieve him near.

2 We may not touch his hands and side,
nor follow where he trod;
yet in his promise we rejoice,
and cry 'My Lord and God!'

3 Help then, O Lord, our unbelief,
and may our faith abound;
to call on you when you are near,
and seek where you are found:

4 That when our life and faith is done
   in realms of clearer light
   we may behold you as you are
   in full and endless sight.

5 We walk by faith, and not by sight:
   no gracious words we hear
   of him who spoke as none e'er spoke,
   but we believe him near.

Henry Alford (1810–71) alt. Music by Marty Haugen

285

1 Sing of one who walks beside us
   and this day is living still,
   one who now is closer to us
   than the thoughts our hearts distill.
   One who once upon a hilltop
   raised against the power of sin,
   died in love as his own creatures
   crucified their God and King!

2 Strangers we have walked beside him
   the long journey of the day,
   and have told him of the darkness
   that has swept our hope away.
   He has offered words of comfort,
   words of energy and light,
   and our hearts have blazed within us
   as he saved us from the night.

3 Stay with us, dear Lord, and raise us,
   once again the night is near.
   Dine with us and share your wisdom,
   free our hearts from every fear.
   In the calm of each new evening,
   in the freshness of each dawn,
   if you hold us fast in friendship
   we will never be alone.

Ralph Wright, O.S.B.

Tune: American, 19th C.)

Sing of one who walks be - side us and this day is li - ving still,
one who now is clo - ser to us than the thoughts our hearts dis - till.

One who once u - pon a hill - top raised a - gainst the power of sin,

died in love as his own crea - tures cru - ci - fied their God and King!

286

1 This joyful Eastertide,
   away with sin and sorrow,
   my love, the Crucified,
   hath sprung to life this morrow:
   Had Christ, that once was slain,
   ne'er burst his three–day prison,
   our faith had been in vain:
   but now hath Christ arisen.

2 My flesh in hope shall rest,
   and for a season slumber:
   till trump from east to west
   shall wake the dead in number:

3 Death's flood hath lost his chill,
   since Jesus crossed the river:
   lover of souls, from ill
   my passing soul deliver:

G.R. Woodward (1849–1934)

287

1 Thine be the glory, risen conquering Son,
endless is the victory thou o'er death hast won;
angels in bright raiment rolled the stone away,
kept the folded grave–clothes, where thy body lay.
Thine be the glory, risen, conquering Son,
endless is the victory thou o'er death hast won.

2 Lo, Jesus meets us risen from the tomb;
lovingly he greets us, scatters fear and gloom;
let the church with gladness hymns of triumph sing,
for her Lord is living, death has lost its sting.

3 No more we doubt thee, glorious Prince of life;
life is nought without thee; aid us in our strife;
make us more than conquerors, through thy deathless love;
bring us safe through Jordan to thy home above.
E.L. Budry (1854–1932) tr. R.B. Hoyle (1875–1939)

288

1. On the jour - ney to Em - ma - us with our hearts cold as
2. And our hearts burned wi - thin us as we talked on the

stone - the One who would save us had left us a - lone. Then a
way, how all that was pro - mised was ours on that day. So we

stran - ger walks with us and, to our sur - prise, he
begged him, 'Stay with us and grant us your word.' We

o - pens our sto - ries and he o - pens our eyes.
wel - comed the stran - ger and we wel - comed the Lord.

3 And that evening at table
as he blessed and broke bread,
we saw it was Jesus
aris'n from the dead;
though he vanished before us
we knew he was near -
the life in our dying
and the hope in our fear.

4 On our journey to Emmaus,
in our stories and feast,
with Jesus we claim that the
greatest is least:
and his words burn within us -
let none be ignored -
who welcomes the stranger
shall welcome the Lord.

Marty Haugen

The Ascension

289

1 Praise him as he mounts the skies,
   alleluia!
   Christ, the Lord of paradise, *alleluia!*
   Cry hosanna in the height, *alleluia!*
   as he rises out of sight, *alleluia!*

2 Now at last he takes his throne,
   from all ages his alone!
   with his praise creation rings:
   'Lord of lords and king of kings!'

3 Hands and feet and side reveal
   wounds of love, high priesthood's seal!
   Advocate, for us he pleads;
   Heavenly Priest, he intercedes!

4 Christians, raise your eyes above!
   He will come again in love,
   on that great and wondrous day
   when this world will pass away!

5 At his word new heavens and earth
   will in glory spring to birth!
   Risen Lord, our great Amen,
   come Lord Jesus, come again!
   James Quinn, S. J.

290

1 The head that once was crowned with
   thorns
   is crowned with glory now:
   a royal diadem adorns
   the mighty victor's brow.

2 The highest place that heaven affords
   is his, is his by right.
   The King of kings and Lord of lords,
   and heaven's eternal light;

3 The joy of all who dwell above,
   the joy of all below,
   to whom he manifests his love,
   and grants his name to know.

4 To them the cross, with all its shame
   with all its grace is given;
   their name an everlasting name,
   their joy the joy of heaven.

5 They suffer with their Lord below,
   they reign with him above,
   their profit and their joy to know
   the mystery of his love.

6 The cross he bore is life and health,
   though shame and death to him;
   his people's hope, his people's wealth,
   their everlasting theme.
   Thomas Kelly (1769–1854)

291

1 Hail the day that sees him rise, *alleluia!*
   To his throne above the skies; *alleluia!*
   Christ, the Lamb for sinners given,
   alleluia!
   Enters now the highest heaven,
   alleluia!

2 There for him high triumph waits;
   lift your heads, eternal gates!
   He hath conquered death and sin;
   take the king of glory in!

3 Circled round with angel–powers,
   their triumphant Lord and ours;
   wide unfold the radiant scene,
   take the king of glory in!

4 Lo, the heaven its Lord receives,
   yet he loves the earth he leaves;
   though returning to his throne,
   he calls humankind his own.

5 See! He lifts his hands above.
   See! He shows the prints of love;
   hark! His gracious lips bestow,
   blessings on his Church below.

6 Still for us he intercedes,
   his prevailing death he pleads;
   near himself prepares our place,
   he the first–fruits of our race.

7 Lord, though parted from our sight,
far above the starry height,
grant our hearts may thither rise,
seeking thee above the skies.

8 Ever upward let us move,
wafted on the wings of love;
looking when our Lord shall come,
longing, sighing after home.

Charles Wesley (1707–88), Thomas Cotterill (1779–1823), and others

292

1 New praises be given to Christ newly crowned,
who back to his heaven a new way hath found;
God's blessedness sharing before us he goes,
what mansions preparing, what endless repose!

2 His glory still praising on thrice holy ground
the apostles stood gazing, his mother around;
with hearts that beat faster, with eyes full of love,
they watched while their master ascended above.

3 No star can disclose him', the bright angels said;
Eternity knows him, your conquering head;
those high habitations, he leaves not again,
till, judging all nations, on earth he shall reign.'

4 Thus spoke they and straightway, where legions defend
heaven's glittering gateway, their Lord they attend,
and cry, looking thither, 'Your portals let down
for him who rides hither in peace and renown.'

5 They asked, who keep sentry in that blessed town,
'Who thus claimeth entry, a king of renown?'
'The Lord of all valiance', that herald replied,
'Who Satan's battalions laid low in their pride.'

6 Grant, Lord, that our longing may follow thee there,
on earth who are thronging thy temples with prayer;
and unto thee gather, Redeemer, thine own
where thou with thy Father dost sit on the throne.
St. Bede (673–735) tr. R. A. Knox (1888–1957)

293

1 Abba, Father, send your Spirit.
Glory, Jesus Christ.
Abba, Father, send your Spirit.
Glory, Jesus Christ.

Glory hallelujah, glory, Jesus Christ.
Glory hallelujah, glory, Jesus Christ.

2 I will give you living water …

3 If you seek me you will find me …

4 If you listen you will hear me …

5 Come, my children, I will teach you …

6 I'm your shepherd, I will lead you …

7 Peace I leave you, peace I give you …

8 I'm your life and resurrection …

9 Glory Father, glory Spirit …
Sister Virginia Vissing, S.S.M.N.

294 Gospel Acclamation & Song of Praise

James Walsh

Je- sus is Lord, Al- le- lu - ia! Je- sus is Lord, Al- le- lu - ia!

1. Come,— Ho - ly Spi - rit of God, come, re - new the face of the earth.
2. Send— forth your light and your truth. Guide us with your pow- er- ful love.
3. Ho - ly Spi - rit, make— us one. Al - le - lu - ia, al - le- lu - ia!

Pentecost

295 Litany of the Spirit

Music: Paul Inwood
Words: Paul Inwood & Michael Shaw

Refrain

Spi - rit of God, come in - to our hearts, make us your new cre - a- tion.

1 Spirit of light: let your wisdom shine on us.
2 Spirit of silence: make us aware of God's presence.
3 Spirit of courage: dispel the fear in our hearts.
4 Spirit of fire: inflame us with Christ's love.
5 Spirit of peace: help us be still and listen to God's word.
6 Spirit of joy: inspire us to proclaim the good news.
7 Spirit of love: help us to open ourselves to the needs of others.
Confirmation only:
8 Spirit of power: give your help and strength to those who are to be confirmed.
9 Spirit of power: give us all your help and strength.
10 Spirit of truth: guide us all in the way of Christ.

296

1 Come, Holy Ghost, Creator, come
from thy bright heavenly throne,
come, take possession of our souls,
and make them all thine own.

2 Thou who art called the Paraclete,
best gift of God above,
the living spring, the living fire,
sweet unction and true love.

3 Thou who art sev'nfold in thy grace,
finger of God's right hand;
his promise, teaching little ones
to speak and understand.

4 O guide our minds with thy blest light,
with love our hearts inflame;
and with thy strength, which ne'er decays,
confirm our mortal frame.

5 Far from us drive our deadly foe;
true peace unto us bring;
and through all perils lead us safe
beneath thy sacred wing.

6 Through thee may we the Father know,
through thee th'eternal Son,
and thee the Spirit of them both,
thrice–blessed Three in One.

last verse overleaf

7 All glory to the Father be,
  with his co–equal Son:
  the same to thee, great Paraclete,
  while endless ages run.

Veni Creator Spiritus, Ascribed to
Rabanus Maurus (776–856), tr. Anon.

297

1. Ve- ni, Cre— a - tor— Spi - ri - tus, men- tes tu - o - rum—
2. Qui di - ce - ris Pa - ra - cli - tus, al - tis - si - mi do -
3. Tu sep - ti— for- mis— mu - ne - re, dig'- tus pa- ter- nae—
4. Ac-cen- de lu - men— sen - si - bus, in- fund' a- mo- rem—
5. Hostem re— pel - las— lon - gi - us, pa- cem- que do - nes—
6. Per te sci— a - mus,— da, Pa- trem, nos - ca - mus at - que—

vi - si - ta, im - ple— su— per— na— gra - ti - a
num De - i, fons vi - vus, ig - nis,— ca - ri - tas
dex - te - rae, tu ri— te— pro— mis— sum Pa - tris,
cor - di - bus, in - fir - ma nos - tri— cor - por - is,
pro - ti - nus: duc to— re— sic— te— prae - vi - o,
Fi - li - um, te - qu'u— tri— us— que— Spi - ri - tum

quae— tu cre— as - ti— pec - to - ra. A - men.—
et— spi- ri - ta - lis— unc - ti - o.
ser— mo- ne— di - tans— gut - tu - ra.
vir - tu - te— fir-mans— per - pe - ti.
vi— te-mus— om - ne— no - xi- um.
cre - da-mus— om - ni— tem - po - re.

Ascribed to Rabanus
Maurus (776–856)

298 Veni Creator Spiritus   *Taizé chant by Jacques Berthier*

Ve- ni cre - a - tor   Spi- ri - tus.

299 Responsorial Psalm for Pentecost (Ps 103 (104))   *Christopher Walker*

Send   forth your Spi - rit, O Lord, and   re - new   the face of the earth!

Opposite: Pentecost Sequence

300

1. Ve - ni san - cte spi - ri - tus et e - mit - te cae - li - tus
2. Ve - ni pa - ter pau - pe-rum, ve - ni da - tor mu - ne - rum,

Ho - ly Spi - rit, Lord___ of light, from the clear ce - les - tial height,
Come, thou Fa - ther of___ the poor, come with trea- sures which___ en - dure;

lu - cis tu - ae ra - di - um. 3. Con - so - la - tor op - ti - me,
ve - ni lu - men cor - di - um. 4. In la - bo - re re - qui - es,

thy pure bea-ming ra - diance give; Thou, of all con - sol - ers best,
come, thou Light of all___ that live! Thou in toil art com - fort sweet;

dul - cis hos - pes a - ni - mae, dul - ce re - fri - ge - ri - um.
in ae - stu___ tem - pe - ri - es, in fle - tu so - la - ti - um.

thou, the soul's___ de - light - some guest, dost re - fre - shing peace___ be- stow:
plea- sant cool - ness in___ the heat; sol - ace in___ the midst___ of woe.

5. O lux be - a - tis - si - ma, re - ple cor - dis in - ti - ma
6. Si - ne tu - o nu - mi - ne, ni - hil est in ho - mi - ne,

Light im - mor - tal, light___ div - ine, vis - it thou these hearts of thine,
If thou take___ thy grace___ a - way, no - thing pure in us will stay;

tu - o - rum fi - de - li - um; 7. La - va quod___ est sor - di - dum,
ni - hil est in - no - xi - um. 8. Fle - cte quod___ est ri - gi - dum,

and___ our in- most be - ing fill: Heal our wounds,. our strength_ re - new;
all___ our good is turned___ to ill. Bend the stub - born heart___ and will;

ri - ga quod___ est a - ri - dum, sa - na quod est sau - ci - um.
fo - ve quod___ est fri - gi - dum, re - ge quod est de - vi - um.

on our dry - ness pour___ thy dew; wash the stains of guilt a - way:
melt the fro - zen, warm___ the chill; guide the steps that go a - stray.

9. Da tu - is fi - de - li - bus in te con - fi - den - ti - bus
10. Da vir - tu - tis me - ri - tum, da sa - lu - tis e - xi - tum,

Thou, on those who e - ver-more thee con - fess___ and thee a - dore,
Give them com - fort when they die; give them life___ with thee on high;

sa - crum sep - te - na - ri - um; A - men.___
da pe - ren - ne gau - di - um.

in thy seven - fold gifts des - cend:
give them joys that ne - ver end.

Ascr. to Stephen Langton, c.1160-1228.
Tr. by E. Caswall (1814-78)

301

1 Holy Spirit, Lord of light,
from the clear celestial height,
thy pure beaming radiance give;
come, thou Father of the poor,
come with treasures which endure;
come, thou Light of all that live!

2 Thou, of all consolers best,
thou, the soul's delightsome guest,
dost refreshing peace bestow:
thou in toil art comfort sweet;
pleasant coolness in the heat;
solace in the midst of woe.

3 Light immortal, light divine,
visit thou these hearts of thine,
and our inmost being fill:
if thou take thy grace away,
nothing pure in us will stay;
all our good is turned to ill.

4 Heal our wounds, our strength renew;
on our dryness pour thy dew;
wash the stains of guilt away:
bend the stubborn heart and will;
melt the frozen, warm the chill;
guide the steps that go astray.

5 Thou, on those who evermore
thee confess and thee adore,
in thy sevenfold gifts descend:
give them comfort when they die;
give them life with thee on high;
give them joys that never end.
Ascribed to Stephen Langton (d. 1228)
tr. Edward Caswall (1814–78)

302

1 Breathe on me, Breath of God,
fill me with life anew,
that I may love what thou dost love,
and do what thou wouldst do.

2 Breathe on me, Breath of God,
until my heart is pure:
until with thee I have one will
to do and to endure.

3 Breathe on me, Breath of God.
till I am wholly thine,
until this earthly part of me
glows with thy fire divine.

4 Breathe on me, Breath of God,
so shall I never die,
but live with thee the perfect life
of thine Eternity.
Edwin Hatch (1835–89)

303

1 Come down, O love divine,
seek thou this soul of mine,
and visit it with thine own ardour
glowing;
O comforter, draw near, within my heart
appear,
and kindle it, thy holy flame bestowing.

2 O let it freely burn,
till earthly passions turn
to dust and ashes in its heat consuming;
and let thy glorious light shine ever on
my sight,
and clothe me round, the while my path
illuming.

3 Let holy charity
mine outward vesture be,
and lowliness become mine inner
clothing;
true lowliness of heart, which takes the
humbler part,
and o'er its own shortcomings weeps
with loathing.

4 And so the yearning strong,
with which the soul will long,
shall far outpass the power of human
telling,
for none can guess its grace,
till he become the place
wherein the Holy Spirit makes a
dwelling.
Bianco da Siena (d. 1434), tr. R.F. Littledale
(1833–90)

304

Come, Ho-ly Spi - rit, des-cend on us, des - cend on us, we

except last time / *Last time*

gath-er here in Je - sus' name. *(hum* name.

1. Come, Holy Spirit.
2. Come, Breath of Heaven.
3. Come, Word of Mercy.
4. Come, Fire of Judgement,
5. Come, Great Creator,
6. Come to unite us.
7. Come to disturb us.
8. Come to inspire us.
(other invocations ad lib.)

John Bell & Graham Maule

305

1. She sits like a bird, brooding on the wa-ters, hov'ring on the
2. She wings o-ver earth, res-ting where she wi-shes, light-ing close at

cha-os of the world's first day; she sighs and she sings, mo - the - ring cre -
hand or soar-ing through the skies; she nests in the womb, wel-com-ing each

a-tion, wai-ting to give birth to all the Word will say.
wonder, nou-rish-ing po-ten-tial hid-den to our eyes.

3. She dances in fire, startling her spectators,
   waking tongues of ecstasy where
       dumbness reigned;
   she weans and inspires all whose hearts
       are open,
   nor can she be captured, silenced or
       restrained.

4. For she is the Spirit, one with God in
       essence,
   gifted by the Saviour in eternal love;
   she is the key opening the scriptures,
   enemy of apathy and heavenly dove.
       John L. Bell and Graham Maule

306

Spirit of the living God, fall afresh on me.
Spirit of the living God, fall afresh on me.
Break me, melt me, mould me, fill me.
Spirit of the living God, fall afresh on me.
       Daniel Iverson (1890-1972)

307

Ve - ni sanc - te Spi - ri-tus, ve - ni sanc - te Spi - ri-tus,
ve - ni, ve - ni sanc-te Spi - ri - tus, ve - ni sanc - te Spi - ri-tus.

Christopher Walker

308

1. The Spi - rit of the Lord has brought new life to earth,
2. Bap-tized in God's own breath, made pure by fire and oil,

whose breath, as seed out - poured, now calls all things to birth.
our hope of life in death, our strength in thirst and toil.

God's Spi - rit now re - vives, our hearts of stone it thaws,
Who knows from where it flows, this gen - tle light so warm,

re - buil-ding bro - ken lives, our shat - tered world res - tores.
which deep with - in us glows, to heal and make us one.

3 The Spirit finds a home in every human breast,
    that God's own chosen Son may guide us to our rest,
    may save us from the storm, and raise us from the dust.
    Creator Spirit, come, complete your work in us.

Huub Oosterhuis, tr. Tony Barr. Dutch traditional melody, arr. Bernard Huijbers

309

Spi - rit of God, rest on your peo - ple:
wa - ken your song deep in our hearts.

1. Spirit of the quiet earth,
   spirit breathing hope to birth:
   sustain in us the fire of your love.

2. Spirit blowing through creation, love
   that cannot be contained: bring forth for
   us the wonders you proclaim.

3. Song that echoes through our story,
   music of our restless souls: resound
   with joy in those you call your own.

4. Spirit moving through our lives,
   work in our mem-'ries:

continues overleaf

healing and restoring,
teaching and revealing,
strengthening and bringing to life.

5 Spirit breaking through our selfhood,
spirit tearing down our walls:
challenge and disturb us;
be the voice that questions and calls.

Bernadette Farrell

310

1. Spi - rit of God with - in me, pos - sess my hu - man frame;
2. Spi - rit of truth with - in me, pos - sess my thought and mind;

fan the dull em - bers of my heart, stir up the liv - ing— flame:
ligh-ten a - new the in - ward eye by Sa - tan ren - dered— blind:

strive till that im - age A - dam lost, new min - ted and res-tored,
shine on the words that wis - dom speaks and grant me power to see

in shi - ning splen - dour bright-ly bears the like-ness of the Lord.
the truth made known to all in Christ, and in that truth be free.

3 Spirit of love within me,
   possess my hands and heart;
   break through the bonds of self concern
   that seeks to stand apart:
   grant me the love that suffers long,
   that hopes, believes and bears,
   the love fulfilled in sacrifice
   that cares as Jesus cares.

4 Spirit of life within me,
   possess this life of mine;
   come as the wind of heaven's breath,
   come as the fire divine!
   Spirit of Christ, the living Lord,
   reign in this house of clay,
   till from its dust with Christ I rise
   to everlasting day.

Timothy Dudley Smith. Music: Michael Joncas

311

1 Holy Spirit, come confirm us
  in the truth that Christ makes known;
  we have faith and understanding
  through your promised light alone.

2 Holy Spirit, come, console us,
  come as Advocate to plead;
  loving Spirit from the Father,
  grant in Christ the help we need.

3 Holy Spirit, come renew us,
  come yourself to make us live;
  holy through your loving presence,
  holy through the gifts you give.

4 Holy Spirit, come possess us,
  you the love of Three in One,
  Holy Spirit of the Father,
  Holy Spirit of the Son.

Brian Foley

The Holy Trinity

312

1 I bind unto myself today
the strong name of the Trinity
by invocation of the same,
the Three in One, and One in Three.

2 I bind this day to me forever,
by power of faith, Christ's incarnation;
his baptism in the Jordan river;
his death on cross for my salvation;
his bursting from the spicèd tomb;
his riding up the heavenly way;
his coming at the day of doom;
I bind unto myself today.

3 I bind unto myself today
the power of God to hold and lead,
his eye to watch, his might to stay,
his ear to hearken to my need,
the wisdom of my God to teach,
his hand to guide, his shield to ward,
the word of God to give me speech,
his heavenly host to be my guard.

4 Christ be with me, Christ within me,
Christ behind me, Christ before me,
Christ beside me, Christ to win me,
Christ to comfort and restore me,
Christ beneath me, Christ above me,
Christ in quiet, Christ in danger,
Christ in hearts of all that love me,
Christ in mouth of friend and stranger.

5 I bind unto myself the name,
the strong name of the Trinity,
by invocation of the same,
the Three in One, and One in Three,
of whom all nature hath creation,
eternal Father, Spirit, Word.
Praise to the Lord of my salvation:
salvation is of Christ the Lord. Amen.

Attributed to St Patrick (c. 386–c.460),
tr. Cecil Frances Alexander (1818–95)

313

1 Father in heaven,
grant to your children
mercy and blessing,
songs never ceasing,
love to unite us,
grace to redeem us,
Father in heaven,
Father our God.

2 Jesus, Redeemer,
may we remember
your gracious Passion,
your resurrection.
Worship we bring you,
praise we shall sing you
Jesus, Redeemer,
Jesus our God.

3 Spirit descending
whose is the blessing -
strength for the weary,
help for the needy,
sealed in our service
yours be our worship -
Spirit unending,
Spirit adored.   *D.T.Niles (1908-70)*

314

1 Father, Lord of earth and heaven
King to whom all gifts belong,
give your greatest Gift, your Spirit,
God the holy, God the strong.

2 Son of God, enthroned in glory,
send your promised Gift of grace,
make your Church your holy Temple,
God the Spirit's dwelling-place.

3 Spirit, come, in peace descending
as at Jordan, heav'nly Dove,
seal your Church as God's anointed,
set our hearts on fire with love.

4 Stay among us, God the Father,
stay among us, God the Son,
stay among us, Holy Spirit,
dwell within us, make us one.

James Quinn, S.J.

315

1 Lead us, heav'nly Father, lead us
  o'er the world's tempestuous sea:
  guard us, guide us, keep us, feed us,
  for we have no help but thee;
  yet possessing ev'ry blessing
  if our God our Father be.

2 Saviour, breathe forgiveness o'er us,
  all our weakness thou dost know,
  thou didst tread this earth before us,
  thou didst feel its keenest woe;
  lone and dreary, faint and weary,
  through the desert thou didst go.

3 Spirit of our God, descending,
  fill our hearts with heavenly joy,
  love with every passion blending,
  pleasure that can never cloy;
  thus provided, pardoned, guided,
  nothing can our peace destroy.
      J. Edmeston (1791–1867)

316

How great is our God,
how great is his name!
How great is our God,
for ever the same!

1 He rolled back the waters
  of the mighty Red Sea,
  and he said 'I'll never leave you.
  Put your trust in me.'

2 He sent his son, Jesus,
  to set us all free,
  and he said 'I'll never leave you.
  Put your trust in me.'

3 He gave us his Spirit,
  and now we can see.
  And he said 'I'll never leave you.
  Put your trust in me.'
      Author unknown

317

1 Father, in my life I see,
  you are God, who walks with me.
  You hold my life in your hands:
  close beside you I will stand.
  I give all my life to you:
  help me, Father, to be true.

2 Jesus, in my life I see …

3 Spirit, in my life I see …
      Frank Anderson, M.S.C.

Corpus Christi

318

1 At this great feast of love
  let joyful praise resound,
  let heartfelt homage now ascend
  to heaven's height:
  ring out the reign of sin;
  ring in the reign of grace;
  a world renewed acclaims its King,
  though veiled from sight.

2 Recall that night when Christ
  proclaims his law of love,
  and shows himself as Lamb of God
  and great high priest:
  the sinless One, made sin,
  for sinners gives his all,
  and shares with us his very self
  as Paschal feast.

3 The bread that angels eat
  becomes our food on earth,
  God sends his manna, living Bread,
  from heav'n above;
  what wonders now we see:
  those who are last and least
  receive their Lord as food and drink,
  his pledge of love.

4 Three persons, yet one God,
be pleased to hear our prayer:
come down in pow'r to seek your own,
dispel our night;
teach us your word of truth:
guide us along your way;
bring us at last to dwell with you
in endless light.

St Thomas Aquinas (1227-74)
tr. James Quinn, S.J.

➤ *Communion Processional songs (613-635);*
Post-Communion (636-653); and Eucharistic
Devotion (654-667). Psalm 114/5 (55).

ChRIST The KING

319

1 Christ is King of earth and heaven!
Let his subjects all proclaim,
in the splendour of his temple,
honour to his holy name.

2 Christ is King! No soul created
can refuse to bend the knee
to the God made man who reigneth
as 'twas promised, from the tree.

3 Christ is King! Let humble sorrow
for our past neglect atone,
for the lack of faithful service
to the Master whom we own.

4 Christ is King! Let joy and gladness
greet him; let his courts resound
with the praise of faithful subjects
to his love in honour bound.

5 Christ is King! In health and sickness,
till we breathe our latest breath,
till we greet in highest heaven,
Christ the victor over death.

Ivor J. E. Daniel (1883–1967)

320

1 Hail, Redeemer, King divine!
Priest and Lamb, the throne is thine,
King, whose reign shall never cease,
Prince of everlasting peace.
Angels saints and nations sing:
'Praised be Jesus Christ, our King;
Lord of life, earth, sky and sea,
King of love on Calvary.'

2 King whose name creation thrills,
rule our minds, our hearts, our wills,
till in peace each nation rings
with thy praises, King of kings.

3 King most holy, King of truth,
guide the lowly, guide the youth;
Christ thou King of glory bright,
be to us eternal light.

4 Shepherd–King, o'er mountains steep,
homeward bring the wandering sheep,
shelter in one royal fold
states and kingdoms, new and old.
Patrick Brennan C.Ss.R., (1877–1952)

321

1 Crown him with many crowns,
the Lamb upon his throne;
hark, how the heav'nly anthem drowns
all music but its own:
awake, my soul, and sing
of him who died for thee,
and hail him as thy matchless King
through all eternity.

2 Crown him the Virgin's Son,
the God incarnate born,
whose arm those crimson trophies won,
which now his brow adorn;
fruit of the mystic rose,
as of that rose the stem,
the root, whence mercy ever flows,
the babe of Bethlehem.

3 Crown him the Lord of love;
  behold his hands and side,
  rich wounds, yet visible above,
  in beauty glorified:
  no angel in the sky
  can fully bear that sight,
  but downward bends his burning eye
  at mysteries so bright.

4 Crown him the Lord of peace,
  whose powers a sceptre sways,
  from pole to pole, that wars may cease,
  absorbed in prayer and praise:
  his reign shall know no end,
  and round his piercèd feet
  fair flowers of Paradise extend
  their fragrance ever sweet.

5 Crown him the Lord of heaven,
  one with the Father known,
  and the blest Spirit through him given
  from yonder triune throne:
  all hail, Redeemer, hail,
  for thou hast died for me;
  thy praise shall never, never fail
  throughout eternity.
    Matthew Bridges (1800–94)

322

1 Jesus shall reign where'er the sun
  does his successive journeys run;
  his kingdom stretch from shore to shore,
  till moons shall wax and wane no more.

2 People and realms of ev'ry tongue
  dwell on his love with sweetest song,
  and infant voices shall proclaim
  their early blessings on his Name.

3 Blessings abound where Jesus reigns;
  the prisoner leaps to lose his chains;
  the weary find eternal rest,
  and all who suffer want are blessed.

4 To him shall endless prayer be made,
  and praises throng to crown his head;
  his Name like incense shall arise
  with ev'ry morning sacrifice.

5 Let all creation rise and bring
  blessing and honour to our King;
  angels descend with songs again,
  and earth repeat the loud Amen.
    Isaac Watts (1674-1748), alt.
    Based on Psalm 72

323

1 All hail the pow'r of Jesus' name!
  let angels prostrate fall;
  bring forth the royal diadem
  To crown him, crown him, crown him,
  crown him Lord of all.

2 Crown him, ye martyrs of your God,
  who from his altar call;
  praise him whose way of pain ye trod,
  and crown him Lord of all.

3 Ye prophets who our freedom won,
  ye searchers, great and small,
  by whom the work of truth is done,
  now crown him Lord of all.

4 Sinners, whose love can ne'er forget
  the wormwood and the gall,
  go spread your trophies at his feet,
  and crown him Lord of all.

5 Bless him, each poor oppressèd race
  that Christ did upward call;
  his hand in each achievement trace,
  and crown him Lord of all.

6 Let every tribe and every tongue
  to him their hearts enthral:
  lift high the universal song,
  and crown him Lord of all.
    Edward Perronet (1726–92) and others

324

1 Jesus is Lord! Creation's voice
   proclaims it,
   for by his power each tree and flower
   was planned and made.
   Jesus is Lord! The universe declares it–
   sun, moon and stars in heaven cry:
   Jesus is Lord!'
   Jesus is Lord, Jesus is Lord!
   Praise him with alleluias,
   for Jesus is Lord.

2 Jesus is Lord! Yet from his throne eternal
   in flesh he came to die in pain on
   Calvary's tree.
   Jesus is Lord! From him all life
   proceeding –
   yet gave his life a ransom thus setting
   us free.

3 Jesus is Lord! O'er sin the mighty
   conqueror;
   from death he rose and all his foes shall
   own his name.
   Jesus is Lord! God sends his Holy Spirit
   to show by works of power that Jesus
   is Lord.
   D.J. Mansell

325

Christ is our king, let the whole world
   rejoice!
May all the nations sing out with one voice!
Light of the world, you have helped us to
   see
that we are one people and one day we all
   shall be free.

1 He came to open the eyes of the blind,
   letting the sunlight pour into their minds.
   Vision is waiting for those who have hope.
   He is the light of the world.

2 He came to speak tender words to the poor,
   he is the gateway and he is the door.
   Riches are waiting for all those who hope.
   He is the light of the world.

3 He came to open the doors of the jail,
   he came to help the downtrodden and
   frail.
   Freedom is waiting for all those who hope.
   He is the light of the world.

4 He came to open the lips of the mute,
   letting them speak out with courage
   and truth.
   His words are uttered by all those
   who hope.
   He is the light of the world.

5 He came to heal all the crippled
   and lame,
   sickness took flight at the sound
   of his name.
   Vigour is waiting for all those who hope.
   He is the light of the world.

6 He came to love everyone on this earth
   and through his Spirit he promised rebirth.
   New life is waiting for all those who hope.
   He is the light of the world.
   Estelle White

326

1 Rejoice! The Lord is King!
   Your Lord and King adore;
   mortals, give thanks and sing,
   and triumph evermore:
      Lift up your heart, lift up your voice;
      rejoice, again I say, rejoice.

2 Jesus the Saviour reigns,
   the God of truth and love;
   when he had purged our stains,
   he took his seat above:

3 His kingdom cannot fail;
   he rules o'er earth and heaven;
   the keys of death and hell
   are to our Jesus given:

4 He sits at God's right hand
   till all his foes submit,
   and bow to his command,
   and fall beneath his feet:
      Charles Wesley (1707–88)

327

Refrain: Cantors then All

Chri-stus_ vin - cit: Chri stus re - gnat: Chri- stus im - - pe - rat.

Cantor: **All:**

Ex - au - di Chri - ste. Ex - au - di Chri - ste.

Sum- mo Pon-ti-fi-ci et u - ni-ver-sa-li Pa- pae vi - ta._

Sal- va-tor mun - di:___ tu il-lum_ ad - ju - va.

San-cta Ma-ri - a:___ tu il-lum_ ad - ju - va.
San-cte Pe - tre:___
San-cte Pau - le:___
San-cte Gre-go - ri:___

Refrain (All):

Chri-stus vin - cit: Chri - stus re - gnat: Chri- stus im - pe - rat.

Cantor: All:

Rex_ re - gum! Chri-stus_ vin - cit. *Rex_ no - ster!* Chri- stus_ re - gnat

Glor - ri-a__ no - stra! Chri-stus_ im - pe - rat. *Ip-si so-li im-pe-ri-um*

glo-ri- a et po - tes-stas, per im-mor-ta-li-a sae cu-la sae-cu - lo-rum. A-men.

Final Refrain (All):   Christus vincit: Christus regnat, Christus imperat.

Mary

Conceived Immaculate

328

1 Holy light on earth's horizon,
hope to us the fallen, bring;
light amid a world of shadows,
dawn of God's redemption, sing.

2 Chosen from eternal ages,
you alone of all our race,
by your Son's atoning merits
were conceived in perfect grace.

3 Mother of the world's redeemer,
promised from the dawn of time;
how could one so highly favoured
share the guilt of Adam's crime?

4 Sun and moon and stars adorn you,
sinless Eve, triumphant sign;
you are she who crushed the serpent,
Mary, pledge of life divine.

5 Earth below and highest heaven
praise the splendour of your state:
you who now are crowned in glory
were conceived immaculate.

6 Hail, beloved of the Father,
Mother of his only Son,
Mystic bride of Love eternal,
Hail, most fair and spotless one.
Edward Caswall (1814-78) alt

Chosen One

329

1 Oh Mary, when our God chose you
to bring his dear Son to birth,
a new creation made in you
gave joy to all the earth.
Alleluia, alleluia, alleluia, alleluia,
A new creation made in you
gave joy to all the earth.

2 When he was born on Christmas night
and music made the rafters ring,
the stars were dancing with delight;
now all God's children sing.

3 One winter's night, a heap of straw
becomes a place where ages meet
when kings come knocking at the door
and kneeling at your feet.

4 In you, our God confounds the strong
and makes the crippled dance with joy
and to our barren world belong
his mother and her boy.

5 In empty streets and broken hearts
you call to mind what he has done;
where all his loving kindness starts
in sending you a son.

6 And Mary, while we stand with you,
may once again his Spirit come,
and all his brothers follow you
to reach our Father's home.
Damian Lundy (1944-1997)

The Promise and Annunciation

330
➤ *See also Advent section (113-115)*

1 An angel came from heaven,
from heaven, from heaven,
an angel came from heaven
to bring good news.
The angel's name was Gabriel,
the angel's name was Gabriel,
the angel's name was Gabriel
to bring good news.

2 He came to see a lady..
the lady's name was Mary..

3 He said, 'You'll have a baby...'
The baby's name was Jesus.

(Christmas)   4   And Mary had a baby...
The baby's name was Jesus.
Christopher Walker

331

1 For Mary, mother of the Lord
God's holy name be praised,
who first the Son of God adored
as on her child she gazed.

2 The angel Gabriel brought the word
she should Christ's mother be;
Our Lady, handmaid of the Lord,
made answer willingly.

3 The heavenly call she thus obeyed,
and so God's will was done;
The second Eve love's answer made
which our redemption won.

4 She gave her body for God's shrine,
her heart to piercing pain,

and knew the cost of love divine
when Jesus Christ was slain.

5 Dear Mary, from your lowliness
and home in Galilee,
there comes a joy and holiness
to every family.

6 Hail, Mary, you are full of grace
above all women blest;
blest in your Son, whom your embrace
in birth and death confessed.
J.R. Peacey (1896-1971)

332

Abbey of Tamié tr, Pamela Stotter

Like ri-vers in the de-sert, like springs from the rock, new hope came through Ma ry,—

when the Word be-came flesh   and our hu-ma-ni-ty re-gained its for-mer glo-ry.

REFRAIN (All)

Bles-sed Ma-ry, spring of new hope, from your Son   flow the wa-ters of life.

1. *The song   of the spring   will glo-ri-fy   the Lord.*   Refrain (All)

2 *The freshness of the clear cooling spring
will quench our burning thirst.*
All: Blessed Mary....

3 *This river in our desert
will fill our hearts with joy.*
All: Blessed Mary....

To conclude, Cantor repeats from 'Like Rivers' and all sing refrain.

333

REFRAIN   repeated as required.

A-ve Ma-ri - a.   A-ve Ma-ri - a.

Hail, full of grace, the Lord is with you
how blest are you,
how blest are you among women.
Blest is the fruit of your womb, Jesus.

O holy Mary, O mother of God,
pray now for us sinners,
and at the hour of our death.
Amen. Amen
Tony Barr

334

A - ve Ma - ri - a, gra - ti - a ple - na, Do - mi - nus te - cum,

be - ne - dic - ta tu in__ mu - li - e - ri - bus, et be - ne - dic - tus fruc - tus ven tris

tu - i,__ Je - sus.__ Sanc - ta Ma - ri - a, Ma - ter De - i, o - ra pro no - bis

pec - ca - to - ri - bus, nunc et in__ ho - ra mor - tis nos - trae.__ A - men.

Plainsong

The Magnificat (Luke 1:46-55)

335 **Magnificat (Canon)**

Taizé chant by Jacques Berthier

A   B

Mag - ni - fi - cat, mag - ni - fi - cat, mag - ni - fi - cat a - ni - ma me - a Do - mi - num.

C   D

Mag - ni - fi - cat, mag - ni - fi - cat, mag - ni - fi - cat a - ni - ma me - a!

336 Refrain

My soul re - joi - ces____ in God my__ Sa - viour.

My spi - rit finds its joy in God, the li - ving God.

Verses

1. My soul pro - claims your migh - ty deeds. My spi - rit sings the great - ness of your name.

2 Your mercy flows throughout the land
and ev'ry generation knows your love.

3 You cast the mighty from their thrones
and raise the poor and lowly to new life.

4 You fill the hungry with good things.
With empty hands you send the rich away.

5 Just as you promised Abraham,
you come to free your people, Israel.

Owen Alstott

337

REFRAIN *repeat as required*

The Al-migh-ty works mar-vels for me.

Ho-ly his name, Ho-ly his name.

338

1. My soul pro-claims the great-ness of the Lord, my spi-rit sings to God, my sa-ving God, who on this day a-bove all oth-ers fa-voured me and raised me up, a light for all to see.

2 Through me great deeds will God make manifest,
and all the earth will come to call me blest.
Unbounded love and mercy sure will I proclaim
for all who know and praise God's holy name.

3 God's mighty arm, protector of the just,
will guard the weak and raise them from the dust.
But mighty kings will swiftly fall from thrones corrupt,
the strong brought low, the lowly lifted up.

4 Soon will the poor and hungry of the earth
be richly blest, be given greater worth:
and Israel, as once foretold to Abraham,
will live in peace throughout the promised land.

5 All glory be to God, Creator blest,
to Jesus Christ, God's love made manifest,
and to the Holy Spirit, gentle Comforter,
all glory be, both now and evermore.
Owen Alstott. Music by Bernadette Farrell

339

1 My soul is filled with joy
as I sing to God my Saviour:
he has looked upon his servant,
he has visited his people.
And holy is his name
through all generations!
everlasting is his mercy
to the people he has chosen,
and holy is his name!

2 I am lowly as a child,
but I know from this day forward
that my name will be remembered,
for all men will call me blessed.

3 I proclaim the pow'r of God!
He does marvels for his servants;
though he scatters the proud-hearted
and destroys the might of princes.

4 To the hungry he gives food,
sends the rich away empty.
In his mercy he is mindful
of the people he has chosen.

5 In his love he now fulfills
what he promised to our fathers.
I will praise the Lord, my saviour.
Everlasting is his mercy.

Anonymous

340

1 My soul proclaims you, mighty God,
my spirit sings your praise.
You look on me, you lift me up,
and gladness fills my days.

➤ *See also Tell out, my soul (880); Magnificat*
for Evening Prayer (23-24); Great is the Lord (25)

2 All nations now will share my joy;
your gifts you have outpoured.
Your little one you have made great;
I magnify my God.

3 For those who love your holy name,
your mercy will not die.
Your strong right arm puts down the proud
and lifts the lowly high.

4 You fill the hungry with good things,
the rich you send away.
The promise made to Abraham
is filled to endless day.

5 Then let all nations praise our God,
the Father and the Son,
the Spirit blest who lives in us,
while endless ages run.

Anne Carter (1944-1993)

Mary's Life and sorrows

341

1 Sing of Mary, pure and lowly
Virgin-Mother undefiled,
Sing of God's own Son most holy,
who became her little child.
Fairest child of fairest mother,
God the Lord who came to earth,
Word made flesh, our very brother,
Takes our nature by his birth.

2 Sing of Jesus, Son of Mary,
in the home at Nazareth.
Toil and labour cannot weary
Love enduring unto death.
Constant was the love he gave her,
though it drove him from her side,[1]
forth to preach, and heal, and suffer,
till on Calvary he died.

3 Sing of Mary, sing of Jesus,
holy Mother's holier Son.
From his throne in heaven he sees us,
thither calls us ev'ry one.

Where he welcomes home his mother
to a place at his right hand,
there his faithful servants gather,
there the crownèd victors stand.

4 Joyful Mother, full of gladness,
in your arms your Lord was borne.
Mournful Mother, full of sadness,
all your heart with pain was torn.
Glorious Mother, now rewarded
with a crown at Jesus' hand,
Age to age your name recorded
shall be blest in every land.

5 Glory be to God the Father;
Glory be to God the Son;
Glory be to God the Spirit;
Glory to the Three in One.
From the heart of blessèd Mary,
From all saints the song ascends,
And the Church the strain re-echoes
Unto earth's remotest ends.

Roland F. Palmer S.S.J.E. (1891-1985)

---

[1] *cf. Mark 1:12*

342

Refrain

Mag-ni - fi - cat! Mag-ni - fi - cat! Your song proclaims the glo-ry of the Lord.

Verses

1. Wo - man asked to bear a son; a child who would com- pare with
2. Wo - man in the tem - ple stands; old man takes the child in his
3. Wo - man at the wed - ding meal, see the mi - ra - cle re -

[v.5: of the]

none. Did you know the pain that lay a - head?
hands. Did his words breathe fear in - to your heart?
veal the glo - ry of your Son to all a - round.

4 Woman waiting at the door;
   your Son is now your Son no more;
   to all the world he gives his life.

5 Woman standing by the cross
   with those around you mourn the loss
   of the child that you had once borne in
      your womb.

6 Woman in the upper room;
   in the frightened air and gloom,
   see your Son in glory now appear.

7 Woman standing on the rock,
   through the child who tends the flock
   speak to the world that we may know
      your Son.

Anne Ward

343

Where are you bound, Mary, Mary?
Where are you bound, Mother of God?

1 Beauty is a dove sitting on a sunlit bough,
   beauty is a pray'r without the need of words.
   Words are more than sounds falling off
      an empty tongue:
   let it be according to his word.

2 Mary heard the word spoken in her
      inmost heart;
   Mary bore the Word and held him in her
      arms.
   Sorrow she has known, seeing him upon
      the cross
   – greater joy to see him rise again.

3 Where are we all bound, carrying the
      Word of God?
   Time and place are ours to make his
   glory known.
   Mary bore him first, we will tell the
   whole wide world;
   let it be according to his word.
      John Glynn

344

1. Sing we of the blessèd Mother
   who received the angel's word,
   and obedient to his summons
   bore in love the infant Lord;
   sing we of the joys of Mary
   at whose breast that child was fed
   who is Son of God eternal
   and the everlasting Bread.

2 Sing we, too, of Mary's sorrows,
of the sword that pierced her through,
when beneath the cross of Jesus
she his weight of suffering knew,
looked upon her Son and Saviour
reigning high on Calvary's tree,
saw the price of our redemption
paid to set the sinner free.

3 Sing again the joys of Mary
when she saw the risen Lord,
and in prayer with Christ's apostles,
waited on his promised word:

from on high the blazing glory
of the Spirit's presence came,
heavenly breath of God's own being,
manifest through wind and flame.

4 Sing the chiefest joy of Mary
when on earth her work was done,
and the Lord of all creation
brought her to his heavenly home:
virgin Mother, Mary blessèd,
raised on high and crowned with grace,
may your Son, the world's redeemer,
grant us all to see his face.

G. B. Timms

345

Music by Christopher Willcock

Verses

1. There is no-thing told a-bout this wo-man but that she had once be-come en-gaged, and an an-gel ad-dressed her and said: 'You are bles-sed a-mong all your kind.'

2. There is no-thing told a-bout this wo-man but that she had brought in-to the world in the land of Ju-de-a, her son; for some shep-herds have passed on this tale.

Refrain

On this day all__ earth and all pa-ra-dise join in na-ming you hap-py and blessed, Vir-gin Ma-ry, bles-sed are you.

3 There is nothing told about this woman
but that she had searched for three long
  days
for her child who was busy elsewhere,
and her heart then did not understand.

4 There is nothing told about this woman
but that she at Cana was a guest,
and that Jesus changed water to wine,
so that all might believe who he was.

5 There is nothing told about this woman
but that she was standing by the cross
when her son stretched his arms out on
  high,
and met death with a thief on each side.

6 There is nothing told about this woman
but that she was one in prayer with those
upon whom tongues of fire did descend,
and the Spirit baptised them with flame.

Didier Rimaud, tr. Christopher Willcock, S.J.

346

1 Maiden, the angel spoke to you
   with words of reverence and grace;
   you, in reply said, 'Let it be!'
   and gave to God a human face.

2 Virgin-with-child, you went to meet
   Elizabeth who carried John:
   held in his mother's womb, he leapt
   in recognition of your son.

3 Mary, you trudged to Bethlehem
   and there you brought a child to birth;
   One, for whom all creation groaned,
   as helpless infant came to earth.

4 Lady, you heard from Simeon
   the prophecy of joy and pain:
   words, which you treasured in your heart,
   of Israel's hope and gentiles' gain.

5 Mother, you stood beside your Son
   while he was stripped and crucified;
   born of your labour, there you shared
   the agony as Jesus died.

6 Queen, you rejoiced to see the Lord
   who first had risen from your womb,
   triumphing over sin and death,
   now rise in glory from the tomb.

Patrick Lee

Melody by Stephen Dean

Maiden, the angel spoke to you with words of reverence and grace;
you, in reply, said 'Let it be!' and gave to God a human face.

Motherhood of Mary

347

1 O purest of creatures! Sweet mother, sweet maid;
   the one spotless womb wherein Jesus was laid.
   Dark night hath come down on us, mother, and we
   look out for thy shining, sweet star of the sea.

2 Deep night hath come down on this rough–spoken world.
   And the banners of darkness are boldly unfurled;
   and the tempest–tossed Church, all her eyes are on thee.
   They look to thy shining, sweet star of the sea.

3 He gazed on thy soul, it was spotless and fair;
   for the empire of sin, it had never been there;
   none ever had owned thee, dear mother, but he,
   and he blessed thy clear shining, sweet star of the sea.

4 Earth gave him one lodging; 'twas deep in thy breast,
   and God found a home where the sinner finds rest,
   his home and his hiding–place, both were in thee;
   he was won by thy shining, sweet star of the sea.

5 Oh, blissful and calm was the wonderful rest
   that thou gavest thy God in thy virginal breast;
   for the heaven he left he found heaven in thee,
   and he shone in thy shining, sweet star of the sea.

F.W.Faber (1814–63)

348

1 The God whom earth, and sea, and sky,
adore and praise and magnify,
whose might they claim, whose love
   they tell,
in Mary's body comes to dwell.

2 The God whose will by moon and sun,
and all things in due course is done,
is borne upon a maiden's breast
by fullest heavenly grace possessed.

3 O mother blest! the chosen shrine
wherein the Architect divine,
whose hand contains the earth and sky,
has come in human form to lie!

4 Blest in the message Gabriel brought;
blest by the work the Spirit wrought;
most blest, to bring to human birth
the long desired of all the earth.

5 O Lord, the Virgin–born, to you
eternal praise and laud are due,
whom with the Father we adore
and Spirit blest for evermore.
Ascribed to Venantius Fortunatus (530–
609) tr. J. M. Neale (1818–66) alt.

Mary in glory

349

1 Mother of God's living Word
glorifying Christ your Lord;
full of joy, God's people sing,
grateful for your mothering.

2 Virgin soil, untouched by sin,
for God's seed to flourish in;
watered by the Spirit's dew,
in your womb the Saviour grew.

3 Sharing his humility,
Bethlehem and Calvary,
with him in his bitter pain,
now as queen with him you reign.

4 We are God's new chosen race,
new-born children of his grace,
citizens of heaven who
imitate and honour you.

5 We, God's people on our way,
travelling by night and day,
moving to our promised land,
walk beside you hand in hand.

6 Christ, your Son, is always near,
so we journey without fear,
singing as we walk along:
Christ our joy and Christ our song!

7 Sing aloud to Christ with joy,
who was once a little boy:
sing aloud to Mary, sing,
grateful for her mothering.
Damian Lundy (1944-1997)

350

1 A sign is seen in heaven,
a maiden–mother fair;
her mantle is the sunlight,
and stars adorn her hair.
The maiden's name is Mary;
in love she brings to birth
the Lord of all the ages,
the King of all the earth.

2 Like moonlight on the hilltops
she shines on all below,
like sunlight on the mountains
her Child outshines the snow.
O Mary, Queen of mothers,
still smile on young and old;
bless hearth and home and harvest,
bless farm and field and fold.

3 Pray, Mother, Queen in glory,
before the Father's throne;
praise God's eternal Wisdom,
the Child who is your own;
rejoice in God the Spirit,
whose power let you conceive
the Child of Eden's promise,
O new and sinless Eve.
James Quinn, S.J.

351

1 This is the image of the Queen
who reigns in bliss above;
of her who is the hope of men,
whom men and angels love.
Most holy Mary, at thy feet
I bend a suppliant knee;
in this thy own sweet month of May,
do thou remember me.

2 The homage offered at the feet
of Mary's image here
to Mary's self at once ascends
above the starry sphere.
Most holy Mary, at thy feet
I bend a suppliant knee;
in all my joy, in all my pain,
do thou remember me.

3 How fair so ever be the form
which here your eyes behold,
its beauty is by Mary's self
excell'd a thousandfold.
Most holy Mary, at thy feet,
I bend a suppliant knee;
in my temptations each and all,
do thou remember me.

4 Sweet are the flow'rets we have culled,
this image to adorn;
but sweeter far is Mary's self,
that rose without a thorn.
Most holy Mary, at thy feet
I bend a suppliant knee;
when on the bed of death I lie,
do thou remember me.

5 O lady, by the stars that make
a glory round thy head;
and by the pure uplifted hands,
that for thy children plead;
when at the judgement–seat I stand,
and my dread saviour see;
when waves of night around me roll
O then remember me.
Edward Caswall (1814-78)

352

1 Hail, Mary, our icon of trust in God's
Word;
in faith you conceived, and God's life in
you stirred.
O woman of wisdom, now show us the way:
Let our hearts be open to God day by day.

1 Hail, mother of Jesus, of all mothers blest,
to you joyful praises and prayers are
addressed.
The saints and the angels your glory
proclaim;
the faithful in confidence call on your
name.

3 We pray you, O woman of all women blest
to care for the homeless, the poor and
oppressed.
Be with us, your people, in joy and in pain;
be near us to cheer us till heaven we gain.

4 To God, your creator, glad hymns with us
raise.
To Jesus, your Son, and the Spirit, give
praise.
And pray for the churches, that all may be
one:
On earth as in heaven, may God's will be
done!
Delores Dufner, O.S.B.

Praise of Mary

353

1 Daily, daily, sing to Mary,
sing my soul, her praises due;
all her feasts, her actions honour,
with the heart's devotion true.
Lost in wond'ring contemplation
be her majesty confessed:
call her Mother, call her Virgin,
happy Mother, Virgin blest.

2 Sing, my tongue, the Virgin's trophies,
who for us her Maker bore;
for the curse of old inflicted,
peace and blessings to restore.
Sing in songs of praise unending,
sing the world's majestic Queen;
weary not nor faint in telling
all the gifts she gives to men.

3 All my senses, heart, affections,
strive to sound her glory forth;
spread abroad the sweet memorials,
of the Virgin's priceless worth,
where the voice of music thrilling,
where the tongues of eloquence,
that can utter hymns beseeming
all her matchless excellence?

4 All our joys do flow from Mary,
all then join her praise to sing;
trembling sing the Virgin Mother,
Mother of our Lord and King,
while we sing her awful glory,
far above our fancy's reach,
let our hearts be quick to offer
love the heart alone can teach.

Ascribed to St. Bernard of Cluny (12th C),
tr. Henry Bittleston (1818–1886)

354

1 O Mary, conceived in the grace of your
Son,
the firstfruits of vict'ry on Calvary won!
He chose you as Mother to bring him
to birth,
the one fitting shrine for his dwelling
on earth!

2 Immaculate Virgin, with motherhood
blest,
true God is the child that in your womb
did rest!
With you shall we ever Magnificat
sing,
whose Son is our Maker and Saviour
and King!

3 O Mother, who stood by your Son till
his death,
still stand by your children till life's
dying breath!
O pray for us all as in glory you share
your Son's resurrection, his
masterpiece fair!

James Quinn, S.J.

355

1 I'll sing a hymn to Mary,
the Mother of my God,
the Virgin of all virgins,
of David's royal blood.
O teach me, holy Mary,
a loving song to frame,
O may I imitate thee
and magnify God's name.

2 O noble Tower of David,
of gold and ivory,
the Ark of God's own promise,
the gate of heav'n to me,
to live and not to love thee,
would fill my soul with shame;
O may I imitate thee
and magnify God's name.

3 The Saints are high in glory,
with golden crowns so bright;
but brighter far is Mary,
upon her throne of light.
O that which God did give thee,
let mortal ne'er disclaim;
O may I imitate thee
and magnify God's name.

4 But in the crown of Mary,
there lies a wondrous gem,
as Queen of all the Angels,
which Mary shares with them:
no sin hath e'er defiled thee,
so doth our faith proclaim;
O may I imitate thee
and magnify God's name.

John Wyse (1825–98)

356

1 Hail, Queen of heav'n, the ocean star!
Guide of the wand'rer here below!
Thrown on life's surge, we claim thy care;
save us from peril and from woe.
Mother of Christ, star of the sea,
pray for the wanderer, pray for me.

2 O gentle, chaste and spotless maid,
we sinners make our prayers through thee;
remind thy son that he has paid
the price of our iniquity.
Virgin most pure, star of the sea,
pray for the sinner, pray for me.

3 Sojourners in this vale of tears,
to thee, blest advocate, we cry;
pity our sorrows, calm our fears,
and soothe with hope our misery.
Refuge in grief, star of the sea,
pray for the mourner, pray for me.

4 And while to him who reigns above,
in Godhead One, in Persons Three,
the source of life, of grace, of love,
homage we pay on bended knee,
do thou, bright Queen, star of the sea,
pray for thy children, pray for me.
John Lingard (1771–1851)

357

1 Star of sea and ocean,
gateway to God's haven,
Mother of our Maker,
hear our prayer, O maiden.

2 Welcoming the Ave,
Gabriel's simple greeting,
you have borne a Saviour
far beyond all dreaming.

3 Loose the bonds that hold us
bound in sin's own blindness
that with eyes now opened
God's own light may guide us.

4 Show yourself our mother;
he will hear your pleading
whom your womb has sheltered
and whose hand brings healing.

5 Gentlest of all virgins,
that our love be faithful
keep us from all evil,
gentle, strong and grateful.

6 Guard us through life's dangers,
never turn and leave us.
May our hope find harbour
in the calm of Jesus.

7 Sing to God our Father
through the Son who saves us,
joyful in the Spirit,
everlasting praises.
Anon, 9th Cent. tr E. Caswall (1814-78)

358

1 Ave maris stella
Dei Mater alma,
atque semper virgo,
felix caeli porta.

2 Sumens illud Ave
Gabrielis ore,
funda nos in pace,
mutans Hevae nomen.

3 Solve vincla reis,
profer lumen caecis,
mala nostra pelle,
bona cuncta posce.

4 Monstra te esse matrem,
sumat per te preces,
qui pro nobis natus
tulit esse tuus.

5 Virgo singularis,
inter omnes mitis,
nos culpis solutos
mites fac et castos.

6 Vitam praesta puram,
iter para tutum,
ut videntes Jesum,
semper collaetemur.

7 Sit laus Deo Patri,
  summo Christo decus,
  Spiritui sancto,
  tribus honor unus.
  Anon, 9th Cent

359

1 All who keep the faith of Jesus,
  sing the wonders that were done,
  when the love of God the Father
  o'er our sin the vict'ry won,
  when he made the Virgin Mary
  Mother of his only Son.
  Hail, Mary, full of grace!

2 Blesséd were the chosen people
  out of whom the Lord did come,
  blesséd was the land of promise
  fashioned for his earthly home;
  but more blesséd far the Mother,
  she who bore him in her womb.

3 Wherefore let all faithful people
  tell the honour of her name,
  let the Church in her foreshadowed
  part in her thanksgiving claim;
  what Christ's Mother sang in gladness
  let Christ's people sing the same.

4 May the Mother's intercessions
  on our homes a blessing win,
  that the children all be prospered,
  strong and fair and pure within,
  following our Lord's own footsteps,
  firm in faith and free from sin.

5 For the sick and for the agèd,
  for our dear ones far away,
  for the hearts that mourn in secret,
  all who need our prayers today,
  for the faithful gone before us,
  may the holy Virgin pray:

5 Praise, O Mary, praise the Father,
  praise your Saviour and your Son,
  praise the everlasting Spirit,
  who has made you ark and throne;
  o'er all creatures high exalted,
  lowly praise the Three in One.
  V.S.S. Coles (1845-1929)

360

1 As I kneel before you,
  as I bow my head in prayer,
  take this day, make it yours
  and fill me with your love.
  Ave Maria, gratia plena,
  Dominus tecum, benedicta tu.

2 All I have I give you,
  ev'ry dream and wish are yours;
  mother of Christ, mother of mine,
  present them to my Lord.

3 As I kneel before you,
  and I see your smiling face,
  ev'ry thought, ev'ry word
  is lost in your embrace.
  Maria Parkinson

361

1 Blessed Virgin Mother,
  daughter of your Son,
  highest of all women,
  humbler there is none.
  When you bore the Saviour
  by divine decree,
  you gave all creation
  new nobility.

2 When the Source of Hope sprang
  forth against Despair,
  and the God of Love was
  nourished by your care,
  Then the fire of grace did
  flourish and increase,
  spreading through the nations
  news of heavenly peace.

3 You are loving kindness,
  ever know our need;
  you are all compassion,
  gladly intercede,
  you are all perfection
  in the human race,
  through your mediation
  we can share God's grace.
  from Dante's Paradiso, *Canto 33, para-*
  phrased by A. G. Petti (1932-1985)

362

1. Of one that is so fair and bright, *ve - lut ma - ris stel - la,*
2. In sor - row, coun - sel thou art best, *fe - lix fe - cun - da - ta:* for

brigh - ter than the day is light, *pa - rens et pu - el - la;* I
all the wea - ry thou art rest, *ma - ter ho - no - ra - ta:* be -

cry to thee to turn to me, La - dy, pray thy Son for me, *tam*
seech him in thy mil - dest mood, who for us did shed his blood *in*

pi - a, that I may come to thee,_____ *Ma - ri - a.*
cru - ce, that we may come to him_____ *in lu - ce.*

3 All this world was forlorn,
      Eva peccatrice,
   till our Saviour Lord was born
      de te genetrice;
   with thy ave sin went away,
   dark night went and in came day
      salutis.
   The well of healing sprang from thee,
      virtutis.

4 Lady, flower of everything,
      rosa sine spina,
   thou borest Jesus, heaven's king,
      gratia divina.
   Of all I say thou bore the prize,
   Lady, Queen of Paradise,
      electa;
   maiden mild, Mother
      es effecta.

Anon., medieval. Music by Francis Duffy

363

1 Mary immaculate, star of the morning,
   chosen before the creation began,
   chosen to bring, for thy bridal adorning,
   woe to the serpent and rescue to man.

2 Here, in an orbit of shadow and sadness
   veiling thy splendour, thy course thou
      hast run;
   now thou art throned in all glory and
      gladness,
   crowned by the hand of thy saviour and Son.

3 Sinners, we honour thy sinless perfection,
   fallen and weak, for thy pity we plead;
   grant us the shield of thy sovereign
      protection,
   measure thine aid by the depth of our need.

4 Frail is our nature, and strict our
      probation,
   watchful the foe that would lure us to
      wrong,
   succour our souls in the hour of
      temptation,
   Mary immaculate tender and strong.

5 Bend from thy throne at the voice of
      our crying;
   bend to this earth which thy footsteps
      have trod;
   stretch out thine arms to us living and
      dying,
   Mary immaculate, mother of God.

F.W. Weatherell

364

1 O Mother blest, whom God bestows
   on sinners and on just,
   what joy, what hope thou givest those
   who in thy mercy trust.
   Thou art clement, thou art chaste,
   Mary, thou art fair;
   of all mothers sweetest, best;
   none with thee compare.

2 O heavenly mother, mistress sweet!
   It never yet was told
   that suppliant sinner left thy feet
   unpitied, unconsoled.

3 O mother pitiful and mild,
   cease not to pray for me;
   for I do love thee as a child,
   and sigh for love of thee.

4 Most powerful mother, we all know
   thy Son denies thee nought;
   thou askest, wishest it, and lo!
   His power thy will hath wrought.

5 O mother blest, for me obtain
   ungrateful though I be,
   to love that God who first could deign
   to show such love for me.
   St. Alphonsus Liguori (1699–1787),
   tr. Edmund Vaughan (1827–1908)

365

1 Immaculate Mary!
   Our hearts are on fire,
   that title so wondrous
   fills all our desire.
   Ave, ave, ave Maria!
   Ave, ave, ave Maria!

2 We pray for God's glory,
   may his kingdom come!
   We pray for his vicar,
   our father, and Rome.

3 We pray for our mother
   the church upon earth,
   and bless, sweetest Lady,
   the land of our birth.

4 For poor, sick, afflicted
   thy mercy we crave;
   and comfort the dying
   thou light of the grave.

5 In grief and temptation,
   in joy or in pain,
   we'll ask thee, our mother,
   nor seek thee in vain.

6 In death's solemn moment,
   our mother, be nigh;
   as children of Mary –
   help us when we die.

7 And crown thy sweet mercy
   with this special grace,
   to behold soon in heaven
   God's ravishing face.

8 To God be all glory
   and worship for aye,
   and to God's virgin mother
   an endless Ave.
   Traditional

366

1 Holy Virgin, by God's decree,
   you were called eternally;
   that he could give his Son to our race.
   Mary, we praise you, hail full of grace.
   Ave, ave, ave, Maria.

2 By your faith and loving accord,
   as the handmaid of the Lord,
   you undertook God's plan to embrace.
   Mary, we thank you, hail full of grace.

3 Joy to God you gave and expressed,
   of all women none so blessed,
   when in mankind your Son took his place,
   Mary, we love you, hail full of grace.

4 Refuge for your children so weak,
   sure protection all can seek.
   Problems of life you help us to face.
   Mary, we trust you, hail full of grace.

5 To our needy world of today
   love and beauty you portray,
   showing the path to Christ we must trace,
   Mary, our mother, hail, full of grace.
   J. P. Lécot, tr. W. Raymond Lawrence

Author unknown (11th century)

Sal - ve Re - gi - na, Ma - ter mi - se - ri - cor - di - æ, vi - ta, dul - ce - do,

et spes nos - tra, sal - ve. Ad te cla - ma - mus, ex - u - les fi - li - i He - væ.

Ad te sus - pi - ra - mus, ge - men - tes et flen - tes, in hac la - cri - ma - rum val - le.

E - ia er - go, Ad - vo - ca - ta nos - tra, il - los tu - os mi - se - ri - cor - des o - cu -

los ad nos con - ver - te. Et Je - sum be - ne - dic - tum fruc - tum ven - tris tu - i,

no - bis post hoc ex - si - li - um os - ten - de. O_____ cle - mens,

O_____ pi - a, O_____ dul - cis Vir - go Ma - ri - a.

367A

1 Hail, our Queen and Mother blest!
Joy when all was sadness,
life and hope you brought to birth,
Mother of our gladness!
Children of the sinful Eve,
sinless Eve, befriend us,
exiled in this vale of tears:
strength and comfort send us!

2 Pray for us, O patroness,
be our consolation!
Lead us home to see your Son,
Jesus, our salvation!
Gracious are you, full of grace,
loving as none other,
Joy of heaven and joy of earth,
Mary, God's own Mother!

tr. James Quinn, S.J.

368A

Joy fill your heart, O Queen most high,
alleluia!
Your Son who in the tomb did lie,
alleluia!

Has risen as he did prophesy, alleluia!
Pray for us, Mother, when we die,
Alleluia, alleluia, alleluia!

Regina celi, tr. James Quinn, S.J.

➤ *Original version overleaf*

368

Re-gi-na Coe-li lae-ta-re, al-le-lu-ia; qui-a quem me-ru-i-sti por-ta-re, al-le-lu-ia,

re-sur-re-xit si-cut di-xit, al-le-lu-ia, O-ra pro no-bis De-um, al-le-lu-ia.

The Saints

369

Saints of God, come to our aid! Pray for us, O pray for us all!

Saints of God, come to our aid, hear us when we call.

James Walsh

370

REFRAIN

As a tree plan-ted by streams of wa-ter is the

one who de-lights in the word of the Lord.

1 Blessed are the poor in spirit,
theirs is the Kingdom of heaven;
blessed are the ones who mourn,
for they shall be comforted.

2 Blessed are the meek and lowly,
they shall inherit the earth;
blessed are those who thirst for good,
for they shall be satisfied.

3 Blessed are the merciful,
for they shall have mercy shown them;
blessed are the pure in heart,
for they shall see their God.

4 Blessed are the peaceful hearts,
for they shall be called God's children;
bless'd those suff'ring for righteousness,
the Kingdom of heaven is theirs.

Matt 5:1-12, versified by Marty Haugen

➤ *Beatitudes: see also 615, 814-7*

371

1 For all the saints who from their labours
rest,
who thee by faith before the world
confessed,
thy name, O Jesus be for every blest.
Alleluia!

2 Thou wast their rock, their fortress, and
their might;
thou, Lord, their captain in the
well-fought fight;
thou in the darkness drear their one
true light.

3 O may thy soldiers, faithful, true and bold,
  fight as the saints who nobly fought
      of old,
  and win, with them, the victor's crown
      of gold.

4 O blest communion! Fellowship divine!
  We feebly struggle, they in glory shine;
  yet all are one in thee, for all are thine.

5 And when the strife is fierce, the
      warfare long,
  steals on the ear the distant triumph–song,
  and hearts are brave again, and arms are
      strong.

6 The golden evening brightens in the west;
  soon, soon to faithful warriors cometh rest:
  sweet is the calm of paradise the blest.

7 But lo! There breaks a yet more
      glorious day;
  the saints triumphant rise in bright array:
  the king of glory passes on his way.

8 From earth's wide bounds,
      from ocean's farthest coast,
  through gates of pearl streams in the
      countless host,
  singing to Father, Son and Holy Ghost.
                    W.W. How (1823–97)

372

1 By all your saints still striving,
  for all your saints at rest,
  your holy Name, O Jesus,
  for evermore be blessed.
  You rose, our King victorious,
  that they might wear the crown
  and ever shine in splendour
  reflected from your throne.

*2 Apostles, prophets, martyrs,
  and all the noble throng
  who wear the spotless raiment
  and raise the ceaseless song:
  For them and those whose witness
  is only known to you
  By walking in their footsteps
  we give you praise anew.
    or appropriate verse from selection opposite

3 Then let us praise the Father
  and worship God the Son
  and sing to God the Spirit,
  e ternal Three in One.
  Till all the ransomed number
  who stand before the throne
  ascribe all pow'r and glory
  and praise to God alone.

Substitute one of the following as v.2 as appropriate:

January 25: Conversion of Paul
  Praise for the light from heaven
  and for the voice of awe:
  praise for the glorious vision
  the persecutor saw.
  O Lord, for Paul's conversion,
  we bless your Name today.
  Come shine within our darkness
  and guide us in the Way.

February 22: Chair of Peter
  We praise you, Lord, for Peter,
  so eager and so bold:
  thrice falling, yet repentant,
  thrice charged to feed your fold.
  Lord, make your pastors faithful
  to guard your flock from harm
  and hold them when they waver
  with your almighty arm.

March 19: Joseph, Husband of Mary
  All praise, O God, for Joseph,
  the guardian of your Son,
  who saved him from King Herod,
  when safety there was none.
  He taught the trade of builder,
  when they to Naz'reth came,
  and Joseph's love made 'Father'
  to be, for Christ, God's name.

March 25: Annunciation of Our Lord
  We sing with joy of Mary
  whose heart with awe was stirred
  when, youthful and unready,
  she heard the angel's word;
  Yet she her voice upraises
  God's glory to proclaim,
  as once for our salvation
  your mother she became.

April 25: Mark

For Mark, O Lord, we praise you,
the weak by grace made strong:
his witness in his Gospel
becomes victorious song.
May we, in all our weakness,
receive your power divine,
and all, as faithful branches,
grow strong in you, the Vine.

May 3: Philip and James

We praise you, Lord, for Philip,
blest guide to Greek and Jew,
and for young James the faithful,
who heard and followed you,
O grant us grace to know you,
the victor in the strife,
that we with all your servants
may wear the crown of life.

June 24: Birth of John the Baptist

All praise for John the Baptist,
forerunner of the Word,
Our true Elijah, making
a highway for the Lord.
The last and greatest prophet,
he saw the dawning ray
of light that grows in splendor
until the perfect day.

June 29: Peter and Paul

We praise you for Saint Peter;
we praise you for Saint Paul.
They taught both Jew and Gentile
that Christ is all in all.
To cross and sword they yielded
and saw the kingdom come:
O God, your two apostles
won life through martyrdom.

July 3: Thomas

All praise, O Lord, for Thomas
whose short-lived doubtings prove
your perfect twofold nature,
the depth of your true love.
To all who live with questions
a steadfast faith afford;
and grant us grace to know you,
made flesh, yet God and Lord.

July 22: Mary Magdalene

All praise for Mary Magd'lene,
whose wholeness was restored
by you, her faithful Master,
her Saviour and her Lord.
On Easter morning early,
a word from you sufficed:
her faith was first to see you,
her Lord, the risen Christ.

July 25: James

O Lord, for James we praise you
who fell to Herod's sword.
He drank the cup of suff'ring
and thus fulfilled your word.
Lord, curb our vain impatience
for glory and for fame,
equip us for such suff'rings
as glorify your Name.

September 21: Matthew

We praise you, Lord, for Matthew
whose gospel words declare
that, worldly gain forsaking,
your path of life we share.
From all unrighteous mammon,
O raise our eyes anew,
that we, whate'er our station
may rise and follow you.

October 18: Luke

For Luke, beloved physician,
all praise, whose Gospel shows
the healer of the nations,
the one who shares our woes.
Your wine and oil, O Saviour,
upon our spirits pour,
and with true balm of Gilead
anoint us evermore.

November 30: Andrew

All praise, O Lord, for Andrew,
the first to follow you;
he witnessed to his brother,
'This is Messiah true.'
You called him from his fishing
upon Lake Galilee;
he rose to meet your challenge,
'Leave all and follow me'.

    All praise, O Lord, for Stephen
who, martyred, saw you stand
to help in time of torment,
to plead at God's right hand.
Like you, our suff'ring Saviour,
his enemies he blessed,
with 'Lord, receive my spirit,'
his faith, in death, confessed.

    For John, your loved disciple
exiled to Patmos' shore,
and for his faithful record,
we praise you evermore;
praise for the mystic vision
his words to us unfold.
Instill in us his longing,
your glory to behold.

Jerry D. Godwin, based on H. Nelson (1823-1913)

373

1 Jerusalem, my happy home
    when shall I come to thee?
    When shall my sorrows have an end?
    Thy joys when shall I see?

2 Thy saints are crowned with glory great;
    they see God face to face;
    they triumph still, they still rejoice
    in that most happy place.

3 There David stands with harp in hand
    as master of the choir:
    ten thousand times would one be blest
    who might this music hear.

4 Our Lady sings Magnificat
    with tunes surpassing sweet,
    and all the virgins join the song
    while sitting at her feet.

5 There Magdalene has left her tears,
    and cheerfully doth sing
    with blessed saints, whose harmony
    doth ring in every street.

6 Jerusalem, Jerusalem,
    God grant that I may see
    thine endless joy, and of the same
    partaker ever be!

'F.B.P. '(c. 16th C.), alt.

Apostles

374

1 The eternal gifts of Christ the King,
    the apostles' glory, let us sing,
    and all with hearts of gladness, raise
    due hymns of thankful love and praise.

2 Their faith in Christ, the Lord, prevailed;
    their hope, a light that never failed;
    their love ablaze o' er pathways trod
    to lead them to the eternal God.

3 In them the Father's glory shone,
    in them the will of God the Son,
    in them exults the Holy Ghost,
    through them rejoice the heavenly host.

4 To you, Redeemer, now we cry,
    that you would join to them on high
    your servants, who this grace implore
    for ever and for evermore.

St Ambrose (c.340-397), tr. J.M.Neale (1818-66), alt.

Martyrs

375

1 Blessed feasts of blessed martyrs,
    holy women, holy men,
    with our love and admiration
    greet we your return again.
    Worthy deeds are theirs, and wonders,
    worthy of the name they bore;
    we, with joyful praise and singing
    honour them for evermore.

2 Faith prevailing, hope unfailing,
    loving Christ with single heart,
    thus they, glorious and victorious,
    bravely bore the martyr's part,
    by contempt of every anguish,
    by unyielding battle done;
    victors at the last, they triumph,
    with the host of angels one.

3 Therefore, all that reign in glory,
   strong and sure with Christ on high,
   join to ours your supplication
   when before him we draw nigh,
   praying that, this life completed,
   all its fleeting moments past,
   by his grace we may be worthy
   of eternal bliss at last.

   Latin, 12th C., tr. J.M.Neale (1818-66) alt.

St Joseph

376

1 Come now, and praise the humble saint
   of David's house and line;
   the carpenter whose life fulfilled
   our gracious God's design.

2 The Architect's high miracles
   he saw, and what was done,
   the Virgin's spouse, the guardian of
   great David's greater Son.

3 For him there was no glory here,
   no crown or martyr's fame,
   for him there was the patient life
   of faith and humble name.

4 But now within the Father's grace
   where saints and angels throng,
   beside his spouse, before the Son,
   he joins the heavenly song.

   G. W. Williams

377

1 Hail, holy Joseph, hail!
   Husband of Mary, hail!
   Chaste as the lily flower
   in Eden's peaceful vale.

2 Hail, holy Joseph, hail!
   Father of Christ esteemed,
   Father be thou to those
   thy foster Son redeemed.

3 Hail, holy Joseph, hail!
   Prince of the house of God,
   may his blest graces be
   by thy pure hands bestowed.

4 Hail, holy Joseph, hail!
   Comrade of angels, hail:
   cheer thou the hearts that faint,
   and guide the steps that fail.

5 Hail, holy Joseph, hail!
   God's choice wert thou alone;
   to thee the Word made flesh
   was subject as a Son.

6 Mother of Jesus, bless,
   and bless, ye saints on high,
   all meek and simple souls
   that to Saint Joseph cry.

   F.W. Faber (1814–1863)

St John the Baptist

378

1 The great fore-runner of the morn
   the herald of the Word, is born;
   and faithful hearts shall never fail
   with thanks and praise his light to hail.

2 With heavenly message Gabriel came,
   that John should be that herald's name,
   and with prophetic utterance told
   his actions great and manifold.

3 John, still unborn, yet gave aright
   his witness to the coming light;
   and Christ, the sun of all the earth,
   fulfilled that witness at his birth.

4 Of woman born shall never be
   a greater prophet than was he,
   whose mighty deeds exalt his fame
   to greater than a prophet's name.

5 All praise to God the Father be,
   and to the Son eternally,
   whom with the Spirit we adore
   for ever and for evermore.

   Bede the Venerable (673-733),
   tr. J.M.Neale (1818-1866), alt

➤ *See also On Jordan's Bank (94); When John
baptised (173); Behold the Lamb of God (98);
Benedictus (83)*

379

1 O Peter, you were named by Christ
the guardian-shepherd of his flock:
protect the Church he built on you
to stand unyielding, firm on rock.

2 Your weakness Christ exchanged for
strength;
you faltered, but he made you true:
he knew the greatness of your love,
and gave the keys of heaven to you.

3 Apostle of the gentiles, Paul,
the greatest witness of them all,
you turned to Christ, the risen Lord,
when out of light you heard him call.

4 You journeyed far and wide to tell
that Christ was risen from the dead;
that all who put their faith in him
would live for ever, as he said.

5 Unseen, eternal Trinity,
we give you glory, praise your name:
your love keeps faith with faithless hearts;
through change and stress you are the same.
The Benedictines of Stanbrook

380

1 Into a world of darkness since the fall,
new light had dawned, two champions
heard the call:
Peter the rock, and Paul once known as
Saul!
Alleluia, alleluia.

2 First Peter stared in wonder at the sight,
Jesus, transfigured, clothed in glorious
light,
then heard God praise his Son from
heaven's height.

3 Beside a desert road a different sign,
Saul saw a blinding light in splendour
shine
and Jesus told him, 'These you hurt are
mine!'

4 On each a lifelong mission was
conferred,
'Go tell the nations all that you have
heard
of God made known through Christ,
th'incarnate Word.'

5 Their work accomplished, called to
their reward,
one crucified, one martyred by the
sword,
their deaths bore witness to the risen
Lord:
Alleluia, alleluia!
Patrick Lee

381

1 Lord, who in thy perfect wisdom
times and seasons dost arrange -
working out thy changeless purpose
in a world of ceaseless change;
thou didst form our ancient nation
in remote barbaric days,
to unfold in it thy purpose
to thy glory and thy praise.

2 To our shores remote, benighted,
washed by distant western waves,
tidings in thy love thou sentest,
tidings of the Cross that saves.
Men of courage strove and suffered
here thy holy Church to plant;
glorious in the roll of heroes
shines the name of Dewi Sant.

3 Lord, we hold in veneration
all the saints our land has known,
bishops, priests, confessors, martyrs,
standing now around thy throne;
Dewi, Dyfrig, Deiniol, Teilo -
all the gallant saintly band,
who of old by prayer and labour
hallowed all our fatherland.

4 Still thy ancient purpose standeth
every change and chance above;
still thy ancient church remaineth -
witness to thy changeless love.
Vision grant us, Lord, and courage
to fulfill thy work begun;
in the church and in the nation
Lord of Lord, thy will be done.

Timothy Rees, C.R. (1874-1939)

St David

382

1 O Great Saint David, still we hear thee
call us,
unto a life that knows no fear of death;
Yea, down the ages, will thy words
enthral us,
strong happy words: 'Be joyful, keep
the faith.'
On Cambria's sons stretch out thy hands
in blessing;
for our dear land thy help we now
implore.
Lead us to God, with humble hearts
confessing
Jesus, Lord and King for evermore.

2 Christ was the centre rock of all thy
teaching,
God's holy will – the splendour of its
theme.
His grace informed, his love inflamed
thy preaching;
Christ's sway on earth, the substance of
thy dream.

3 In early childhood, choosing Jesus only,
thy fervour showed his yoke was light
and sweet!
And thus for thee, life's journey was not
lonely –
the path made plain by prints of
wounded feet.

4 O glorious saint, we wander in the dark;
with thee we seek our trusted guide in
Rome.

Help him to steer on earth Saint Peter's
barque,
that we may safely reach our heavenly
home.

Archbishop Francis Mostyn (1860–1939)

St Patrick

383

1 Hail, glorious Saint Patrick, dear saint
of our isle,
on us thy poor children bestow a
sweet smile;
and now thou art high in the mansions
above,
on Erin's green valleys look down in
thy love.
On Erin's green valleys,
on Erin's green valleys,
on Erin's green valleys look down in
thy love.

2 Hail, glorious Saint Patrick! Thy words
were once strong
against Satan's wiles and an infidel throng;
not less is thy might where in heaven
thou art;
O, come to our aid in our battle take part.

3 In the war against sin, in the fight for
the faith,
dear saint, may thy children resist unto
death;
may their strength be in meekness, in
penance, in prayer,
their banner the Cross which they glory
to bear.

4 Thy people, now exiles on many a shore,
shall love and revere thee till time be no
more;
and the fire thou hast kindled shall ever
burn bright,
its warmth undiminished, undying its light.

5 Ever bless and defend the sweet land of
our birth,
where the shamrock still blooms as when
thou wert on earth,

and our hearts shall yet burn,
  wheresoever we roam,
for God and Saint Patrick, and our native
  home.
  Sister Agnes

➤ *See also : St Patrick's Breastplate (312);
Christ be near on either hand (812)*

384

1 We praise you and thank you our Father
  above,
  who offer us peace in your kingdom of
    love.
  Your people are saved by the death of
    your Son
  who leads us to glory where all will be
    one.
  Accepting this Gospel we honour Saint
    Patrick,
  who taught in our land what your
    kindness has done.

2 Your Word has revealed what our future
  will be,
  Raised up from earth I draw all men to me.'
  May we, like Saint Patrick, bear witness
    to you,
  reflecting your love in whatever we do.
  He came to our country which once had
    enslaved him,
  to preach the good news that God makes
    all things new.
  Donal Murray

St Andrew

385

1 Great Saint Andrew, friend of Jesus,
  lover of his glorious cross,
  early by his voice effective
  called from ease to pain and loss,
  strong Saint Andrew, Simon's brother,
  who with haste fraternal flew,
  fain with him to share the treasure
  which, at Jesus' lips, he drew.

2 Blest Saint Andrew, Jesus' herald,
  true apostle, martyr bold,
  who, by deeds his words confirming,
  sealed with blood the truth he told.
  Ne'er to king was crown so beauteous,
  ne'er was prize to heart so dear,
  as to him the cross of Jesus
  when its promised joys drew near.

3 Loved Saint Andrew, Scotland's patron,
  watch thy land with heedful eye,
  rally round the cross of Jesus
  all her storied chivalry!
  To the Father, Son, and Spirit,
  fount of sanctity and love,
  give we glory, now and ever,
  with the saints who reign above.
  Frederick Oakeley (1802–80)

St George

386

1 Leader now on earth no longer,
  soldier of th'eternal king,
  victor in the fight for heaven,
  we thy loving praises sing.
  *Great Saint George, our patron, help us,
  in the conflict be thou nigh;
  help us in that daily battle,
  where each one must win or die.*

2 Praise him who in deadly battle
  never shrank from foeman's sword,
  proof against all earthly weapon,
  gave his life for Christ the Lord.

3 Who, when earthly war was over,
  fought, but not for earth's renown;
  fought, and won a nobler glory,
  won the martyr's purple crown.

4 Help us when temptation presses,
  we have still our crown to win,
  help us when our soul is weary
  fighting with the powers of sin.

5 Clothe us in thy shining armour,
  place thy good sword in our hand;
  teach us how to wield it, fighting
  onward towards the heavenly land.

6 Onward, till, our striving over,
on life's battlefield we fall,
resting then, but ever ready,
waiting for the angel's call.
Joseph W. Reeks (1849–1900)

Everyday Saints

387

1 For all the saints who showed your love
in how they lived and where they moved,
for mindful women, caring men,
accept our gratitude again.

2 For all the saints who loved your name,
whose faith increased the Saviour's fame,
who sang your songs and shared your
word,
accept our gratitude, good Lord.

3 For all the saints who named your will,
and saw your kingdom coming still
through selfless protest, prayer and praise,
accept the gratitude we raise.

4 Bless all whose will or name or love
reflects the grace of heaven above.
Though unacclaimed by earthly powers,
your life through theirs has hallowed ours.
John L.Bell & Graham Maule

Holy Souls

388

1 Help, Lord, the souls that thou hast made,
the souls to thee so dear,
in prison for the debt unpaid
of sin committed here.

2 These holy souls, they suffer on,
resigned in heart and will,
until thy high behest is done,
and justice has its fill.

3 For daily falls, for pardoned crime
they joy to undergo
the shadow of thy cross sublime,
the remnant of thy woe.

4 Oh, by their patience of delay,
their hope amid their pain,
their sacred zeal to burn away
disfigurement and stain;

5 Oh, by their fire of love, not less
in keenness than the flame;
oh, by their very helplessness,
oh, by thy own great name;

6 Good Jesus, help! Sweet Jesus, aid
the souls to thee most dear,
in prison for the debt unpaid
of sins committed here.
J.H. Newman (1801–90)

The Triumph of the Cross (14 September)

389

*Lift high the cross, the love of Christ
proclaim
till all the world adore his sacred name.*

1 Come, Christians, follow where the
Master trod,
our King victorious, Christ the Son of God:

2 Each new–born soldier of the Crucified
is signed with the cross, the seal of him
who died:

3 This is the sign which Satan's armies
fear, and angels veil their faces to revere:

4 Saved by the cross on which their Lord
was slain,
see Adam's children their lost home regain:

5 From north and south, from east and
west they raise
in growing unison their songs of praise:

6 Let every race and every language tell
of him who saves our souls from death
and hell:

7 O Lord, once lifted on the tree of pain,
draw all the world to seek you once again:

8 So shall our song of triumph ever be:
praise to the Crucified for victory!
*G.W. Kitchin (1827–1912) & M.R. Newbolt (1874–
1956) alt.by Jubilate Hymns and others*

CHRISTIAN INITIATION

The passage of a person into the Christian community takes place over an extended period of time. The members of the local church, the catechists and sponsors, the clergy and the bishop, all take part in the journey from inquiry through the catechumenate to baptism, confirmation and the eucharist.

The journey is marked by liturgical rites: Acceptance into the Order of Catechumens (celebrated in the parish), the Rite of Election (usually in the Cathedral), Scrutinies and other rites with the elect, and finally the celebration of the Sacraments of Initiation (baptism, confirmation, first eucharist), ideally at the Easter Vigil.

Acceptance into the Order of Catechumens

Introductory Rites

The priest greets the assembly. The candidates are asked what it is they seek and each replies. After each candidate has responded, an acclamation such as the following may be sung.

390   Marty Haugen

We praise you, Lord, we praise you, Lord, we praise you, Lord, and we bless you.

Signing of the Candidates with the Cross

The priest signs each candidate with the cross on the forehead, praying that the catechumens may share in the cross's saving power. Sponsors and others may also sign them. Ears, eyes and other senses may also be signed. An acclamation such as the following may be sung.

391   **Refrain 1**   Marty Haugen

In the cross of Christ, our glo-ry, Christ, our sto-ry, Christ our song.

Refrain II   Marty Haugen

Glo-ry and praise to you, Lord Je-sus Christ.

392   Stephen Dean

ff Glo-ry and praise to you, Lord Je-sus Christ!

*Sing this note only the last time

Response to the Intercessions   *See nos. 547-551; 928*

The Rite of Election

This is celebrated by the Bishop on the 1st Sunday of Lent, and the readings are those of the mass of the day. Psalms: Year A: Psalm 50(51), no. 48 B: Psalm 24 (25), e, no. 43 C: Psalm 90 (91), no. 51

The Scrutinies

The Scrutinies occur on the 3rd, 4th & 5th Sundays of Lent. The elect are called before the community for exorcism and prayer. This rite may conclude with a refrain or a psalm, sung prior to dismissal of the elect, e.g. 25(26) nos.43 or 393; 32(33), nos.45 or 394; 50(51), no.48; 129(130), no.59; 138(139), nos. 777-779

Celebration of the Sacraments of Initiation
outside the Easter Vigil

Responsorial Psalms

22(23), The Lord is my shepherd, no. 42; 41(42) Like the deer, no. 47; 50(51), R. A pure heart create for me, no. 48; 62(63), My soul is thirsting, no. 49; 125(126) When the Lord delivered Zion, no. 57

Baptismal Acclamations

Up from the waters, no. 396; You have put on Christ, no. 400; Awake from your sleep, no. 403

The Baptism of Infants

22(23), The Lord is my shepherd, no. 42; 32(33), nos. 45 or 394; 26 (27), R.The Lord is my light and my help. ACCLAMATIONS no. 396, 400, 403

Reception into Full Communion with the Church

Responsorial Psalms

26(27), The Lord is my light, no. 44; 41(42), Like the deer, no. 47; 62(63), My soul is thirsting, no. 49

Confirmation

Responsorial Psalms

22 (23), The Lord is my shepherd, no. 42; 103(104), Send forth your spirit, no.299; 144 (145), I will bless your name for ever, no. 62

Psalms for Initiation

393

Christopher Walker

Those who seek your face, Lord, with a pure— heart shall stand in your ho - ly place.

Psalm 26 (27) (Acceptance Rite)

1 Lord, you are my light and my help.
   With you there is no-one I fear.
   For you are the stronghold of my life.
   I will not be afraid.

2 My God, there is one thing I ask:
   to live in your house all my life.
   To savour your sweetness and to ask you
   Lord, to guide my ways

3. O Lord, hear my voice when I call.
   O Lord, in your mercy give answer.
   Of you I have spoken in my heart,
   O God, I seek your face.

4. O Lord, do not turn me away,
   O Lord, do not leave me alone!
   Teach me, to do what is your will
   and lead me in your paths.

5. I know in this life I will see
   the goodness of God all around me.
   Have trust in the Lord, do not despair
   but have faith in your God.

6. To you our Creator we pray;
   to you, God the Son, we give glory.
   To you, Holy Spirit we give praise
   both now and evermore.

Verses: Psalm 32 (33) (Scrutinies)

1. O happy are those you forgive,
   the people whose sin you have pardoned,
   O happy the guiltless for their hearts
   are free from all deceit.

2 O God when I grieved at my guilt
   my days were exhausted with crying;
   your hand was upon me night and day,
   my strength drained away.

3 But then I confessed all my sins,
   I did not conceal my wrongdoings.
   To you I confessed them and in love
   you have forgiven me.

4 God, you are the place where I hide.
   When I am in trouble you save me.
   Aloud I will sing of your salvation.
   God, protect my soul.
   Adapted by Christopher Walker

394   *Psalm 32 (33), no. 45, with response : May your love be upon us O Lord, or :*

Hap-py the peo-ple the Lord has cho-sen, cho-sen as his own.

Hap-py the peo-ple the Lord has cho-sen, cho-sen as his own.

Stephen Dean

395

In love you sum-mon, in love I fol-low, li-ving to-day for your to-mor-row, Christ to re-lease me, Christ to en-fold me, Christ to re-strain me, Christ to up-hold me.

John L. Bell

{Priest: I baptise you in the name of the Father, and of the Son, and of the Holy Spirit..}
All: *(music below)* Praise to the One who called and named you up from the waters into life.

Baptismal or Sprinkling song

Up from the wa-ters God has claimed you, up_ from the wa-ters, child of light.

Praise to the One who called and named you up_ from the wa-ters in-to life.

1 Always proclaim the wonderful story:
   Up from the waters, child of light.
   How you were raised from death into glory:
   Up from the waters into life.

2 Now you have crossed the River of Jordan:
   Now you behold God's mercy and pardon:

3 No more shall sin have power to hold you:
   now let the grace of Jesus enfold you:

4 Come and praise the God of the living:
   Now let your song ring out with
   thanksgiving:

5 Water of life and grace and salvation:
   Water that heals the heart of creation:

6 This is the life that rains down from
   heaven:
   this is the new life Jesus has given:

397

Refrain

No lon-ger I,   but Christ who lives with-in_ me:

Last time: repeat

this po-ver-ty,   a trea-sure rich be-yond com-pare.

Verses

1. The life we live is not our own.   Christ lives with-in us,   the
2. We have been clothed_ in_ Christ,   chil-dren of free-dom,   of
3. Then may we bear the cross of Christ,   and wear the brand-marks of

seed that must be sown.   Formed in the pat-tern of God's love,
jus-tice and new life.   To him whose dy-ing set us free,
Je-sus in our flesh;   as woun-ded hea-lers we be-come

we die to rise_ with the Lord.
we give our lives, our li-ber-ty.
i-ma-ges of the ri-sen one.

Bob Hurd

398

We are God's work of art, fash-ioned in Christ, fash-ioned to shine with good-ness and light. As it was from the start formed by this great, great love, we are God's great, won-drous work of art.

1 When we were dead in sin, you brought
   us to life in Christ,
   and raised us up, up to the heavens.

2 How rich is the grace of God, how
   strong is the love of God,
   to send us Christ for our salvation.

3 We are strangers no longer, outcasts no
   longer,
   we are saints in the house of God.

4 We are the temple that our God has
   fashioned,
   in Christ we are the dwelling place of
   love.

5 From the foundation of the world you
   have chosen us,
   destined in love to be your sons and
   daughters,
   You have revealed to us the mystery of
   grace, to unite all things in Christ.

Ephesians 2:1. 4-7. 10. 19. 21-22, versified by Marty Haugen

399

Refrain

With joy you shall draw wa-ter,__ with joy you shall draw wa-ter from the foun-tain of God's mer-cy, from the well-spring of love.

Fine

Verses

1. Come, all who are thir-sty, come and drink this liv-ing wa-ter, come and rest be-side the riv-er of heal-ing love.__
2. I saw wa-ter flow-ing from the side of God's own tem-ple, from the woun-ded heart of Je-sus, who died for us.__

D.C.

Bob Hurd

3 This water I give you
   shall become a flowing river,
   welling up from deep within you,
   eternal life.

4 May this living water
   confirm us in our calling
   to be Christ to one another
   and all the world.

400

REFRAIN: You have put on Christ; in him you have been baptized. Al-le-lu-ia, al-le-lu-ia, al-le-lu - ia!

1. We who were dead are now re-born. We who were bur-ied now are raised. We who were dwel-ling in the dark now see light.
2. For though in A-dam all have sinned, in Je-sus Christ are all made clean. The grace a-boun-ding of his death sets us free.

3 One Lord we serve who died for us;
  one faith we hold, in life to come;
  one God and Father of us all we proclaim.

4 And this we know, that nothing ill,
  no price nor power, nor death nor sin,
  can separate us from God's love
      shown in Christ.

Refrain from the Rite of Baptism;   Verses from Scripture, arr. by Stephen Dean

401

1 God, at creation's dawn,
  over a world unborn,
  your Spirit soared.
  By word and water deign
  that this same Spirit reign
  in those now born again,
  through Christ our Lord.

2 We, who in Adam fell,
  are, as the Scriptures tell,
  saved and restored.
  For, when these rites are done,
  dying we are made one,
  rising we overcome,
  with Christ our Lord.

3 Hear us, your Church, rejoice,
  singing with grateful voice,
  Father adored;
  telling our faith anew,
  greeting with welcome true
  children new born to you,
  in Christ our Lord.
        Denis E. Hurley

402

1 O come let us follow the voice we have
      heard
    for our God is faithful, and faithful
      God's word.
    As pilgrims we journey, by faith
      through the night,
    for God's Son is our sun; we walk in
      the light.

2 Yes, now is the hour to rise from our sleep,
    to follow the road, though both narrow
      and steep,
    to leave works of darkness and hasten
      toward day.
    O see how Christ Jesus in love shows
      the way!

3 So let us set out with the gospel as guide,
    for God will go with us and stay at our
      side,
    and love shall impel us to climb
      every height,
    our hearts overflowing with joy and delight
        Delores Dufner, O.S.B.

403

A - wake from your sleep, rise up from the dead and Christ will shine up - on you.

1 In the beginning, before all creation,
   Christ was the eternal word of God.

2 Born in the flesh, preached to the nations,
   he makes our peace by his death on the cross.

3 Risen from the dead, raised up in glory,
   all things created in him are restored.

4 My redeemer, victorious!
   Mighty Saviour, now reigning!
   Where, death, is thy power,
   where, grave, thy sting?

Stephen Dean, from scripture

404

1. A lit - tle child in a bed of night long,— long a - go,
2. A lit - tle child from her mo - ther's knee squeezed through a space
3. A lit - tle child in a ran - dom crowd tired— and un - fed,

con - vinced the world of its need for light and how to glow.
to find her - self in a trades - man's arms, smile on her face.
ar - rived to place in a stran - ger's hands fish - es and bread.

Oh, child in the bor - rowed shed, clear - ly you show how
Oh, child saved from ad - ult scorn, cen - tral your place when
Oh, child by your self - less - ness, oth - ers you've led to

God in splen - dour re - veals for earth Love from be - low.
Christ em - bra - ces you as the key to hea - ven's grace.
share with all what they called their own as Je - sus said.

4 A little child to the font we bring
   here to entwine
   his/her life with that of the Lord of Love,
   Jesus, the Vine.
   Oh, child as you're christened here
   through word and sign,
   God's finger writes in your heart the words
   'Now you are mine.'

If several children are to be baptised:

[4a These children now to the font we bring
   here to entwine
   their lives with that of the Lord of Love,
   Jesus, the Vine.
   On all who are christened here
   through word and sign,
   God's finger writes in their hearts the words
   'Now you are mine.'

John L.Bell & Graham Maule

405

In - to the fam-ily of God we welcome this child.___
(Adults) 1a. In - to the fam-ily of God we welcome you now.___

In - to the fam-ily of God we wel-come this child. Child of the
In - to the fam-ily of God we wel-come you now. Peo-ple of

pro-mise, child of grace, ⎱
pro-mise, filled with grace, ⎰ come to the Spi - rit's dwel-ling place, come to

Christ's own lo-ving em - brace, come to the Lord.

2 Set on a journey of faith with the people of God;
   led into paths that the saints before you have trod:
   Oil of rejoicing grace your head,
   At the Lord's feast may you be fed
   Christ's own life in wine and bread,
   strength for the way.

for children:

3 God who created us all,
      we give thanks for this child.
   Help us to cherish what Christ
      by blood reconciled.
   Help us to teach what he has taught,
   train for the fight which he has fought,
   seek the life his victory bought,
   teach us to strive.

4 Into the family of God we welcome this
      child;
   into the family of God we welcome this
      child;
   risen with Christ and dead to sin
   after new birth, new life begin
   Christ the Saviour welcomes you in:
   come to the Lord!

for adult initiation:

3a God who created us all,
       we give thanks for this day.
    Help us to cherish new friends
       now sharing our way.
    Help us to teach what Christ has taught,
    strengthen the faith which they have
       sought,
    live the life Christ's victory bought,
    teach us to strive.

4a Into the family of God we welcome
       you now;
    into the family of God we welcome
       you now;
    risen with Christ and dead to sin,
    after new birth, new life begin
    Christ the Saviour welcomes you in:
    come to the Lord!

Stephen Dean

406

1 O praise ye the Lord!
Praise him in the height;
rejoice in his word,
ye angels of light;
ye heavens, adore him,
by whom ye were made,
and worship before him,
in brightness arrayed.

2 O praise ye the Lord!
praise him upon earth,
in tuneful accord,
ye sons of new birth.
Praise him who hath brought you
his grace from above,
praise him who hath taught you
to sing of his love.

3 O praise ye the Lord,
all things that give sound;
each jubilant chord
re–echo around;
loud organs, his glory
forth tell in deep tone,
and, sweet harp, the story
of what he hath done.

4 O praise ye the Lord!
Thanksgiving and song
to him be outpoured
all ages along;
for love in creation,
for heaven restored,
for grace of salvation,
O praise ye the Lord!
H.W. Baker (1821–77)

407

1 Baptised in water, sealed by the Spirit,
cleansed by the blood of Christ our King:
trusting his promise, heirs of salvation,
faithfully now God's praises we sing.

2 Baptised in water, sealed by the Spirit,
dead in the tomb with Christ our King:
one with his rising, freed and forgiven,
thankfully now God's praises we sing.

3 Baptised in water, sealed by the Spirit,
marked with the sign of Christ our King:
born of one Father, we are his children,
joyfully now God's praises we sing.
Michael Saward

408

1 O let all who thirst,
let them come to the water.
And let all who have nothing,
let them come to the Lord:
without money, without price.
Why should you pay the price
except for the Lord?

2 And let all who seek,
let them come to the water.
And let all who have nothing,
let them come to the Lord:
without money, without strife.
Why should you spend your life,
except for the Lord?

3 And let all who toil,
let them come to the water.
And let all who are weary,
let them come to the Lord:
all who labour, without rest.
How can your soul find rest,
except for the Lord?

4 And let all the poor,
let them come to the water.
Bring the ones who are laden,
bring them all to the Lord:
bring the children without might.
Easy the load and light:
come to the Lord!
John Foley, S.J. based on Isaiah 55:1-12

Marriage

Refrain I

409

Blest are those who love you, hap - py those who fol - low you,

blest are those who seek you, O God.

from Psalm 127 (128),
Marty Haugen

Refrain II

May the Lord bless us, may the Lord pro - tect us,

all the days, all the days of our life.

1 Happy all those who fear the Lord, and walk in God's pathway;
you will find what you long for: the riches of our God.

2 Your spouse shall be like a fruitful vine in the midst of your home,
your children flourish like olive plants rejoicing at your table.

3 May the blessings of God be yours all the days of your life,
may the peace and the love of God live always in your heart.

➤ *see also: The Lord fills the earth with his love, 45; O blessed are those, 58*

410 Wedding Acclamation

Repeated after each verse.

Bles-sed be God, bles-sed be God, bles-sed be God for e - ver.

1 Blessed are you, heavenly Father: you give joy to bridegroom and bride.

2 Blessed are you, Lord Jesus Christ: you have brought new life to the world.

3 Blessed are you, Holy Spirit of God: you bring us together in love.

4 Blessed are you, source of all grace, one God to be praised for ever.

From the Rite of Marriage, Alternative Service Book. Music by Paul Inwood

411

May God bless you, hold and keep you; may God's mer-cy shine on you, guide your work and guard your rest-ing, keep your love for ev-er new.

1 May God satisfy your longing, be refreshment at your table,
and provide your daily bread,
guard your going and your coming, be the solace in your silence:
life within the lives you wed.

2 May God join your hopeful spirits, fill your hearts with truth and courage,
trust to share both joy and tears,
teach love to your children's children, may your household learn to witness
living faith through all your years.

3 May God find your home a refuge where you warmly welcome strangers
and the lowly find a place;
make you caring, kind companions, help you meet the needs of neighbours,
finding Christ in ev'ry face.

Michael Joncas

412

1. O let there be songs of— joy on this our day of—
2. His ca-ring hand has led us here, his word un-ites us—
3. May it be con-stant as the stars with love no flood can—

days and for this feast of life and love to God let us— give praise.
now, the Christ that once graced Ca-na's feast will bless our mar-riage vow.
drown, my love a seal up-on your heart and yours for me— a crown.

4 Now where you go I will go,
and with you I will dwell;
in laughter, sorrow, rich or poor
for God does all things well.

5 So let there be songs of joy
on this our day of days,
and for this feast of life and love
to God let us give praise.

Liam O'Carroll C.Ss.R.

413

1 Jesus, Lord, we pray,
be our guest today!
Gospel story has recorded
how your glory was afforded
to a wedding day:
be our guest, we pray.

2 Lord of love and life,
blessing man and wife:
as they stand, their need confessing,
may your hand take theirs in blessing.
You will share their life:
bless this man and wife.

3 Lord of hope and faith,
  faithful unto death:
  let the ring serve as a token
  or a love sincere, unbroken:
  love more strong than death -
  Lord of hope and faith!
  Basil E. Bridge

414

1 God in the planning and purpose of life,
  hallowed the union of husband and wife:
  this we embody where love is displayed,
  rings are presented and promises made.

2 Jesus was found at a similar feast,
  taking the roles of both waiter and priest,
  turning the worldly towards the divine,
  tears into laughter and water to wine.

3 Therefore we pray that his spirit preside
  over the wedding of bridegroom and
      bride,
  fulfilling all that they've hoped will
      come true,
  lighting with love all they dream of and do.

4 Praise then the Maker, the Spirit, the Son,
  source of the love through which two
      are made one.
  God's is the glory, the goodness and grace
  seen in this marriage and known in
      this place.
  John L.Bell & Graham Maule

415

1 O perfect love, all human thought
      transcending,
  lowly we kneel in prayer before thy
      throne.
  That theirs may be the love which
      knows no ending,
  whom thou for evermore dost join in one.

2 O perfect life, be thou their full assurance
  of tender charity and steadfast faith,
  of patient hope, and quiet, brave endurance,
  with childlike trust that fears not pain nor
      death.

3 Grant them the joy which brightens
      earthly sorrow,
  grant them the peace which calms all
      earthly strife;
  and to life's day the glorious unknown
      morrow
  that dawns upon eternal love and life.
  Dorothy Francis Gurney (1858–1932)

416

1 When love is found and hope comes home
  sing and be glad that two are one.
  When love explodes and fills the sky
  praise God and share our Maker's joy.

2 When love has flow'red in trust and care,
  build both each day that love may dare
  to reach beyond home's warmth and light,
  to serve and strive for truth and right.

3 When love is tried, as loved-ones change,
  hold still to hope though all seems strange,
  till ease returns and love grows wise
  through list'ning ears and opened eyes.

4 When love is torn and trust betrayed,
  pray strength to love till torments fade,
  till lovers keep no score of wrong
  but hear through pain love's Easter song.

5 Praise God for love, praise God for life,
  in age or youth, in calm or strife,
  Lift up your hearts! Let love be fed
  through death and life in broken bread.
  Brian Wren

417

1 Lord of all loving, we stand before you,
  asking your blessing on us today.
  Love in our union this day beginning,
  life–long communion every new day.

2 Lord of our living, grant in good measure
  grace for forgiving each fault we find.
  Holding together in time of trouble
  strength for each other, loving and kind.

3 Lord of salvation, daily we offer
   fresh consecration, blessing and praise.
   Find you in work–life, friends for our
      sharing,
   joy in our home–life through all our days.

4 Lord of all power, joy is our crowning,
   faith is our strong tower, hope is our peace.
   Love is the promise golden before us,
   grant that our gladness never may cease.
   Averil Norton

418

1 Surprised by joy no song can tell,
   no thought can compass, here we stand
   to celebrate eternal Love,
   to reach for God's almighty hand.

2 Beyond an angel's mind is this,
   best gift, alone to mortals given;
   the love of parent, lover, friend
   brings straight to earth the bliss of heaven.

3 Faith, hope and love here come alive,
   God's very being is made known,
   when giving and forgiving all
   two are inseparably one.

4 For all this splendour, all this joy
   is ours because a Father's care -
   large, generous, patient, strong as death
   showed us in Christ what love can dare.

5 Your banner over us be love,
   your grace refresh our travelling days,
   your power sustain, your beauty cheer,
   our words, our home, our lives be praise.
   Erik Routley (1917-82)

419

Refrain

God of ten - der mer - cy, God of love,
God of glo - rious light from heav'n a - bove: in your light we see light, in
your love we feel love: Light e - ter - nal, love which ne - ver ends.

Verses

1. Liv - ing God, cre - a - tor of all life, heav'n and earth pro - claim your migh - ty
2. Word of God, in - vi - ting us to trust, bid - ding us to pledge our hope–filled

pow'r. Man and wo - man you have fash-ioned in your lo - ving kind - ness,
vow, son and daugh - ter by your grace in one flesh now u - ni - ted,

set - ting them to pros - per and to grow.
called to live the sa - cra - ment of love.

Verses 3 & 4 overleaf

3 Spirit of our God and bond of peace,
   day by day you call us to be one.
   Hopes and fears we bring to you
   in sorrow and rejoicing,
   strengthened by the promise of your love.

4 Age to age shall raise its voice in song,
   as your Church rejoices in your name:
   singing to the God of life
   and source of ev'ry blessing:
   praise and glory now and ever more!

Ernest Sands

420

1. O Father all creating, whose wisdom, love and power first bound two lives together in Eden's dawning hour, today to these your children your earliest gifts renew: a home by you kept happy, a love by you kept true.

2. With good wine, Lord, at Cana the wedding feast you blessed. Grant them your saving presence and be their dearest guest. Their store of earthly treasure transform to heav'nly wine, and teach them in the testing to know the gift divine.

If another tune is sung:

1 O Father all creating
   whose wisdom, love and power
   first bound two lives together
   in Eden's dawning hour,
   today to these your children
   your earliest gifts renew:
   a home by you kept happy,
   a love by you kept true.

2 With good wine, Lord, at Cana
   the wedding feast you blessed.
   Grant them your saving presence
   and be their dearest guest.
   Their store of earthly treasure
   transform to heav'nly wine,
   and teach them in the testing
   to know the gift divine.

3 O Spirit, bond of union
   breathe on them from above
   so mighty in your coming,
   so tender in your love,
   that guarded by your presence
   and kept from strife and sin,
   their hearts may sense your guidance
   and know you dwell within.

4 Unless you build it, Father,
   the house is built in vain;
   unless you, Saviour, bless it,
   the joy will turn to pain,
   but nothing breaks a marriage
   of hearts in you made one.
   The love your Spirit hallows
   is endless love begun.

John Ellerton (1826-1893)

Melody: traditional Irish, arranged by Margaret Daly-Denton

421

1 Hear us now, Our God and Father,
   send your Spirit from above
   on this Christian man and woman
   who here make their vows of love!
   Bind their hearts in true devotion
   endless as the seashore's sands,
   boundless as the deepest oceans,
   blest and sealed by your own hands.

2 Give them joy to lighten sorrow!
   Give them hope to brighten life!
   Go with them to face the morrow,
   stay with them in every strife.
   As your Word has promised, ever
   fill them with your strength and grace,
   so that each may serve the other
   till they see you face to face.

3 May the grace of Christ, our Saviour,
   and the Father's boundless love,
   with the Holy Spirit's favour
   rest upon them from above.
   Thus may they abide in union
   with each other and the Lord,
   and possess in sweet communion
   joys which earth cannot afford.

   Vv. 1,2, Harry N. Huxhold (b.1922)
   V.3, John Newton (1725-1807), alt

422

1 Father, we come in prayer
   to witness to your love,
   to make two hearts as one.
   Father, we give ourselves to you,
   we give our lives anew
   for all time.
   Wherever you must go
   I'll be always at your side.
   Wherever you live you'll find me there,
   for your God is mine.

2 Jesus, we ask your help
   to conquer for all time
   the darkness in our land.
   Jesus, where we live you live too,
   unite our hearts with you
   in your love.

3 Spirit, we feel your pow'r
   your presence in our hearts:
   be with us in each day,
   Spirit, may we be one in you,
   make all we say and do
   give you praise.
   Anthony Sharpe. Refrain: Ruth 1:16

➢ *See also: Love for one another (918-927)*
e.g. 918 Where there is love; 919 Not for
tongues of heaven's angels

MINISTRY, SERVICE, ORDINATION

423

O Lord, you are the centre of my life: I will al-ways praise you,
I will al-ways serve you, I will al-ways keep you in my sight.

1 Keep me safe, O God, I take refuge in you.
   I say to the Lord: 'You are my God.
   My happiness lies in you alone;
   my happiness lies in you alone.'

2 I will bless the Lord who gives me counsel,
   who even at night directs my heart.
   I keep the Lord ever in my sight:
   since he is at my right hand, I shall stand
   firm.

Verses 3 & 4 overleaf

3 And so my heart rejoices, my soul is glad;
   even in safety shall my body rest.
   For you will not leave my soul among
      the dead,
   nor let your beloved know decay.

4 You will show me the path of life,
   the fullness of joy in your presence,
   at your right hand, at your right hand
   happiness for ever.

Ps 15 (16); Refrain by Paul Inwood

424

Go in - to the world,— al- le - lu - ia; make dis - ci- ples of all the na - tions, al- le - lu - ia.

Psalm 95 (96), refrain Matt 28:19. Music:Stephen Dean

➤ *see also: Ps 22 (23), no. 42; Ps 24 (25), no.53;; Ps 84 (85), no. 50; Ps 115(116), no. 55*

425

1 You are called to tell the story
   passing words of life along,
   then to blend your voice with others
   as you sing the sacred song.
      Christ be known in all our singing
      filling all with songs of love.

2 You are called to teach the rhythm
   of the dance that never ends,
   then to move within the circle,
   hand in hand with strangers, friends.
      Christ be known in all our dancing,
      touching all with hands of love.

3 You are called to set the table,
   blessing bread as Jesus blessed,
   then to come with thirst and hunger,
   needing care like all the rest,
      Christ be known in all our sharing,
      feeding all with signs of love.

4 May the One whose love is broader
   than the measure of all space
   give us words to sing the story,
   move among us in this place.
      Christ be known in all our living
      filling all with gifts of love.
                        Ruth Duck

426

1 Go to the world! Go into all the earth.
   Go preach the cross where Christ
      renews life's worth,
   baptising as the sign of our rebirth,
      Alleluia.

2 Go to the world! Go into every place.
   Go live the Word of Christ's redeeming
      grace.
   Go seek God's presence in each time
      and space
      Alleluia.

3 Go to the world! Go struggle, bless and
      pray;
   the nights of tears give way to joyous day.
   As servant Church, you follow Christ's
      own way.
      Alleluia.

4 Go to the world! Go as the ones I send,
   for I am with you 'til the age shall end,
   when all the hosts of glory cry 'Amen!'
      Alleluia.

Sylvia Dunstan (1955-93)

➤ *See also Church (777-798); Sending out/ discipleship/commitment (815-841); Laudate Dominum (730); Out of Darkness (835)*

Healing

Psalms *24(25), To you, O Lord, no.43; 33(34), Taste and see, no. 46; 41(42), Like the deer that yearns, no. 47; 62(63) For you my soul is thirsting, no.49; 102(103) The Lord is compassion and love, no. 54; and other settings of these psalms listed on p.409*

427

REFRAIN

Hea - ler of our ev' - ry ill, light of each to - mor - row,

give us peace be - yond our fear, and hope be-yond our sor - row.

Verses

1. You who know our fears and sad - ness, grace us with your
2. In the pain and joy be - hol - ding, how your grace is

peace and glad - ness, Spi- rit of all com - fort: fill our hearts.
still un - fol - ding, give us all your vi - sion: God of love.

3 Give us strength to love each other,
   ev'ry sister, ev'ry brother,
   Spirit of all kindness: be our guide.

4 You who know each thought and feeling,
   teach us all your way of healing,
   Spirit of compassion: fill each heart.
   Marty Haugen

428

1 By gracious powers so wonderfully
      sheltered
   and confidently waiting, come what may,
   we know that God is with us night and
      morning,
   and never fails to greet us each new day.

2 Yet is this heart by its old foe tormented
   still evil days bring burdens hard to bear;
   O give our frightened souls the sure
      salvation
   for which, O God, you taught us to prepare.

3 And when this cup you give is filled to
      brimming
   with bitter suffering, hard to understand,
   we take it thankfully and without trembling,
   out of so good, and so beloved, a hand.

4 Yet when again, in this same world, you
      give us
   the joy we had, the brightness of your sun,
   we shall remember all the days we lived
      through,
   and our whole life shall then be yours
      alone.

5 Now, when your silence deeply spreads
      around us,
   O let us hear all your creation says -
   that world of sound which soundlessly
      invades us,
   and all your children's highest hymns of
      praise.

*F. Pratt Green, based on the German of
Dietrich Bonhoeffer (1906-45)*

429

1 Great God of mercy, God of consolation,
   look on your people, gathered here to
      praise you!
   Pity our weakness, come in power to
      aid us,
   source of all blessing.

2 Jesus Redeemer, Lord of all creation,
   come as our Saviour, Jesus, friend of
      sinners:
   grant us forgiveness, lift our downcast
      spirit,
   heal us and save us.

3 Joy-giving Spirit, be our light in darkness,
   come to befriend us, help us bear our
      burdens:
   give us true courage, breathe your
      peace around us,
   stay with us always.

4 God in three persons, Trinity eternal,
   come to renew us, fill your Church with
      glory:
   grant us your healing, pledge of
      resurrection,
   foretaste of heaven.
                              James Quinn, S.J.

430

1 O Christ, the Healer, we have come
   to pray for health, to plead for friends.
   How can we fail to be restored,
   when reached by love that never ends?

2 From every ailment flesh endures
   our bodies clamour to be freed;
   yet in our hearts we would confess
   that wholeness is our deepest need.

3 How strong, O Lord, are our desires,
   how weak our knowledge of ourselves!
   Release in us those healing truths
   unconscious pride resists or shelves.

4 In conflicts that destroy our health
   we recognise the world's disease;
   our common life declares our ills:
   is there no cure, O Christ, for these?

5 Grant that we all, made one in faith,
   in your community may find
   the wholeness that, enriching us,
   shall reach the whole of human kind.
                              F. Pratt Green

431

1 Your hands O Lord, in days of old
   were strong to heal and save;
   they triumphed over pain and death,
   fought darkness and the grave.
   To you they went, the blind, the mute,
   the palsied and the lame,
   the leper set apart and shunned,
   the sick and those in shame.

2 And then your touch brought life
      and health,
   gave speech, and strength, and sight;
   and youth renewed and health restored,
   claimed you, the Lord of light:
   and so, O Lord, be near to bless,
   Almighty now as then,
   in ev'ry street, in ev'ry home,
   in ev'ry troubled friend.

3 O be our mighty healer still,
   O Lord of life and death;
   restore and strengthen, soothe and bless,
   with your almighty breath;
   on hands that work and eyes that see,
   your healing wisdom pour,
   that whole and sick, and weak and strong
   may praise you evermore.
                       E. H. Plumtree (1821-1891), alt.

432

Lay your hands gently upon us,
let their touch render your peace;
let them bring your forgiveness and
   healing,
lay your hands, gently lay your hands.

1 You were sent to free the broken hearted.
   You were sent to give sight to the blind.
   You desire to heal all our illnesses.
   Lay your hands, gently lay your hands.

2 Lord, we come to you through one
    another.
Lord, we come to you in all our need.
Lord, we come to you seeking wholeness.
Lay your hands, gently lay your hands.
    Carey Landry

433

1 We cannot measure how you heal
or answer every sufferer's prayer,
yet we believe your grace responds
where faith and doubt unite to care.
Your hands, though bloodied on the cross,
survive to hold and heal and warn,
to carry all through death to life
and cradle children yet unborn.

2 The pain that will not go away,
the guilt that clings from things long past,
the fear of what the future holds,
are present as if meant to last.
But present too is love which tends
the hurt we never hoped to find,
the private agonies inside,
the memories that haunt the mind.

3 So some have come who need your help
and some have come to make amends,
as hands which shaped and saved the
    world
are present in the touch of friends.
Lord, let your Spirit meet us here
to mend the body, mind and soul,
to disentangle peace from pain
and make your broken people whole.
    John L. Bell & Graham Maule

434

1 We give God thanks for those who knew
the touch of Jesus' healing love;
they trusted him to make them whole,
to give them peace, their guilt remove.

2 We offer prayer for all who go
relying on his grace and power,
to help the anxious and the ill,
to heal their wounds, their lives restore.

3 We dedicate our skills and time
to those who suffer where we live,
to bring such comfort as we can
to meet their need, their pain relieve.

4 So Jesus' touch of healing grace
lives on within our willing care;
by thought and prayer and gift we prove
his mercy still, his love we share.
    Michael Perry (1942-96)

435

1 He healed the darkness of my mind
the day he gave my sight to me:
it was not sin that made me blind;
it was no sinner made me see.

2 Let others call my faith a lie,
or try to stir up doubt in me:
Look at me now! None can deny
I once was blind, and now I see!

3 Ask me not how! But I know who
has opened up new worlds to me:
this Jesus does what none can do –
I once was blind, and now I see.
    F. Pratt Green (1903-2000)

435 *melody by David Haas*

1. He healed the dark - ness of my mind the day he gave my sight to me:— It

was not sin that made me blind; It was no sin-ner made me see.

436   *David Haas*

Refrain

Jes-us heal us: Je-sus. Je-sus, hear us now.

Verses

1. All who fear the Lord: wait for God's mer-cy.
2. All who fear the Lord: fol-low the way.
3. All who fear the Lord: keep your hearts pre-pared.
4. All who trust the Lord: God will up-hold you.*

continue below

All who love the Lord: come, he will fill you.
All who love the Lord: hope in God's good-ness.
All who love the Lord: be hum-bled in God's pre-sence.

4. *Let us cling to our God; let us fall in the arms of the Lord!

437

Lord Je-sus Christ, lo-ver of all, trail wide the hem of your gar-ment, bring hea-ling, bring peace.

John l.Bell & Graham Maule

Funerals

438

Re-qui-em ae-ter-nam do-na e-is Do-mi-ne, et lux per-pe-tu-a lu-ce-at e-is.

Te— de - cet— hym- nus, De - us, in Si- on: et ti - bi red- de -
tur vo-tum in— Ie-ru - sa- lem. *Requiem..* Qui— au - dis— o- ra- ti - o-nem,
ad te— om- nis ca- ro ve - ni - et prop- ter in - i - qui - ta- tem.
Requiem..

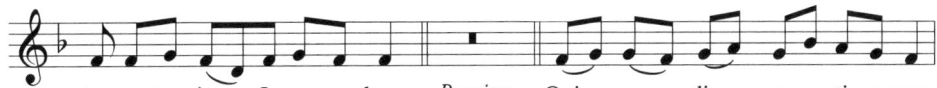

Owen Alstott

439

REFRAIN

Grant them e - ter - nal rest, O Lord, and let per - pe - tu- al
light shine up - on them.

Verses
1. Out of the depths I cry to
2. One thing I ask, just one thing
3. Hear me, O God, hide not your

you, O Lord, I know you are my on - ly hope. Save me, O God!
do I seek: to dwell for - e - ver in your house, Lord, God of Hosts!
face from me. Re - mem- ber that your mer-cies, Lord, are from of old.

Responsorial Psalms

22(23) The Lord's my shepherd, no 42; 24(25), To you, O Lord, no.43; 41(42), Like the deer that yearns, no. 47; 62(63) For you my soul is thirsting, no.49; 121(122) I rejoiced, no.56; 129(130) nos. 59, 60 or 452. Complete Psalm list: p.409

Gospel Acclamation

Settings of the Alleluia: nos 534-46. Lenten Acclamation: 184-87. A suitable verse:
I am the resurrection and the life, says the Lord;
whoever believes in me will never die.   *Jn 11:25-26*

Songs of Farewell

440

1 I know that my Redeemer lives,
   and on that final day of days
   his voice shall bid me rise again:
   unending joy, unceasing praise.

2 This hope I cherish in my heart:
   to stand on earth, my flesh restored,
   and, not a stranger but a friend
   behold my Saviour and my Lord.
                          John Hatton (d.1793?)

441

Refrain

I know that my Re - dee- mer lives, and on the last day I will rise a- gain;

I know that my Re - dee- mer lives, and on the last day I will rise a- gain.

Verses

1. With my own eyes I shall gaze on my God, face to face.
2. And this one hope I will che- rish, this pro - mise he gives:

It is my Sa - viour who calls me: I trust in his grace.
that though this bo - dy will pe- rish in Christ I will live.

3 And nothing evil can touch us,
   no danger befall;
   God watches over his people,
   and answers their call.

4 And though we go into darkness
   all hidden from sight;
   God's arms are open to welcome
   and lead us to light.

Stephen Dean

442

In pa- ra - di- sum de - du- cant te an - ge - li: in tu - o ad -
May an- gels guide you and bring you in- to pa - radise: and may all the

ven - tu sus - ci- pi- ant te mar- ty - res,— et per - du- cant te in
mar - tyrs come— forth to wel- come you— home;— and may they lead you in-

ci - vi- ta- tem sanc- tam— Je - ru- sa- lem. Cho - rus an - ge-
to the ho- ly ci - ty,— Je - ru- sa- lem. May— the an - gel

lo - rum te— sus - ci- pi- at, et cum La - za- ro quondam
cho- rus sing— to— wel- come you, and like La - za- rus, for- got -

pau- pe - re ae- ter - nam— ha- be- as— re- qui- em
ten and poor, you shall— have— e - ver - lasting rest.

From the liturgy, English translation by Owen Alstott

443

Ernest Sands, from Psalm 27

May the choirs of an-gels come to greet you. May they speed you to pa-ra-dise.

May the Lord en-fold you in his mer-cy. May you find e - ter - nal life.

1 The Lord is my light and my help;
it is he who protects me from harm.
The Lord is the strength of my days;
before whom should I tremble with fear?

2 There is one thing I ask of the Lord;
that he grant me my heartfelt desire.
To dwell in the courts of our God
ev'ry day of my life in his presence.

3 O Lord, hear my voice when I cry;
have mercy on me and give answer.
Do not cast me away in your anger,
for you are the God of my help.

4 I am sure I shall see the Lord's goodness;
I shall dwell in the land of the living.
Hope in God, stand firm and take heart,
place all your trust in the Lord.

444

1 Go, silent friend,
your life has found its ending;
to dust returns
your weary mortal frame.
God, who before birth
called you into being,
now calls you hence,
his accent still the same.

2 Go, silent friend,
your life in Christ is buried;
for you he lived
and died and rose again.
Close by his side
your promised place is waiting
where, fully known,
you shall with God remain.

3 Go, silent friend,
forgive us if we grieved you;
safe now in heaven,
kindly say our name.
Your life has touched us,
that is why we mourn you;
our lives without you
cannot be the same.

4 Go, silent friend,
we do not grudge you glory;
sing, sing with joy
deep praises to your Lord.
You, who believed
that Christ would come back for you,
now celebrate
that Jesus keeps his word.

John L.Bell and Graham Maule

445

1 May God the Father look on you with love,
and call you to himself in bliss above.
May God the Son, good Shepherd of his
sheep,
stretch out his hand and waken you from
sleep.
May God the Spirit breathe on you his peace,
where joys beyond all knowing never cease.

2 May flights of angels lead you on your way
to paradise, and heaven's eternal day!
May martyrs greet you after death's dark
night,
and bid you enter into Zion's light!
May choirs of angels sing you to your rest,
with once poor Lazarus, now for ever blest.

In paradisum, tr. James Quinn, S.J.

446

1 Jesu, Son of Mary, fount of life alone
here we hail thee present, we who are
    thine own.
Think, O Lord, in mercy on the souls of
    those
who, in faith gone from us, now in
    death repose.

2 Often they were wounded in the deadly
    strife;
heal them, Good Physician, with the
    balm of life.
Every taint of evil, frailty and decay,
good and gracious Saviour, cleanse and
    purge away.

3 Rest eternal grant them, after weary fight;
shed on them the radiance of the
    heavenly light.
Lead them onward, upward, to the holy
    place,
where thy saints made perfect gaze
    upon thy face.

Swahili, tr. E.S. Palmer (1857-1931)

447

1 Word of God from Mary's womb,
born to die for our salvation,
laid to rest within the tomb,
risen Lord of all creation:
bread of life, with new life feed us,
bread from heav'n, to heaven
    lead us.

2 Shepherd-King, for us you bled,
guard your sheep in love's safe
    keeping:
welcome home your faithful dead,
where no sound is heard of weeping:
Loving Shepherd, walk beside them,
through death's darkness safely
    guide them.

3 Living Lord, you conquered death,
come and take away our sadness;
breathe on us the Spirit's breath,
give us hope of heaven's gladness:
word of peace, all sorrow healing,
speak, your Father's love revealing.

James Quinn, S.J.

448

1. Since we are sum-moned to a si-lent place, strug-gling to
   find some words to fill the space; Christ be be-side us as we
   grieve, da - ring to doubt or to be - lieve.

2. Since we are sa - vaged by the pain of loss, stopped at a
   bar - rier we have yet to cross; Christ be be-side us as we
   mourn, bro - ken, dis - con - so - late and torn.

3 Since we are forced to face this last
    farewell,
saddened to depths we never could foretell;
Christ be beside us as we weep,
loosening our hold on whom you'll keep.

4 Christ be beneath us, Christ be all above,
Christ take the hand of *her* we've lost
    and love;
Take *her* to paradise and then
Christ be beside us once again.

John L.Bell and Graham Maule

Remembrance Sunday

449

1. What shall we pray for those who died, those on whose
2. What shall we pray for those who mourn friend-ships and

death our lives re - lied? Si - lenced by war but not de -
love, their fruit un - born? Though years have passed, hearts still are

Verses 1-5   *Verse 6*

nied, God give them peace.   peace that lasts.
torn; God give them peace.

3 What shall we pray for those who live
tied to the past they can't forgive,
haunted by terrors they relive?
God give them peace.

4 What shall we pray for those who know
nothing of war, and cannot show
grief or regret for friend or foe?
God give them peace.

5 What shall we pray for those who fear
war, in some guise, may reappear
looking attractive and sincere?
God give them peace.

6 God give us peace, and, more than this,
show us the path where justice is;
and let us never be remiss
working for peace that lasts.
John Bell & Graham Maule

Songs of Hope

450

1 As longs the deer for cooling streams,
in parched and barren ways,
so longs my soul for you, my God,
and your refreshing grace.

2 For you, my God, the living God,
my thirsting soul will pine:
O when shall I behold your face,
your majesty divine?

3 My tears have been my constant food,
in sorrow I have prayed,
I know the taunts: where is your God,
and where his promised aid?

4 Why restless, why cast down, my soul?
Hope still, and you shall sing
the praise of him who is your God,
your health's eternal spring.

5 To Father, Son and Holy Ghost,
The God whom we adore,
be glory as it was, is now,
and shall be evermore.
Based on Psalm 42 in the New Version

451

1 Sing with all the saints in glory,
sing the resurrection song!
Death and sorrow, earth's dark story,
to the former days belong.
All around the clouds are breaking,
soon the storms of time shall cease;
in God's likeness we awaken,
knowing everlasting peace.

2 O what glory, far exceeding
   all that eye has yet perceived!
   Holiest heart for ages pleading,
   never that full joy conceived.
   God has promised, Christ prepares it,
   there on high our welcome waits;
   Ev'ry humble spirit shares it,
   Christ has passed the eternal gates.

3 Life eternal! heaven rejoices:
   Jesus lives who once was dead;
   Shout with joy, O deathless voices!
   Child of God, lift up your head!

Patriarchs from distant ages,
saints all longing for their heaven,
prophets, psalmists, seers and sages,
all await the glory giv'n.

4 Life eternal! O what wonders
   crowd on faith; what joy unknown,
   when, amidst earth's closing thunders,
   saints shall stand before the throne!
   O to enter that bright portal,
   see that growing firmament,
   know, with you, O God immortal,
   'Jesus Christ whom you have sent!'

William J. Irons (1812-83), alt.

452

Out of the depths I cry to you, O Lord.

1 From out of the depths, I cry to you, Lord:
   O hear the sound of my voice.
   Lord, open your ears and listen to me;
   I plead for your kindness, O God.

2 If you, O Lord, should number our sins,
   then Lord, who would survive?
   But you are forgiveness for our sins;
   for this we adore you, O God.

3 I trust in you, Lord, my soul looks to you
   as watchmen wait for the dawn.
   And more than the watchman wait for
      the dawn,
   let Israel wait for the Lord.

4 For with you is found forgiveness of sin;
   you show your mercy to all.
   And you will deliver your chosen ones;
   deliver your people, O God.

Psalm 129(130), adapted by Scott Soper

453

Like a child rests in its mother's arms, so will I rest in you.

Like a child rests in its mo-ther's arms, so will I rest in you.

Verses

1. My God, I am not proud. I do not look for things too great.
2. My God, I trust in you. You care for me, you give me peace.
3. O Is - rael, trust in God, now and al - ways trust in God.

Ps 130(131), Christopher Walker

➤ *Funerals: See also Trust, Hope Guidance (948-973); May you walk with Christ (994); One thing I ask of
the Lord ((990) . Another setting of Ps 130(131): My soul is longing for your peace (950)*

The House of God, Dedication of a Church

Psalms *18(19): Your words are spirit, no 41; 83(84) below; 121(122) Let us go to God's house, no. 56*

454

Refrain 1 *Psalm 84:3-6.11, adapted by Stephen Dean*

They are hap-py who— dwell in your house,— O— Lord.

Refrain 2

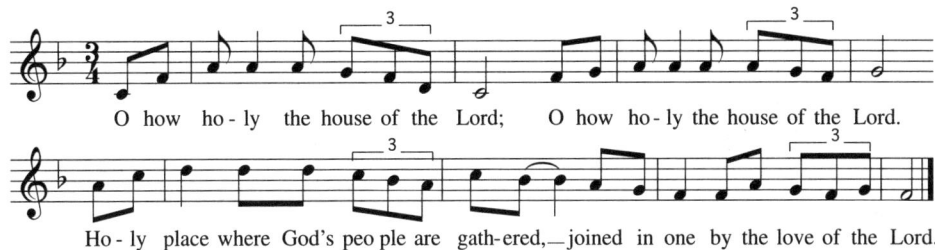

O how ho-ly the house of the Lord; O how ho-ly the house of the Lord.

Ho-ly place where God's peo ple are gath-ered,—joined in one by the love of the Lord.

1 O my soul is longing and yearning,
is yearning for the courts of the Lord;
my heart rings out its joy
to God, the living God.

2 See, the sparrow herself finds a home,
the swallow a nest for her brood,
she lays her young by your altars,
O Lord, my God and King.

3 They are happy who dwell in your temple
for ever singing your praise,
whose strength is you, O God,
who love the road to Sion.

4 Just one day to spend in your courts
surpasses far a thousand elsewhere,
the house of God I love,
the wicked I treat with scorn.

455

1 Christ the rock is our foundation
on his word we firmly build;
for in him is God's own wisdom,
and in him all doubt is stilled.
Come and praise him for the promise
that in him has been fulfilled.

2 On this rock that is his temple,
here was poured the oil of might,
that the dreams which stirred in Jacob
in the watches of the night,
may be found in us his people
here made holy in God's sight.

3 Here the living stones, his people,
consecrated to his name,
burn the incense of their praises,
offer thanks and then proclaim
joyfully that Christ is risen
and one day will come again.

4 Offer praise to God the Father
in whose love we came to be.
Praise the Son, whose might is gentle
and whose power can make us free
if we live in his own Spirit.
Praise our God, both One and Three.
Ralph Wright, O.S.B.

456

1 Christ is made the sure foundation,
  Christ the head and corner–stone,
  chosen of the Lord, and precious,
  binding all the Church in one,
  holy Sion's help for ever,
  and her confidence alone.

2 All that dedicated city,
  dearly loved of God on high,
  in exultant jubilation
  pours perpetual melody,
  God the One in Three adoring
  in glad hymns eternally.

3 To this temple where we call you
  come, Almighty Lord, today;
  with your wonted loving kindness
  hear your people as they pray,
  and your fullest benediction
  shed within its walls alway.

4 Grant, we pray, to all your servants
  what they ask of you to gain,
  what they gain of you forever
  with the blessed to retain,
  and hereafter in your glory
  evermore with you to reign.

5 Praise and honour to the Father,
  praise and honour to the Son,
  praise and honour to the Spirit,
  ever Three and ever One,
  consubstantial, co-eternal,
  while unending ages run.

Latin, c. 8th C. tr. J .M. Neale (1818–66), alt.

➤ *see also What is this place, no. 476; All are welcome, no. 458; God, you call us to this place, no. 469; Church on Earth (822-836), e.g. Sing a new church, no. 836*

457

O how love-ly is your dwel-ling place, dwel-ling of the Lord of hosts! How we long for your house, O Lord, sing-ing out a song of joy to the li - ving God!

1 Even sparrows find a home with you,
  and swallows lay their young to rest.
  Blessed are those who dwell in you
  and sing your praise, O God!

2 Bless'd are those who find their strength
    in you,
  whose hearts are highways for your will.
  Bringing joy to those around them,
  they go from strength to strength.

3 Hear our prayer, O Lord God of hosts;
  receive our life into your hands!
  Look into the hearts of those you love
  and grant us all we need!

4 For one day within your house exceeds
  a thousand spent away from you.
  We would rather serve within your house
  than wealth and power receive.

5 For our God protects us from all harm;
  he gives his favour and his love.
  All good things will come to those
    who love
  the Lord, and walk with him.

Randall DeBruyn, based on Psalm 83(84)

Music for the Eucharist

Gathering

458

1. Let us build a house where love can dwell and all can safe-ly__ live,
a__ place where saints and chil-dren__ tell how__ hearts learn__ to for-give.
Built of hopes and dreams and vi-sions, rock of faith and vault of grace;
here the love of Christ shall end di-vi-sions, All are wel-come,
all are wel-come, all are wel-come in this place.____

2 Let us build a house where prophets
     speak,
   and words are strong and true,
   where all God's children dare to seek
   to dream God's reign anew.
   Here the cross shall stand as witness
   and as symbol of God's grace;
   here as one we claim the faith of Jesus:
   All are welcome, all are welcome,
   all are welcome in this place.

3 Let us build a house where love is found
   in water, wine and wheat:
   a banquet hall on holy ground
   where peace and justice meet.
   Here the love of God through Jesus
   is revealed in time and space;
   as we share in Christ the feast that frees us:

4 Let us build a house where hands will reach
   beyond the wood and stone
   to heal and strengthen, serve and teach,
   and live the Word they've known.
   Here the outcast and stranger
   bear the image of God's face;
   let us bring an end to fear and danger:

5 Let us build a house where all are named,
   their songs and visions heard
   and loved and treasured, taught and claimed
   as words within the Word.
   Built of tears and cries and laughter,
   prayers of faith and songs of grace,
   let this house proclaim from floor to
        rafter:

Marty Haugen

459

REFRAIN

God, our fountain of sal-va-tion, re-new the spring of your life in us. In li-ving wa-ter wash a-way our sin, that we may come to you— in ho-li-ness, God, our foun-tain of sal-va-tion.— God our fountain of sal-va-tion.—

Verses

1. Tru-ly now— God is my Sa-viour. I have trust, I will— not fear.
2. Draw with joy from wells of sal-va-tion. Praise the Lord, call on— God's name.
3. Sing out loud— praise for God's won-ders, let the whole world hear the news.

rall. - - - -

God my song, God my sal-va-tion.— God a-lone my pow'r— and strength!
What God does, tell all the na-tions:— God has done great things— for us!
Shout and sing. peo-ple of Zi-on:— God the ho-ly, God— with us!

(Isaiah 12:2-6)

Lent verses

1 God, my God, I have kept faithful,
even when in fear I said:
'God I feel crushed with affliction,
there is no-one I can trust.'

2 God, my God, how can I thank you!
All that you have done for me!
I will raise the cup of salvation,
thanking you for saving me.

3 Now, before all of your people,
I will keep my vows to you.
In your sight precious the death of
one who has kept faith in you.

4 In my heart I am your servant;
you, my God, save me from death.
To you now I bring thanksgiving,
on my lips I speak your name.

5 Now before all of your people
I will keep my vows to you.
In your temple singing your praises,
even in Jerusalem.

6 Praise to God, Creator almighty,
praise to Christ, God's only Son.
Praise to God, the Holy Spirit,
now and evermore. Amen.

(Psalm 116)

Christopher Walker

460

REFRAIN

All the earth pro-claim the Lord, sing your praise to God.

Verses

1. Serve you the Lord, heart filled with glad-ness. Come in-to God's pre-sence,
2. Know that the Lord is our cre-a-tor. Yes, God is our Fa-ther;

sing-ing for joy!
we are his own.

3 We are the sheep of his green pasture,
for we are God's people, chosen by God.

4 Come to the gates bringing thanksgiving,
O enter the courts while singing in praise.

5 Our Lord is good, with love enduring,
God's word is abiding now with us all.

6 Honour and praise be to the Father,
the Son, and the Spirit, world without end.

Lucien Deiss, based on Psalm 99 (100)

461

Cantor: Praise the Lord, all you na-tions,
All: Praise the Lord, all you na-tions,

Cantor: Ac-claim him all you peo-ples!
All: Ac-claim him all you peo-ples!

Cantor: *Strong is his love for us, he is faithful for ever.*
Alleluia, alleluia; alleluia, alleluia.
All: Alleluia, alleluia; alleluia, alleluia.

1 *O sing a new song to the Lord,*
sing to the Lord all the earth,
O sing to the Lord, bless his name.
All: Alleluia, alleluia; alleluia, alleluia.

2 *Proclaim his help day by day,*
tell among the nations his glory,

and his wonders among all the peoples.
All: Alleluia, alleluia; alleluia, alleluia.

3 *Bring an offering and enter his courts,*
worship the Lord in his temple,
O earth tremble before him.
All: Alleluia, alleluia; alleluia, alleluia.

Cantor: *Praise the Lord, all you nations!*   All repeat.
Acclaim him all you peoples!   All repeat.
Cantor: *Strong is his love for us, he is faithful for ever.*
Alleluia, alleluia; alleluia, alleluia.
All: Alleluia, alleluia; alleluia, alleluia.

Psalm 116 & 96, arr. Fintan O'Carroll

462

REFRAIN

Ga-ther your peo-ple, O Lord,_____ Ga-ther your peo-ple, O Lord. One_____ bread, one_ bo - dy, one_ spi - rit of love._____ Ga - ther your peo - ple, O Lord.

Verses

1. Draw us forth to the ta - ble of life: bro-thers and sis-ters, each of us called to walk in your light._____

2. We are parts of the bo - dy of Christ, nee-ding each o - ther, each of the gifts the Spi - rit pro - vides._____

3 No more harm on the mountain of God;
   swords into ploughshares,
   free us, O Lord, from hardness of heart.

Bob Hurd, Based on 1 Cor 12, Is 2:3-4, 11:9

Extra verse (as a sprinkling song)

4 Wash us, Lord, in the waters of life;
   waters of mercy,
   waters of hope that flow from your side.

463

Refrain 1 Cantors then All repeat

Fa - ther, we come to you, God of all power and might. Show us your glo - ry: give us your life.

Cantor   You have united us, bound us in love and peace:
            God in the midst of us, holy, unseen.

Refrain 2 All

Bles-sed is he who comes, pier-cing our night of sin. O - pen your hearts to him. Great is his name.

Cantor   Bread of life shared with us, body of Christ the Lord,
            broken and died for us: life for the world.

All: **R1:** Father, we come to you, God of all power and might.
Show us your glory: give us your life.

R2: Blessed is he who comes piercing our night of sin.
Open our hearts to you: great is your name.
Open our hearts to you: great is your name!

James Walsh

464

1 On this day, the first of days,
God the Father's name we praise
who creation's Lord and spring,
did the world from darkness bring.

2 On this day th'eternal Son
over death his triumph won;
on this day the Spirit came
with the gifts of living flame.

3 On this day his people raise
one pure sacrifice of praise,
and with all the saints above,
tell of Christ's redeeming love.

4 Praise, O God, to you be given,
praise on earth and praise in heaven,
Praise to the eternal Son,
who this day our victory won.

*H.W. Baker (1821-77) (vv.1-2), and
editors of The New English Hymnal*

465

1 This is the day (2)
that the Lord has made. (2)
We will rejoice, (2)
and be glad in it. (2)
This is the day that the Lord has made.
We will rejoice and be glad in it.
This is the day (2)
that the Lord has made.

2 This is the day.. when he rose again …

3 This is the day.. when the Spirit came…

Les Garrett

466

1 All people that on earth do dwell,
sing to the Lord with cheerful voice;
him serve with fear, his praise forth tell,
come ye before him and rejoice.

2 The Lord, ye know, is God indeed,
without our aid he did us make;
we are his folk, he doth us feed
and for his sheep he doth us take.

3 O enter then his gates with praise,
approach with joy his courts unto,
praise, laud, and bless his name always,
for it is seemly so to do.

4 For why? The Lord our God is good:
his mercy is for ever sure;
his truth at all times firmly stood,
and shall from age to age endure.

5 To Father, Son and Holy Ghost,
the God whom heaven and earth adore,
from us and from the angel–host
be praise and glory evermore.

W. Kethe (d 1594), from 'Day's Psalter' (1560–61).

467

1 Sing, all creation, sing to God in gladness!
Joyously serve him, singing hymns of
homage!
Chanting his praises, come before his
presence!
Praise the Almighty!

2 Know that our God is Lord of all the ages!
He is our maker, we are all his creatures,
people he fashioned, sheep he leads to
pasture!
Praise the Almighty!

3 Enter his temple, ringing out his praises!
Sing in thanksgiving as you come
before him!
Blessing his bounty, glorify his greatness!
Praise the Almighty!

4　Great in his goodness is the Lord we
　　　worship;
　　steadfast his kindness, love that knows
　　　no ending!
　　Faithful his word is, changeless, everlasting!
　　Praise the Almighty!
　　　　　James Quinn, S.J. from Psalm 99 (100)

468

1　Holy, holy, holy! Lord God almighty!
　　Early in the morning our song shall rise
　　　to thee;
　　holy, holy, holy! Merciful and mighty!
　　God in three persons, blessed Trinity!

2　Holy, holy, holy! All the saints adore thee.
　　Casting down their golden crowns
　　　around the glassy sea;
　　cherubim and seraphim falling down
　　　before thee,
　　God ever living through eternity.

3　Holy, holy, holy! Though the darkness
　　　hide thee,
　　though the eye made blind by sin thy
　　　glory may not see;
　　only thou art holy, there is none beside thee
　　perfect in power, in love and purity.

4　Holy, holy, holy! Lord God almighty!
　　All thy works shall praise thy name, in
　　　earth, and sky and sea;
　　holy, holy, holy! Merciful and mighty!
　　God in three persons, blessed Trinity!
　　　　　Reginald Heber (1783–1875)

469

1　God, you call us to this place
　　where we know your love and grace.
　　Here your hospitality
　　makes of us one family,
　　makes our rich diversity
　　richer still in unity,
　　makes our many voices one,
　　joined in praise with Christ your Son.

2　Now assembled in Christ's name,
　　all your mercies to proclaim -
　　In the hearing of your word,
　　in the gospel of the Lord,
　　in the breaking of the bread,
　　in the meal where we are fed -
　　in the Spirit let us be
　　one in faith and unity.

3　In the water we were born
　　of the Spirit in the Son.
　　Now a priestly, royal race
　　rich in every gift of grace -
　　called, forgiven, loved and freed,
　　for the world we intercede:
　　Gather into unity
　　all the human family.
　　　　　Delores Dufner, O.S.B.

470

1　God is here! As we his people
　　meet to offer praise and prayer,
　　may we find in fuller measure
　　what it is in Christ we share.
　　Here as in the world around us,
　　all our varied skills and arts
　　wait the coming of his Spirit
　　into open minds and hearts.

2　Here are symbols to remind us
　　of our lifelong need of grace;
　　here are table, font, and pulpit,
　　here the cross has central place:
　　Here in honesty of preaching,
　　here in silence as in speech,
　　here in newness and renewal
　　God the Spirit comes to each.

3　Here our children find a welcome
　　in the Shepherd's flock and fold;
　　here, as bread and wine are taken,
　　Christ sustains us, as of old;
　　here the servants of the Servant
　　seek in worship to explore
　　what it means in daily living
　　to believe and to adore.

4 Lord of all, of Church and Kingdom,
in an age of change and doubt,
keep us faithful to the gospel,
help us work your purpose out:
Here, in this day's dedication,
all we have to give, receive:
we who cannot live without you,
we adore you! We believe!

F. Pratt Green

471

Jubilate, ev'rybody,
serve the Lord in all your ways, and
come before his presence singing;
enter now his courts with praise.
For the Lord our God is gracious,
and his mercy everlasting.
Jubilate, jubilate, jubilate Deo!

Fred Dunn (1907–1979)

472

1 Open your ears, O Christian people,
open your ears and hear Good News.
Open your hearts O royal priesthood
God has come to you.
God has spoken to his people, alleluia.
And his words are words of wisdom,
alleluia.

2 Israel comes to greet the Saviour,
Judah is glad to see his day.
From East and West the people travel,
he will show the way.

3 Those who have ears to hear his message;
those who have ears, then let them hear.
Those who would learn the way of wisdom,
let them hear God's words.

W. F. Jabusch

473

REFRAIN

We come to share our story, we come to break the
bread, we come to know our rising from the dead.

Verses

1. We come as your people, we come as your
   own, united with each other, love finds a home.
2. We are called to heal the broken, to be hope for the
   poor, we are called to feed the hungry at our door.
3. Bread of life and cup of promise, in this meal we all are
   one. In our dying and our rising, may your kingdom come.

4 You will lead and we shall follow,
you will be the breath of life;
living water, we are thirsting
for your light.

5 We will live and sing your praises,
'Alleluia' is our song.
May we live in love and peace
our whole life long.

David Haas

474

REFRAIN

Let us go to the al-tar of God, the God of our glad-ness and joy! Let us en-ter the courts of the house of the Lord and sing to the glo-ry of God.

Verses

1. Give praise with blast of trum - pet, with no - ble sound of the horn.
2. Give praise with lyre and tim - brel, with lute and sound of the harp.

With the clash of the clang - ing cym - bal, give glo - ry to the Lord!
With the dance of the flute and o - boe, give glo - ry to the Lord!

3 Give praise with pipe and organ,
   with rousing beat of the drum,
   with the call of bell and bagpipe,
   give glory to the Lord!

4 Give praise, all creatures of heaven,
   and all that dwell on the earth.
   Come to worship the God who made us,
   and dance before the Lord!

Based on Pss 42, 150. Daniel L. Schutte

475

1. Here in this place, new light is strea-ming, now is the dark - ness
2. We are the young – our lives are a mys - t'ry, we are the old– who

4. a - way, but

va - nished a - way, see, in this space, our fears and our drea-mings,
yearn for your face, we have been sung through-out all of his - t'ry,

v.4 king - dom

brought here to you in the light of this day.
called to be light to the whole hu - man race.

Ga - ther us in the lost and for - sa - ken,
ga - ther us in the blind and the lame; call to us now, and we shall a - wa - ken,
we shall a - rise at the sound of our name.

Ga - ther us in the rich and the haugh- ty,
ga - ther us in the proud and the strong; give us a heart so meek and so low - ly,
give us the cou- rage to en - ter the song.

3 Here we will take the wine and the water,
here we will take the bread of new birth,
here you shall call your sons and your
        daughters,
call us anew to be salt for the earth.
Give us to drink the wine of compassion,
give us to eat the bread that is you;
nourish us well, and teach us to fashion,
lives that are holy and hearts that are true.

4 Not in the dark of buildings confining,
not in some heaven, light years away,
but here in this place the new light is
        shining,
now is the Kingdom, now is the day.
Gather us in and hold us for ever,
gather us in and make us your own;
gather us in all peoples together,
fire of love in our flesh and our bone.

Marty Haugen

476

1 What is this place where we are meeting?
Only a house, the earth its floor,
walls and a roof, sheltering people,
windows for light, an open door.
Yet it becomes a body that lives
when we are gathered here,
and know our God is near.

2 Words from afar, stars that are falling,
sparks that are sown in us like seed:
names for our God, dreams, signs and
        wonders
sent from the past are all we need.
We in this place remember and speak
again what we have heard:
God's free redeeming word.

3 And we accept bread at his table,
broken and shared, a living sign.
Here in this world, dying and living,
we are each other's bread and wine.
This is the place where we can receive
what we need to increase:
God's justice and God's peace.

Huub Oosterhuis, tr. David Smith

477

1 All who hunger, gather gladly;
   holy manna is our bread.
   Come from wilderness and wand'ring.
   Here in truth, we will be fed.
   You that yearn for days of fullness,
   all around us is our food.
   Taste and see the grace eternal,
   taste and see that God is good.

2 All who hunger, never strangers,
   seeker, be a welcome guest.
   Come from restlessness and roaming.
   Here in joy we keep the feast.

We that once were lost and scattered
in communion's love have stood.
Taste and see the grace eternal.
Taste and see that God is good.

3 All who hunger, sing together;
   Jesus Christ is living bread.
   Come from loneliness and longing.
   Here in peace, we have been led.
   Blest are those who from this table
   live their lives in gratitude.
   Taste and see the grace eternal.
   Taste and see that God is good.

   Sylvia Dunstan (1955-93)

Melody: 19th century American

1. All who hunger, gather gladly; holy manna is our bread.
Come from wilderness and wand'ring. Here in truth, we will be fed.

You that yearn for days of fullness, all around us is our food.

Taste and see the grace eternal. Taste and see that God is good.

Laudate omnes gentes   *Taizé chant by Jacques Berthier*

478

Lau - da - te om - nes gen - tes, lau - da - te Do - mi -

num. Lau - da - te om - nes gen - tes, lau - da - te Do - mi - num.

Eucharist: Mass Settings

Gathering Mass

Paul Inwood

479
Penitential Rite

Presider:
(Sung, or spoken invocation)

Presider or Cantor:
Lord, have mer - cy:

1st time Cantor. repeated by All:
Ky - ri - e e - le - i - son.

Christ, have mer - cy:
Chri - ste e - le - i - son.

Lord, have mer - cy:
Ky - ri - e e - le - i - son.

Presider (sung or spoken)

May almighty God have mercy on us, forgive
us our sins, and bring us to everlasting life.

1st time Cantor. repeated by All:
A - men.

480
Gloria

REFRAIN: 1st time: Choir then All; each time thereafter: All

Glo - ry, glo - ry to God, glo - ry to God in the high - est heav'ns.

Peace, peace, peace on the earth; peace to God's peo-ple, all peo-ple on earth.

VERSES 1 & 2: Choir

1 Lord God, heavenly King,
almighty God and Father,

we worship you, we give you thanks,
we praise you for your glory. (Refrain)

2 Lord Jesus Christ, Lord Jesus Christ,
only Son of the Father,
Lord God, Lamb of God,
you take away the sin of the world:
have mercy, mercy on us.

All: Have mer - cy, mer - cy on us.

You are seated at the right hand,
at the right hand of the Father:
receive Lord, receive our prayer.

All: Re-ceive, Lord, re - ceive our prayer.

VERSE 3: Choir

For you alone are the Holy One,
you alone are the Lord.
You alone are the Most High, Jesus Christ,

with the Holy Spirit,
in the glory, glory of God,
the glory of God the Father

REFRAIN, *followed by*

Sanctus

481

Ho - ly, ho - ly, ho - ly Lord, God — of pow'r — and God — of might: heav-en and earth, heav-en and earth are full of your glo - ry, your pow'r — and might. Ho - san - na, ho - san - na, ho - san - na in the high - est heav'ns. Ho - san - na, ho - san - na, ho - san - na in the high - est heav'ns.

rit. last time only   *Fine*

Bles-sed, blessed is he — who comes, bles-sed, blessed is he — who comes; bles-sed is he, blessed is he who comes in the name of the Lord. — Ho -

D.S. al fine

482   **Memorial Acclamation 1**

All:

Christ — has died, Christ — is ris'n, Je - sus Christ will come — a - gain.

Ho - san - na, ho - san - na, ho - san - na in the high - est heav'ns!

Memorial Acclamation 2

483

Dy-ing you — de-stroyed — our death, ris-ing you — re-stored — our life.

Lord Je - sus, come. Lord Je - sus, come; Lord Je - sus, come — in glo - ry.

Ho - san - na, ho - san - na, ho - san - na in the high - est heav'ns.

Ho - san - na, ho - san - na, ho - san - na in the high - est heav'ns!

Memorial Acclamation 3

484

When we eat — this liv - ing bread, when we drink — this sav - ing cup,

we — pro - claim your death, — Lord Je - sus, un - til — you come — in glo - ry.

*Hosanna
as above ⊕ after Acclamation 2*

Memorial Acclamation 4

485

Lord, by your cross, Lord, by your cross, Lord, by your cross and

res - ur - rec - tion, you — have set — your peo - ple free.

*Hosanna as ⊕
after Acc. 2*

You are the Sav - iour of the world.

Great Amen

rit.

486

A - men, a - men.

Agnus Dei

487

Je-sus, Lamb of God, Bread of Life for us; Je-sus, Lamb of God,
Source of u - ni - ty;
Bread that makes us one;
Food for hearts and minds;
Build-ing up your Church;

Wine of Joy for us; Je - sus, Lamb of God, bear-ing all our sin:
Pre-cious cor - ner-stone;
Wine that heals our pain;
Giv - ing strength to all;
Source of light and love;

have mer - cy on us, give us your peace.

During the distribution of communion the melody may be hummed while a cantor sings verses of Psalm 34.

Mass of Creation

Marty Haugen

488 **Penitential Rite**

Lord, have mer - cy, Christ, have mer - cy, Lord, have mer - cy.

489 **Gloria**

Glo-ry to God in the high-est,___ and peace___ to his peo - ple on earth.___

1 Lord God, heavenly King,
   almighty God and Father,
   we worship you, we give you thanks,
   we praise you for your glory. *(Refrain)*

2 Lord Jesus Christ, only Son of the
      Father,

Lord God, Lamb of God,
you take away the sin of the world:
have mercy on us.
You are seated at the right hand
   of the Father:
receive our prayer. *(Refrain)*

3 For you alone are the Holy One,
   you alone are the Lord.
   You alone are the Most High, Jesus Christ,

with the Holy Spirit,
in the glory of God the Father.
Amen! Amen!   *(Refrain)*

Sanctus

490

Ho - ly, ho - ly, ho - ly Lord, God of po - wer, God of might,

hea - ven and earth are full of your glo - ry.___ Ho - san - na in the high-est.___

Bles - sed is he who comes in the name of the Lord.__ Ho - san - na

in the high - est,___ ho - san - na in the high - est.

Memorial Acclamation 1

The music is sung twice.

491

Christ has died, Christ is ri - sen, Christ will come a - gain.

Memorial Acclamation 2

492

Cantors

Dy - ing you des - troyed our death,___ ri - sing you re - stored our

All

Dy - ing you des - troyed our death,___

life.___ Lord Je - sus, come in glo - ry.___

ri - sing you re - stored our life.___ Lord Je - sus, come in glo - ry.___

Memorial Acclamation 3

493

When we eat this bread, when we drink this cup, we pro - claim your death, Lord Je - sus,— un - til you come in glo - ry.—

Memorial Acclamation 4

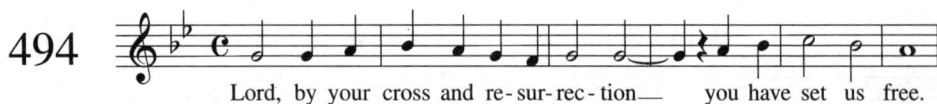

494

Lord, by your cross and re - sur - rec - tion— you have set us free.

You are the Sa-viour of the world.— You are the Sa-viour of the world.

Amen

The music is sung twice.

495

A - men, A - men, A - men.

Agnus Dei

496

1. Je - sus, Lamb of God, you take a - way the
2. Je - sus, Bread of Life,
3. Je - sus, Prince of Peace,

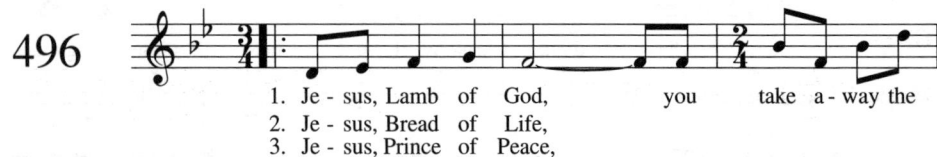

sins of the world: have mer - cy on us.

Other invocations may be sung e.g.: Jesus, word of God... Jesus, Tree of Life...

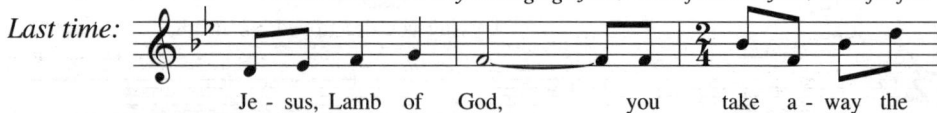

Last time:

Je - sus, Lamb of God, you take a - way the

sins of the world: grant us your— peace.

Communion song

The Lamb of God may lead into the following song
(full version, no. 634)

Come and eat this bread,
come and drink this cup,
come and share the feast our God has spread.
You have promised us, you are here with us
in the breaking of the bread.

Missa de Angelis

Plainsong

Kyrie

497

Cantor then All

Ky-ri - e _____ e - le - i-son.

Cantor then All

Chris te _____ e - le - i-son.

Cantor

Ky-ri - e _____ e - le-ison. Ky-ri-e _____

All

_____ e - le - i-son.

Gloria

498

Glo - ri - a in ex - cel - sis De - o. Et in ter - ra pax ho - mi - ni - bus

bo - nae vo - lun - ta - tis. Lau-da - mus te. Be - ne - di - ci - mus te. _____

A - do - ra - mus te. Glo - ri - fi - ca - mus te. Gra - ti - as a - gi - mus _____

ti - bi prop - ter mag - nam glo - ri - am tu - am. Do - mi - ne De - us, Rex cae - le - stis,

De - us _____ Pa - ter _____ o - mni - po - tens. Do - mi - ne Fi - li u - ni - ge - ni - te

Je - su— Chris - te. Do - mi - ne De - us,— Ag-nus De - i, Fi - li - us—

Pa - tris. Qui tol - lis pec - ca - ta mun - di— mi - se - re -

re— no - bis. Qui tol - lis pec - ca - ta mun - di— sus - ci - pe de - pre - ca - ti -

o - nem nos - tram.— Qui se - des ad dex - te - ram Pa - tris,

mi - se - re - re no - bis. Quo - ni - am tu so - lus sanc - tus, tu so - lus— Do - mi - nus,

tu so - lus— al - tis - si - mus,— Je - su— Chris - te. Cum Sanc - to—

Spi - ri - tu, in glo - ri - a De - i Pa - tris.— A - men.—

Sanctus

499

Sanc - tus, sanc - tus,— sanc - tus,—

Do - mi - nus De - us Sa - ba - oth.

Ple - ni— sunt cae - li et— ter - ra— glo - ri - a—

tu - a. Ho-san - na— in ex - cel - sis.—

Be-ne-dic - tus qui— ve - nit— in no-mi-ne Do - mi-ni.

Hosan - na— in— ex - cel - sis.—

Agnus Dei

500

Ag - nus De - i, qui tol - lis— pec-ca-ta— mun - di,

mi-se - re - re— no - bis. Ag-nus— De - i, qui tol - lis

pec-ca-ta— mun - di, mi se - re - re— no - bis. Ag - nus De - i,

qui tol - lis— pec-ca-ta— mun - di, do-na— no - bis— pa - cem.

Simple Plainchant

Kyrie Orbis Factor

501

Cantor then All   *Cantor then All*

Ky - ri - e— e - le - i-son. Chris - te—

e - le - i-son. Ky - ri - e— e - le - i-son.

Cantor ... *All*

Ky - ri - e e - le - i-son.

Kyrie XVI

502

Cantor then All.

Ky-ri - e e - le - i-son. *Cantor then All* Chris te e - le - i-son.

Cantor ... *All*

Ky-ri - e e - le - i- son. Ky-ri-e e - le - i-son.

Credo III

503

Cre-do in u-num De - um, Pa - trem om - ni - po- ten- tem,

fac- to- rem cae- li et ter-rae, vi - si- bi - li- um om - ni- um et in-vi-si-

bi - li-um. Et in un-um Do- mi-num Je-sum Chris-tum, Fi - li-um De - i

u - ni-ge-ni- tum. Et ex Pa-tre na - tum an- te om- n - ia sae - cu-la.

De um de De-o, lu- men de lu-mi- ne, De-um ve-rum de De-o ve-ro. Ge- ni-tum, non

fac - tum, con-sub-stan- ti - a-lem Pa-tri: per quem om-ni - a fa-cta sunt.

Qui prop-ter nos ho- mi-nes, et prop-ter nos-tram sa - lu- tem de scen-dit de caelis.

Et in-car-na-tus est de Spi-ri-tu Sanc - to ex Ma-ri- a Vir-gi-ne: et ho-mo fac-tus est.

Cruci - fi - xus et- i- am pro no - bis: sub Pon-ti - o Pi-la-to pas-sus, et se-

pul - tus est. Et re-sur-re-xit ter- ti- a di- e, se- cun-dum Scrip tu- ras. Et as-

cen - dit in cae - lum: se- det ad dex-te-ram Pa - tris. Et i-te-rum ven-tu-rus

est cum glo-ri- a, iu-di-ca-re vi- vos et mor-tu- os: cu-ius reg-ni non e- rit fi- nis.

Et in Spi- ri-tum Sanc-tum, Do- mi-num, et vi- vi-fi- can tem: qui ex Pa-tre Fi-li-o-que

pro - ce-dit. Qui cum Pa-tre et Fi- li- o si-mul a- do-ra-tur, et con-glo-ri-fi-ca tur:

qui lo- cu-tus est per Pro - phe-tas. Et u- nam san-ctam ca - tho- li-cam

et a- po-sto- li-cam Ec - cle-si- am. Con-fi- te- or un-um bap - tis-ma

in re-mis-si- o nem pec ca-to- rum. Et exs-pec-to re-surrec-ti- o nem mor-tu- o-rum.

Et vi - tam ven-tu-ri saecu-li. A - men.

Preface Dialogue

504

Priest Do-mi-nus vo - bis - cum. *All* Et cum spi-ri-tu tu - o.

Priest Sur - sum cor - da.__ *All* Ha-be - mus ad Do-mi-num.__ *Priest* Grati - as__ a-

ga - mus Do-mi-no__ De - o nos - tro. *All* Di - gnum et jus - tum est.__

Sanctus XVIII

505

Sanc-tus,__ sanc-tus,__ sanc-tus Do - mi - nus De-us Sa-ba-oth.

Ple-ni sunt cae-li et ter-ra glo-ri-a tu-a. Ho-san-na in ex-cel-sis.

Be-ne-dic-tus qui ve-nit in no-mi-ne Do-mi-ni. Ho-san - na in ex-cel - sis.__

Memorial Acclamation

506

Priest or Deacon Myste - ri-um fi de i. Mortem tu - am an-nun-ti-amus, Do - mine,

et tu - am re-sur-rec-ti-o-nem con-fi-te - mur, do - nec ve - ni - as.

Pater Noster

507

Pa-ter nos-ter, qui es in cae-lis: sanc-ti-fi-ce-tur__ no-men tu - um;

ad-ve-ni-at reg-num tu um; fi-at vo-lun-tas tu - a, si-cut in cae-lo,— et— in ter - ra.

Pa-nem nos-trum co-ti-di-a-num da no-bis ho-di-e; et di-mit-te no-bis

de-bi-ta nos-tra, si-cut et nos di-mit-ti-mus de-bi-to-ri-bus nos-tris;

et ne nos in-du-cas in ten-ta-ti-o-nem, sed li-be-ra nos a ma-lo.

Acclamation after 'Deliver us, Lord..'

508

Priest ...et ad-ven-tum Sal - va - to-ris nos-tri Ie - su Chris - ti.

Qui-a— tu-um est reg-num, et po-tes-tas,— et glo-ri-a in sae-cu-la.

Agnus Dei XVIII

509

Ag nus De - i, qui tol-lis pec-ca-ta mun-di, mi-se-re-re no - bis.

Agnus De - i, qui tol-lis pec-ca-ta mun-di, mi-se-re-re no - bis.

Ag-nus De - i, qui tol-lis pec-ca-ta mun-di, do-na no-bis pa - cem.

Dismissal

Deacon or Priest   *All*

510

I - te, mis - sa est. De - o gra - ti - as.

Rite of Blessing of Water

511

Refrain

Springs of wa-ter, bless the Lord! Give him glo-ry and praise for ev-er!

1. Oceans of earth, sing glory to God!
   Praise to the one who formed you!

   Sound from your depths a hymn that tells
   the wonders God has done! Oh...

All:

(Oh) Bless-ed be God for ev-er! Bless-ed be God for ev-er! *To Refrain*

D.C.

2. Rivers and lakes, sing glory to God!
   Praise, all you ponds and bogs!
   Rich with the life that God creates,
   now let your song be heard! Oh...

3. Brooks of the hills, sing glory to God!
   Praise to the source of life!

   Dancing with joy from peak to valley,
   laughing and clear your song! Oh...

4. Showers and springs, sing glory to God!
   Praise, all you living waters!
   Shower the earth with life and goodness,
   shower the grace of God! Oh...

Marty Haugen

512

Wa-ter of Life, cleanse and re-fresh us; raise us to life in Christ Je - sus.

1. All you who thirst, come to the waters,
   and you will never be thirsty again.

2. As rain from heav'n, so is God's word,
   it waters the earth and brings forth life.

3. Dying with Christ, so we shall rise with him,
   death shall no longer have power over us.

4. Turn to the Lord, cast off your wickedness,
   you will find peace in his infinite love.

Stephen Dean

513

O wash__me__ in the wa - ter__ of re - dee-ming love:

li-ving wa - ter__ from the foun-tain of sal - va - tion.__

1. The water of life renews the soul:
   your gift to us all the source of life.
   O cleanse us! cleanse us Lord and
      refresh us!
   Renew the spring of your spirit in us.

2. Creator of life, of all we are:
   forgive us our weakness and our fear.

   Deliver us from the darkness of evil;
   from danger free us body and soul.

3. You stretched out your hand to calm the sea:
   the people of Israel you set free.
   O Freedom! Lead your people to freedom!
   And Liberty, through the water of life.

Chris O'Hara

514

℀ Refrain

Give us, Lord, a new heart; re-cre-ate your spir-it with-in us.

1 I will cleanse you in living waters,
   I will wash away your sin.
   I will put a new spirit in you
   and you shall live, shall live. *Ez 36:25.26*

2 I will implant my law deep within you,
   I will write it on your hearts.

I will be your God,
and you shall be my people. *Jer 31:33*

3 For all your faults I will grant forgiveness,
   nevermore will I remember your sins.

Jer 31:34

Bernadette Farrell

515

As - per - ges me, Do - mi - ne___

hys-so - po___ et mun - da - bor: la - va - bis___ me,

et___ su - per ni - vem de - al - ba - bor.

the horizontal line indicates a lengthening of these notes.

Ps 50 (51):1

Mi - se - rere   me - i De - us,
Glo - ri - a Patri, et Filio, et Spi - ri - tu - i Sanc - to,

[- -] se - cun -
si - cut___ erat in principio, et nunc, et sem - per,   et___ in___

dum magnam miseri - cor - di - am tu - am.___ *Refrain*
saecula sae - cu - lo-rum A - men.___ *Refrain*

Translation: R. *Purify me, O Lord, with hyssop, and I shall be made clean;*
  wash me, and I shall be clean as new snow.
  V. *Have mercy on me, O God, in your kindness; in your compassion blot out my offence.*
  Glory be to the Father....

➤ *See also: Surrexit Christus (266); I saw springs of water (256); You have put on Christ (400)*

Penitential Rites & Kyries

516

Kyrie, Kyrie eleison, Kyrie, Kyrie eleison. *hmm.*

Kyrie 1.
Taizé chant by
Jacques Berthier

517

Kyrie eleison, Kyrie eleison.

hmm

Kyrie 7.
Taizé chant by
Jacques Berthier

Each invocation: Cantor then all

Alan Smith

518

Jesus, born for us: Lord, have mercy.

Jesus, you died for us: Christ, have mercy.

Jesus, you rose for us: Lord, have mercy.

519

Ky - ri - e e - lei - son, Ky - ri - e e - lei - son,
Chris - te e - lei - son, Chris - te e - lei - son,
Ky - ri - e e - lei - son, Ky - ri - e e - lei - son,

Ky - ri - e e - lei - son.
Chris - te e - lei - son.
Ky - ri - e e - lei - son.

Russian Kyrie

520

1. Je - sus, Lord, have mer - cy on us. Je - sus, Lord,
2. Christ our Lord, have mer - cy on us. Christ our Lord,
3. Je - sus, Lord, have mer - cy on us. Je - sus, Lord,

have mer - cy on us. Je - sus, Lord, have mer - cy on
have mer - cy on us. Christ our Lord,
have mer - cy on us. Je - sus, Lord,

Fine

us, have mer - cy on us all.

Presider: May Almighty God .... and bring us to everlasting life:

Fine

A - men, a - men, a - men.

Jubilee Service: Bill Tamblyn

521

Mass of Hope: Stephen Dean

Presider

Cantor then All

[You came to heal the contrite] Ky - ri - e e - le - i - son.

Chri - ste e - le - i - son.

Ky - ri - e e - le - i - son.

May Almighty God have mercy on us, forgive us our sins, and bring us to ever - las - ting life:

Cantor

A_____ men.

All

A_____ men.

The Gloria no 531 is from the same setting.

522

Canonic Kyrie: Stephen Dean

The final note may be held while invocations are sung or spoken.

Melody

1, 2..

last time

1,3 Ky - ri - e e - lei - son, Ky - ri - e e - lei - son. lei - son.
Lord,___ have mer - cy, Lord,___ have mer - cy. mer - cy.

Optional second part

1, 2..

last time

Ky - ri - e e - lei - son, e - lei - son. lei - son.
Lord,___ have mer - cy. have mer cy. mer - cy.

Verse 2 (or as required): Christe eleison/Christ, have mercy

523

Cantor:

Assembly:

C:

Ky - ri - e e - le - i - son. Ky - ri - e e - le - i - son. Chris - te e - le - i son.

A:

C:

A:

Chris - te e - le - i - son. Ky - ri - e e - le - i - son. Ky - ri - e e - le - i - son.

'New Plainsong': David Hurd

The Gloria no 524 is from the same setting.

Glorias

524

Glo-ry to God in the high-est, and peace to his peo-ple on earth.

Lord__ God, hea-ven-ly King, Al-migh-ty God and Fa-ther,

we wor-ship you, we give__ you thanks, we praise you for your glo-ry.

Lord Je-sus Christ, on-ly Son of the Fa-ther, Lord God, Lamb_ of God,

you take a-way the sin of the world: have mer-cy on us;

you are sea-ted at the right hand of the Fa-ther: re-ceive our prayer.

For you a-lone are the Ho-ly One, you a-lone are the Lord,

you a-lone are the Most High, Je - sus Christ, with the Ho-ly

Spi-rit, in the glo-ry of God the Fa-ther. A - men.

'New Plainsong' by David Hurd

525

Refrain

Anne Ward

Glo ry to God! Glo-ry in the high-est and peace to his peo-ple on earth.

Verses

1. Lord God, heav - en-ly King, al-migh - ty God— and— Fa - ther,

D.S.

we wor - ship you, we give— you thanks,— we praise you for your glo - ry. ℟.

2. Lord Je-sus Christ, on-ly Son of the Fa-ther,— Lord God Lamb— of— God,

D.S.

you take— a-way the sin of the world:— have mer - cy on us. ℟.

3. You are seated at the right hand of the Father: re - ceive our prayer.

D.S.

You a-lone— are the Ho - ly One and you a-lone are Lord: ℟.

4. You a - lone— are the Most High, Je - sus— Christ, with the Ho - ly—

D.S.

Spi-rit in the glo - ry of God— the Fa - ther. A - men. ℟.

526 **Coventry Gloria**

Peter Jones

Refrain 1: Cantor then All

Glo-ry to God, glo-ry in the high-est. Peace to his peo-ple, peace on earth.

Cantor: *Lord God, heavenly King, almighty God and Father.*

All: Glory to God, glory in the highest, peace to his people, peace on earth.

C: *We worship you,*

All :

glo-ry in the high - est.

C: *Give you thanks,*
Glory in the highest.
Praise you for your glory.

All: Glory to God, glory in the highest, peace to his people, peace on earth.

C: *Lord Jesus Christ, only Son of the Father,*
Lord God, Lamb of God,
you take away the sin of the world,
have mercy on us.

All:

have mer - cy on us.

C: *You are seated at the right hand of the Father:*
receive our prayer

All:

re - ceive our prayer.

C : *Glory to God, glory in the highest, peace to his people, peace on earth.*

All: Glory to God, glory in the highest, peace to his people, peace on earth.

C: *For you alone are the Holy One,*
you alone are the Lord,
you alone are the Most High, Jesus Christ,
with the Holy Spirit, in the glory of God
the glory of God the Father.

All: Glory to God, glory in the highest, peace to his people, peace on earth.

C: *Amen.*

All:

A - men!

527

Glo - ri - a, glo - ri - a in ex - cel - sis De - o;

Glo - ri - a, glo - ri - a in ex - cel - sis De - o.

1 Glory to God in the highest, and peace to his people on earth.
Lord God, heavenly King, almighty God and Father.
We worship you, we give you thanks, we praise you for your glory.

2 Lord Jesus Christ, only Son of the Father, Lord God, Lamb of God,
you take away the sin of the world, have mercy on us.
You are seated at the right hand of the Father: receive our prayer.

3 For you alone are the Holy One, you alone are the Lord,
you alone are the Most High, Jesus Christ,
with the Holy Spirit, in the glory of God the Father.

Gloria for Cantor & Congregation: Francis Duffy

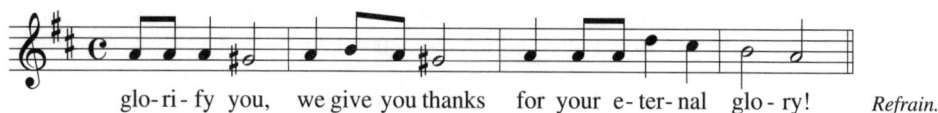

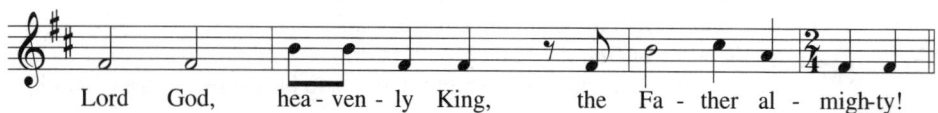

528

Refrain

Glo - ry to God in the high-est, peace on earth to his peo - ple;

Glo - ry to God in the high-est, peace on earth to his peo - ple.

We praise you, we bless you, we a - dore you! We

glo-ri-fy you, we give you thanks for your e - ter-nal glo-ry! *Refrain.*

Lord God, hea - ven - ly King, the Fa - ther al - migh-ty!

Lord God, Lamb of God, Son of the Fa - ther! *Refrain.*

You take a-way the sins of the world: have mer-cy on us. You are
sea-ted at the right hand of the Fa-ther: re-ceive our prayer.— *Refrain*

You a-lone are ho-ly, are Lord, you are Most High,
Je-sus Christ, with the ho-ly Spi-rit, one in the glo-ry of the Fa-ther.

Refrain

Glory to God: Jacques Berthier

529

Glo-ry to God in the high - est, and peace to his friends.

1 Lord God, heavenly King,
  almighty God and Father.
  We worship you, we give you thanks,
  we praise you for your glory.

2 Lord Jesus Christ, only Son of the
  Father, Lord God, Lamb of God,
  you take away the sin of the world,
  have mercy on us.

You are seated at the right hand of the
Father: receive our prayer

3 For you alone are the Holy One,
  you alone are the Lord,
  you alone are the Most High,
    Jesus Christ,
  with the Holy Spirit,
    in the glory of God the Father. Amen

Kelvinhall Mass Gloria: Gerry Fitzpatrick

530

Glo-ri-a,— *(claps)* glo-ri-a— in ex-cel-sis De-o.

1. Lord God, heavenly King,
   peace you bring to us;
   we worship you, we give you thanks,
   we sing our song of praise.

2. Jesus, Saviour of all,
   Lord God, Lamb of God,
   you take away our sins, O Lord,
   have mercy on us all.

3. At the Father's right hand,
   Lord, receive our prayer,
   for you alone are the Holy One,
   and you alone are Lord.

4. Glory Father and Son,
   glory Holy Spirit,
   to you we raise our hands up high,
   we glorify your name.

Gloria: Mike Anderson

531

Glo - ri - a   in ex - cel - sis De - o;   pax ho - mi - ni - bus bo - nae vo - lun - ta - tis.

1st time: Cantor then all.
After verses the refrain is always sung twice

1 Lórd God, heavenly Kíng,
   almíghty God and Fáther:
   we wórship you, we give you thánks,
   we práise you for your glóry!
Refrain

2 Lórd Jesus Chríst, only Són of the Fáther,
   Lórd Gód, Lámb of Gód,
   yóu take away the sin of the wórld:
   have mércy on ús.
      You are séated at the right hand of the
         Fáther: recéive our práyer.
Refrain.

3 Fór you alone are the Hóly One,
   yóu alóne are the Lórd,
   you alóne are the Móst High, Jésus Chríst,
   with the Hóly Spírít,
   in the glóry of Gód the Fáthér.

Final Refrain
Gloria in excelsis Deo .... *followed by Amen:*

Much slower

A - men.

Mass of Hope Gloria: Stephen Dean

532

Refrain   ¡Glo - ria!   ¡Glo - ria!   ¡Glo - ria al Se - ñor.
            Glo - ry!   Glo - ry!   Glo - ry   to   God!

¡Glo - ria!   ¡Glo - ria!   ¡Glo - ria a mi Dios.
Glo - ry!   Glo - ry!   Glo - ry   to   God!

1. Glo - ry   to   God   in   the heights of   the hea - vens.
2. Son   of   the   Fa - ther, all glo - ry and   wor - ship;
3. You   take   a - way___ the   sin   of   the world;___
4. Sea - ted   in   pow'r   at   the right of   the Fa - ther,
5. And   with   the   Spi - rit   of love e - ver - las - ting,

Peace   to   God's   peo - ple,   all   peo - ple   on   earth.
praise and   thanks - gi - ving   to   you, Lamb of   God.
have   mer - cy   on   us,   re - ceive___   our   prayer.
Je - sus   a - lone   is   the   Lord, the   Most High.
reig - ning in   glo - ry   for   e - ver.   A - men.

George Salazar, tr. Paul Inwood

533

1. Glo-ry be to God in hea-ven, peace on earth to hu-man-kind.

Fa-ther, heav'n-ly King, Cre-a-tor, God of po-wer un-de-fined,

praise and ho-nour, thanks we of-fer, wor-ship you with heart and mind

2 Jesus Christ, our Saviour, only
Son of God by faith we know;
Lamb of God, the world's Redeemer,
love and mercy to us show;
seated at the Father's right hand,
intercede for us below.

3 You alone, O Lord, are holy,
Jesus Christ, you are Most High
with the Father and the Spirit;
Trinity, to you we cry:
'Alleluia, alleluia!' –
you, O God, we glorify.

Gloria in excelsis, *versified by John Ainslie*

Gospel Acclamation: Alleluia

534

Al - le - lu - ia, al - le - lu - ia, al - le - lu - ia.

Al - le - lu - ia, al - le - lu - ia, al - le - lu - ia.

Salisbury Alleluia : Christopher Walker

535

Al - le - lu - ia, al - le - lu - ia, al - le - lu - ia.

Colin Mawby

536

Al - le - lu - ia, al - le - lu - ia, al - le - lu - ia.

Laurence Bévenot, O.S.B.

537

Al - le - lu - ia, al - le - lu - ia, al - le - lu - ia!

Stephen Dean

538

Al - le-lu - ia, al - le-lu - ia,

al - le-lu - ia, al - le-lu - ia, al - le-lu - ia.

Richard Proulx

539

Al - le-lu - ia, al - le - lu - ia, al - le - lu - ia. Al-le-

(Al - le-lu - ia)

D.C.

lu - ia, al - le - lu - ia, al - le - lu - ia.*

* *last time finish here.*

Taizé Alleluia 7: Jacques Berthier

540

(Alle-lu-i - a)

D.C.

Al-le-lu - i - a, al - le-lu - i - a, al - le-lu - i - a.

* *last time finish here.*

Taizé Alleluia 41: Russian Orthodox

541

Al - le - lu - ia, al - le - lu - ia, Praise to Christ, the Word of Life.

Glo - ry, praise and ju - bi - la - tion. Al - le - lu - ia.

Jubilee Alleluia: James Walsh

542

Al - le - lu - ia, al - le - lu - ia!

The Priory Mass, Mick Truman

543

Al - le - lu - ia, al - le - lu - ia.

Al - le - lu - ia, al - le - lu - ia. Al - le - lu - ia, al -

le - lu - ia. Al - le - lu - ia, al - le - lu - ia.

Alleluia from South Africa

544

Al - le - lu - ia, al - le - lu - ia, al - le - lu - ia.

Russian Alleluia

➤ *See also Seasonal sections: Advent (69-72), Christmas (122), Easter (261-3).*
Halle, halle, halle: 178. Lent Gospel Acclamations: 184-7.

Profession of Faith

545

Refrain We be-lieve in one— God, we be-lieve in one Lord,

we be - lieve in one Spi - rit.____

1 We believe in God the Father Almighty,
   creator of heaven and earth.

2 We believe in Jesus, his Son, our Lord,
   who was born of the Virgin Mary.

3 Who was crucified on a cross,
   and for us he suffered death.

4 We believe he rose from the dead,
   and is seated at the Father's right hand.

5 And in the Holy Spirit,
      the holy catholic Church,
   the communion of saints.

6 And the forgiveness of sins,
   the resurrection and life for evermore.
   Adapted by Christopher Walker

546

Refrain: We be-lieve,— we be-lieve.— Lord, help our un-be-lief.—

We be-lieve,— we be-lieve.— Lord, help our un-be-lief.—

Christopher Walker

➤ *See also Credo III (503)*

General Intercessions

547

(Intercessions) Let us pray to the Lord. Lord, hear our prayer.

Russian chant

548

Cantor: Lord, in your mer-cy, All: hear our prayer.

Millennium Mass: Paul Inwood.

549

f Hear our prayer! Hear our prayer! Lord, hear our prayer.

Stephen Dean

550

Cantor: We ask you, Lord, All: lis-ten to our prayer. Cantor: We ask you, Lord, All: lis-ten to our prayer.

Millennium Mass: Paul Inwood

551

God ev-er-faith-ful, God ev-er mer-ci-ful, God of your peo-ple, hear our prayer.

from Mass of John Carroll: Michael Joncas

552

slowly

Through our lives and by our prayers, your King-dom come.

John L. Bell

☞ *See also 26-29, 740, 928-930*

The Eucharistic Prayer

A Celtic Liturgy

Christopher Walker

553

Priest .and so, with all the choirs of an-gels in heaven we proclaim your

glo - ry and join in their un - en - ding hymn of praise:

Ho - ly, ho-ly, ho - ly Lord, God of po - wer and might.

Hea - ven and earth are full of your glo - ry. Ho - san-na, ho-

san-na, in the highest. Bles-sed is he who

comes in the name of the Lord. Ho - san-na in the

high - est, ho - san - na in the high - est.

Memorial Acclamation

554

Deacon or priest Let us proclaim the my-ste-ry of faith:

Acclamation *Sung twice.*   *Descant may be added on repeat.*

Christ   has died,   Christ   is   ri-sen,   Christ   will

come   a - gain.

come   a - gain,   Christ   will   come   a - gain.

Doxology and Great Amen

555

Through him, with him, in him,   in the   u-ni-ty   of the   Spi-rit,   all

glo-ry and honour is   yours,   al-migh-ty   Fa-ther,   for   e - ver and   e-ver.

A - men,   a - men,   a - men,   a - men.

A Mass of Peace

Seoirse Bodley

556

Ho - ly,   ho - ly,   ho - ly Lord,   God   of power   and

might.   Hea - ven and   earth   are   full   of your   glo - ry.   Ho -

san - na   in the high - est.   Bles - sed is___   he   who   comes in   the

name   of the Lord.   Ho - san - na   in the   high - est.

Acclamation A & Doxology

557

Christ has died,— Christ is ris'n, Christ will come a - gain.
A - men,— a - men, a - men.

Acclamation B

558

Dy - ing you des - troyed our death, ri - sing—

you re - stored our life, Lord Je - sus, come in glo-ry!

Eucharistic Acclamations

Bernadette Farrell

559

cresc.

Ho-ly ho-ly, ho-ly Lord God of pow'r, Lord God of

mf

might, Lord God of pow'r and might.___ Heav'n and earth are full of your

glo-ry. Ho - sanna___ in the high - est.___ Ho-san - na, ho-san - na, ho-

p

san-na___ in the high-est.___ Blessed, blessed, blessed, blessed is

cresc.

he who comes in the name, who comes in the Lord's own name!___

Ho-san - na, ho-san - na, ho-san - na___ in the high - est;

ho-san - na, ho-san - na, ho-san-na___ in the high - est.___

Acclamation B

may be sung responsorially

560

optional repeat

Dy - ing you de-stroyed our death,___ ris - ing you re-

optional repeat

stored our life.__ Lord Je - sus, come,___ come in glo - ry.___

Lord Je - sus, come.
*if sung responsorially

Acclamation C

561

When we eat this bread and drink this cup,___

we pro - claim your death, Lord Je - sus Christ,___ un - til you

come__ in glo ry,___ un - til you come in glo - ry,___ un -

til you come in glo - ry, Je - sus Christ!___

Doxology and Amen

562

Presider:

Through him, with him, in him___ in the u - ni - ty__

of the Ho - ly Spi - rit all glo - ry and hon - our is yours, al -

All: *Presider:*

migh - ty Fa - ther,___ for ev - er, A - men, for

All: *Presider:* *All:*

ev - er, A - men, for ev - er, A - men.

Community Mass

Richard Proulx

563

Ho-ly, ho-ly, ho-ly Lord, God of pow-er and might.

Heav'n_____ and earth_____ are full___ of your glo-ry. Ho-

san-na in the high-est, ho-san-na in the high-est.

Blest is he who comes___ in the name___ of the Lord. Ho-

san-na in the high-est, ho-san-na in the high-est._____

564 **Memorial Acclamation A, Great Amen**

Christ has died, Christ is ri-sen, Christ will come a-gain.
A - men, A - men, A - men.

St Andrew's Mass

Stephen Dean

565

Ho - ly,___ ho - ly,___ ho - ly,___ Lord, God of

power and might! Heav'n and earth are full of your glo - ry. Ho-

san - na, ho - san - na, ho-san-na in the high-est, ho-

san - na. Blest is he who comes in the name of the Lord.

Blest is he who comes in the name of the Lord. Ho-san - na, ho-san - na, ho-san-na in the high-est, ho - san - na.

566 **Memorial Acclamation A**

May be sung twice (Cantor then All.)

Christ has died, Christ is risen, Christ will come a-gain!

567 **Memorial Acclamation A for Eastertide**

May be sung twice, first time by cantor and second by all

Christ has died, al-le-lu - ia, Christ is ris-en, al-le-lu - ia, Christ will come a - gain, al-le-lu - ia, al-le-lu - ia.

Memorial Acclamation B

568

Dy-ing you des-troyed our death, ri - sing you re-stored our life. Lord Je-sus come, Lord Je-sus come, Lord Je-sus come in glo-ry.

Lord Je-sus come, Lord Je-sus come, Lord Je-sus come in glo-ry!

Memorial Acclamation C

569

When we eat this bread, and drink this cup, we pro-claim your death, Lord Je-sus Christ, un-til you come in glo - ry!

Doxology and Amen

570

Through him, with him, in him, in the unity of the Holy Spirit,

all glory and honour is yours, al-migh-ty Fa-ther, for ever and ever.

A - men, a - men, a - men!

Millennium Mass

Paul Inwood

571

Ho-ly, ho-ly, ho-ly, Lord, God of pow'r and God of might,

heav'n and earth are full, heav'n and earth are full of your glo - ry.

Ho-san-na in the high-est, ho-san-na in the high est.

Blest is he who comes in the name of the Lord. Ho-san-na in the high-est,

ho-san-na in the high-est, ho-san - na— in the high- est, in the high est!

Memorial Acclamations

572

Intro

Let us proclaim the myste-ry of faith:

A. Christ has died,— Christ is ri-sen, Christ has died,— Christ is ri-sen,
B. Dy-ing you des-troyed our death, ri-sing you re-stored our life.—
C. When we eat this li-ving bread, when we drink this sav-ing cup,—
D. By your cross and re-sur-rec-tion, you have set your peo-ple free.—

Christ will come a-gain, Christ will come a-gain— in glo-ry.
Come, Lord Je-sus, come; come, Lord Je-sus, come— in glo-ry.
we pro-claim your death, un-til you come— in glo-ry.
Sa-viour of the world, come in glo-ry, come— in glo-ry!

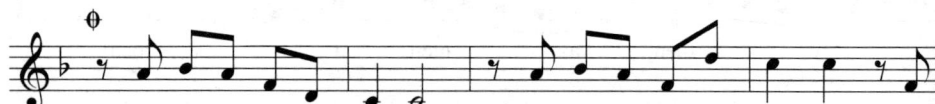

Ho-san-na in the high-est, ho-san-na in the high-est, ho-

san - na— in the high-est, in the high - est!

Doxology and Amen

573

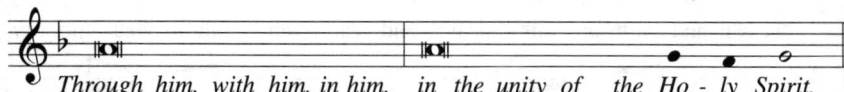

Through him, with him, in him, in the unity of the Ho - ly Spirit,

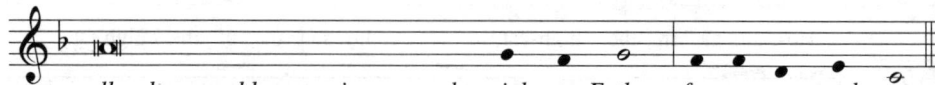

all glory and honour is yours, al - migh - ty Father, for e - ver and ever.

A - men, A - men.—

Coventry Acclamations

Paul Inwood

574

Ho-ly ho - ly, ho-ly Lord, God of power and God of might.

Heav'n and earth are full, heav'n and earth are full, heav'n and earth are full — of your

glo - ry. Ho - san - na, ho - san - na, ho - san - na in the

high-est; Ho-san - na, ho - san - na, ho - san - na in the

high - est. Blest is he who comes, blest is

Choir: (Blest is he who comes...

he who comes in the name of the Lord. *in the name of the Lord.)*
is he who comes

Ho-san - na, ho - san - na, ho - san - na in the high-est; Ho-

san - na, ho - san - na, ho - san - na in the high-est.

Memorial Acclamation A (outside Lent)

575

Christ has died, al - le - lu - ia; Christ is ris'n, al - le -

lu - ia, Christ will come a-gain — in — glo-ry! *(Choir: Alleluia!)*

Repeat Hosannas
as above.

Memorial Acclamation C

576

When we eat this li- ving bread, when we drink this sa- ving cup, we proclaim your death, Lord Je- sus Christ, un - til you come__ in__ glo - ry.

Repeat Hosannas as above.

Amen

577

A - men, a - men, a - men!

German Mass

*(Franz Schubert, 1797-1828,
arranged by Richard Proulx)*

578

mp Slowly

Ho-ly, ho-ly, ho- ly Lord, God of pow'r and might.__

Ho - ly, ho - ly, ho - ly Lord, God of pow'r and might.__ *mf*

f

Heav - en and earth are full,__ full__ of your glo - ry. Ho-

san - na in the high - est, ho - san - na in the high - est.

f *mf*

Bless - ed is he who comes__ in the name of the Lord.__ Ho-

dim.

san - na in the high - est, ho - san - na in the high - est.

Memorial Acclamation A

579

Christ has died, Christ is ris-en, Christ will come a - gain.

Christ has died, Christ is ris-en, Christ will come a - gain.

Amen

mp

580

A - men, A - men, A - men, A - men, A - men.

Annunciation Mass

Nigel Kerry

581

Ho - ly, ho - ly, ho - ly Lord,

God of power and God of might, ho - ly, ho - ly Lord.

Verses

D.C.

Heaven and earth are full of your glo - ry. Ho-san-na in the high est.
Blessed is He who comes in the name of the Lord. Ho-san-na in the high est.

582 **Memorial Acclamation A**

Christ has died, Christ is ri - sen, Christ will come a - gain.

583 **Amen**

A - men, a - men, a - men.

Eucharistic Acclamations

John Lillis

584

Cantor sings first (words in italics) and All repeat.

Ho - ly, ho - ly,_ ho - ly, Ho - ly, ho - ly,_ ho - ly,

God of po-wer and might! God of po-wer and might! *Your glo - ry fills all_*

hea - ven and earth. Your glo - ry fills all_ hea - ven and earth.

Ho - san - na in_ the high-est. Ho - san - na in_ the high-est.

Bles - sed is he who comes in the name of the Lord.

Ho - san - na in_ the high-est. Ho - san - na in_ the high-est.

Memorial Acclamation A & Doxology

Repeat each phrase after the Cantor

585

Christ has died! Christ is ri-sen! Christ will come a- gain!
A - men! A - men. A - men!

St Anne's Mass

586

Ho - ly, ho - ly, ho - ly_ Lord, God of_ power_ and_

might._ Heav'n and earth are_ full of your glo - ry. Ho - san - na

(musical notation)

in— the— high - est. Bles-sed is he, O bles-sed is— he who—

comes in the name— of the Lord.——— Ho - san - na in the—

high - est, ho - san - na in— the high - est.

Mass of St Anne by James MacMillan © 1997 Boosey & Hawkes Ltd. Used by permission

---

The Lord's Prayer

587

(musical notation)

Our Fa-ther, who art in heav'n, hallowed be thy name, thy kingdom come, thy

will be done, on earth as it is in heav'n. Give us this day our dai-ly bread,

and forgive us our trespasses, as we for-give those who tres-pass a-gainst us;

and lead us not in-to temp-ta-tion, but de-li-ver us from e-vil.

At Mass, the Priest continues: Deliver us O Lord from every evil...

... as we wait in joyful hope
for the coming of our Saviour, Jesus Christ

(musical notation)

For the king-dom, the power, and the glo-ry are yours, now and for e-ver.

Russian Our Father: Nicolai Rimsky-Korsakov (1844 -1908)

588

Our Fa-ther, who art in hea-ven, hallowed be thy name, thy

king-dom come, thy will be done, on earth as it is in hea-ven. Give

us this day our dai-ly bread, and for-give us our tres-pas-ses, as

we for-give those who tres-pass a-gainst us; and

lead us not— in-to temp-ta-tion, but de-li-ver us from e-vil.

At Mass, the priest continues with the prayer, which concludes:

for the coming of our Saviour, Je-sus Christ. For the king-dom, the

pow-er, and the glo-ry are yours, now and for e - ver.

Celtic Mass Our Father: Christopher Walker

Prayer and Doxology after the Our Father

589

Priest

......we wait in joyful hope for the coming of our Sa-viour Je-sus Christ

For the king - dom, the power, and the glo-ry are yours, now and for e - ver.

From the Roman Missal

➤ *See also Pater noster (507)*

Lamb of God

590 1 Jesus, Lamb of God, bearer of our sin;
Jesus, Saviour:

REFRAIN

[Musical notation]

Hear our prayer, hear our prayer; through this bread and wine we share, may we be your sign of peace ev'-ry-where.

2 Jesus, Lamb of God, bearer of our pain;
Jesus, healer:

3 Jesus, Lamb of God, broken as our bread,
here among us:

4 Jesus, Lamb of God, poured our as our wine,
shared in gladness:

other verses may be sung.

Jesus, Lamb of God: Bernadette Farrell

591

[Musical notation]

O Lamb of God, O Lamb that was slain, O Lamb of God, have mer - cy on us, O Lamb of God, O Lamb that was slain, O Lamb of God, grant— us your peace.

Jacques Berthier, arr. Martin Foster

592

first & last time

[Musical notation]

1,3 O Lamb of God, you take a-way the sins of the world: Have
        3. *world*

Fine

mer - cy, have mer - cy u - pon— us. 2. O Lamb of God, you
Grant us peace, grant us peace, Lord, grant us peace.

D.C.

take a-way the sins of the world: Have mer - cy, have mer-cy u - pon— us.

Mass of Hope: Stephen Dean

593

Litany for the Breaking of Bread: Paul Inwood

Hear our prayer, have mer-cy; hear our prayer, have mer-cy, give us your peace.

GENERAL

1 Jesus, Lamb of God and source of life,
  Jesus, loving bearer of our sins:
2 Jesus, Son of God and Son of Man;
  Jesus, true redeemer of the world:
*3 Jesus, Christ, our Way, our Truth, our Life:
  Jesus Christ, our living Cornerstone:
4 Jesus, Lord of life and Lord of light:
  Jesus, here in form of bread and wine:

ADVENT

5=1
6 Jesus, coming near to bring us joy:
  Jesus, Son of God, Emmanuel:
7 Jesus, bringing hope to all who fear:
  Jesus, bringing strength to all who mourn:
*8 Jesus, Saviour heralded by John:
  Jesus, son of David's house and line:
*9=4

CHRISTMAS

10 Jesus, Lamb of God, the Word made flesh:
  Jesus, Son of God come down on earth:
11 Jesus, King of glory, Prince of Peace:
  Jesus, shining in our darkened world:
12 Jesus, King of angels, Lord of joy:
  Jesus, born to save the world from sin:
12=4

LENT

14 Jesus, source of everlasting life:
  Jesus, source of reconciling love:

15 Jesus, by whose suffering we are healed:
  Jesus, man of sorrows, friend of grief:
16 Jesus, crucified, transcending time:
  Jesus, Saviour, by whose death we live:

EUCHARISTIC *(Maundy Thursday, Corpus Christi)*

17 Jesus, Lamb of God and bread of life:
  Jesus, blood that cleanses us from sin:
18 Jesus, showing how we ought to serve:
  Jesus, teaching how we ought to love:
*19 Jesus Christ, our true, eternal priest:
  Jesus, food and drink that makes us one:
20=4

EASTER

21 Jesus, risen Lord, triumphant King:
  Jesus, true redeemer of the world:
22 Jesus, Morning Star which never sets:
  Jesus, Paschal Lamb and sacrifice:
23 Jesus, bursting from the shattered tomb:
  Jesus, mighty Victor over death:
24=4

PENTECOST *(Spirit, healing)*

25 Jesus, glorious brightness, flame of love:
  Jesus, filling hearts and minds with life:
26 Jesus, healing strength, redeeming power:
  Jesus, burning out the mark of sin:
27 Jesus, by whose truth we are inspired:
  Jesus, present here among us now:
28=4

594

Communion song 4: Paul Inwood

Cantor; All repeat

Je - sus, Lamb of God, have mer - cy on us.
Je - sus, Bread of Life, have mer - cy on us.
Je - sus, Lamb of God, have mer - cy on us.

Cantor
Je - sus, Word made flesh, bea - rer of our sins:
Je - sus, Mor - ning Star, Je - sus, Prince of Peace:
Je - sus, King of kings; Je - sus, Lord of all:

All
Je - sus, Lamb of God, have mer - cy on us.
Je - sus, Bread of Life, have mer - cy on us
Je - sus, Lamb of God,_____ give us your peace.

595

Cantor
O Lamb of___ God, All you take a - way the
O bread of___ life...
O Son of___ God...

other verses may be added. Last time begins O Lamb of God...

sins of the world: have mer - cy, have mer - cy on us.
Last time: grant us,___ grant_ us_ peace.

Mass of Thanksgiving: Stephen Dean

596

Cantor:

Lamb of God, you take a - way the sins of the
Bread of life...

All:

world; have mer - cy on us, mer - cy on us, give us your peace.

Communion Song: Martin Foster

597

Mi - se - re - re no - bis, Do - na no - bis pa - cem.

John Schiavone

598

Be - hold the Lamb of God, be - hold the Lamb_ of God. He

takes a - way the sin, the sin_____ of the world.

John L. Bell

Preparation of Gifts

599

Refrain

The Lord is now a-bout to en-ter his Tem-ple, he who is and who was, and is to come. 'God— a-mong us' comes to make his dwel-ling.

1 The Word that brings peace is now proclaimed,
   the salvation that was promised is now in our midst.
   May all strife and hate be banished from our hearts,
   may the love of Christ our Lord dwell in them!

2 All you servants of the Lord, give praise to the Lord!
   with the heavenly hosts, sing his glory and his holiness.
   All you faithful, gathered round the altar of the Holy King,
   come, worship Christ among us, with all the saints of heaven.

3 We look up to you, Christ, and we implore you,
   remember not our sins, in your love, Lord, have mercy!
   With the angels we bless you,
   with all the saints, we give you glory!

After the Armenian Liturgy, by André Gouzes, O.P. Translated by Jean Clément

600

1 All that I am, all that I do,
   all that I'll ever have, I offer now to you.
   Take and sanctify these gifts
   for your honour, Lord.
   Knowing that I love and serve you
   is enough reward.
   All that I am, all that I do,
   all that I'll ever have I offer now to you.

2 All that I dream, all that I pray,
   all that I'll ever make, I give to you today.
   Take and sanctify these gifts
   for your honour, Lord.
   Knowing that I love and serve you
   is enough reward.
   All that I am, all that I do,
   all that I'll ever have I offer now to you.

Sebastian Temple (1928-97)

601

1 Praise to the Lord, the Almighty,
   the King of creation;
   O my soul, praise him,
      for he is your health and salvation:
   All you who hear, now to his altar draw
      near,
   join in profound adoration.

2 Praise to the Lord, let us offer
      our gifts at his altar;
   let not our sins and transgressions
      now cause us to falter.
   Christ, the High Priest,
      bids us all join in his feast.
   Gathered with him at the altar.

3 Praise to the Lord! O let all that
      is in us adore him!
   All that has life and breath,
      come now in praises before him!
   Let the Amen sound from
      his people again:
   now as we worship before him.
   Joachim Neander (1650–80), Vv 1,3 tr.
   C. Winkworth (1827–78), v.2 unknown
   ➤ *See also no 706*

602

1 Almighty Father, Lord most high,
   who madest all, who fillest all,
   thy name we praise and magnify,
   for all our needs on thee we call.

2 We offer to thee of thine own,
   ourselves and all that we can bring,
   in bread and cup before thee shown,
   our universal offering.

3 All that we have we bring to thee,
   yet all is naught when all is done,
   save that in it thy love can see
   the sacrifice of thy dear Son.

4 By this command in bread and cup,
   his body and his blood we plead;
   what on the cross he offer'd up
   is here our sacrifice indeed.

5 For all thy gifts of life and grace,
   here we thy servants humbly pray
   that thou would'st look upon the face
   of thine anointed Son today.
   V.S.S. Coles (1845–1929)

603

1 Blest are you, Lord, God of all creation,
   thanks to your goodness this bread we
      offer:
   fruit of the earth, work of our hands,
   it will become the bread of life.
   Blessed be God! Blessed be God!
   Blessed be God forever! Amen!
   Blessed be God! Blessed be God!
   Blessed be God forever! Amen!

2 Blest are you, Lord, God of all creation,
   thanks to your goodness this wine we
      offer:
   fruit of the earth, work of our hands,
   it will become the cup of life.
   Aniceto Nazareth

604

1 Lord accept the gifts we offer
   at this Eucharistic feast;
   bread and wine to be transformed now
   through the action of thy priest.
   Take us too, Lord, and transform us,
   be thy grace in us increased.

2 May our souls be pure and spotless
   as the host of wheat so fine;
   may all stain of sin be crushed out,
   like the grape that forms the wine,
   as we, too, become partakers
   in this sacrifice divine.

3 Take our gifts, almighty Father,
   living God, eternal, true,
   which we give through Christ, our Saviour,
   pleading here for us anew.
   Grant salvation to all present,
   and our faith and love renew.
   Sister M. Teresine Fonder, O.S.F.

605

1 O King of might and splendour,
   creator most adored,
   this sacrifice we render
   to thee as sovereign Lord.
   May these our gifts be pleasing
   unto thy majesty,
   from sin, O Lord, release us,
   who have offended thee.

2 Thy body thou hast given,
   thy blood thou hast outpoured,
   that sin might be forgiven,
   O Jesus, loving Lord.
   As now with love most tender,
   thy death we celebrate,
   our lives in self–surrender
   to thee we consecrate.

German 19th C., tr A. G. Murray, O.S.B (1905–1992)

606

1 Upon thy table, Lord we place
   these symbols of our work and thine,
   life's food won only by thy grace,
   who giv'st to all the bread and wine.

2 Within these simple things there lie
   the height and depth of human life,
   the thoughts we own, our tears and toil,
   our hopes and fears, our joy and strife.

3 Accept them, Lord; from thee they come;
   we take them humbly at thy hand.
   These gifts of thine for higher use
   we offer, as thou dost command.

4* All life is thine: O give us faith
   to know thee in the broken bread,
   and drink with thee the wine of life,
   Thou Lord supreme of quick and dead.

5 To thee we come; refresh thou us
   with food from thy most holy board,
   until the kingdoms of this world
   become the kingdom of the Lord.
   M.F.C. Willson (1884–1944)
   * Vv 4-5 not found in all editions.

607

1 Let all mortal flesh keep silence,
   and with fear and trembling stand;
   ponder nothing earthly minded:
   for with blessing in his hand
   Christ our God to earth descendeth,
   our full homage to demand.

2 King of kings, yet born of Mary,
   as of old on earth he stood
   Lord of lords, in human vesture –
   in the Body and the Blood:
   he will give to all the faithful
   his own self for heavenly Food.

3 Rank on rank the host of heaven
   spreads its vanguard on the way,
   as the Light of Light descendeth
   from the realms of endless day,
   that the powers of hell may vanish
   as the darkness clears away.

4 At his feet the six–winged seraph;
   cherubim with sleepless eye
   veil their faces to the Presence,
   as with ceaseless voice they cry,
   Alleluia, alleluia,
   alleluia, Lord most high!
   Liturgy of St. James, tr. G. Moultrie (1829–85)

608

1 Take my hands and make them as your own,
   and use them for your kingdom here on
         earth.
   Consecrate them to your care,
   anoint them for your service where
   you may need your gospel to be sown.

2 Take my hands, they speak now for my
         heart,
   and by their actions they will show their love.
   Guard them on their daily course,
   be their strength and guiding force
   to ever serve the Trinity above.

3 Take my hands, I give them to you, Lord.
   Prepare them for the service of your name.
   Open them to human need
   and by their love they'll sow your seed
   so all may know the love and hope you gave.
   Take my hands, take my hands, O Lord.
   Sebastian Temple (1928-1997)

609

1 In bread we bring you, Lord, our bodies' labour.
In wine we offer you our spirits' grief.
We do not ask you, Lord, who is my neighbour?
But stand united now, one in belief.
Oh, we have gladly heard your Word, your holy Word,
and now in answer, Lord, our gifts we bring.
Our selfish hearts make true, our failing faith renew,
our lives belong to you, our Lord and King.

2 The bread we offer you is blessed and broken,
and it becomes for us our spirits' food.
Over the cup we bring your Word is spoken;
make it your gift to us your healing blood.
Take all that daily toil plants in our heart's poor soil
take all we start and spoil, each hopeful dream,
the chances we have missed, the graces we resist,
Lord, in thy Eucharist, take and redeem.
Kevin Nichols

610

Take our bread, we ask you,
take our hearts, we love you,
take our lives, oh Father,
we are yours, we are yours.

1 Yours as we stand at the table you set,
yours as we eat the bread our hearts can't forget.
We are the signs of your life with us yet;
we are yours, we are yours.

2 Your holy people stand washed in your blood,
Spirit filled, yet hungry, we await your food.
Poor though we are, we have brought ourselves to you:
we are yours, we are yours.
Joe Wise

611

Cantor or choir:

1,5 Blest are you who made the u-ni-verse, you who see be-yond our death. Blest are you who dwells in each of us. Blest be you with ev-'ry breath,

All:

Blest be you with ev-'ry breath.

Marty Haugen

2 Through your goodness we have bread to eat,
seeds that died to bring life new.
As the sep'rate grains become one loaf,
gather us as one in you. (2)

3 Through your goodness we have wine to drink,
fruit of vineyard, work of hands.
Let the fruits of all we celebrate
spread your love to ev'ry land. (2)

4 Here the stranger is a welcome guest
Here all hungers shall be fed.
Come, and know the one who brings you life
in the breaking of the bread. (2)

612

Solo or S, A: All:

1. Ho, ev-'ry-one who   thirsts:
   and ev-'ry-one who   la-bours:
2. Ho, ev-'ry-one who   seeks:
   and ev-'ry-one who   mourns:
3. Let all who seek their God: Come to the wa-ters!
   the ev-er-last-ing   stream:
4. And you who are en - slaved:
   To all who live in   fear:
5. And all who are op - pressed:
   and you, the lost and bro - ken:

Solo or S, A: All:

here   is   an   end   to   hun - ger:
all   you who have   no   mon - ey:
hear   me   and   share the   rich - es:
now   is   an   end   to   sad - ness:

heed   now the One   who calls you: Come to the feast!
drink   deep the Cup   that saves you:
this   is   the feast of   free - dom:
join   in   the feast with cour - age:
this   is   the feast of   jus - tice:
this   is   the feast of   heal - ing:

All: Solo or S, A: All:

For this is life: 1. the   wa - ters of the Jor - dan: For this is life:
                  2. the streams of joy and glad-ness:
                  3. the floods that o - ver - whelm you:
                  4. the   wa - ters that have freed you:
                  5. to   die and rise in Je - sus:

Solo or S, A: All: Solo or S, A:

the wa - ters of   your birth: For this is life: the wa - ters that re-new you:
the rains that bring you joy: the wa - ters that re-store you:
the streams of death and life: the wa - ters that sus-tain you:
the sav - ing stream of God: to share a - round the ta - ble:
to share the life of Christ: the bread and wine of jus - tice:

                              All: D.C.

O come to the feast! O come to the feast!

Marty Haugen (based on Isaiah 55)

Communion Processional Songs

613

Ho-ly gifts for ho-ly peo-ple, come, you hun-gry, and be-lieve;

Come and take Christ's bo-dy off-ered, come and be what you receive.

1 This is what we have been told:
that on the night before he died,
after thanksgiving spoken,
bread blest and broken,
Christ sealed his love with his body
and blood.

2 This is what we understand:
that when we eat and drink this feast,
in this bread which we are breaking,
Christ we are partaking,
Christ's death proclaiming until his
return.

3 This is how we are to live:
that being joined by Christ's gifts,
we should be Christ to others,
sisters and brothers,
holding them precious, as saved by
his love.

4 Christ, our way, our truth and life:
we are not worthy to draw near:
but take our praise and thanksgiving,
transform our living,
give us that food which is healing and
strength.

Stephen Dean

614

See this bread; take and eat and live in me.

Fine

See this cup; take and drink, re - mem - ber me.__

1 I am the living bread, come down from
heaven.
All who eat my flesh and drink my blood
will live, will live for ever.

2 I am the living bread: you shall not
hunger.
If you believe in me you shall not thirst,
but live, but live for ever.

3 I am the living bread risen among you.
If you believe in me, though you die,
you will live,
you will live for ever.

4 You are the living bread, life for the world.
O Lord, to whom shall we go?
Your words, they live for ever.

David Haas

615

Hap-py are those who are in - vi - ted to the feast of the

King-dom of hea-ven.

Cantors sing the Beatitudes (Mt 5:3-12)
Music: Russian chant

616

Come, Christ's be-lo-ved, feed____ on Christ's true flesh,____
Drink your re-demp-tion____ in his pre-cious blood.

1 Here is salvation, here, the risen Lord,
  here God's great banquet: let us thank
     our God.

2 Christ, in this myst'ry gives his flesh
     and blood,
  guiding us safely through death's gates
     to life.

3 Son of the Father, Lord of all the world,
  Christ is our Saviour thro' his Cross
     and blood.

4 Christ, priest and victim, gave himself
     for all,
  at once the giver and his gift divine.

5 Priests of the old law, off'ring blood
     outpoured,
  did but foreshadow Christ, the victim
     priest.

6 Christ, our salvation, Christ the light
     of all,
  has yet enriched us by this gift sublime.

7 Bring to his banquet faithful hearts
     sincere,
  take now the safeguard of eternal life.

From the Antiphonary of Bangor (7th Cent.)
tr. based on J.M. Neale (1818-66)
Music by James Walsh

617

Taste and see, taste and see that the Lord is good, the Lord is good.

1 I will bless the Lord at all times,
  his praise always on my lips.
  The Lord shall be the glory of my soul;
  the humble shall hear and be glad.

2 Glorify the Lord with me,
  together let us praise his name.
  I sought the Lord: he answered me;
  he set me free from all my fear.

3 Look upon the Lord and be radiant,
  hide not your face from the Lord.
  He heard the cry of the poor;
  he rescued them from all their woes.

4 The angel of the Lord is with his people
  to rescue those who trust in him.

Taste and see the goodness of the Lord;
seek refuge in him and be glad.

5 Saints of the Lord, revere him;
  those who fear him lack nothing.
  Lions suffer want and go hungry,
  but those who seek him lack no blessing.

6 Children of the Lord, come and hear,
  and learn the fear of the Lord.
  Who is he who longs for life,
  whose only love is for his wealth?

7 Keep evil words from your tongue,
  your lips from speaking deceit.
  Turn aside from evil and do good;
  seek and strive after peace.

Psalm 34, versified by Stephen Dean

618

Taste and see, taste and see the good-ness of the Lord.___ O taste and see, taste and see the good-ness of the Lord,___ of the Lord.

1. I will bless the Lord at all times.
   Praise shall always be on my lips.
   my soul shall glory in the Lord
   for God has been so good to me.

2. Glorify the Lord with me.
   Together let us all praise God's name.

   I called the Lord who answered me;
   from all my troubles I was set free.

3. Worship the Lord, all you people.
   You'll want for nothing if you ask.
   Taste and see that the Lord is good;
   in God we need put all our trust.

   Psalm 34, versified by James Moore

619

Stephen Dean, from Ps 116

How can I re-pay the Lord for all the good-ness he shows to me?

620

Lord, how can I re-pay all you e-ver give to me? your end-less love an e-ter-nal flame: Lord, if you say the word, I will take your bles-sing cup and I will call on your ho-ly name.

Last time repeat 'and I will call on your holy name.'

1. I trusted, went on trusting
   through the night of pain;
   in my anguish and affliction
   human help was vain.

2. In the service of your people
   I will spend my days,
   giving freely of my lifeblood
   as I walk your ways.

3. You unbound me, gave me freedom:
   you I gladly serve.
   In thanksgiving I will offer
   praise without reserve.

4. In the service of your people
   I will spend my days,
   in your temple, in your Church, Lord,
   singing endless praise.
   John Glynn, from Psalm 116

Another setting of Ps 116: Our blessing cup (55)

621

We hold the death of the Lord deep in our hearts.

Li-ving, now we re-main with Je-sus, the Christ.

1. Once we were peo-ple a-fraid, lost in the night.
2. Some-thing which we have known, some-thing we've touched,
3. He chose to give of him-self, be-came our bread.
4. We are the pre-sence of God; this is our call.

Then by your cross we were saved; dead be-came li-ving, life from your
what we have seen with our eyes: this we have heard; life-gi-ving
Bro-ken that we might live. Love be-yond love, pain for our
Now to be-come bread and wine: food for the hun-gry, life for the

1-3 to R. | *V.4*

giving.
Word.
pain.
wea ry, for to live with the Lord, we must die with the Lord.

David Haas

622

Refrain   Sung twice   *Rob Glover*

We know and be-lieve in God's love for us. Make us one in

love and peace.

1 Nourish us well with this bread of the
   kingdom,
   the gift of yourself so freely given.
   To make us all one you call us to the table,
   to eat and drink of your flesh and blood.

2 Happy are we who eat at your table.
   Happy are we who drink of this cup.
   Your blood once shed, your body once
   broken,
   now call us to rise again daily with you.

3 God's love we embrace in each brother
   and sister.
   The signs of your presence are
   constantly new.
   Though many we are, we become one
   in Jesus,
   one body one bread, we are sign of you.

4 Neither Jew nor Greek, male nor female,
   we are all one in your presence, O Lord.
   All fighting and discord will melt in
   your mercy.
   We are one in your Spirit and one in
   your peace.

623

Marty Haugen

Now in this banquet, Christ is our bread; here shall all hun-gers be fed.

Advent *God of our jour-neys, daybreak to night; Lead us to jus-tice and light.*

Lent *Lord, you can o-pen hearts that are stone; live in our flesh and our bone.*

Bread that is bro-ken, wine that is poured, Love is the sign of our Lord.

Grant us com-pas-sion, strength for the day, Wis-dom to walk in your way.

Lead us to won-der, mys-t'ry and grace, one in your lo-ving em-brace.

1 You who have touched us and graced us
  with love,
  make us your people of goodness and light.

2 Let our hearts burn with the fire of your love;
  open our eyes to the glory of God.

3 God who makes the blind to see,
  God who makes the lame to walk,
  bring us dancing into day,
  lead your people in your way.

4 Hope for the hopeless, light for the blind,
  'Strong' is your name, Lord, 'Gentle'
  and 'Kind'.

5 Call us to be your light,
  call us to be your love,
  make us your people again.

5 Come, O Spirit! Renew our hearts!
  We shall arise to be children of light.

See no 80 (for Advent) and 192 (for Lent)

624

REFRAIN

Verses

In___ the brea-king___ of___ the bread___

1. Bread for the jour-ney,___ ⸭ strength for our years,___
2. Bread of the pro-mise,___ ⸭ peo-ple of hope,___

we___ have known___ him; we have been fed.___

man-na of a-ges of strug-gle and tears.___

wine of com-pas-sion, life for the world.___

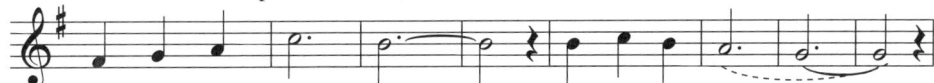

Je-sus the stran-ger,___ Je-sus the Lord,___

Cup of sal-va-tion,___ fruit of the land,___

Ga-thered at ta-ble,___ joined as his bo-dy,___

be our com-pa-nion; — be___ our hope.___

bless and re-ceive now___ the work of our hands.___ *(to refrain)*

sealed in the Spi-rit,___ sent by the Word.___ *(to refrain)*

Bob Hurd

625

Bread for the world: a world of hun-ger, wine for all peo-ples: peo-ple who thirst. May we who eat be bread for oth-ers. May we who drink pour out our love.— *Fine*

1 Lord Jesus Christ, you are the
   bread of life,
  broken to reach and heal the wounds
   of human pain.
  Where we divide your people you are
   waiting there
  on bended knee to wash our feet
   with endless care.

2 Lord Jesus Christ, you are the wine of
   peace,
  poured into hearts once broken and
   where dryness sleeps.

Where we are tired and weary you are
 waiting there
to be the way which beckons us
 beyond despair.

3 Lord Jesus Christ, you call us to your feast,
  at which the rich and pow'rful have
   become the least.
  Where we survive on others in our
   human greed
  you walk among us begging for your
   ev'ry need.
    Bernadette Farrell

626

Stephen Dean

One bread we break in the love of Christ, one cup we share in the life of Christ; one faith we hold, one Lord we serve, one Spi-rit ga-thers us here.

1 Many the grains but one the bread;
  many the grapes but one the wine;
  many the gifts, but one same Lord;
  many the parts, but all are joined
  in Jesus Christ, who makes us One.

2 We who were scattered on the hills;
  we who were shaken by the wind;
  we who were wandering and lost
  we who were separate and alone
  in Jesus Christ are all made One.

3 No longer slaves, we are set free;
  no longer lost, we are redeemed;
  no longer servants, we are friends
  no longer we that live our life
  but Jesus Christ, who lives in us.

4 Open our eyes to see your light;
  open our ears to hear your word;
  open our lips to sing your praise;
  open our hearts to find the love
  of Jesus Christ, who makes us One.

627

1 This is my body, broken for you,
bringing you wholeness, making
    you free.
Take it and eat it, and when you do,
do it in love for me.

2 This is my blood poured out for you,
bringing forgiveness, making you free.
Take it and drink it, and when you do,
do it in love for me.

3 Back to my Father soon I shall go.
Do not forget me; then you will see
I am still with you, and you will know
you're very close to me.

4 Filled with my Spirit, how you will grow!
You are my branches; I am the tree.
If you are faithful, others will know
you are alive in me.

5 Love one another – I have loved you,
and I have shown you how to be free;
serve one another, and when you do,
do it in love for me.
Verses 1 and 2 Jimmy Owens;
verses 3–5 Damian Lundy

628

1 Draw nigh, and take the body of our Lord;
and drink the holy blood for you
    outpoured;
saved by that body, hallowed by that
    blood,
whereby refreshed we render thanks to
    God.

2 Salvation's giver, Christ the only Son,
who by his cross and blood the victory
    won,
gave his own life for greatest and for least;
himself the Victim, and himself the Priest.

3 Victims were offered by the law of old,
that, in a type, celestial mysteries told.
He, ransomer from death
    and light from shade,
bestows his holy grace his saints to aid.

4 Approach ye then with faithful hearts
    sincere,
and take the safeguard of salvation here,
he that in this world rules his saints and
    shields,
to all believers life eternal yields.

5 With heav'nly bread he makes the
    hungry whole
gives living waters to the thirsty soul,
Alpha and Omega, to whom shall bow
all nations at the doom, is with us now.
From the Antiphonary of Bangor (7th
century) tr. J. M. Neale (1818–66), alt.

629

1 I am the Bread of life.
You who come to me shall not hunger;
and who believe in me shall not thirst.
No–one can come to me
unless the Father draw him.
And I will raise you up,
and I will raise you up,
and I will raise you up on the last day.

2 The bread that I will give
is my flesh for the life of the world,
and if you eat of this bread,
you shall live for ever,
you shall live for ever.

3 Unless you eat of the flesh of the
    Son of Man,
and drink of his blood,
and drink of his blood,
you shall not have life within you.

4 I am the Resurrection, I am the Life.
If you believe in me,
even though you die,
you shall live for ever.

5 Yes, Lord, I believe,
that you are the Christ,
the Son of God,
who have come into the world.
Suzanne Toolan, RSM

630

1. We come as guests in-vi-ted when Je-sus bids us dine, his friends on earth u-ni-ted to share the bread and wine; the bread of life is bro-ken, the wine is free-ly poured for us, in sol-emn to-ken of Christ our dy-ing Lord.

2 We eat and drink, receiving
from Christ the grace we need,
and in our hearts believing
on him by faith we feed;
with wonder and thanksgiving
for love that knows no end,
we find in Jesus living
our ever-present friend.

3 One bread is ours for sharing,
one single fruitful vine,
our fellowship declaring
renewed in bread and wine –
renewed, sustained and given
by token, sign and word,
the pledge and seal of heaven,
the love of Christ our Lord.

Timothy Dudley-Smith. Music by James Walsh

631

Joanne Boyce & Mike Stanley

Bread of Life, Truth e-ter-nal,___ bro-ken now to set us___ free,_ the ri-sen Christ, his sa-ving power,___ is here in bread___ and wine___ for me.___

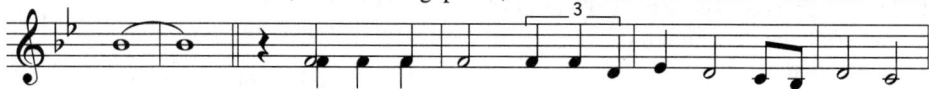

1. Lord,___ I know I am not wor-thy to re-ceive you.
2. Lord, by your cross you re-con-ciled us to the Fa-ther,
3. Lord,___ you gave your peo-ple man-na in the de-sert;

You speak the words and I am healed. Here at your ta-ble,
We have on-ly to be-lieve. Your sa-cri-fice,___
still you ful-fil our eve-ry need. Lord when we hun-ger,

love's my-ste-ry, one bread, one cup one fa-mi-ly.___ Bread of..
our vic-to-ry; now by your blood we are redeemed.___ Bread of..
Lord, when we thirst, we come to you and we re-ceive___ (the) bread of..

632

Refrain

Come to the feast___ of hea - ven and earth!
Come to the ta - ble of plen - ty! God will pro - vide___ for

Fine

all that we need, here at the ta - ble of plen - ty!___

Verses

1. O come and sit at my ta - ble___ where saints and
2. O come and eat with-out mo-ney;___ come to

sin - ners are friends.___ I wait to wel-come the lost and
drink with - out price.___ My feast of glad-ness will feed your

lone-ly to share the cup of my love.___
spi - rit with faith and full-ness of life.___

3 My bread will ever sustain you
  through days of sorrow and woe.
  My wine will flow like a sea of gladness
  to flood the depths of your soul.

4 Your fields will flower in fullness;
  your homes will flourish in peace.
  For I, the giver of home and harvest,
  will send my rain on the soil.

Daniel L. Schutte

Eat this bread

633

p Eat this bread, drink this cup, come to me and ne - ver be hun - gry.
(or) Je - sus Christ, bread of life, those who come to you will not hun - ger.

mf

Eat this bread, drink this cup, trust in me and you will not thirst.
Je - sus Christ, Ri - sen Lord, those who trust in you will not thirst.

Taizé chant by Jacques Berthier

634

Come and eat this bread, come and drink this cup, come and share the feast our God has spread. You have pro-mised us, you are here with us in the brea-king of the bread.

1 This is the bread of life, for all to share,
bread of hope and redemption,
bread to feed a world of hungers.

2 This is the cup of Christ's own sacrifice,
blood of love and compassion,
blood to heal the world's divisions.

3 Just as the scattered grains become one
bread,
make us one in your Spirit,
all one Body in Christ Jesus.

4 And as we share one cup of covenant
make us one in communion
at the table of Christ Jesus.

5 Each time we eat this bread and drink
this cup,
we remember your death, Lord
and we celebrate your rising.
Marty Haugen

See below for Post-communion version.

➤ *Other Communion songs: See Bread of life (78), O Christe Domine Jesu (757) and seasonal sections (Advent, Lent, Eastertide)*

Communion Thanksgiving

635

Praise the li - ving God, praise to Christ the Son, praise, O migh - ty Spi - rit, Ho - ly Breath. For our whole life through we shall sing to you God of life be - yond all death.

Now from this table to the ends of earth,
gather all of your people
in this feast of all creation.
Marty Haugen

This may be sung to conclude no 634 when communion has finished.

636

Refrain

I re-ceived the liv-ing God, and my heart is full of joy.—

I re-ceived the liv-ing God, and my heart is full of joy.

Verses

1. Je-sus said: 'I am the Bread knead-ed long to give you life;
2. Je-sus said: 'I am the Way, and my Fa-ther longs for you;

D.C.

You who will par-take of me need not ev-er fear to die.'
so I come to bring you home to be one with him a-new.'

3 Jesus said: I am the Truth;
   if you follow close to me,
   you will know me in your heart,
   and my word shall make you free.

4 Jesus said: I am the Life
   far from whom no thing can grow,
   but receive this living bread,
   and my Spirit you shall know.

Anonymous

637

Refrain

Seed, scat-tered and sown, wheat, gath-ered and grown, bread, bro-ken and

shared as one, the Liv-ing Bread of God. Vine, fruit of the land, wine, work of our

hands. One cup that is shared by all; the Li-ving Cup, the Li-ving Bread of God.

Verses

1. Is not the bread we break a sha-ring in our Lord?
2. The seed which falls on rock will wi-ther and will die.
3. As wheat u-pon the hills was gath-ered and was grown,

Is not the cup we bless the blood of Christ out-poured?
The seed wi-thin good ground will flo-wer and have life.
so may the church of God be gath-ered in-to one.

Dan Feiten

638

1 The time was early evening, the place a room upstairs;
the guests were the disciples, few in number and few in prayers.

REFRAIN

Oh the food comes from the baker, the drink comes from the vine, the
words come from the Saviour, 'I will meet you in bread and wine.'

2 The company of Jesus
had met to share a meal,
but he, who made them welcome,
had much more to reveal.

3 'The bread and body broken
the wine and blood outpoured,
the cross and kitchen table
are one by my sign and word'.

4 On both sides of the table,
on both sides of the grave,
the Lord joins those who love him
to serve them and to save.

5 Lord Jesus, now among us,
confirm our faith's intent,
as, with your words and actions,
we unite in this sacrament.

John Bell & Graham Maule

639

1. We have gathered round your table, laid with wine and living bread;
now we rise to praise the Giver from whose riches we are fed.

2 Who has laid this banquet for us?
Who has brought us to this feast?
Christ, who seeks out all who hunger,
from the greatest to the least.

3 Love's the lesson, Lord, you gave us,
love the teaching we must learn.
Gifts of love you spread before us,
love you ask us in return.

4 Greater love no one can offer,
more than life no-one can give;
In these symbols we remember:
Jesus died that we might live.

5 Rich ones in a world of hunger,
let us go and do the same:
giving up our lives for others,
feeding them in Jesus's name.

Stephen Dean

640

Plen-ty of *bread at the feast of life, plen-ty of *bread* to share;
plen-ty of *bread* at the feast of life, there is plen-ty of *bread* to share.

*sing 'bread', 'fish', 'wine' or 'room' according to previous verse

Verses

Cantor:
1. Bread for ev'-ry hun-ger: *All:* you have plen-ty to share. the bread of joy and
2. Bread for those who sor-row: and bread of life and
3. Bread for ev'-ry sis-ter: and bread for ev'-ry
4. Bread of hope and kind-ness: the bread of your com
5. Fish for those who hun-ger: and joy for all who
6. Wine of our re-mem brance: the wine of dreams and
7. Wine of our for-give-ness: the wine of our re

glad-ness: you have plen-ty to share. the bread of grace and mer-cy:
laugh-ter: the bread of strength and jus-tice:
bro-ther: and bread for free-dom's jour-ney:
pas-sion: the bread of love and wel-come:
sor-row: amd faith for un-be-lie-vers:
vi-sions: the wine of ce-le-bra-tion:
demp-tion: the wine of our to-mor-rows:

you have plen-ty to share, you have plen-ty of bread to share.

8 Room for those forgotten:
and room for those rejected:
and room for all the outcasts:

9 Room for all the children:
and room for all the elders:
and room for all the lonely:

10 Room for those who suffer:
and room for all the dying:
and room that sings for
new life:

Marty Haugen

641

Verses: cantor/choir

1. Come now, the ta-ble's spread, in Je-sus' name we
Come take this ho-ly food, re-ceive the bo-dy

All
break the bread, here shall we all be fed with-in the reign of God.
and the blood, grace is a migh-ty flood.

Refrain

Bles-sed are they who will feast in the Reign of God! Bles-sed are they who will share the bread of life! Bles-sed are they who are least in the Reign of God! They shall re - joice at the feast of life!

2 Stand up and do not fear,
   for Christ is truly present here.
   heaven is truly near *within the reign...*
   Now at this wedding feast,
   the greatest here shall be the least.
   All bonds shall be released *within the reign...*

3 Welcome the weak and poor,
   the sinner finds an open door,
   none judged, and none ignored *within...*
   Here shall the weary rest,
   the stranger be a welcome guest.
   So shall we all be blest *within the reign...*

4 All fear and hatred ends
   and foes become our faithful friends,
   just as our God intends *within the reign...*

All you who seek God's face
are welcome in this holy place;
join in the feast of grace: *within the reign..*

5 Sing out the jubilee
   when those enslaved are all set free,
   children of God are we *within the reign...*
   No more can we forget
   the ones who bear life's crushing debt;
   God's justice guides us yet *within the reig*

6 One earth, one holy band,
   one fam'ly as our God has planned,
   all share the promised land *within the reig*
   Come now, the feast is spread;
   in Jesus's name we break the bread.
   Here shall we all be fed *within the reign...*

Marty Haugen

642

1.Praise now your God, ev'ry tongue, ev'ry na - tion, tell the good news to the next ge-ne - ra - tion: Christ, the Re - dee - mer, who rose from the dead, stays with his peo - ple as life - gi - ving Bread.

Al - le - lu - ia, God is great! Al - le - lu - ia, God is good!

2 Christ gave his word at the multiplication.
   Bread and sweet wine are now Christ
       our oblation.
   Cross and Last Supper are with us today.
   Life now abounds, and God's will we obey.
   Alleluia, God is great!
   Alleluia, God is good!

3 Here is your Saviour, give deep adoration,
   sing of his glory in glad celebration.
   Come, for his manna is food for the road,
   strength for the journey, our glory
       foreshowed.

C.J. Marivoet

643

1 Gifts of bread and wine, gifts we've
      offered,
  fruits of labour, fruits of love:
  taken, offered, sanctified,
  blessed and broken; words of one who
      died:
  'Take my body; take my saving blood.'
  Gifts of bread and wine: Christ our Lord.

2 Christ our Saviour, living presence here,
  as he promised while on earth:
  'I am with you for all time,
  I am with you in this bread and wine.
  Take my body, take my saving blood.'
  Gifts of bread and wine: Christ our Lord.

3 Through the Father, with the Spirit,
  one in union with the Son,
  for God's people, joined in prayer
  faith is strengthened by the food we
      share.
  'Take my body, take my saving blood.'
  Gifts of bread and wine: Christ our
      Lord.
    Christine McCann

644

1 Alleluia, sing to Jesus,
  his the sceptre, his the throne,
  alleluia, his the triumph,
  his the victory alone:
  hark! the songs of peaceful Sion
  thunder like a mighty flood;
  Jesus, out of every nation,
  has redeemed us by his blood.

2 Alleluia, not as orphans
  are we left in sorrow now;
  alleluia, he is near us,
  faith believes, nor questions how;
  though the cloud from sight received him
  when the forty days were o'er,
  shall our hearts forget his promise,
  'I am with you evermore'?

3 Alleluia, Bread of Angels,
  thou on earth our food, our stay;
  alleluia, here the sinful
  flee to thee from day to day;
  intercessor, friend of sinners,
  earth's Redeemer, plead for me,
  where the songs of all the sinless
  sweep across the crystal sea.

4 Alleluia, King eternal
  thee the Lord of lords we own;
  alleluia, born of Mary,
  earth thy footstool, heaven thy throne;
  thou within the veil hast entered,
  robed in flesh, our great High Priest;
  thou on earth both priest and victim
  in the Eucharistic Feast.
    W. Chatterton Dix (1837–98)

645

1 Father, we give you thanks, who planted
  your holy name within our hearts.
  knowledge and faith and life immortal
  Jesus your Son to us imparts.
  Lord, you have made all for your pleasure,
  and giv'n us food for all our days,
  giving in Christ the Bread eternal,
  yours is the pow'r, be yours the praise.

2 Watch o'er your Church, O Lord, in mercy,
  save it from evil, guard it still,
  And in your love unite, perfect it,
  cleanse and conform it to your will.
  As grain, once scattered on the hillsides
  was in the broken bread made one,
  so from all lands your Church be gathered
  into your kingdom by your Son.
    F. Bland Tucker (1895-1984), alt.

646

1 Welcome all you noble saints of old,
  as now before your very eyes unfold
  the wonders all so long ago foretold.
  God with us at table is sat down.
  God with us at table is sat down.

2 Elders, martyrs, all are falling down,
   prophets, patriarchs are gath'ring round;
   what angels longed to see, now we
      have found.

3 Who is this who spreads the vict'ry feast?
   Who is this who makes our warring cease?
   Jesus risen, Saviour, Prince of Peace.

4 Beggars lame, and harlots also here;
   repentant publicans are drawing near;
   wayward sons come home without a fear.

5 Worship in the presence of the Lord
   with joyful songs, and hearts in one accord,
   and let our host at table be adored.

6 When at last this earth shall pass away,
   when Jesus and his bride are one to stay,
   the feast of love is just begun that day.
   Robert J. Stamp

647

1 Now let us from this table rise
   renewed in body, mind, and soul;
   with Christ we die and rise again,
   his selfless love has made us whole.

2 With minds alert, upheld by grace,
   to spread the Word in speech and deed,
   we follow in the steps of Christ,
   at one with us in hope and need.

3 To fill each human house with love,
   it is the sacrament of care;
   the work that Christ began to do
   we humbly pledge ourselves to share.

4 Then give us grace, Companion-God,
   to choose again the pilgrim way,
   and help us to accept with joy
   the challenge of tomorrow's day.
   Fred Kaan

648

1 See us, Lord, about thine altar;
   though so many, we are one;
   many souls by love united
   in the heart of Christ thy Son.

2 Hear our prayers, O loving Father,
   hear in them thy Son, our Lord;
   hear him speak our love and worship,
   as we sing with one accord.

3 Once were seen the blood and water;
   now he seems but bread and wine;
   then in human form he suffered,
   now his form is but a sign.

4 Wheat and grape contain the meaning;
   food and drink he is to all;
   one in him, we kneel adoring,
   gathered by his loving call.

5 Hear us yet; so much is needful
   in our frail, disorded life;
   stay with us and tend our weakness
   till that day of no more strife.

6 Members of his mystic body
   now we know our prayer is heard,
   heard by thee, because thy children
   have received th' eternal word.
   John Greally

649

1 I come with joy, a child of God,
   forgiven, loved and free,
   the life of Jesus to recall
   in love laid down for me.

2 I come with Christians far and near
   to find, as all are fed,
   the new community of love
   in Christ's communion bread.

3 As Christ breaks bread, and bids us share
   each proud division ends.
   The love that made us, makes us one,
   and strangers now are friends.

4 The Spirit of the risen Christ,
   unseen, but ever near,
   is in such friendship better known,
   alive among us here.

5 Together met, together bound
   by all that God has done,
   we'll go with joy, to give the world
   the love that makes us one.
   Brian Wren

650

1 The Son of God proclaim,
  the Lord of time and space;
  the God who bade the light break forth
  now shines in Jesus' face.

2 He, God's creative Word,
  the Church's Lord and head,
  here bids us gather as his friends
  and share his wine and bread.

3 Behold his outstretched hands;
  though all was in his power
  He took the towel and basin then,
  and serves us in this hour.

4 The Lord of life and death,
  with wond'ring praise we sing;
  we break the bread at his command
  and name him God and King.

5 We take this cup in hope;
  for he, who gladly bore
  the shameful cross, is ris'n again
  and reigns for evermore.
  Basil E. Bridge

651

1 My God, and is thy table spread,
  and does thy cup with love o'erflow?
  Thither be all thy children led,
  and let them all thy sweetness know.

2 Hail, sacred feast, which Jesus makes!
  Rich banquet of his flesh and blood!
  Thrice happy those, who here partake
  that sacred stream, that heavenly food.

3 O let thy table honoured be,
  and furnished well with joyful guests;
  and may each soul salvation see,
  that here its sacred pledges tastes.
  Philip Doddridge (1702–51)

Blessing and Dismissal

652

1 Go, the Mass is ended,
  children of the Lord.
  Take God's Word to others
  as you've heard it spoken to you.
  Go, the Mass is ended,
  go and tell the world
  the Lord is good, the Lord is kind,
  and loves us ev'ry one.

2 Go, the Mass is ended,
  take God's love to all.
  Gladden all who meet you,
  fill their hearts with hope and courage.
  Go, the Mass is ended,
  fill the world with love,
  and give to all what you've received
  – the peace and joy of Christ.

3 Go, the Mass is ended,
  strengthened in the Lord,
  lighten ev'ry burden,
  spread the joy of Christ around you.
  Go, the Mass is ended,
  take God's peace to all.
  This day is yours to change the world
  – to make God known and loved.
  Sister Marie Lydia Pereira

653

May God bless and keep *you*,* may God's face
shine on you: May God be kind to you and give you peace.

* '*Us*' may be substituted. *Numbers 6:22-23, music by Christopher Walker*

654

1 Glory to thee, Lord God!
In faith and hope we sing.
Through this completed sacrifice
our love and praise we bring.
We give thee for our sins
a price beyond all worth,
which none could ever fitly pay
but this thy Son on earth.

2 Here is the Lord of all,
to thee in glory slain;
of worthless givers, worthy gift
a victim without stain.

Through him we give thee thanks,
with him we bend the knee,
in him be all our life, who is
our one true way to thee.

3 So may this sacrifice
we offer here this day,
be joined with our poor lives in all
we think and do and say.
By living true to grace,
for thee and thee alone,
our sorrows, labours, and our joys
will be his very own.

John Greally

➤ *See also Sending out/Discipleship (852-879)*

Euchaelstic Adoeation

655

1 O salutaris hostia,
quae caeli pandis ostium,
bella premunt hostilia,
da robur, fer auxilium.

2 Uni trinoque Domino
sit sempiterna gloria,
qui vitam sine termino
nobis donet in patria. Amen.

St Thomas Aquinas (1227–74)

655a

1 O saving victim, opening wide,
the gate of heav'n to man below,
Our foes press on from ev'ry side:
thine aid supply, thy strength bestow.

2 To thy great name be endless praise,
Immortal Godhead, one in three;
O grant us endless length of days
in our true native land with thee. Amen.

Translation by J.M. Neale (1818–66),
E Caswall (1814–78), and others

656

1 Tantum ergo Sacramentum
veneremur cernui:
et antiquum documentum
novo cedat ritui:
praestet fides supplementum
sensuum defectui.

2 Genitori, genitoque
laus et jubilatio,
salus, honor, virtus quoque
sit et benedictio;
procedenti ab utroque
compar sit laudatio. Amen.

St Thomas Aquinas (1227–74)

657

1 Come, adore this wondrous presence,
bow to Christ, the source of grace.
Here is kept the ancient promise
of God's earthly dwelling–place.
Sight is blind before God's glory,
faith alone may see his face.

2 Glory be to God the Father,
praise to his co–equal Son,
adoration to the Spirit,
bond of love, in Godhead one.
Blest be God by all creation
joyously while ages run.

Translation by James Quinn, S.J.

658

1 O food of travellers, angels' bread,
manna wherewith the blest are fed,
come nigh, and with thy sweetness fill
the hungry hearts that seek thee still.

2 O fount of love, O well unpriced,
outpouring from the heart of Christ,
give us to drink of very thee,
and all we pray shall answered be.

3 O Jesus Christ, we pray to thee
that this presence which we see,
though now in form of bread concealed,
to us may be in heaven revealed.

Maintzisch Gesangbuch, 1661,
tr. Walter H. Shewring and others

659

1 Father and life–giver,
grace of Christ impart;
he, the Word incarnate –
food for mind and heart.
Children of the promise,
homage now we pay;
sacrificial banquet
cheers the desert way.

2 Wine and bread the symbols –
love and life convey,
offered by your people,
work and joy portray.
All we own consigning,
nothing is retained;
tokens of our service,
gifts and song contain.

3 Transformation wondrous
water into wine;
mingled in the Godhead
we are made divine.
Birth into his body
brought us life anew,
total consecration –
fruit from grafting true.

4 Christ, the head and members
living now as one,
offered to the Father
by this holy Son;
and our adoration
will be purified,
by the Holy Spirit breathing
through our lives.

A.J. Newman (adapted)

660

1 Godhead here in hiding, whom I do
adore,
masked by these bare shadows, shape
and nothing more,
see, Lord, at thy service low lies here a
heart
lost, all lost in wonder at the God thou art.

2 Seeing, touching, tasting are in thee
deceived;
how says trusty hearing? That shall be
believed;
what God's Son hath told me, take for
truth I do;
truth himself speaks truly, or there's
nothing true.

3 On the cross thy Godhead made no sign
to men;
here thy very manhood steals from
human ken;
both are my confession, both are my
belief;
and I pray the prayer of the dying thief.

4 I am not like Thomas, wounds I cannot
see,
but can plainly call thee Lord and God
as he;
this faith each day deeper be my
holding of,
daily make me harder hope and dearer
love.

5 O thou our reminder of Christ crucified,
living Bread, the life of us for whom he
died,

lend this life to me then; feed and feast
    my mind,
there be thou the sweetness man was
    meant to find.

6 Jesu, whom I look at shrouded here
    below,
I beseech thee send me what I long for so,
some day to gaze on thee face to face in
    light
and be blest for ever with thy glory's sight.

Adoro te devote, ascr. to St. Thomas Aquinas
(1227–74), tr. G.M. Hopkins (1844–89)

661

1 O Godhead hid, devoutly I adore thee,
who truly art within the forms before me;
to thee my heart I bow with bended knee,
as failing quite in contemplating thee.

2 Sight, touch, and taste in thee are each
    deceived,
the ear alone most safely is believed:
I believe all the Son of God has spoken;
than truth's own word there is no truer
    token.

3 God only on the cross lay hid from view;
but here lies hid at once the manhood too:
and I, in both professing my belief,
make the same prayer as the repentant
    thief.

4 Thy wounds, as Thomas saw, I do not see;
yet thee confess my Lord and God to be;
make me believe thee ever more and more,
in thee my hope, in thee my love to store.

5 O thou memorial of our Lord's own
    dying!
O bread that living art and vivifying!
Make ever thou my soul on thee to live:
ever a taste of heavenly sweetness give.

6 Jesus, whom for the present veiled I see,
what I so thirst for, oh, vouchsafe to me:
that I may see thy countenance unfolding,
and may be blest thy glory in beholding.

Adoro te devote, ascr. to St. Thomas Aquinas
(1227–74) tr. E.Caswall (1814–78)

662

1 O bread of heaven, beneath this veil
thou dost my very God conceal;
my Jesus, dearest treasure, hail;
I love thee and adoring kneel;
each loving soul by thee is fed
with thine own self in form of bread.

2 O food of life, thou who dost give
the pledge of immortality;
I live; no, 'tis not I that live;
God gives me life, God lives in me:
he feeds my soul, he guides my ways,
and every grief with joy repays.

3 O bond of love, that dost unite
the servant to his living Lord;
could I dare live, and not requite
such love - then death were meet reward
I cannot live unless to prove
some love for such unmeasured love.

4 Belovèd Lord in heaven above,
there, Jesus, thou awaitest me;
to gaze on thee with changeless love,
yes, thus I hope, thus shall it be:
for how can he deny me heaven
who here on earth himself hath given?

St Alphonsus Liguori (1696–1787),
tr. Edmund Vaughan (1827–1908)

663

1 Sweet sacrament divine,
hid in thy earthly home,
lo! Round thy lowly shrine,
with suppliant hearts we come;
Jesus, to thee our voice we raise,
in songs of love and heartfelt praise,
sweet sacrament divine.

2 Sweet sacrament of peace,
dear home of every heart,
where restless yearnings cease,
and sorrows all depart,
there in thine ear all trustfully
we tell our tale of misery,
sweet sacrament of peace.

3　Sweet sacrament of rest,
　　Ark from the ocean's roar,
　　within thy shelter blest
　　soon may we reach the shore,
　　save us, for still the tempest raves;
　　save, lest we sink beneath the waves
　　sweet sacrament of rest.

4　Sweet sacrament divine,
　　earth's light and jubilee,
　　in thy far depths doth shine
　　thy Godhead's majesty;
　　sweet light, so shine on us, we pray,
　　that earthly joys may fade away,
　　sweet sacrament divine.
　　　　　Francis Stanfield (1835–1914)

664

1　O praise our great and gracious Lord
　　and call upon his name;
　　to strains of joy tune every chord,
　　his mighty acts proclaim;
　　tell how he led his chosen race
　　to Canaan's promised land;
　　tell how his covenant of grace
　　unchanged shall ever stand.

2　He gave the shadowing cloud by day,
　　the moving fire by night;
　　to guide his Israel on their way,
　　he made their darkness light;
　　and have not we a sure retreat,
　　a Saviour ever nigh,
　　the same clear light to guide our feet,
　　the dayspring from on high?

3　We, too, have manna from above,
　　the bread that came from heaven;
　　to us the same kind hand of love
　　hath living waters given.
　　A rock we have, from whence the spring
　　in rich abundance flows;
　　that rock is Christ, our priest, our king,
　　who life and health bestows.

4　O let us prize this blessèd food,
　　and trust our heavenly guide;
　　so shall we find death's fearful flood
　　serene as Jordan's tide,
　　and safely reach that happy shore,
　　the land of peace and rest,
　　where angels worship and adore,
　　in God's own presence blest.
　　　　　Harriet Auber (1773–1862)

665

1　Shepherd of souls, in love, come feed us
　　life–giving bread for hungry hearts!
　　To those refreshing waters lead us
　　where dwells that grace your peace
　　　　imparts.
　　May we, the wayward in your fold,
　　by your forgiveness rest consoled.

2　Life–giving vine, come, feed and nourish,
　　strengthen each branch with life divine.
　　Ever in you, O may we flourish,
　　fruitful the branches of the vine.
　　Lord, may our souls be purified
　　so that in Christ we may abide.

3　Following you, O Lord, who led them,
　　multitudes thronged the mountainside;
　　filled with compassion, Lord, you fed them,
　　fed them with loaves you multiplied.
　　Come, feed us now, O Lord, we pray:
　　life–giving bread give us this day.

4　Father, who fed the Hebrew nation,
　　giving them manna from the sky,
　　give now the bread of our salvation
　　that we who eat shall never die.
　　We are your people, God, in need;
　　may we on living bread now feed.

5　Help us, dear Lord, prepare a dwelling
　　worthy of you who made us all;
　　cleanse then our hearts, our guilt dispelling,
　　purify us who heed your call.
　　'Take this and eat' were words you said;
　　so do we gather for this bread.
　　　　　Omer Westendorf (1916-1997)

666

A - ve ve-rum cor-pus na-tum de Ma-ri - a Vir - gi-ne:___
Je - sus' Bo-dy, here we greet you, vir-gin-born of Da - vid's line,—

Ve - re pas-sum im-mo-la-tum in cru-ce pro ho - mi - ne:___
pas - chal vic-tim, giv'n to save us un - der forms of bread— and wine,—

Cu-jus la-tus per-fo-ra - tum flu-xit_____ a-qua_ et_ san-gui-
bo - dy bro-ken, life-blood flo - wing, wa-ter_____ strea-ming from— woun-ded

ne:___ Es-to no-bis prae-gus-ta - tum mor-tis_____ in e -
side:___ ri-sen bo-dy, when we jour - ney home from_____ ex - ile,—

xa - mi - ne.___ O___ Je - su dul - cis! O___ Je - su
be our guide! Way___ of truth, lead___ us! Bread of life,

pi - e! O_____ Je - su fi - li_ Ma - ri - ae.
feed___ us! Ma - ry's Son, show us— your mer - cy!___

Latin, 14th C., tr. James Quinn, S.J. Music: plainchant

667 **Adoramus te, Domine/We adore you, Lord, Jesus Christ**

(hum)_____ A - do - ra - mus te, Do - mi - ne.
We a - dore you, Lord Je - sus Christ.

1 With the angels and archangels:

2 With the patriarchs and prophets:

3 With the Virgin Mary, mother of God:

4 With the Apostles and evangelists:

5 With all the martyrs of Christ:

6 With all who witness to the Gospel of the Lord:

7 With all your people of the Church throughout the world:

Taizé chant by Jacques Berthier

➤ *See also Communion (613-651), Praise, Church*

Morning

668

1. From the night of a-ges wa-king morning comes to heart and mind,
2. Christ in light im-mortal dwel-ling, Word by whom the worlds were made;

day of grace in splen-dour brea - king, mists and sha-dows fall be - hind;
Light of lights, our dark dis - pel - ling, Lord of lords in light ar - rayed;

in the bright-ness of his glo - ry Christ the Light of life has shined.
in the bright-ness of his glo - ry see the Fa-ther's love dis-played.

3 Risen Lord in radiance splendid,
   Christ has conquered Satan's sway;
   sin and shame and sorrow ended,
   powers of darkness flee away;
     in the brightness of his glory
   walk as children of the day.

4 Light to lighten every nation,
   shining forth from shore to shore,
   Christ who won the world's salvation
   now let all the earth adore;
     in the brightness of his glory
   Light of life for evermore.

Timothy Dudley-Smith. Music by James Walsh

669

1. Lord, as the day be - gins lift up our hearts in praise;
2. Christ be in work and skill, ser - ving each o - ther's need;

take from us all our sins, guard us in all our ways: our ev - ery
Christ be in thought and will, Christ be in word and deed; our minds be

step di - rect and guide that Christ in all be glo - ri - fied!
set on things a - bove in joy and peace, in faith_ and love.

3 Grant us the Spirit's strength,
   teach us to walk his way;
   so bring us all at length
   safe to the close of day:
   from hour to hour sustain and bless
   and let our song be thankfulness.

4 Now as the day begins
   make it the best of days;
   take from us all our sins,
   guard us in all our ways;
   our every step direct and guide
   that Christ in all be glorified!

Timothy Dudley-Smith. Music by Stephen Dean

670

1 Christ, whose glory fills the skies,
   Christ, the true, the only Light,
   Sun of Righteousness, arise,
   triumph o'er the shades of night;
   Day-spring from on high, be near;
   day-star, in my heart appear.

2 Dark and cheerless is the morn
   unaccompanied by thee;
   joyless is the day's return
   till thy mercy's beams I see,
   till they inward light impart,
   glad my eyes, and warm my heart.

3 Visit then this soul of mine;
   pierce the gloom of sin and grief;
   fill me, radiancy divine;
   scatter all my unbelief;
   more and more thyself display,
   shining to the perfect day.
                Charles Wesley (1707-88)

671

1 Morning has broken like the first morning,
   blackbird has spoken like the first bird.
   Praise for the singing! Praise for the
      morning!
   Praise for them, springing fresh from the
      Word!

2 Sweet the rain's new fall sunlit from heaven,
   like the first dew-fall on the first grass.
   Praise for the sweetness of the wet garden,
   sprung in completeness where his feet pass.

3 Mine is the sunlight! Mine is the morning
   born of the one light Eden saw play!
   Praise with elation, praise ev'ry morning,
   God's re-creation of the new day!
                Eleanor Farjeon (1881–1965)

672

1 Lord as I wake I turn to you,
   yourself the first thought of my day:
   my King, my God, whose help is sure,
   yourself the help for which I pray.

2 There is no blessing Lord, from you
   for those who make their will their way;
   no praise for those who will not praise,
   no peace for those who will not pray.

3 Your loving gifts of grace to me,
   those favours I could never earn,
   call for my thanks in praise and prayer,
   call me to love you in return.

4 Lord, make my life a life of love,
   keep me from sin in all I do;
   Lord, make your law my only law,
   your will my will, for love of you.
                Brian Foley, from Psalm 5

673

1 This day God gives me
      strength of high heaven,
   sun and moon shining, flame in my hearth,
   flashing of lightning, wind in its
      swiftness,
   deeps of the ocean, firmness of earth.

2 This day God sends me
      strength as my steersman,
   might to uphold me, wisdom as guide.
   Your eyes are watchful,
      your ears are listening,
   your lips are speaking, friend at my side.

3 God's way is my way,
      God's shield is round me,
   God's host defends me, saving from ill.
   Angels of heaven, drive from me always
   all that would harm me, stand by me still.

4 Rising, I thank you, mighty and
      strong One,
   King of creation, giver of rest,
   firmly confessing Threeness of Persons,
   Oneness of Godhead, Trinity blest.
                Adapted from St Patrick's Breastplate,
                by James Quinn, S.J.

1. This day God gives me strength of high heaven,
sun and moon shining, flame in my hearth, flashing of lightning,
wind in its swiftness, deeps of the ocean, firmness of earth.

Melody by David Haas

Evening

674

1. Now the evening gives way to darkness, now the stars of the night appear;
shed your light and your peace around us; be among us who gather here.

2 For the brightness of passing daylight,
   for the fruits of the earth this day,
   it is good that we make thanksgiving,
   that we praise you in every way.

3 Work is over, the day completed,
   in the silence, your word is near;
   be the future of all who seek you,
   be a stronghold in every fear.

4 As we rest safe within your keeping,
   earth is wrapped in the robe of night;
   but when daybreak sends out its greeting,
   we rejoice in the newborn light.

5 Be among us, our promised Daystar,
   give your hope to the poor who cry;
   be our strength in this world of weakness,
   be the light which shall never die.

Tony Barr

675

1. Now it is evening lights of the city bid us remember Christ is our Light. Many are lonely, who will be neighbour? Where there is caring Christ is our Light.

2. Now it is evening little ones sleeping bid us remember Christ is our Peace. Some are neglected, who will be neighbour? Where there is caring Christ is our Peace.

3 Now it is evening
food on the table
bid us remember
Christ is our Life.
Many are hungry,
who will be neighbour?
Where there is sharing
Christ is our Life.

4 Now it is evening
here in our meeting
may we remember
Christ is our Friend.
Some may be strangers,
who will be neighbour?
Where there's a welcome
Christ is our Friend.

F. Pratt Green

676

1. Now the day has drawn to en - ding and we look u - pon the night,
hear, O God, our glad thanks - gi - ving for the bles - sings— of the light.
(4. com-for-ter)

2 In the darkness that surrounds us,
give us calm and quiet sleep,
Guard us safe from every danger,
loving shepherd of the sheep.

3 Every day brings joy and sorrow,
times to dance and times to mourn,
May we rise refreshed tomorrow
fit to work for your kingdom's dawn.

4 Loving Father and Creator,
Jesus Christ, who walked our way;
Holy Spirit, friend and comforter,
be with us till the break of day.

Stephen Dean

677

1. O glad - some light, O grace of God the Fa - ther's face,
the e - ter - nal splen - dour wea - ring; ce - les - tial, ho - ly, blest,
Our Sa - viour, Je - sus Christ, joy - ful in your ap - pear - ing.

2 As fades the day's last light
we see the lamps of night,
our common hymn outpouring,
O God of might unknown,
you, the incarnate Son,
and Spirit blest adoring.

3 To you of right belongs
all praise of holy songs,
O Son of God, lifegiver;
You, therefore, O Most High,
the world does glorify
and shall exalt for ever.

Greek, before 4th Century, tr Robert Bridges (1844-1930)

678

1 Day is done, but Love unfailing
  dwells ever here;
  shadows fall, but hope, prevailing,
  calms every fear.
  Loving Father, none forsaking,
  take our hearts, of Love's own making,
  watch our sleeping, guard our waking,
  be always near!

2 Dark descends, but Light unending
  shines through our night;
  you are with us, ever lending
  new strength to sight;
  one in love, your truth confessing,
  one in hope of heaven's blessing,
  may we see, in love's possessing,
  love's endless light!

3 Eyes will close, but you, unsleeping,
  watch by our side;
  death may come: in love's safe keeping
  still we abide.
  God of love, all evil quelling,
  sin forgiving, fear dispelling,
  stay with us, our hearts indwelling,
  this eventide!
  James Quinn, S.J.

679

1 The day thou gavest, Lord, is ended:
  the darkness falls at thy behest;
  to thee our morning hymns ascended;
  thy praise shall sanctify our rest.

2 We thank thee that thy Church
  unsleeping,
  while earth rolls onward into light,
  through all the world her watch is
  keeping,
  and rests not now by day or night.

3 As o'er each continent and island
  the dawn leads on another day,
  the voice of prayer is never silent,
  nor dies the strain of praise away.

4 The sun that bids us rest is waking
  our brethren 'neath the western sky
  and hour by hour fresh lips are making
  thy wondrous doings heard on high.

5 So be it, Lord; thy throne shall never,
  like earth's proud empire, pass away;
  thy kingdom stands, and grows for ever,
  till all thy creatures own thy sway.
  John Ellerton (1826–93)

680

1 Sweet Saviour, bless us ere we go,
  thy word into our minds instil;
  and make our lukewarm hearts to glow
  with lowly love and fervent will.
    *Through life's long day
    and death's dark night,
    O gentle Jesus, be our light.*

2 The day is done; its hours have run,
  and thou hast taken count of all,
  the scanty triumphs grace has won,
  the broken vow, the frequent fall.

3 Grant us, dear Lord, from evil ways,
  true absolution and release;
  and bless us more than in past days
  with purity and inward peace.

4 Do more than pardon; give us joy,
  sweet fear and sober liberty,
  and loving hearts without alloy,
  that only long to be like thee.

5 Labour is sweet, for thou hast toiled,
  and care is light, for thou hast cared;
  let not our works with self be soiled,
  nor in unsimple ways ensnared.

6 For all we love – the poor, the sad,
  the sinful – unto thee we call;
  oh let thy mercy make us glad,
  thou art our Jesus and our all.
  F.W. Faber (1814–63)

681

1. As the set-ting sun sinks in-to the West, and its
2. On our lips the song all Cre - a - tion sings as it
3. So ac - cross the earth, and in ev - 'ry age, count-less

gol - den flame fades a - way, we raise our hearts in thank-ful praise as
yearns to grow in-to birth, to Christ, the First Born in - to life, who
hearts and voi - ces u - nite to sing your praise, O Son of God, for

ev' - ning fol - lows day. When the dy - ing light yields be -
shat - ter'd death's long curse; Christ who trod our path, Christ who
peace and joy and light, till the praise of God through cre -

fore the night and our world is lost in deep shade, then
shared our pain, once in si - lent dark - ness en - tombed: whose
a - tion rings, till the dawn of Life's glo - rious day, when

Fine

hear the prayer, O Sa - ving God, of those your hand has made.
ri - sing fills the world with light, and scat - ters sin's dread gloom. ▼*below*
all will be re-newed in light in Love's e - ter - nal Reign.

After v.2, O Ra-diant light! O Joy-ful light! Our Sa - viour Je - sus Christ! The

To verse 3

glo-rious shi - ning of our God, ar - ise u-pon our night!

Peter McGrail

682

1 Round me falls the night,
Saviour be my light;
through the hours in darkness shrouded
let me see thy face unclouded.
Let thy glory shine
in this heart of mine.

2 Earthly work is done,
earthly sounds are none;
rest in sleep and silence seeking,
let me hear thee softly speaking;

in my spirit's ear
whisper: 'I am near'.

3 Blessed heav'nly light
shining through earth's night;
voice that oft of love has told me,
arms, so strong, to clasp and hold me;
thou thy watch wilt keep,
Saviour, o'er my sleep.

W. Romanis (1824-99)

God the Creator

683

1 O worship the King
    all glorious above;
O gratefully sing
    his power and his love:
our shield and defender,
    the ancient of days,
pavilioned in splendour,
    and girded with praise.

2 O tell of his might,
    O sing of his grace,
whose robe is the light,
    whose canopy space.
His chariots of wrath, the
    deep thunderclouds form,
and dark is his path
    on the wings of the storm.

3 This earth, with its store
    of wonders untold,
almighty, thy power
    hath founded of old;
hath stablished it fast
    by a changeless decree;
and round it hath cast,
    like a mantle, the sea.

4 Thy bountiful care
    what tongue can recite?
It breathes in the air,
    it shines in the light;
it streams from the hills,
    it descends to the plain,
and sweetly distils
    in the dew and the rain.

5 Frail children of dust,
    and feeble as frail,
in thee do we trust,
    nor find thee to fail;
thy mercies how tender!
    How firm to the end!
Our maker, defender,
    redeemer, and friend.

6 O measureless might,
    ineffable love,
while angels delight
    to hymn thee above,
thy humbler creation,
    though feeble their lays,
with true adoration
    shall sing to thy praise.
      Robert Grant (1779–1838)

684

1 I sing the almighty power of God
    that made the mountains rise,
that spread the flowing seas abroad
    and built the lofty skies.
I sing the wisdom that ordained
    the sun to rule the day;
the moon shines full at God's command
    and all the stars obey.

2 I sing the goodness of the Lord
    that filled the earth with food;
that formed the creatures with a word
    and then pronounced them good.
Lord, how your wonders are displayed
    where-e'er I turn my eye;
if I survey the ground I tread,
    or gaze upon the sky!

3 There's not a plant or flower below
    but makes your glories known;
and clouds arise, and tempests blow,
    by order from your throne;
while all that borrows life from you
    is ever in your care,
and everywhere that I may be,
    O God, be present there.
      Isaac Watts, 1674-1748, alt.

685

All things bright and beautiful,
all creatures great and small,
all things wise and wonderful,
the Lord God made them all.

1 Each little flower that opens,
  each little bird that sings,
  he made their glowing colours,
  he made their tiny wings.

2 The purple–headed mountain,
  the river running by,
  the sunset and the morning,
  that brightens up the sky.

3 The cold wind in the winter,
  the pleasant summer sun,

the ripe fruits in the garden,
  he made them every one.

4 The tall trees in the greenwood,
  the meadows for our play,
  the rushes by the water,
  to gather every day.

5 He gave us eyes to see them,
  and lips that we may tell
  how great is God Almighty,
  who has made all things well.

Cecil Frances Alexander (1818–95)

686

1. God be-yond our dreams, you have stirred in us a mem-'ry; you have placed your pow'r-ful spi-rit in the hearts of hu-man-kind. *Refrain* All a-round us we have known you, all cre-a-tion lives to hold you, in our li-ving and our dy-ing we are bring-ing you to birth.

2 God, beyond all names,
  you have made us in your image;
  we are like you, we reflect you;
  we are woman, we are man.

3 God, beyond all words,
  all creation tells your story;
  you have shaken with our laughter,
  you have trembled with our tears.

4 God, beyond all time,
  you are labouring within us;
  we are moving, we are changing
  in your spirit ever new.

5 God of tender care,
  you have cradled us in goodness,
  you have mothered us in wholeness,
  you have loved us into birth.

Bernadette Farrell

687

1. God in his love for us lent us this pla-net, gave it a
2. Thanks be to God for its boun-ty and beau-ty, life that sus-

pur - pose in time and in space: small as a spark from the
tains us in bo - dy and mind: plen - ty for all, if we

fire of cre - a - tion, cra - dle of life and the home of our race.
learn how to share it, ri - ches un - dreamed of to fa - thom and find.

3 Long have our human wars ruined its
harvest,
long has earth bowed to the terror of
force;
long have we wasted what others have
need of,
poisoned the fountain of life at its source.

4 Earth is the Lord's, it is ours to enjoy it;
ours, as his stewards, to farm and defend.
From its pollution, misuse and
destruction,
Good Lord, deliver us, world without end!

F. Pratt Green.
Music by Valerie Ruddle

688

1. We can - not own the sun - lit sky,___ the moon, the
wild - flow'rs grow - ing,___ for we are part of all that is with -
in life's riv - er flow - ing.___ with o - pen hands re - ceive and
share___ the gifts of God's cre - a - tion,___ that all may have a -

Last time

bun - dant life___ in ev - 'ry earth - ly na - tion.___

2 When bodies shiver in the night
and weary, wait for morning,
when children have no bread but tears,
and warhorns sound their warning,
God calls humanity to wake,
to join in common labor,
that all may have abundant life
in oneness with their neighbour.

3 God calls humanity to join
as partners in creating
a future free from want or fear,
life's goodness celebrating,
that new world beckons from afar,
invites our shared endeavour,
that all may have abundant life
and peace endure forever.

Ruth Duck

PRaise of The CReaToR

689

Bénissez le Seigneur/Let us sing to the Lord

(Cantor)

Let us sing to the Lord! *(Cantor)*
Bé - nis - sez le Seig - neur!

Let us sing to the Lord! *(Cantor)*
Bé - nis - sez le Seig - neur!

Let us sing to the Lord, let us sing to the Lord!
Bé - nis - sez le Seig - neur, bé - nis - sez le Seig - neur!

Taizé chant by Jacques Berthier

1 All creation bless the Lord;
  and you, angels of the Lord,
  praise and glorify the Lord.

2 Sun and moon, bless the Lord;
  and you, night and day, bless the Lord;
  and you, light and darkness, bless the Lord.

3 All you heavens, bless the Lord,

spirits and souls of the just,
saints and the humble of heart.

4 Praised be Christ, he is our hope.
  He is the joy of our hearts.
  Compassionate and gracious is our God.

5 Christ is always with us,
  and loves us before we love him.
  God's love will never pass away.

690

1. Hea - ven is sing - ing for joy,— Al - le - lu - ia!
2. Hea - ven is sing - ing for joy,— Al - le - lu - ia!
3. Hea - ven is sing - ing for joy,— Al - le - lu - ia!

For in your life and— mine is shi - ning the glo - ry of God.
For your— life and— mine are one— in the love of— God.
For your— life and mine will al - ways pro - claim the— Lord.

*Pablo
Sosa*

Al - le - lu - ia, al - le-lu - ia; al - le - lu - ia, al - le-lu - ia!
Al - le - lu - ia, al - le-lu - ia; al - le - lu - ia, al - le-lu - ia!

691 **Jubilate, servite** *canon*

Taizé chant by Jacques Berthier

Ju - bi - la - te De - o, om - nis ter - ra, Ser - vi - te Do - mi - no in lae - ti - ti - a.

Al - le - lu - ia, al - le - lu - ia, in lae - ti - ti - a! Al - le - lu - ia, al - le - lu - ia, in lae - ti - ti - a!

Cry out with joy to the Lord, all the earth; serve the Lord with gladness. Ps 100:1.

692

Paul Inwood, from Isaiah 12:1-6

We shall draw water joy-ful-ly, sing-ing joy-ful-ly, singing joy-ful-ly:

we shall draw wa-ter joy-ful-ly from the well-springs of sal-va-tion.

1 Truly God is our salvation;
we trust, we shall not fear.
For the Lord is our strength,
the Lord is our song;
he became our saviour.

2 Give thanks, O give thanks to the Lord;
give praise to his holy name!
Make his mighty deeds known
to all of the nations,
proclaim his greatness.

3 Sing a psalm, sing a psalm to the Lord
for he has done glorious deeds.
Make known his works to all of the
earth;
people of Zion, sing for joy,
for great in your midst, great in
your midst
is the Holy One of Israel.

693

Refrain

The heav-ens are tell-ing the glo-ry of God, and all cre-a-tion is shou-ting for joy. Come, dance in the for-est, come, play in the field, and sing, sing to the glo-ry of the Lord.

Verses

1. Praise for the sun, the bring-er of day, he car-ries the
2. Praise for the wind that blows through the trees, the seas might-y

1. light of the Lord in his rays; the moon and the stars who
2. storms, the gen-tl-est breeze; they blow where they will, they

D.C.

light up the way un-to your throne. _____
blow where they please to please the Lord. _____

3 Praise for the rain that waters our fields,
and blesses our crops so all the earth yields;
from death unto life her myst'ry revealed
springs forth in joy.

4 Praise for the fire who gives us his light,
the warmth of the sun to brighten our night;
he dances with joy, his spirit so bright,
he sings of you.

5 Praise for the earth who makes life to grow,
the creatures you made to let your life show;
the flowers and the trees that help us to know
the heart of love.

6 Praise for our death that makes our life real,
the knowledge of loss that helps us to feel;
the gift of yourself, your presence revealed
to lead us home.

Marty Haugen

694

1 All creatures of our God and King,
lift up your voice and with us sing
alleluia, alleluia!
Thou burning sun with golden beam,
thou silver moon with softer gleam:
O praise him, O praise him,
alleluia, alleluia, alleluia.

2 Thou rushing wind that art so strong,
ye clouds that sail in heaven along,
O praise him, alleluia!
Thou rising morn, in praise rejoice,
ye lights of evening, find a voice:

3 Thou flowing water, pure and clear,
make music for thy Lord to hear,
alleluia, alleluia!
Thou fire so masterful and bright,
that givest us both warmth and light:

4 Dear mother earth, who day by day
unfoldest blessings on our way,
O praise him, alleluia!
The flowers and fruits that in thee grow
let them his glory also show.

5 And all who are of tender heart,
forgiving others, take your part,
O sing ye, alleluia!
Ye who long pain and sorrow bear,
praise God and on him cast your care.

6 And thou, most kind and gentle death,
waiting to hush our latest breath,
O praise him, alleluia!
Thou leadest home the child of God,
and Christ our Lord the way hath trod:

7 Let all things their Creator bless,
and worship him in humbleness,
O praise him, alleluia!
Praise, praise the Father, praise the Son,
and praise the Spirit, Three in One.

W.H Draper (1855–1933) based on St.
Francis of Assisi's 'Cantico di Frate Sole'

695

Glory and praise to our God,
who alone gives light to our days.
Many are the blessings he bears
to those who trust in his ways.

1 We, the daughters and sons of God
who built the valleys and plains,
praise the wonders our God has done
in ev'ry heart that sings.

2 In his wisdom he strengthens us,
like gold that's tested in fire,
though the power of sin prevails,
our God is there to save.

3 Ev'ry moment of ev'ry day
our God is waiting to save,
always ready to seek the lost,
to answer those who pray.

4 God has watered our barren land
and spent his merciful rain.
Now the rivers of life run full
for anyone to drink.

Daniel L. Schutte, from Pss. 65, 66

696

Deep down I know, I must thank God, Oh— deep down I
know, I must thank God! God!—

David Haas

1 Lost in the night, I feel the hand of God;
   deep in my soul, I know God is near!
   When I awake to greet the sweet morning.
   I see the holy light shine before me!

2 My heart is glad, leaping for happiness;
   my God will walk with me, and I'll
        never die,

for God will destroy the demons that
     haunt me;
forgiving with mercy: giving me peace!

3 Stand up my friends, and feel the power
        of God
   stirring within you; answer the call!
   Look all around you, and you'll see the
        face of God!
   Bound to each other, we will be free!

697

Sing a new song unto the Lord;
let your song be sung from mountains high.
Sing a new song unto the Lord,
singing alleluia.

1 Yahweh's people dance for joy.
   O come before the Lord
   and play for him on glad tambourines,
   and let your trumpet sound.

2 Rise, O children, from your sleep;
   your Saviour now has come.
   He has turned your sorrow to joy,
   and filled your soul with song.

3 Glad my soul for I have seen
   the glory of the Lord.
   The trumpet sounds; the dead shall be
        raised.
   I know my Saviour lives.

   Daniel L. Schutte, from Psalm 98

Laudate Dominum

698

Lau-da-te Do-minum, lau-da-te Do-mi-num, om-nes

First time gen-tes al-le-lu-ia. *Second time* al-le-lu-ia.

Praise the Lord, all you nations. Ps 117:1.   *Taizé chant by Jacques Berthier*

1 Praise the Lord, all you nations,
   praise God all you peoples. Alleluia!

2 Strong is God's love and mercy,
   always faithful for ever. Alleluia! *(Ps 117)*

699

Ps 117, arr. Paul Inwood

Last time: sing refrain twice

Ref. 1   2

Ho-ly is God, Ho-ly and strong! God e-ver - li-ving, al-le-lu - ia.

Verses

1. Sing the Lord's praise, ev'-ry na-tion,_____ give him all
2. Praise to the Fa-ther al-migh-ty;_____ praise to his

ho-nour and glo-ry,_____ strong is his love for his
son, Christ the Lord;_____ praise to the life-gi-ving

D.C.

peo-ple,_____ his faith-ful-ness_____ is e - ter-nal._____
Spi-rit;_____ both now and for ev-er, A - men._____

700

1 Come, praise the Lord, the almighty,
  the King of all nations!
  Tell forth his fame, O ye peoples,
  with loud acclamations!
  His love is sure;
  faithful his word shall endure,
  steadfast through all generations!

2 Praise to the Father most gracious,
  the Lord of creation!
  Praise to his Son, the Redeemer
  who wrought our salvation!
  O heav'nly Dove,
  praise to thee, fruit of their love.
  Giver of all consolation!

James Quinn, S.J., from Ps 117

Confitemini Domino

701

Con-fi-te-mi-ni Domi-no quo - ni - am bo-nus.

Con - fi - te - mi - ni Do - mi - no, Al - le - lu - ia!

Give thanks to the Lord, who is good, alleluia (Ps 118:1),   *Taizé chant by Jacques Berthier*

702

1 God, my King, your might confessing,
ever will I bless your Name;
day by day your throne addressing,
still will I thy praise proclaim.

2 Highest praise to God is fitting;
who his majesty can reach?
Age to age his works transmitting,
age to age his power shall teach.

3 They shall talk of all your glory,
on your might and greatness dwell,
speak of your dread acts the story,
and your deeds of wonder tell.

4 Nor shall fail from mem'ry's treasure
works by love and mercy wrought,
works of love surpassing measure,
works of mercy passing thought.

5 Full of kindness and compassion,
slow to anger, vast in love,
God is good to all creation;
all his works his goodness prove.

6 All your works, O Lord, shall bless you;
You alone your saints adore:
King supreme shall they confess you,
and proclaim your sovereign power.

R. Mant (1776-1848), from Psalm 145

703

1 Fill your hearts with joy and gladness,
sing and praise your God and mine!
Great the Lord in love and wisdom,
might and majesty divine!
He who framed the starry heavens
knows and names them as they shine.

2 Praise the Lord, his people, praise him!
wounded souls his comfort know;
those who fear him find his mercies,
peace for pain and joy for woe;
humble hearts are high exalted,
human pride and power laid low.

3 Praise the Lord for times and seasons,
cloud and sunshine, wind and rain;
spring to melt the snows of winter
till the waters flow again;
grass upon the mountain pastures,
golden valleys thick with grain.

4 Fill your hearts with joy and gladness,
peace and plenty crown your days;
love his laws, declare his judgements,
walk in all his words and ways;
he the Lord and we his children -
praise the Lord, all people, praise!

Timothy Dudley-Smith, from Psalm 147

704

1 Praise the Lord! Ye heavens, adore him;
praise him, angels, in the height;
sun and moon, rejoice before him,
praise him, all ye stars and light.
Praise the Lord! For he hath spoken;
worlds his mighty voice obeyed:
laws, which never shall be broken,
for their guidance he hath made.

2 Praise the Lord! For he is glorious;
never shall his promise fail:
God hath made his saints victorious;
sin and death shall not prevail.
Praise the God of our salvation;
hosts on high, his power proclaim;
heaven and earth and all creation,
laud and magnify his name!

3 Worship, honour, glory, blessing,
Lord, we offer to thy name;
young and old, thy praise expressing,
join their Saviour to proclaim.
As the saints in heaven adore thee,
we would bow before thy throne;
as thine angels serve before thee,
so on earth thy will be done.

From Psalm 148. Vv. 1-2 from the
Foundling Hospital Collection (1796);
v. 3 by E. Osler (1798–1863)

705

1 Bring to the Lord a glad new song,
children of grace extol your king:
your love and praise to God belong -
to instruments of music, sing!
Let those be warned
  who spurn God's name,
let rulers all obey God's word,
for justice shall bring tyrants shame -
let every creature praise the Lord!

2 Sing praise within these hallowed walls,
worship beneath the dome of heaven;
by cymbals' sounds and trumpets' calls
let praises fit for God be given:
with strings and brass and wind rejoice-
then, join our song in full accord
all living things with breath and voice;
let every creature praise the Lord!

Michael Perry (1942-96) from Pss149/150

706

1 Praise to the Lord, the Almighty,
  the King of creation!
O my soul, praise him, for he is your
  health and salvation.
All you who hear, now to his temple
  draw near,
join in profound adoration.

2 Praise to the Lord, above all things
  so mightily reigning.
Keeping us safe at his side, and so
  gently sustaining.
Have you not seen
  all you have needed has been
met by his gracious ordaining?

3 Praise to the Lord, who will
  prosper our work and defend us;
surely his goodness and mercy
  here daily attend us;
ponder anew what the Almighty can do,
who with his love will befriend us.

4 Praise to the Lord, O let all that
  is in us adore him!
All that has life and breath,
  come now in praises before him.
Let the Amen sound from
  his people again,
now as we worship before him.

Joachim Neander (1650–80),
tr. C. Winkworth (1827–78), alt
➤ *See also no 601*

707

1 Let us, with a gladsome mind,
praise the Lord, for he is kind:
For his mercies aye endure,
ever faithful, ever sure.

2 Let us blaze his name abroad,
for of gods he is the God;

3 He, with all–commanding might,
filled the new–made world with light;

4 He the golden–tressèd sun
caused all day his course to run:

5 And the hornèd moon at night,
'mid her spangled sisters bright:

6 All things living he doth feed,
his full hand supplies their need:

7 Let us, with a gladsome mind,
praise the Lord, for he is kind.

John Milton (1608–75), from Ps 136

708

1 Holy God, we praise thy name;
Lord of all, we bow before thee!
All on earth thy sceptre own,
all in heaven above adore thee.
Infinite thy vast domain,
everlasting is thy reign.

2 Hark! The loud celestial hymn,
angel choirs above are raising;
cherubim and seraphim,
in unceasing chorus praising,
fill the heavens with sweet accord,
holy, holy, holy Lord.

3 All the apostles join the strain
   as thy sacred Name they hallow;
   prophets swell the loud refrain,
   and the white-robed martyrs follow;
   and from morn to set of sun,
   through the Church the song goes on.

4 Holy Father, holy Son,
   Holy Spirit, three we name thee,
   while in essence only one
   undivided God we claim thee;
   and, adoring, bend the knee
   while we own the mystery.

5 Spare thy people, Lord, we pray,
   by a thousand snares surrounded;
   keep us without sin today;
   never let us be confounded.
   Lo, I put my trust in thee,
   never, Lord, abandon me.

C. A. Walworth (1820–1900) based on Te Deum Laudamus

709

1. We praise you O God; acclaim you as Lord.
2. Apostles and prophets, the martyrs for Christ,
3. Lord Jesus the Christ, your death brings us life.
4. Lord, grant us salvation, protect us from harm.

All of creation resounds to the voice of the
sing of your goodness while bathed in the beams of your
Come with your judgement and grant us a place in the
Free us from evil and bless us with mercy as

heavenly host, united in song, praising your
infinite love, your splendour and light,
Kingdom of God, at one with your saints,
daily in you we trust and we hope,

majesty, praising your glory. Alleluia, alle-

luia. Holy is God, holy and strong. Allelu-

ia, alleluia. Holy Immortal One.

Peter Jones, from Te Deum Laudamus

710

Alleluia, alleluia! Alleluia, alleluia!

1 Father we praise you as Lord,
all of the earth gives you worship,
for your majesty fills the heavens,
fills the earth.

2 Blessed apostles sing praise;
prophets and martyrs give glory;
'For your majesty praise the Spirit,
praise the Son!'

3 You are the Christ everlasting,
born for us all of a Virgin,
you have conquered death,
opened heaven to all believers.

4 Help those you saved by your blood,
raise them to life with your martyrs.
Save your people, Lord, as their ruler
raise them up.

Christopher Walker, from Te Deum Laudamus

711

Great is the po-wer we pro-claim now, as we wor-ship_ and
praise God's name. For the glo-ry_ of God is re-vealed when we pray:
_ Come, Lord, come Lord,_ and live in us to-day. *fine*

Verses

1. God's peo-ple called to serve_____ as dis-ci-ples of the
2. God's peo-ple called to bring_____ to the world, the peace of
3. God's peo-ple called to pray_____ for the Church to be made

Lord._____ Gifts of the Spi-rit_ are gifts_ we in-he-rit_ to
Christ._____ Love for our neigh-bour,_ and jus-tice in our la-bour,_ com-
one._____ One Ho-ly Na-tion_ in hope_ of sal-va-tion,_

build up the bo-dy_ of Christ._____
pelled by the love_____ of Christ._____
bro-thers and sis-ters_ in Christ._____

Christopher Walker

4. God's people called to-day
to make known the love of God.
Seeds we are sowing
with faith that is growing
strong in the power of Christ.

5. God's people called to share
in the blessing cup of Christ:
Bread that is broken,
and Word that is spoken,
one in the Body of Christ.

712

1 The God of Abraham praise
who reigns enthroned above,
Ancient of everlasting Days,
and God of love:
the Lord,the great I AM,
by earth and heaven confessed;
we bow and bless the sacred name
for ever blessed.

2 The God of Abraham praise,
at whose supreme command
from earth we rise, and seek the joys
at his right hand:
we all on earth forsake
its wisdom, fame, and power;
and him our only portion make,
our shield and tower.

3 The Lord our God has sworn,
I on that oath depend;
I shall, on eagle's wings upborne,
to heaven ascend:
I shall behold God's face,
I shall God's power adore,
and sing the wonders of God's grace
for evermore.

4 There dwells the Lord our King,
the Lord our Righteousness,
triumphant o'er the world of sin,
the Prince of peace:
on Sion's sacred height
his kingdom he maintains,
and glorious with the saints in light
for ever reigns.

5 The God who reigns on high
the great archangels sing,
and 'Holy, Holy, Holy,' cry,
'almighty King,
who was, and is the same,
and evermore shall be:
Immortal God, the great I AM,
we worship thee.'

> *Thomas Olivers (1725-99) based on the*
> *Hebrew Yigdal*

713

1 Sing of the Lord's goodness,
Father of all wisdom,
come to him and bless his name.
Mercy he has shown us, his love is for ever,
faithful to the end of days.
> *Come then all you nations,*
> *sing of your Lord's goodness,*
> *melodies of praise and thanks to God.*
> *Ring out the Lord's glory,*
> *praise him with your music,*
> *worship him and bless his name.*

2 Power he has wielded,
honour is his garment,
risen from the snares of death.
His word he has spoken,
one bread he has broken,
new life he now gives to all.

3 Courage in our darkness,
comfort in our sorrow,
Spirit of our God most high;
solace for the weary,
pardon for the sinner,
splendour of the living God.

4 Praise him with your singing,
praise him with the trumpet,
praise God with the lute and harp;
praise him with the cymbals,
praise him with your dancing,
praise God till the end of days.
> *Ernest Sands*

714

1 Holy, holy, holy is the Lord;
holy is the Lord God almighty!
Holy, holy, holy is the Lord;
holy is the Lord God almighty!
Who was, and is, and is to come!
Holy, holy, holy is the Lord!

2 Jesus, Jesus, Jesus is the Lord...

3 Worthy, worthy, worthy is the Lord..

4 Glory, glory, glory to the Lord;
glory to the Lord God almighty!
> *Author unknown*

715

1 King of glory, king of peace,
    I will love thee;
    and that love may never cease,
    I will move thee.
    Thou hast granted my request,
    thou hast heard me;
    thou didst note my working breast,
    thou hast spared me.

2 Wherefore with my utmost art,
    I will sing thee.
    And the cream of all my heart
    I will bring thee,
    though my sins against me cried,
    thou didst clear me;
    and alone, when they replied,
    thou didst hear me.

3 Seven whole days, not one in seven,
    I will praise thee;
    in my heart, though not in heaven,
    I can raise thee.
    Small it is, in this poor sort
    to enrol thee:
    e'en eternity's too short
    to extol thee.
        George Herbert (1593–1633)

716

1 Let all the world in every corner sing,
    my God and King!
    The heav'ns are not too high,
    God's praise may thither fly;
    the earth is not too low,
    God's praises there may grow.
    Let all the world in every corner sing,
    my God and King!

2 Let all the world in every corner sing,
    my God and King!
    The church with psalms must shout,
    no door can keep them out;
    but, above all, the heart
    must bear the longest part.
    Let all the world in every corner sing,
    my God and King!
        George Herbert (1593–1633)

717

1 I will sing, I will sing a song unto the Lord
    I will sing, I will sing a song unto the Lord
    I will sing, I will sing a song unto the Lord
    Alleluia, glory to the Lord.
        Allelu, alleluia, glory to the Lord,
        allelu, alleluia, glory to the Lord,
        allelu, alleluia, glory to the Lord,
        alleluia, glory to the Lord.

2 We will come, we will come as one
        before the Lord...
    Alleluia, glory to the Lord.

3 If the Son, if the Son shall make you free.
    you shall be free indeed.

4 They that sow in tears shall reap in joy...
    Alleluia, glory to the Lord.

5 Ev'ry knee shall bow and ev'ry tongue
        confess...
    that Jesus Christ is Lord.

6 In his name, in his name we have the
        victory...
    Alleluia, glory to the Lord.
        Max Dyer

718

1 Father, we adore you,
    lay our lives before you,
    how we love you.

2 Jesus, we adore you …

3 Spirit, we adore you …
        Terry Coelho

719

1 To God be the glory, great things he has
        done!
    So loved he the world that he gave us his
        Son.
    Who yielded his life in atonement for sin,
    and opened the life–gate that all may go in
        Praise the Lord! Praise the Lord!
        Let the earth hear his voice!
        Praise the Lord! Praise the Lord!
        Let the people rejoice!

O come to the Father through Jesus
*   his Son;*
*   and give him the glory, great things he*
*   has done!*

2 O perfect redemption, the purchase of
        blood,
    to every believer the promise of God!
    And every offender who truly believes,
    that moment from Jesus a pardon
        receives.

3 Great things he has taught us, great things
        he has done,
    and great our rejoicing through Jesus the
        Son;
    but purer, and higher, and greater will be
    our wonder, our rapture, when Jesus we see.
                    Fanny Crosby (1820–1915)

720

1 Be still, for the presence of the Lord,
        the Holy One is here.
    Come, bow before him now,
        with reverence and fear.
    In him no sin is found,
        we stand on holy ground.
    Be still, for the presence of the Lord,
        the Holy One is here.

2 Be still, for the glory of the Lord
        is shining all around;
    He burns with holy fire,
        with splendour he is crowned.
    How awesome is the sight,
        our radiant King of light!
    Be still, for the glory of the Lord
        is shining all around.

3 Be still, for the power of the Lord
        is moving in this place,
    He comes to cleanse and heal,
        to minister his grace.
    No work too hard for him,
        in faith receive from him;
    Be still, for the power of the Lord
        is moving in this place.
            David J. Evans

721

1 O Lord, my God, when I in awesome
        wonder
    consider all the worlds thy hand has made,
    I see the stars, I hear the rolling thunder,
    thy power throughout the universe
        displayed.
    Then sings my soul, my Saviour God to thee:
    how great thou art, how great thou art.
    Then sings my soul, my Saviour God to thee:
    how great thou art, how great thou art.

2 When through the woods and
        forest glades I wander
    and hear the birds sing sweetly
        in the trees,
    when I look down from lofty mountain
        grandeur
    and hear the brook and feel the gentle
        breeze:

3 And when I think that God, his Son not
        sparing,
    sent him to die, I scarce can take it in
    that on the cross, my burden gladly bearing,
    he bled and died to take away my sin.

3 When Christ shall come with shout of
        acclamation
    and take me home, what joy shall fill my
        heart;
    then I shall bow in humble adoration,
    and there proclaim; my God, how great
        thou art.
        Stuart K. Hine (1898-1989), based on a
        hymn by Carl Boberg (1850–1940)

722

1 Give me joy in my heart, keep me praising,
    give me joy in my heart I pray.
    Give me joy in my heart, keep me praising.
    keep me praising till the break of day.
        Sing hosanna! Sing hosanna!
        Sing hosanna to the King of Kings!
        Sing hosanna! Sing hosanna!
        Sing hosanna to the King!

2 Give me peace in my heart, keep me resting,
   give me peace in my heart I pray.
   Give me peace in my heart, keep me resting.
   keep me resting till the end of day.

3 Give me love in my heart, keep me
      serving,
   give me love in my heart, I pray.

Give me love in my heart, keep me
   serving,
keep me serving till the end of day.

3 Give me oil in my lamp, keep me burning,
   give me oil in my lamp, I pray.
   Give me oil in my lamp, keep me burning,
   keep me burning till the end of day.

Traditional

723

San - to, san - to, san - to, mi co - ra - zon te a - do - ra! Mi
Ho - ly, ho - ly, ho - ly, my heart, my heart a - dores you! My

co - ra - zon te sa - be de - cir: san - to e - res, Se - ñor.
heart is glad to say the words: you are ho - ly, Lord.

Holy, holy, holy, my heart, my heart adores you!
My heart is glad to say the words: you are holy, Lord.

Song from Argentina, arranged by Geoff Weaver

724

1 Angel–voices ever singing
   round thy throne of light,
   angel–harps, for ever ringing,
   rest not day nor night;
   thousands only live to bless thee
   and confess thee Lord of might.

2 Thou who art beyond the farthest
   mortal eye can see,
   God almighty, thou regardest
   all our song to thee;
   and we know that thou art near us,
   and wilt hear our ev'ry plea.

3 Yes, we know that thou rejoicest
   o'er each work of thine;
   thou didst ears and hands and voices
   for thy praise design;
   craftsman's art and music's measure
   for thy pleasure all combine.

4 In thy house, great God, we offer
   of thine own to thee;
   and for thine acceptance proffer,
   all unworthily,
   hearts and minds and hands and voices
   in our choicest psalmody.

5 Honour, glory, might and merit
  thine shall ever be,
  Father, Son and Holy Spirit,
  Blessed Trinity!
  Of the best that thou hast given
  earth and heaven render thee.
  Francis Pott (1832–1909)

725

1 Immortal, invisible, God only wise,
  in light inaccessible hid from our eyes,
  most blessed, most glorious, the
      Ancient of Days,
  almighty, victorious, thy great name we
      praise.

2 Unresting, unhasting, and silent as light;
  nor wanting, nor wasting, thou rulest in
      might –
  thy justice like mountains high–soaring
      above
  thy clouds which are fountains of
      goodness and love.

3 To all life thou givest, to both great and
      small;
  in all life thou livest, the true life of all;
  we blossom and flourish as leaves on the
      tree,
  and wither and perish; but naught
      changeth thee.

4 Great Father of glory, pure Father of light,
  thine angels adore thee, all veiling their
      sight;
  all laud we would render: O help us to see
  'tis only the splendour of light
      hideth thee.
  W. Chalmers Smith (1825–1908)

726

1 For the beauty of the earth,
  for the beauty of the skies,
  for the love which from our birth
  over and around us lies,
  Christ our God, to you we raise
  this our sacrifice of praise.

2 For the beauty of each hour
  of the day and of the night,
  hill and vale, and tree and flower,
  sun and moon and stars of light.
  Christ our God, to you we raise
  this our sacrifice of praise.

3 For the joy of ear and eye,
  for the heart and mind's delight,
  for the mystic harmony
  linking sense to sound and sight.
  Christ our God, to you we raise
  this our sacrifice of praise.

4 For the joy of human love,
  brother, sister, parent, child,
  friends on earth and friends above,
  pleasures pure and undefiled,
  Christ our God, to you we raise
  this our sacrifice of praise.

5 For each perfect gift divine
  to our race so freely given,
  joys bestowed by love's design,
  flowers of earth and fruits of heaven,
  Christ our God, to you we raise
  this our sacrifice of praise.
  F.S. Pierpoint (1835–1917)

727

1 My God, how wonderful thou art,
  thy majesty how bright
  how beautiful thy mercy–seat
  in depths of burning light.

2 How dread are thine eternal years
  O everlasting Lord!
  By prostrate spirits day and night
  incessantly adored.

3 How wonderful, how beautiful
  the sight of thee must be,
  thine endless wisdom, boundless power
  and awesome purity!

4 Oh, how, I fear thee, living God!
  with deepest, tenderest fears,
  and worship thee with trembling hope
  and penitential tears.

5 Yet I may love thee too, O Lord,
almighty as thou art,
for thou hast stooped to ask of me
the love of my poor heart.

6 No earthly father loves like thee,
no mother e'er so mild
bears and forbears as thou hast done
with me thy sinful child.

7 Father of Jesus, love's reward,
what rapture will it be
prostrate before thy throne to lie,
and gaze and gaze on thee!
F. W. Faber (1814–63)

728

1 O God beyond all praising,
we worship you today
and sing the love amazing
that songs cannot repay;
for we can only wonder
at every gift you send,
at blessings without number
and mercies without end:
we lift our hearts before you
and wait upon your word,
we honour and adore you,
our great and mighty Lord.

2 The flower of earthly splendour
in time must surely die,
its fragile bloom surrender
to you, the Lord most high;
but hidden from all nature
the eternal seed is sown;
though small in mortal stature,
to heaven's garden grown:
For Christ the man from heaven
from death has set us free,
and we through him are given
the final victory.

3 Then hear, O gracious Saviour,
accept the love we bring,
that we who know your favour
may serve you as your king;
and whether our tomorrows
be filled with good or ill,
we'll triumph through our sorrows
and rise to bless you still:
to marvel at your beauty
and glory in your ways,
and make a joyful duty
our sacrifice of praise.
Michael Perry (1942-96)

729

1 When, in our music, God is glorified,
and adoration leaves no room for pride,
it is as though the whole creation cried:
Alleluia!

2 How often, making music, we have found
a new dimension in the world of sound,
as worship moved us to a more profound
Alleluia!

3 So has the Church, in liturgy and song,
in faith and love, through centuries of
wrong,
borne witness to the truth in every tongue:
Alleluia!

4 And did not Jesus sing a Psalm that night
when utmost evil strove against the Light?
Then let us sing, for whom he won the
fight:
Alleluia!

5 Let every instrument be tuned for praise!
Let all rejoice who have a voice to raise!
and may God give us faith to sing always:
Alleluia!
F. Pratt Green

730

Lau - da - te, lau - da - te Do - mi - num, om - nes
We praise you, we praise your ho - ly name, God of

gen - tes, lau - da - te Do - mi - num. Ex - sul - ta - te, ju - bi -
jus - tice, e - ter - nal - ly the same. May our li - ving be thanks-

la - te per an - nos Do - mi - ni, om - nes gen - tes. Lau - gen - tes.
gi - ving, re - joi - cing in your name now and al - ways.

Verses

1. In the faith of Christ we walk hand in hand, light be - fore our path as the
2. In the name of Christ we will spread the seed; share the Word of God with all

Lord has planned; shi - ning the torch of faith in our land:
those in need, faith - ful in thought and word and deed:

in the name of Christ Je - sus.

3 In the power of Christ we proclaim one
      Lord.
   All who put on Christ are by faith
      restored;
   sharing new life, salvation's reward.
   in the name of Christ Jesus.

4 In the life of Christ, through the blood
      he shed,
   we are justified, and by him are fed,
   nourished by word and living bread:
   in the name of Christ Jesus.

5 In the Church of God we are unified,
   by the Spirit's power we are sanctified,
   temples of grace, where God may abide:
   by the pow'r of the Spirit.

6 Praise to God the Father while ages run
   praise to Christ the Saviour, God's only
      Son,
   praise to the Holy Spirit be sung:
   omnes gentes, laudate.
                    Christopher Walker

For ordination:

1 In the Church we answer the Saviour's
      call,
   serving, as he showed us, both great
      and small.
   sharing the Lord's compassion for all:

2 In the name of Christ we baptize and
      teach,
   truth upon our lips in the way we preach:
   raising the cup of blessing for each:

731

1 For the fruits of all creation,
thanks be to God;
for these gifts to every nation,
thanks be to God;
for the ploughing, sowing, reaping,
silent growth while we are sleeping,
future needs in earth's safe keeping,
thanks be to God.

2 In the just reward of labour,
God's will is done;
in the help we give our neighbour,
God's will is done;
in our world–wide task of caring
for the hungry and despairing
in the harvests we are sharing,
God's will is done.

3 For the harvests of the Spirit,
thanks be to God;
for the good we all inherit,
thanks be to God;
for the wonders that astound us,
for the truths that still confound us,
most of all, that love has found us,
thanks be to God.
F. Pratt Green

732

1 Loving Father, from your bounty
choicest gifts unnumbered flow:
all the blessings of salvation,
which to Christ thy Son we owe,
all the gifts that by your bidding
nature's hands on us bestow!

2 Here your grateful children gather,
offering gifts of bread and wine;
these we give to you in homage,
of your love the loving sign,
and restore to you creation,
through this fruit of earth and vine.

3 Soon will come Christ's loving presence,
on our love to set his seal!
Sacred body, precious life-blood,
bread and wine will then reveal!
Bread and wine, though these no longer,
flesh and blood will yet conceal.
James Quinn, S.J.

733

1 God whose farm is all creation,
take the gratitude we give;
Take the finest of our harvest,
crops we grow that all may live.

2 Take our ploughing, seeding, reaping,
hopes and fears of sun and rain,
all our thinking, planning, waiting,
ripened in this fruit and grain.

3 All our labour, all our watching,
all our calendar of care,
in these crops of your creation,
take, O God: they are our prayer.
John Arlott (1914-91)

734

1 Reap me the earth as a harvest to God,
gather and bring it again,
all that is his, to the Maker of all.
Lift it and offer it high.
*Bring bread, bring wine,
give glory to the Lord;
whose is the earth but God's,
whose is the praise but his?*

2 Go with your song and your music
with joy,
go to the altar of God.
Carry your offerings, fruits of the earth,
work of your labouring hands.

3 Gladness and pity and passion and pain,
all that is mortal in man,
lay all before him, return him his gift,
God, to whom all shall go home.
Peter Icarus

735

1 We plough the fields and scatter
the good seed on the land,
but it is fed and watered
by God's almighty hand;
he sends the snow in winter,
the warmth to swell the grain,
the breezes and the sunshine,
and soft refreshing rain.
All good gifts around us
are sent from heav'n above,
then thank the Lord,
O thank the Lord, for all his love.

2 He only is the maker
of all things near and far;
he paints the wayside flower,
he lights the ev'ning star.
The winds and waves obey him,
by him the birds are fed:
much more to us his children,
he gives our daily bread.

3 We thank thee then, O Father,
for all things bright and good:
the seed–time and the harvest,
our life, our health, our food.
No gifts have we to offer
for all thy love imparts,
but that which thou desirest,
our humble, thankful hearts.
M. Claudius (1740–1815),
tr. Jane M. Campbell (1817-78)

736

1 Come, ye thankful people, come,
raise the song of harvest–home!
All be safely gathered in,
ere the winter storms begin;
God, our maker, doth provide
for our wants to be supplied;
come to God's own temple come;
raise the song of harvest–home!

2 We ourselves are God's own field,
fruit unto his praise to yield;
wheat and tares together sown,
unto joy or sorrow grown;
first the blade and then the ear,
then the full corn shall appear:
grant, O harvest Lord, that we
wholesome grain and pure may be.

3 For the Lord our God shall come,
and shall take his harvest home;
from his field shall purge away
all that doth offend, that day,
give his angels charge at last
in the fire the tares to cast,
but the fruitful ears to store
in his garner evermore.

4 Then, thou Church triumphant, come,
raise the song of harvest–home
all be safely gathered in,
free from sorrow, free from sin,
there for ever purified
in God's garner to abide;
come, ten thousand angels, come,
raise the glorious harvest–home!
Henry Alford (1810–71)

737

Ag Críost an síol; ag Críost an fómhar;
in ioth lainn Dé go dtugtar sinn.
Ag Críost an mhuir; ag Críost an t-iasc,
i líonta Dé go gcastar sinn.
Ó fhás go haois, is ó aois go bás,
Do dhá láimh, a Chríost, anall tharainn.
Ó bhás go críoch, ní críoch ach athfhás,
i bPharthas na nGrást go rabhaimid.
Irish Traditional

The seed is Christ's, the harvest his:
may we be stored within God's barn.

The sea is Christ's, the fish are his:
may we be caught within God's net.

From birth to age, from age to death,
enfold us, Christ, within your arms.

Until the end, the great rebirth,
Christ be our joy in paradise.

English version by James Quinn, S.J.

JESUS CHRIST, THE WORD MADE FLESH

Jesus, Word of God

738

1. Be - fore the world be - gan, One Word was there; groun- ded in
2. Life found in him its source, death found its end; Light found in

God he was, roo - ted in care; By him all things were made, In him was
him its course, dark-ness its friend. For nei-ther death nor doubt nor dark-ness

love dis - played, through him God spoke, and said, 'I AM FOR YOU'.
can put out the glow of God, the shout, 'I AM FOR YOU'.

3 The Word was in the world
which from him came;
unrecognised he was,
unknown by name;
one with all humankind,
with the unloved aligned,
convincing sight and mind,
'I AM FOR YOU'.

4 All who received the Word
by God were blessed;
sisters and brothers they
of earth's fond guest.
So did the Word of Grace
proclaim in time and space
and with a human face,
'I AM FOR YOU'.

John Bell & Graham Maule

739

1 In a byre near Bethlehem,
passed by many a wand'ring stranger,
the most precious Word of Life
was heard gurgling in a manger,
for the good of us all.
  And he's here when we call him,
  bringing health, love and laughter
  to life now and ever after
  for the good of us all.

2 By the Galilean Lake
where the people flocked for teaching,
the most precious Word of Life
fed their mouths as well as preaching,
for the good of us all.

3 Quiet was Gethsemane,
camouflaging priest and soldier;
the most precious Word of Life
took the world's weight on his shoulder,
for the good of us all.

4 On the hill of Calvary -
place to end all hope of living -
the most precious Word of Life
breathed his last and died, forgiving,
for the good of us all.

5 In a garden, just at dawn,
near the grave of human violence,
the most precious Word of Life
cleared his throat and ended silence,
for the good of us all.

John Bell & Graham Maule

➤ see also Before the earth had yet begun (85)

(Cantor) Word of the Fa-ther, (all)

Hum_____ Come, Lord, come; and take our fear a-way,

and take our fear a-way, re-place it with your love._____

2 Firstborn of Mary,

3 Healer and helper,

4 Servant and sufferer,

5 Jesus, redeemer,

6 Christ resurrected,

7 Maranatha!

John Bell & Graham Maule

741

1 Word of God, come down to earth,
living rain from heav'n descending;
touch our hearts and bring to birth
faith and hope and love unending.
Word almighty, we revere you;
Word made flesh, we long to hear you.

2 Word eternal, throned on high,
Word that brought to life creation,
Word that came from heav'n to die,
crucified for our salvation,
saving Word, the world restoring,
speak to us, your love outpouring.

3 Word that caused blind eyes to see,
speak and heal our mortal blindness;
deaf we are; our healer be;
loose our tongues to tell your kindness.
Be our Word in pity spoken,
heal the world, by our sin broken.

4 Word that speaks your Father's love,
one with him beyond all telling,
Word that sends us from above
God the Spirit, with us dwelling;
Word of truth, to all truth lead us;
Word of life, with one Bread feed us.

James Quinn, S.J.

➤ *see also no 447, Word of God from Mary's womb*

742

1 God has spoken - by his prophets,
spoken his unchanging word,
each from age to age proclaiming
God, the one, the righteous Lord.
'Mid the world's despair and turmoil
one firm anchor holds us fast:
God is King, his throne eternal.
God the first, and God the last.

2 God has spoken - by Christ Jesus.
  Christ, the everlasting Son,
  brightness of the Father's glory,
  with the Father ever one;
  spoken by the Word incarnate,
  God from God, before time was;
  Light from Light to earth descending.
  He reveals our God to us.

3 God is speaking - by his Spirit,
  speaking to the hearts of all,
  in the age-long word expounding
  God's own message for us all.
  Through the rise and fall of nations
  one sure faith yet standing fast;
  God still speaks, his word unchanging.
  God the first, and God the last.

G.W. Briggs (1875-1959), alt.

Jesus Christ: his Ministry

743

1. If you would fol-low me,— fol-low where life will lead;—
2. If you would ho-nour me,— ho-nour the least of these:— you

do not look for me a-mong the dead,— for I am hid-den in pain,—
will not find me dressed in fi-ne-ry.— My Word cries out to be heard;—

ri-sen in love;— there is no har-vest with-out sow-ing of grain.—
breaks through the world:— my Word is on your lips and lives in your heart.—

Refrain: All that is hid-den will be made clear.— All that is dark now— will

be re-vealed. What you have heard in the dark— pro-claim in the light;—

—— what you hear in whis-pers——— pro-claim from the house- tops.—

3 If you would speak of me
  live all your life in me:
  my ways are not the ways that you
  would choose;
  my thoughts are far beyond yours,
  as heaven from earth:
  if you believe in me my voice will be
  heard.

4 If you would rise with me,
  rise through your destiny:
  do not refuse the death
  which brings you life,
  for as the grain in the earth
  must die for re-birth,
  so I have planted your life deep within
  mine.

Bernadette Farrell

744

1 Christ is the world's Light, he and no
    other;
  born in our darkness, he became our
    brother.
  If we have seen him, we have seen the
    Father:
  Glory to God on high.

2 Christ is the world's Peace, he and no
    other;
  no–one can serve him and despise
    another.
  Who else unites us, one in God the
    Father?

3 Christ is the world's Life, he and no other,

  sold once for silver, murdered here, our
    Brother -
  he who redeems us, reigns with God the
    Father:

4 Give God the glory, God and no other;
  give God the glory, Spirit, Son and Father;
  give God the glory, God in man my
    brother:
        F. Pratt Green (1903-2000)

745

1 O changeless Christ, for ever new,
  who walked our earthly ways,
  still draw our hearts as once you drew
  the hearts of other days.

2 As once you spoke by plain and hill
  or taught by shore and sea,
  so be today our teacher still,
  O Christ of Galilee.

3 As wind and storm their master heard
  and his command fulfilled,
  may troubled hearts receive your word,
  the tempest–tossed be stilled.

4 And as of old to all who prayed
  your healing hand was shown,
  so be your touch upon us laid,
  unseen but not unknown.

5 In broken bread, in wine outpoured,
  your new and living way
  proclaim to us, O risen Lord,
  O Christ of this our day.

6 O changeless Christ, till life is past
  your blessing still be given;
  then bring us home, to taste at last
  the timeless joys of heaven.
        Timothy Dudley–Smith

746

1 Jesus the Lord said, 'I am the bread,
  the bread of life for mankind am I.'
  the bread of life for mankind am I.'
  the bread of life for mankind am I.'
  Jesus the Lord said, 'I am the bread,
  the bread of life for mankind am I.'

2 Jesus the Lord said, 'I am the door,
  the way and the door for the poor am I.'

3 Jesus the Lord said, 'I am the light,
  the one true light of the world am I.'..

4 Jesus the Lord said, 'I am the shepherd,
  the one good shepherd of the sheep am I.'..

5 Jesus the Lord said, 'I am the life,
  the resurrection and the life am I.'..
      Urdu, tr Dermott Monahan (1906-57)

747

The light of Christ has come into the world,
The light of Christ has come into the world.

1 We all must be born again
  to see the kingdom of God;
  the water and the Spirit
  bring new life in God's love.

2 God gave up his only Son
  out of love for the world
  so that ev'ryone who believes in him
  will live for ever.

3 The Light of God has come to us
  so that we might have salvation,
  from the darkness of our sins, we walk
  into glory with Christ Jesus.
        Donald Fishel

➤ *See also: He healed the darkness (435), Justice & Peace (887-904)*

748

Un-less a grain of wheat shall fall u-pon the ground__ and die,____ it re-mains____but a sin-gle grain__ with no life.____

Verses

1. If we have died with him then we shall live with him;
2. If a - ny - one serves__ me then they must fol - low me;
3. ⸭ Make your home in me as I make mine in you;
4. If you re - main in me and my word lives in you;
5. ⸭ Those who love me are loved by my Fa - ther;
6. ⸭ Peace I leave with you, my peace I give to you;

if we hold firm we shall reign with him.____
wher - ev - er I am my ser - vants will be.
those who re - main in me bear much fruit.____
then you will be my dis - ci - ples.____
we shall be with them and dwell in them.____
peace which the world can - not give is my gift.

Bernadette Farrell. Words adapted from the Gospel of St John

749

1 From heaven You came, helpless babe,
entered our world, Your glory veiled,
not to be served but to serve,
and give Your life that we might live.
  This is our God, the Servant King,
  He calls us now to follow Him,
  to bring our lives as a daily offering
  of worship to the Servant King.

2 There in the garden of tears
my heavy load He chose to bear;
His heart with sorrow was torn,
'Yet not my will but yours,' He said.

3 Come see His hands and His feet,
the scars that speak of sacrifice,
hands that flung stars into space
to cruel nails surrendered.

4 So let us learn how to serve
and in our lives enthrone Him,
each other's needs to prefer,
for it is Christ we're serving.
  Graham Kendrick

750

1 Glory be to Jesus,
who in bitter pains
poured for me the life–blood,
from his sacred veins.

2 Grace and life eternal
in that blood I find:
blest be his compassion,
infinitely kind.

3 Blest through endless ages
  be the precious stream,
  which from endless torment
  doth the world redeem.

4 There the fainting spirit
  drinks of life her fill;
  there as in a fountain
  laves herself at will.

5 Abel's blood for vengeance
  pleaded to the skies,
  but the blood of Jesus
  for our pardon cries.

6 Oft as it is sprinkled
  on our guilty hearts,
  Satan in confusion
  terror–struck departs.

7 Oft as earth exulting
  wafts its praise on high,
  hell with horror trembles;
  heaven is filled with joy.

8 Lift ye, then, your voices;
  swell the mighty flood;
  louder still and louder,
  praise the precious blood.
        Italian, 18th century,
        tr. Edward Caswall (1814–78)

751

1 Meekness and majesty,
  manhood and deity,
  in perfect harmony,
  the man who is God.
  Lord of eternity
  dwells in humanity,
  kneels in humility
  and washes our feet.

  O, what a mystery,
  meekness and majesty,
  bow down and worship,
  for this is your God.
  This is your God.

2 Father's pure radiance,
  perfect in innocence,
  yet learns obedience
  to death on a cross.
  Suff'ring to give us life,
  conqu'ring through sacrifice;
  and as they crucify prays
  'Father forgive'.

3 Wisdom unsearchable,
  God the invisible;
  love indestructible
  in frailty appears.
  Lord of infinity,
  stooping so tenderly,
  lifts our humanity
  to the heights of his throne.
        Graham Kendrick

752

1 My song is love unknown,
  my Saviour's love to me,
  love to the loveless shown,
  that they might lovely be.
  O who am I, that for my sake,
  my Lord should take, frail flesh and die?

2 He came from his blest throne,
  salvation to bestow;
  but men made strange, and none
  the longed–for Christ would know,
  but O, my friend, my friend indeed,
  who at my need his life did spend!

3 Sometimes they strew his way,
  and his sweet praises sing;
  resounding all the day
  hosannas to their King;
  then 'Crucify!' is all their breath,
  and for his death they thirst and cry.

4 Why, what hath my Lord done?
  What makes this rage and spite?
  He made the lame to run,
  he gave the blind their sight.
  Sweet injuries! Yet they at these
  themselves displease, and 'gainst him
        rise.

5 They rise, and needs will have
my dear Lord made away;
a murderer they save,
the Prince of Life they slay.
Yet cheerful he to suffering goes,
that he his foes from thence might free.

6 In life, no house, no home
my Lord on earth might have:
in death no friendly tomb
but what a stranger gave.
What may I say? Heaven was his home;
but mine the tomb wherein he lay.

7 Here might I stay and sing,
no story so divine,
never was love, dear King,
never was grief like thine.
This is my Friend, in whose sweet praise
I all my days could gladly spend.
Samuel Crossman (c.1624–83)

753

1 To Christ, the Prince of peace,
and Son of God most high,
the father of the world to come,
sing we with holy joy.

2 Deep in his heart for us
the wound of love he bore:
that love wherewith he still inflames
the hearts that him adore.

3 O Jesu, victim blest,
what else but love divine
could thee constrain to open thus
that sacred heart of thine?

4 O fount of endless life,
O spring of water clear,
O flame celestial, cleansing all
who unto thee draw near!

5 Hide us in thy dear heart,
for thither we do fly;
there seek thy grace through life, in
death
thine immortality.

6 Praise to the Father be,
and sole–begotten Son;
praise, holy Paraclete, to thee
while endless ages run.
*Catholicum Hymnolgium Germanicum
(1587) tr. E. Caswall (1814–78)*

754

1 Before the heaven and earth
were made by God's decree,
the Son of God all glorious dwelt
in God's eternity.

2 Though in the form of God
and rich beyond compare,
he did not stop to grasp his prize;
nor did he linger there.

3 From heights of heaven he came
to this world full of sin,
to meet with hunger, hatred, hell,
our life, our love to win.

4 The Son became true man
and took a servant's role;
with lowliness and selfless love,
he came, to make us whole.

5 Obedient to his death
that death upon the cross,
no son had ever shown such love,
nor father known such loss.

6 To him enthroned on high,
by angel hosts adored,
all knees shall bow, and tongues confess
that Jesus Christ is Lord.
Brian Black, from Philippians 2:6-11

755

Ev-ery knee shall bow be - fore him, ev-ery tongue con-fess his glo - ry, Je - sus Christ is Lord a - bove ev - ery name.

Verses

1. Though he was in form of God, Je - sus did not flaunt his
2. Be - ing found in hu - man form, He be - came hum - bler
3. There - fore God has raised him up; gi - ven him the grea - test

state, but emp - tied him - self, be - came as a ser - vant, was
yet; o - be - dient he was, o - be - dient un - to death, he en -
name; all hea - ven and earth con - fess that he is Lord to the

born in the like - ness of a man.
dured e - ven death on a cross.
glo - ry of God the Fa - ther.

Stephen Dean,
from Philippians
2:6-11

756

1 When I survey the wondrous cross
   on which the Prince of Glory died,
   my richest gain I count but loss,
   and pour contempt on all my pride.

2 Forbid it, Lord, that I should boast,
   save in the death of Christ, my God:
   all the vain things that charm me most,
   I sacrifice them to his blood.

3 See from his head, his hands, his feet,
   sorrow and love flow mingled down;
   did e'er such love and sorrow meet,
   or thorns compose so rich a crown?

4 His dying crimson like a robe,
   spreads o'er his body on the Tree;
   then I am dead to all the globe,
   and all the globe is dead to me.

5 Were the whole realm of nature mine,
   that were an offering far too small;
   love so amazing, so divine,
   demands my soul, my life, my all.
   Isaac Watts (1674-1748)

O Christe Domine Jesu

Taizé chant by Jacques Berthier

757

O Chris - te Do - mi - ne Je - su, O Chris - te Do - mi - ne Je - su. O

The Paschal Mystery: Jesus risen in glory

758

God, your glo-ry we have seen in your Son, full of truth, full of heav'n-ly
grace; in Christ make us live,— his love shine on our face, and the na-tions will
see in us the tri-umph you have won.

Verses

1. In the fields of this world his good
2. In his love like a fire that con-
3. He was bro-ken for us, God-for-

news he has sown, and sends us out to reap till the har-vest is done.
sumes he passed by: the flame has touched our lips; let us shout: 'Here am I!'
sa-ken his cry, and still the bread he breaks: to our-selves we must die.

4 He has trampled the grapes
   of new life on his Cross;
   now drink the cup and live:
   he has filled it for us:

5 He has founded a kingdom
   that none shall destroy;
   the corner–stone is laid:
   Go to work, build with joy!

Didier Rimaud, Vv. tr. Brian Wren Refrain tr. Ronald Johnson

759

Join in the dance of the earth's ju-bi-la-tion! This is the
feast of the love of God. Shout from the heights to the ends of cre-a-tion:
Je-sus the Sa-viour is ri-sen from the grave!

Verses

1. Wake, O peo-ple; sleep no lon-ger: greet the brea-king day!__
2. All cre-a-tion, like a mo-ther, la-bours to give birth.__

Christ, Re-dee-mer, Lamb and Li-on, turns the night a-way!__
Soon the pain will be for-got-ten, joy for all the earth!__

3 Now our shame becomes our glory
      on this holy tree.
   Now the reign of death is ended;
      now we are set free!

4 None on earth, no prince or power,
      neither death nor life,
   nothing now can ever part us
      from the love of Christ!

5 Love's triumphant day of vict'ry
      heaven opens wide.
   On the tree of hope and glory
      death itself has died!

6 Christ for ever, Lord of ages,
      Love beyond our dreams:
   Christ, our hope of heaven's glory
      all that yet will be!
                              Daniel L. Schutte

760

1 All heaven declares
      the glory of the risen Lord.
   Who can compare
      with the beauty of the Lord?
   Forever he will be
      the Lamb upon the throne:
   I gladly bow the knee
      and worship him alone.

2 I will proclaim
      the glory of the risen Lord,
   who once was slain
      to reconcile man to God.
   Forever you will be
      the Lamb upon the throne:
   I gladly bow the knee
      and worship you alone.
           Noel Richards and Tricia Richards

761

1 He is Lord, he is Lord.
   He is risen from the dead and he is Lord.
   Ev'ry knee shall bow, ev'ry tongue confess
   that Jesus Christ is Lord.

2 He is King, he is King.
   He is risen from the dead and he is King.
   Ev'ry knee shall bow, ev'ry tongue confess
   that Jesus Christ is King.

3 He is love, he is love.
   He is risen from the dead and he is love.
   Ev'ry knee shall bow, ev'ry tongue confess
   that Jesus Christ is love.
                              Anonymous

762

1 At the name of Jesus
      every knee shall bow,
   every tongue confess him
      King of glory now;
   'tis the Father's pleasure
      we should call him Lord,
   who from the beginning
      was the mighty Word.

2 At his voice creation
      sprang at once to sight,
   all the angel faces,
      all the hosts of light,
   thrones and dominations,
      stars upon their way,
   all the heavenly orders,
      in their great array.

3 Humbled for a season,
      to receive a name
   from the lips of sinners
      unto whom he came,
   faithfully he bore it
      spotless to the last,
   brought it back victorious
      when from death he passed.

4 Bore it up triumphant
      with its human light
   through all ranks of creatures,
      to the central height,
   to the throne of Godhead,
      to the Father's breast,
   filled it with the glory
      of that perfect rest.

5 Name him, Christians, name him,
    with love as strong as death;
but with awe and wonder,
    and with bated breath;
he is God the Saviour,
    he is Christ the Lord,
ever to be worshipped,
    trusted, and adored.

6 In your hearts enthrone him;
    there let him subdue
all that is not holy,
    all that is not true;
crown him as your captain,
    in temptation's hour
let his will enfold you
    in its light and power.

7 Christians, this Lord Jesus
    shall return again,
with his Father's glory,
    with his angel train,
for all wreaths of empire
    meet upon his brow,
and our hearts confess him
    King of glory now.
      Caroline Maria Noel (1817–77)

763

1 Christ triumphant ever–reigning,
Saviour, Master, King,
Lord of heav'n, our lives sustaining,
hear us as we sing.

    Yours the glory and the crown,
    the high renown,
    the eternal name.

2 Word incarnate, truth revealing,
Son of Man on earth!
Power and majesty concealing
by your humble birth:

3 Suffering servant, scorned, ill–treated,
victim crucified!
Death is through the cross defeated,
sinners justified:

4 Priestly King, enthroned for ever
high in heaven above!
Sin and death and hell shall never
stifle hymns of love:

5 So, our hearts and voices raising
through the ages long,
ceaselessly upon you gazing,
this shall be our song:
    Michael Saward

764

1 Colours of day dawn into the mind,
the sun has come up, the night is behind.
Go down in the city, into the street,
and let's give the message to the people
    we meet.
So light up the fire and let the flame burn,
open the door, let Jesus return.
Take seeds of his Spirit, let the fruit grow,
tell the people of Jesus, let his love show.

2 Go through the park, on into the town;
the sun still shines on it never goes down.
The light of the world is risen again;
the people of darkness are needing our
    friend.

3 Open your eyes, look into the sky,
the darkness has come, the sun came to die.
The evening draws on the sun disappears,
but Jesus is living, and his Spirit is near.
    Sue McClellan, John Paculabo
      & Keith Rycroft

765

1 I danced in the morning
    when the world was begun,
and I danced in the moon
    and the stars and the sun,
and I came down from heaven and
    I danced on the earth –
at Bethlehem I had my birth.
Dance, then, wherever you may be,
I am the Lord of Dance, said he.
And I'll lead you all, wherever you may be,
and I'll lead you all in the dance, said he.

2 I danced for the scribe
    and the pharisee
but they would not dance
    and they wouldn't follow me,
I danced for the fishermen,
    for James and John –
they came with me
    and the dance went on:

3 I danced on the Sabbath
    and I cured the lame;
the holy people
    said it was a shame.
They whipped and they stripped
    and they hung me high,
and they left me there
    on a Cross to die.

4 I danced on a Friday
    when the sky turned black –
It's hard to dance
    with the devil on your back.
They buried my body
    and they thought I'd gone,
but I am the Dance
    and I still go on.

5 They cut me down
    and I leapt up high –
I am the life
    that'll never, never die
I'll live in you
    if you'll live in me –
I am the Lord
    of the Dance, said he.
Sydney Carter

766

Jesus, you are Lord.
You are risen from the dead
and you are Lord.
Ev'ry knee shall bow,
and ev'ry tongue confess
that Jesus, you are Lord.
You are the Way.

1 I am the Way.
No one knows the Father but it be
    through me.
I am in my Father, and my Father is in me,
and we come in love to live within your
    hearts.

2 I am the Truth.
And I set my spirit deep within your hearts,
and you will know me, and love me,
and the truth I give to you will set you
    free.

3 I am the Life.
The living waters I pour out for you.
Anyone who drinks of the waters that I
    give
will have eternal life.

4 I am the Word,
    the true light that shines brightly in the
    dark,
a light that darkness could not overpower,
the Word made flesh, risen among you.
Mary Barrett, based on John 14:6

767

Majesty, worship his Majesty;
unto Jesus be glory, honour and praise.
Majesty, kingdom, authority,
flows from his throne unto his own,
his anthem raise.
So exalt, lift upon high,
the name of Jesus,
magnify, come glorify,
Christ Jesus the King.
Majesty, worship his Majesty,
Jesus who died, now glorified,
King of all kings.
Jack W. Hayford

768

1 How lovely on the mountains
are the feet of him
who brings good news, good news,
announcing peace,
proclaiming news of happiness:
our God reigns, our God reigns.

Our God reigns, our God reigns,
our God reigns, our God reigns.

2 You watchmen, lift your voices joyfully
  as one,
shout for your king, your king!
See eye to eye, the Lord restoring Sion:
our God reigns, our God reigns.

3 Wasteplaces of Jerusalem,
break forth with joy!
We are redeemed, redeemed,
the Lord has saved
and comforted his people.
our God reigns, our God reigns.

4 Ends of the earth,
see the salvation of our God!
Jesus is Lord, is Lord!
Before the nations,
he has bared his holy arm.
our God reigns, our God reigns.
Leonard E. Smith Jnr

769

1 Lord, enthroned in heavenly splendour,
first begotten from the dead,
thou alone, our strong defender,
liftest up thy people's head.
 Alleluia, alleluia,
Jesus, true and living bread!

2 Prince of life, for us thou livest,
by thy body souls are healed;
Prince of peace, thy peace thou givest,
by thy blood is pardon sealed;
 alleluia, alleluia,
Word of God, in flesh revealed.

3 Though the lowliest form doth veil thee
as of old in Bethlehem,
here as there thine angels hail thee,
branch and flower of Jesse's stem
 alleluia, alleluia,
we in worship join with them.

4 Paschal Lamb! thine offering, finished
once for all when thou wast slain,
in its fullness undiminished
shall for evermore remain,

alleluia, alleluia,
cleansing souls from every stain.

5 Life–imparting heavenly manna,
stricken rock, with streaming side,
heaven and earth with loud hosanna
worship thee, the Lamb who died;
 alleluia, alleluia,
risen, ascended, glorified!
G.H. Bourne (1840–1925)

770

1 Lord, the light of your love is shining
in the midst of the darkness, shining;
Jesus, Light of the World, shine upon us,
set us free by the truth you now bring us,
shine on me, shine on me.
 Shine, Jesus, shine,
 fill this land with the Father's glory;
 blaze, Spirit, blaze,
 set our hearts on fire.
 Flow, river, flow,
 flood the nations with grace and mercy;
 send forth your word, Lord,
 and let there be light.

2 Lord, I come to your awesome presence,
from the shadows into your radiance;
by the blood I may enter your brightness,
search me, try me, consume all my darkness.
Shine on me, shine on me.

3 As we gaze on your kingly brightness
so our faces display your likeness,
ever changing from glory to glory,
mirrored here may our lives tell your story.
Shine on me, shine on me.
Graham Kendrick

771

1 The Spirit lives to set us free,
walk, walk in the light.
He binds us all in unity,
walk, walk in the light.
 Walk in the light,
 walk in the light,

walk in the light,
walk in the light of the Lord.

2 Jesus promised life to all,
  the dead were wakened by his call.

3 He died in pain on Calvary,
  to save the lost like you and me.

4 We know his death was not the end,
  He gave his Spirit to be our friend.

5 By Jesus' love our wounds are healed,
  the Father's kindness is revealed.

6 The Spirit lives in you and me,
  His light will shine for all to see.
  Damian Lundy

772

1 Lord, Jesus Christ,
  you have come to us
  you are one with us, Mary's son.
  Cleansing our souls from all their sin,
  pouring your love and goodness in,
  Jesus our love for you we sing,
  living Lord.

2 Lord Jesus Christ,
  now and ev'ry day
  teach us how to pray, Son of God.
  You have commanded us to do
  this in remembrance, Lord, of you
  into our lives your pow'r breaks through,
  living Lord.

3 Lord Jesus Christ,
  you have come to us,
  born as one of us, Mary's Son.
  Led out to die on Calvary,
  risen from death to set us free,
  living Lord Jesus, help us see
  you are Lord.

4 Lord Jesus Christ,
  I would come to you,
  live my life for you, Son of God.
  All your commands I know are true,
  your many gifts will make me new,
  into my life your pow'r breaks through,
  living Lord.
  Patrick Appleford

773

Keep in mind that Je-sus Christ has died for us and is ri-sen from the dead. He is our sa-ving Lord, he is joy for all a-ges.

Verses *may be sung singly or in pairs between refrains* Refrain

1. If we die with the Lord, we shall live with the Lord.
(2). If we en-dure with the Lord, we shall reign with the Lord.

Refrain

3. In him all our sor-row, in him all our joy.
(4.) In him hope of glo-ry, in him all our love.
5. In him our re-demp-tion, in him all our grace.
(6.) In him our sal-va-tion, in him all our peace.

Lucien Deiss, from 2 Tim 1:8, 11

God's Love & Mercy

774

Lord, your love has drawn us near; per-fect love which casts out fear;

love has sought us, home-ward brought us, joined us in com-mu-nion here.

Verses

1. How can I re-pay the Lord, who feeds us with his
2. He who calls us to be here, who calms us in our
3. Ev-ery crea-ture that God feeds, Praise him who fills your

word, with bread and wine? Sing in ho-mage all your
fear, will guide our way; he who gave his ve-ry
needs, lift up your voice; ev-ery crea-ture that has

days, a sa-cri-fice of praise will be our sign.
life, who con-quered in the strife, will light our day.
breath, praise him who con-quered death, and still re-joice!

Stephen Dean

775

I have loved you with an e-ver-las-ting love, I have

called you and you are mine; I have loved you with an e-ver-las-ting

love, I have called you and you are mine. 1–3. Seek the face of the

Lord and long for him; he will bring you his light and his peace.
2. he will bring you his joy and his hope.
3. he will bring you his care and his love.

Michael Joncas, from Jer 31:3, Ps 24:3

776

Verses

1. I will come to you in the si-lence,
2. I am hope for all who are hope-less,
3. I am strength for all the des-pai-ring,
4. (I) am the Word that leads all to free-dom, I

I will lift you from all your fear. You will hear my voice, I
I am eyes for all who long to see. In the sha-dows of the night,
hea-ling for the ones who dwell in shame. All the blind will see, the
am the peace the world can-not give. I will call your name, em-

claim you as my choice, be still and know I am here. *(To verse 2)*
I will be your light, come and rest in me. *(To refrain)*
lame will all run free, and all will know my name. *(To refrain)*
brac-ing all your pain, stand up, now walk, and live! *(To refrain)*

Refrain

Do not be a-fraid, I am with you. I have called you each by name. Come and fol-low

D.C.

me, I will bring you home; I love you and you are mine. 4. I

David Haas

777

Yahweh, I know you are near,
standing always at my side.
You guard me from the foe
and you lead me in ways everlasting.

1 Lord, you have searched my heart
and you know when I sit and when I
stand.
Your hand is upon me, protecting me
from death,
keeping me from harm.

2 Where can I run from your love?
If I climb to the heavens, you are there.

If I fly to the sunrise or sail beyond the
sea
still I'd find you there.

3 You know my heart and its ways,
you who formed me before I was born,
in secret of darkness, before I saw the sun,
in my mother's womb.

4 Marvellous to me are your works;
how profound are your thoughts my Lord!
Even if I could count them, they number
as the stars,
you would still be there.

Daniel L. Schutte, from Psalm 139

778

Vv 1,3,5,7: All

1,7. You know me, Lord, you search my heart, my thoughts are o-pen
3. Where could I go to flee from you? How can I shel-ter
5. If dark-ness came to swal-low me and night sur-round me

to your gaze. Pro-tect me, Lord, from e-vil ways and guide me in the
from your face? If hea-ven-ward, I find you there: in earth's dark depths you
in its grasp, no dark-ness would there be for you: the light would be as

Vv 2,4,6: Cantor

path of life. 2. Be-fore a word is on my tongue you
fol-low me. 4. If I could take the wings of dawn and
light as day. 6. For it was you who fash-ioned me; knit

know the se-crets of my heart. Be close to me, sur-
jour-ney to the ends of earth, your hands would still be
bone to bone and flesh on flesh. I thank you, Lord, Cre-

round me, Lord, from all my ter-rors set me free. *(to v.3)*
gui-ding me, your right hand still would hold me fast. *(to v.5)*
a-tor God, that you should think and breathe on me. *(to v.7)*

James Walsh, from Psalm 139

779

1. O God, you search me and you know me. All my

thoughts lie o-pen to your gaze. When I walk or lie down you are be-

fore me: e-ver the ma-ker and kee-per of my days.

2. You know my resting and my rising.
   You discern my purpose from afar.
   And with love everlasting you besiege me:
   in ev'ry moment of life or death, you are.

3. Before a word is on my tongue, Lord,
   you have known its meaning through
   and through.
   You are with me, beyond my understanding:
   God of my present, my past and future, too.

4. Although your Spirit is upon me,
   still I search for shelter from your light.
   There is nowhere on earth I can escape you:
   even the darkness is radiant in your sight.

5. For you created me and shaped me,
   gave me life within my mother's womb.
   For the wonder of who I am, I praise you:
   safe in your hands, all creation is made new.

Bernadette Farrell, from Psalm 139

780

God to en-fold you, Christ to up-hold you, Spi - rit to
keep you in hea-ven's sight; so may God grace you, heal and embrace you, lead you through dark - ness in - to the light.

John L. Bell

781

1. Look and learn from the birds of the air, fly-ing high a-bove wor-ry and fear:
nei - ther sow-ing nor har-ves-ting seed, yet they're gi-ven what-e - ver they need.
If the God of earth and heaven cares for birds as much—— as this,
won't he care— much more— for you, when you put— your trust—— in him?

2 Look and learn from the flowers of the field,
   bringing beauty and colour to life;
   neither sowing nor tailoring cloth,
   yet they're dressed in the finest attire.
   If the God of earth and heaven
   cares for flowers as much as this,
   won't he care much more for you
   when you put your trust in him?

3 What God wants should be our will;
   where God calls should be our goal.
   When we seek the kingdom first,
   all we've lost is ours again.
   Let's be done with anxious thoughts,
   set aside tomorrow's cares,
   live each day that God provides
   putting all our trust in him.

Nah Young-Soo, from Matt 6:23-24. English version by John L. Bell

Toi, tu nous aimes/Lord God, you love us — *Taizé chant by Jacques Berthier*

782

Lord God, you love us, source of com - pas - sion.
Toi, tu nous ai - mes, sour - ce de vie.

783

1 Lord of life we come to you;
   Lord of all, our Saviour be;
   come to bless and to heal
   with the light of your love.

2 Through the days of doubt and toil,
   in our joy and in our pain,
   guide our steps in your way,
   make us one in your love.
   Catherine Walker

784

1 Praise we our God with joy
   and gladness never ending;
   angels and saints with us
   their grateful voices blending.
   He is our Father dear,
   o'er filled with parent's love;
   mercies unsought, unknown,
   he showers from above.

2 He is our shepherd true;
   with watchful care unsleeping,
   on us, his erring sheep
   an eye of pity keeping;
   he with a mighty arm
   the bonds of sin doth break,
   and to our burden'd hearts
   in words of peace doth speak.

3 Graces in copious stream
   from that pure fount are welling,
   where, in our heart of hearts,
   our God hath set his dwelling.
   His word our lantern is;
   his peace our comfort still;
   his sweetness all our rest;
   our law, our life, his will.
   Frederick Oakeley (1802–80), and others

785

*Though the mountains may fall, and the
   hills turn to dust,
yet the love of the Lord will stand
as a shelter for all who will call on his
   name.
Sing the praise and the glory of God.*

1 Could the Lord ever leave you?
   Could the Lord forget his love?
   Though the Mother forsake her child,
   he will not abandon you.

2 Should you turn and forsake him,
   he will gently call your name.
   Should you wander away from him,
   he will always take you back.

3 Go to him when you're weary;
   he will give you eagle's wings.
   You will run, never tire,
   for your God will be your strength.

4 As he swore to your Fathers,
   when the flood destroyed the land.
   He will never forsake you;
   he will swear to you again.
   *Daniel L. Schutte,
   based on Isaiah 54:6-10; 49:15; 40:31-32*

786

*Turn to me, O turn, and be saved,
says the Lord, for I am God
there is no other, none beside me.
I call your name.*

1 I am God who comforts you;
   who are you to be afraid,
   of flesh that fades,
   is made like the grass of the field
   soon to wither.

2 Listen to me, my people;
   give ear to me, my nation:
   a law will go forth from me,
   and my justice for a light to the people.

3 Lift up your eyes to the heavens,
   and look at the earth down below.
   The heavens will vanish like smoke,
   and the earth will wear out like a
      garment.

John Foley, S.J., based on Isaiah 45, 51

787

Sing it in the valleys,
shout it from the mountain tops;
Jesus came to save us,
and his saving never stops.
He is King of Kings,
and new life he brings,
sing it in the valleys,
shout it from the mountain tops, (Oh!)
shout it from the mountain tops.

1 Jesus you are by my side,
   you take all my fears.
   If I only come to you,
   you will heal the pain of years.

2 You have not deserted me,
   though I go astray.
   Jesus take me in your arms,
   help me walk with you today.

3 Jesus, you are living now,
   Jesus, I believe.
   Jesus, take me, heart and soul,
   yours alone I want to be.

Mike Anderson

788

1 Praise to the Holiest in the height,
   and in the depth be praise,
   in all his words most wonderful,
   most sure in all his ways.

2 O loving wisdom of our God!
   When all was sin and shame,
   a second Adam to the fight,
   and to the rescue came.

3 O wisest love! That flesh and blood
   which did in Adam fail,
   should strive afresh against the foe,
   should strive and should prevail;

4 And that a higher gift than grace
   should flesh and blood refine,
   God's presence and his very self,
   and Essence all divine.

5 O generous love! That he who smote
   in man for man the foe,
   the double agony in man
   for man should undergo;

6 And in the garden secretly
   and on the Cross on high,
   should teach his brethren, and inspire
   to suffer and to die.

7 Praise to the Holiest in the height,
   and in the depth be praise,
   in all his words most wonderful,
   most sure in all his ways.

John Henry Newman (1801–90)

789

1 Trust is in the eyes of a tiny babe
   leaning on his mother's breast.
   In the eager beat of a young bird's wings
   on the day it leaves the nest.
   It is the living Spirit
   filling the earth, bringing to birth
   a world of love and laughter,
   joy in the light of the Lord.

2 Hope is in the rain that makes crystal
      streams
   tumble down a mountain side,
   and in every man who repairs his nets,
   waiting for the rising tide.

3 Love is in the hearts of all those who
      seek
   freedom for the human race.
   Love is in the touch of the hand that
      heals,
   and the smile that lights a face.

4 Strength is in the wind as it bends the
      trees,
   warmth is in the bright red flame,
   light is in the sun and the candle–glow,
   cleansing are the ocean's waves.
                    Estelle White

790

1 And can it be that I should gain
   an interest in the Saviour's blood?
   Died he for me, who caused his pain;
   for me, who him to death pursued?
   Amazing love! – How can it be
   that thou, my God, shouldst die for me?

2 'Tis mystery all! – The Immortal dies –
   who can explore his strange design?
   In vain the first–born seraph tries
   to sound the depths of love divine!
   'Tis mercy all! – Let earth adore,
   let angel minds inquire no more.

791

1 Come to me, O weary traveller;
   come to me with your distress;
   Come to me, you heavy burdeneed;
   come to me and find your rest.

2 Do not fear, my yoke is easy;
   do not fear, my burden's light;
   do not fear the path before you;
   do not run from me in fright.

3 He left his Father's throne above,
   so free, so infinite his grace;
   emptied himself of all but love,
   and bled for Adam's helpless race.
   'Tis mercy all, immense and free;
   for, O my God, it found out me.

4 Long my imprisoned spirit lay
   fast bound in sin and nature's night:
   thine eye diffused a quickening ray;
   I woke – the dungeon flamed with light.
   My chains fell off, my heart was free;
   I rose, went forth, and followed thee.

5 No condemnation now I dread;
   Jesus, and all in him, is mine!
   Alive in him, my living Head,
   and clothed in righteousness divine,
   bold I approach the eternal throne,
   and claim the crown through Christ
      my own.
                  Charles Wesley (1707–88)

3 Take my yoke and leave your troubles;
   take my yoke and come with me.
   Take my yoke, I am beside you;
   take and learn humility.

4 Rest in me, O weary traveller;
   rest in me and do not fear.
   Rest in me, my heart is gentle,
   rest and cast away your care
             Sylvia G. Dunstan (1955-93)   Mt 11:28-30

*Music by
Bob Moore*

1. Come to me, O wea-ry trav'-ler; come to me with your dis-tress;
Come to me, you hea-vy burdened; come to me and find your rest.

792

Eye has not seen, ear has not heard what God has read-y for
those who love him; Spir - it of love, come, give us the

mind of Je - sus,____ teach us the wis - dom of God.____

Verses

1. When pain and sor - row weigh us down, be near to us, O Lord, for -
2. Our lives are but a sin - gle breath, we flow - er and we fade, yet
3. To those who see with eyes of faith, the Lord is ev - er near, re -
4. We sing a mys - t'ry from the past in halls where saints have trod, yet

Verses 1-3

give the weak - ness of our faith, and bear us up with - in your peace - ful word.
all our days are in your hands, so we re - turn in love what love has made.
flect - ed in the fac - es of all the poor and low - ly of the world.
ev - er new the

D.C. *Verse 4* *D.C.*

_____ mu - sic rings to Je - sus, Liv - ing Song of God._____

Marty Haugen

793

If God is for us, who can be against,
if the Spirit of God has set us free?
If God is for us, who can be against,
if the Spirit of God has set us free?

1 I know that nothing in this world
   can ever take us from his love.

2 Nothing can take us from his love,
   poured out in Jesus, the Lord.

3 And nothing present or to come
   can ever take us from his love.

4 I know that neither death nor life
   can ever take us from his love.
          John B. Foley, S.J., based on Romans 8

794

1 God is love: his the care,
   tending each, everywhere.
   God is love, all is there!
   Jesus came to show him,
   that we all might know him!

Sing aloud, loud, loud!
Sing aloud, loud, loud!
God is good! God is truth!
God is beauty!
Praise him!

2 None can see God above;
   humankind we can love;
   thus may we Godward move,
   finding God in others,
   sisters all, and brothers:

3 Jesus shared all our pain:
   strove and died, rose again,
   rules our hearts now as then,
   for he came to save us
   by the truth he gave us:

4 To our Lord praise we sing,
   light and life, friend and king,
   coming down love to bring,
   pattern for our duty,
   showing God in beauty:
          Percy Dearmer (1867–1936), alt.

795

1 I heard the voice of Jesus say,
'Come unto me and rest;
lay down, you weary one, lay down
your head upon my breast.'
I came to Jesus as I was,
weary, and worn, and sad;
I found in him a resting-place
and he has made me glad.

2 I heard the voice of Jesus say,
'Behold, I freely give
the living water, thirsty one;
stoop down, and drink, and live.'
I came to Jesus, and I drank
of that life-giving stream;
my thirst was quenched, my soul
    revived,
and now I live in him.

3 I heard the voice of Jesus say,
'I am this dark world's Light;
look unto me, your morn shall rise
and all your day be bright.'
I looked to Jesus, and I found
in him my Star, my Sun;
and in that light of life I'll walk
till travelling days are done.
Horatius Bonar (1808-89)

796

1 I will never forget you, my people,
I have carved you on the palm of my
    hand.
I will never forget you;
I will not leave you orphaned.
I will never forget my own.

2 Does a mother forget her baby?
Or a woman the child within her womb?
Yet, even if these forget,
yes, even if these forget,
I will never forget my own.

Repeat Verse 1

Carey Landry

797

1 Jesu, lover of my soul!
Let me to thy bosom fly,
while the nearer waters roll,
while the tempest still is high;
hide me, O my Saviour, hide,
till the storm of life is past;
safe into the haven guide,
O receive my soul at last.

2 Other refuge have I none;
hangs my helpless soul on thee;
leave, ah! leave me not alone,
still support and comfort me.
All my trust on thee is stayed,
all my help from thee I bring;
cover my defenceless head
with the shadow of thy wing.

3 Thou, O Christ, art all I want;
more than all in thee I find;
raise the fallen, cheer the faint,
heal the sick and lead the blind.
Just and holy is thy name;
I am all unrighteousness;
false and full of sin I am,
thou art full of truth and grace.

4 Plenteous grace with thee is found,
grace to cover all my sin
let the healing streams abound;
make and keep me pure within.
Thou of life the fountain art,
freely let me take of thee;
spring thou up within my heart,
rise to all eternity.
Charles Wesley (1707–88)

798

1 Jesu, the very thought of thee
with sweetness fills my breast;
but sweeter far thy face to see,
and in thy presence rest.

2 Nor voice can sing, nor heart can frame,
nor can the memory find,
a sweeter sound than thy blest name,
O Saviour of mankind.

3 O hope of every contrite heart,
   O joy of all the meek,
   to those who fall, how kind thou art,
   how good to those who seek!

4 But what to those who find? Ah, this
   nor tongue nor pen can show;
   the love of Jesus, what it is
   none but his lovers know.

5 Jesu, our only joy be thou,
   as thou our prize wilt be;
   Jesu, be thou our glory now,
   and through eternity.

   11th century, tr. Edward Caswall (1814–78)

799

1 O Sacred Heart,
   our home lies deep in thee;
   on earth thou art an exile's rest,
   in heav'n the glory of the blest,
   O Sacred Heart.

2 O Sacred Heart,
   thou fount of contrite tears;
   where'er those living waters flow,
   new life to sinners they bestow,
   O Sacred Heart.

3 O Sacred Heart,
   our trust is all in thee,
   for though earth's night be dark and
   drear,
   thou breathest rest where thou art near,
   O Sacred Heart.

4 O Sacred Heart,
   when shades of death shall fall,
   receive us 'neath thy gentle care,
   and save us from the tempter's snare,
   O Sacred Heart.

5 O Sacred Heart,
   lead exiled children home,
   where we may ever rest near thee,
   in peace and joy eternally,
   O Sacred Heart.

   Francis Stanfield (1835–1914)

800

1 To Jesus' Heart, all burning
   with fervent love for all,
   my heart with fondest yearning
   shall raise its joyful call.

   While ages course along,
     blest be with loudest song
     the sacred heart of Jesus
     by ev'ry heart and tongue.
   The sacred heart of Jesus
     by ev'ry heart and tongue.

2 O Heart, for me on fire
   with love no–one can speak,
   my yet untold desire
   God gives me for thy sake.

3 Too true, I have forsaken
   thy love for wilful sin;
   yet now let me be taken
   back by thy grace again.

4 As thou art meek and lowly,
   and ever pure of heart,
   so may my heart be wholly
   of thine the counterpart.

5 When life away is flying,
   and earth's false glare is done;
   still, Sacred Heart, in dying
   I'll say I'm all thine own.

   Aloys Schlör (1805–52),
   tr. A.J. Christie (1817–1891)

801

1 Love divine, all loves excelling,
   joy of heav'n, to earth come down,
   fix in us thy humble dwelling,
   all thy faithful mercies crown.

2 Jesus, thou art all compassion,
   pure unbounded love thou art;
   visit us with thy salvation,
   enter every trembling heart.

3 Come, almighty to deliver,
   let us all thy life receive;
   suddenly return, and never,
   never more thy temples leave.

4 Thee we would be always blessing,
serve thee as thy hosts above;
pray, and praise thee without ceasing,
glory in thy perfect love.

5 Finish then thy new creation,
pure and sinless let us be;
let us see thy great salvation
perfectly restored in thee.

6 Changed from glory into glory,
till in heaven we take our place,
till we cast our crowns before thee,
lost in wonder, love, and praise.
Charles Wesley (1707–88)

802

1 Loving shepherd of thy sheep,
keep me, Lord, in safety keep;
nothing can thy pow'r withstand,
none can pluck me from thy hand.

2 Loving shepherd, thou didst give
thine own life that I might live;
may I love thee day by day,
gladly thy sweet will obey.

3 Loving shepherd, ever near,
teach me still thy voice to hear;
suffer not my steps to stray
from the strait and narrow way.

4 Where thou leadest may I go,
walking in thy steps below;
then before thy Father's throne,
Jesu, claim me for thine own.
Jane E. Leeson (1809–91)

803

1 Love is his word, love is his way,
feasting with kin, fasting alone,
living and dying, rising again,
love, only love, is his way.
Richer than gold is the love of my Lord:
better than splendour and wealth.

2 Love is his way, love is his mark,
sharing his last Passover feast,
Christ at the table, host to the Twelve,
love, only love, is his mark.

3 Love is his mark, love is his sign,
bread for our strength, wine for our joy,
'This is my body, this is my blood,'
love, only love, is his sign.

4 Love is his sign, love is his news,
'Do this,' he said, 'lest you forget
all my deep sorrow, all my dear blood,'
love, only love, is his news.

5 Love is his news, love is his name,
we are his own, chosen and called,
family, brethren, cousins and kin.
Love, only love, is his name.

6 Love is his name, love is his law.
Hear his command, all who are his:
'Love one another, I have loved you.'
Love, only love, is his law.

7 Love is his law, love is his word:
love of the Lord, Father and Word,
love of the Spirit, God ever one,
love, only love, is his word.
Luke Connaughton (1919–79)

804

1 The King of love my shepherd is,
whose goodness faileth never;
I nothing lack if I am his
and he is mine for ever.

2 Where streams of living water flow
my ransomed soul he leadeth,
and where the verdant pastures grow
with food celestial feedeth.

3 Perverse and foolish oft I strayed
but yet in love he sought me,
and on his shoulder gently laid,
and home, rejoicing, brought me.

4 In death's dark vale I fear no ill
with thee, dear Lord, beside me;
thy rod and staff my comfort still,
thy cross before to guide me.

5 Thou spread'st a table in my sight,
thy unction grace bestoweth:
and O what transport of delight
from thy pure chalice floweth!

6 And so through all the length of days
thy goodness faileth never;
good Shepherd, may I sing thy praise
within thy house for ever.
H.W.Baker (1821–77)

805

1 The living God my shepherd is,
I know no care or need.
You guide me where rich pastures grow
along the verdant mead,
where ev'ry day by pleasant way
my hungering soul may feed.

2 You lead me where cool waters flow
by rippling stream and rill,
where I may taste the springs of life,
my thirsting spirit fill;
you near me bide and homeward guide
my vagrant heart and will.

3 I nothing fear; for you, O Lord
are with me night and day,
intent, with shepherd's staff and rod,
to guide me when I stray,
and in the fold you will uphold
my fainting heart always.

4 And so through all the length of days,
your mercy waits on me,
at last within my Father's house
your glory I shall see;
you evermore will I adore
through all eternity.
J. Driscoll, S.J. ,from Psalm 23

806

1 The Lord's my shepherd, I'll not want,
he makes me down to lie
in pastures green. He leadeth me
the quiet waters by.

2 My soul he doth restore again,
and me to walk doth make
within the paths of righteousness,
e'en for his own name's sake.

3 Yea, though I walk in death's dark vale,
yet will I fear none ill.
For thou art with me, and thy rod
and staff me comfort still.

4 My table thou hast furnishèd
in presence of my foes,
my head thou dost with oil anoint,
and my cup overflows.

5 Goodness and mercy all my life
shall surely follow me.
And in God's house for evermore
my dwelling–place shall be.
Psalm 23 from the Scottish Psalter, 1650

807

1 Praise, my soul, the king of heaven!
To his feet thy tribute bring.
Ransomed, healed, restored, forgiven,
who like me his praise should sing?
     Praise him! Praise him!
     Praise him! Praise him!
Praise the everlasting king!

2 Praise him for his grace and favour
to our fathers in distress;
praise him still the same for ever,
slow to chide and swift to bless.
     Praise him! Praise him!
     Praise him! Praise him!
Glorious in his faithfulness!

3 Father–like he tends and spares us;
well our feeble frame he knows;
in his hands he gently bears us,
rescues us from all our foes.
     Praise him! Praise him!
     Praise him! Praise him!
Widely as his mercy flows!

4 Angels, help us to adore him;
ye behold him face to face;
sun and moon bow down before him,
dwellers all in time and space.
     Praise him! Praise him!
     Praise him! Praise him!
Praise with us the God of grace!
H.F.Lyte (1793–1847) from Psalm 103

808

1 The love I have for you, my Lord,
   is only a shadow of your love for me,
   only a shadow of your love for me:
   your deep abiding love.

2 My own belief in you, my Lord,
   is only a shadow of your faith in me:
   only a shadow of your faith in me:
   your deep and lasting faith.

3 My life is in your hands;
   my life is in your hands.
   My love for you will grow, my God.
   Your light in me will shine.

4 The dream I have today, my Lord,
   is only a shadow of your dreams for me:
   only a shadow of all that will be:
   if I but follow you.

5 The joy I feel today, my Lord,
   is only a shadow of your joys for me:
   only a shadow of your joys for me:
   when we meet face to face.

6 *Repeat v. 3.*

Carey Landry

809

1 There is a green hill far away,
   without a city wall,
   where the dear Lord was crucified
   who died to save us all.

2 We may not know, we cannot tell,
   what pains he had to bear,
   but we believe it was for us
   he hung and suffered there.

3 He died that we might be forgiven,
   he died to make us good;
   that we might go at last to heaven,
   saved by his precious blood.

4 There was no other good enough
   to pay the price of sin;
   he only could unlock the gate
   of heaven, and let us in.

5 O, dearly, dearly has he loved,
   and we must love him too,
   and trust in his redeeming blood,
   and try his works to do.

Mrs C.F. Alexander (1818–95)

810

1 There's a wideness in God's mercy
   like the wideness of the sea;
   there's a kindness in God's justice
   which is more than liberty.
   There is plentiful redemption
   in the blood that has been shed;
   there is joy for all the members
   in the sorrows of the Head.

2 For the love of God is broader
   than the measures of our mind,
   and the heart of the Eternal
   is most wonderfully kind.
   If our love were but more simple
   we should take him at his word,
   and our lives would be thanksgiving
   for the goodness of our Lord.

3 Troubled souls, why will you scatter
   like a crowd of frightened sheep?
   Foolish hearts, why will you wander
   from a love so true and deep?
   There is welcome for the sinner
   and more graces for the good;
   there is mercy with the Saviour,
   there is healing in his blood.

F. W. Faber (1814-63), alt.

811

1 God is Love: let heav'n adore him;
   God is Love: let earth rejoice;
   let creation sing before him,
   and exalt him with one voice.
   God who laid the earth's foundation,
   God who spread the heav'ns above,
   God who breathes through all creation,
   God is Love, eternal Love.

2 God is Love: and he enfoldeth
   all the world in one embrace;
   with unfailing grasp he holdeth
   every child of every race.
   And when human hearts are breaking
   under sorrow's iron rod,
   then they find that selfsame aching
   deep within the heart of God.

3 God is Love; and though with blindness
   sin afflicts all human life,
   God's eternal loving-kindness
   guides us through our earthly strife.
   Sin and death and hell shall never
   o'er us final triumph gain;
   God is Love, so Love for ever
   o'er the universe must reign.

   Timothy Rees (1874-1939)

812

1. Christ be near at ei - ther hand, Christ be - hind, be - fore me stand,—
2. Christ be in my head and mind, Christ with - in— my soul en - shrined,—
3. Christ my life and on - ly way. Christ my lan - tern night and day;—

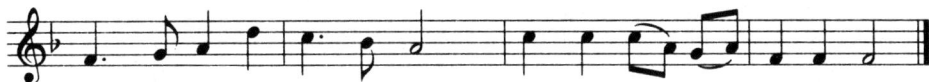

Christ with me where e'er I go, Christ a - round, a - bove, be - low.
Christ con - trol my way-ward heart; Christ a - bide and— ne'er de - part.
Christ be my un - chan-ging friend, guide and shep-herd— to the end.

4 Christ be all my strength and might
   Christ my captain for the fight;
   Christ fulfil my soul's desire;
   Christ ennoble and inspire.

5 Christ the King and Lord of all
   find me ready at his call;
   Christ receive my service whole
   hand and body, heart and soul.

6 Christ the King of kings descend
   and of tyrants make an end;
   Christ on us and all below
   concord, love and peace bestow.

7 Thanks to him, who for our food
   gives his sacred flesh and blood;
   praise to him unceasing rise.
   Christ whose glory fills the skies.

   J. Fennelly (1890-1966). Music: traditional Irish

Bless the Lord   *Taizé chant by Jacques Berthier*

813

Bless the Lord, my soul, and bless God's ho - ly name.—

Bless the Lord, my soul, who leads me in - to life.

The Kingdom

814

David Haas, from Matt. 5:3-10

1 Blest are they, the poor in spirit,
theirs is the kingdom of God.

Blest are they, full of sorrow,
they shall be consoled.

(musical notation)

Re - joice — and be glad! — Bless-ed are you, ho - ly are you! Re - joice — and be glad! — Yours is the king-dom of God! —

2 Blest are they, the lowly ones,
they shall inherit the earth.
Blest are they who hunger and thirst;
they shall have their fill.

3 Blest are they who show mercy,
mercy shall be theirs.
Blest are they, the pure of heart,
they shall see God!

4 Blest are they who seek peace;
they are the children of God.
Blest are they who suffer in faith,
the glory of God is theirs.

5 Blest are you who suffer hate,
all because of me.
Rejoice and be glad, yours is the kingdom
shine for all to see.

The refrain is sung twice at the end.

815

Stephen Dean

(musical notation)

Blessed are they who fol - low God's law and walk in his way: the Kingdom is theirs.

Cantor/Choir sing verses from Matt. 5:3-10 over refrain.

816

*The Kingdom of Heaven
the Kingdom of Heaven is yours.
A new world in Jesus,
a new world in Jesus is yours.*

1 Blessed are you in sorrow and grief:
for you shall all be consoled.
Blessed are you the gentle in heart;
you shall inherit the earth.

2 Blessed are you who hunger for right:
for you shall be satisfied.

Blessed are you the merciful ones:
for you shall be pardoned too.

3 Blessed are you whose hearts are pure:
your eyes shall gaze on the Lord.
Blessed are you who strive after peace:
the Lord will call you his own.

4 Blessed are you who suffer for right:
the Heavenly Kingdom is yours.
Blessed are you who suffer for me:
for you shall reap your reward.

Mike Anderson, from Matt 5:3-10

817

1. Bless - ed are they who are poor in spir - it,
2. Bless - ed are they who are meek and hum - ble,
3. Bless - ed are they who will mourn in sor - row,
4. Bless those who hun - ger and thirst for jus - tice,
5. Bless - ed are they who show oth - ers mer - cy,
6. Bless - ed are hearts that are clean and ho - ly,
7. Bless - ed are they who bring peace a - mong us,
8. Bless those who suf - fer from per - se - cu - tion,

1. Theirs is the king - dom of God. Bless us, O Lord, make us
2. They will in - her - it the earth. Bless us, O Lord, make us
3. They will be com - fort - ed. Bless us, O Lord, when we
4. They will be sat - is - fied. Bless us, O Lord, hear our
5. They will know mer - cy too. Bless us, O Lord, hear our
6. They will be - hold the Lord, Bless us, O Lord, make us
7. They are the chil - dren of God. Bless us, O Lord, may your
8. Theirs is the king - dom of God. Bless us, O Lord, when they

1. poor in spir - it; Bless us, O Lord, our God.
2. meek and hum - ble; Bless us, O Lord, our God.
3. share their sor - row; Bless us, O Lord, our God.
4. cry for jus - tice; Bless us, O Lord, our God.
5. cry for mer - cy; Bless us, O Lord, our God.
6. pure and ho - ly; Bless us, O Lord, our God.
7. peace be with us; Bless us, O Lord, our God.
8. per - se - cute us; Bless us, O Lord, our God.

We are the light of the world, may our light shine be - fore all,

that they may see the good that we do, and give glo - ry to God.

Jean Anthony Greif, from Matt 5:3-10

➤ *See also Russian Beatitudes (615), As a tree (370)*

818

Rejoice! Rejoice! Christ is in you,
the hope of glory in our hearts.
He lives! He lives!
His breath is in you,
arise, a mighty army, we arise.

1 Now is the time for us
to march upon the land,
into our hands
he will give the ground we claim.
He rides in majesty
to lead us into victory,
the world shall see that Christ is Lord!

2　God is at work in us
　　his purpose to perform,
　　building a kingdom
　　of power not of words,
　　where things impossible
　　by faith shall be made possible;
　　let's give the glory
　　to him now.

3　Though we are weak, his grace
　　is everything we need;
　　we're made of clay
　　but this treasure is within.
　　He turns our weaknesses
　　into his opportunities,
　　so that the glory
　　goes to him.

Graham Kendrick

819

1　Make way, make way,
　　for Christ the King in splendour arrives.
　　Fling wide the gates
　　and welcome him into your lives.
　　　Make way! Make way!
　　　for the King of kings.
　　　Make way! Make way!
　　　And let his kingdom in.

2　He comes the broken hearts to heal
　　the prisoners to free.
　　the deaf shall hear, the lame shall dance,
　　the blind shall see.

3　And those who mourn with heavy hearts,
　　who weep and sigh;
　　with laughter, joy and royal crown
　　he'll beautify.

4　We call you now to worship him
　　as Lord of all.
　　To have no gods before him
　　their thrones must fall!

Graham Kendrick

820

1　Seek ye first the Kingdom of God,
　　and his righteousness,

and all these things shall be added unto
　　you;
allelu, alleluia.
Alleluia, alleluia, alleluia,
allelu, alleluia.

2　Ask and it shall be given unto you,
　　seek and ye shall find;
　　knock and it shall be opened unto you;
　　allelu, alleluia.

3　We do not live by bread alone
　　but by ev'ry word
　　that comes forth from the mouth of God:

4　Where two or three are gathered in
　　my name,
　　there am I in your midst;
　　and whatsoever you ask I will do:

V.1 Karen Lafferty, vv 2-4 Anon

821

1　The kingdom of God is justice and joy;
　　for Jesus restores what sin would destroy.
　　God's power and glory in Jesus we know;
　　and here and hereafter the kingdom shall
　　　grow.

2　The kingdom of God is mercy and grace;
　　the captives are freed, the sinners find place,
　　the outcast are welcomed God's banquet
　　　to share;
　　and hope is awakened in place of despair.

3　The kingdom of God is challenge and
　　　choice:
　　believe the good news, repent and rejoice!
　　His love for us sinners brought Christ to
　　　his cross:
　　our crisis of judgement for gain or for
　　　loss.

4　God's kingdom is come, the gift and the
　　　goal;
　　in Jesus begun, in heaven made whole.
　　The heirs of the kingdom shall answer
　　　his call;
　　and all things cry 'Glory!' to God all
　　　in all.

Bryn Rees (1911–83)

The Church on earth

Marty Haugen

822

We are ma-ny parts, we are all one bo-dy,_____ and the gifts we
have we are gi-ven to share._____ May the Spi-rit of love make us one in-deed;
one, the love that we share,_____ one, our hope in des-pair,_____ one, the
cross that we bear._____

Last time / *Verses*

1. God of all, we look to you,_____
2. So my pain is pain for you,_____
3. All you seek-ers, great and small,_____

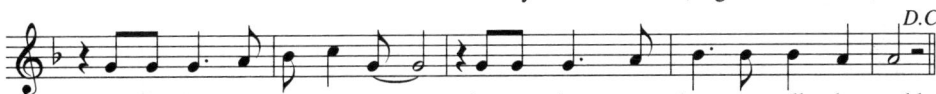

we would be your ser-vants true,_____ let us be your love to all the world.
in your joy is my joy, too;_____ all is brought to-geth-er in the Lord.
seek the grea-test gift of all;_____ if you love, then you will know the Lord.

D.C.

823

Cyprian of Carthage, tr Anders Frostenson. Muisc by Olle Widestrand

1. Ma-ny are the light-beams from the one light. Our one light_ is Je-sus._____
Ma-ny are the light-beams from the one light; we are one in Christ.

2 Many are the branches
of the one tree.
Our one tree is Jesus.
Many are the branches
of the one tree;
we are one in Christ.

3 Many are the gifts giv'n,
love is all one.
Love's the gift of Jesus.
Many are the gifts giv'n,
love is all one;
we are one in Christ.

4 Many ways to serve God,
the Spirit is one;
servant spirit of Jesus.
Many ways to serve God,
the Spirit is one;
we are one in Christ.

5 Many are the members,
the body is one;
members all of Jesus.
Many are the members,
the body is one;
we are one in Christ.

824

1 Awake from your slumber!
Arise from your sleep!
A new day is dawning
for all those who weep.
The people in darkness
have seen a great light.
The Lord of our longing
has conquered the night.
Let us build the city of God.
May our tears be turned into dancing!
For the Lord, our light and our Love,
has turned the night into day!

2 We are sons of the morning;
we are daughters of day.
The One who has loved us
has brightened our way.
The Lord of all kindness
has called us to be
a light for his people
to set their hearts free.

3 God is light; in him there is no darkness.
Let us walk in his light, his children,
    one and all.
O comfort my people;
make gentle your words.
Proclaim to my city
the day of her birth.

4 O city of gladness, now lift up your voice!
Proclaim the good tidings that all may
    rejoice!
Daniel L. Schutte

825

1 Church of God, elect and glorious,
holy nation, chosen race;
called as God's own special people,
royal priests and heirs of grace:
know the purpose of your calling,
show to all his mighty deeds;
tell of love which knows no limits,
grace which meets all human needs.

2 God has called you out of darkness
into his most marvellous light,
brought his truth to life within you,
turned your blindness into sight.
Let your light so shine around you
that God's name is glorified;
and all find fresh hope and purpose
in Christ Jesus crucified.

3 Once you were an alien people,
strangers to God's heart of love;
but he brought you home in mercy,
citizens of heaven above.
Let his love flow out to others,
let them feel a Father's care;
that they too may know his welcome
and his countless blessings share.

4 Church of God, elect and holy,
be the people he intends;
strong in faith and swift to answer
each command your master sends:
royal priests, fulfil your calling
through your sacrifice and prayer;
give your lives in joyful service -
sing his praise, his love declare.
(from 1 Peter 2) J. E. Seddon (1915-1983)

826

1 Christ's church shall glory in his power
and grow to his perfection;
he is our rock, our mighty tower,
our life, our resurrection.
So by his skilful hand
the church of Christ shall stand;
the master–builder's plan
he works, as he began,
and soon will crown with splendour.

2 Christ's people serve his wayward world
to whom he seems a stranger;
he knows its welcome from of old,
he shares our joy, our danger.
So strong, and yet so weak,
the church of Christ shall speak;
his cross our greatest need,
his word the vital seed
that brings a fruitful harvest.

3 Christ's living lamp shall brightly burn,
and to our earthly city
forgotten beauty shall return,
and purify and pity.
To give the oppressed their right
the church of Christ shall fight;
and though the years seem long
God is our strength and song,
and God is our salvation.

4 Christ's body triumphs in his name;
one Father, sovereign giver,
one Spirit, with his love aflame,
one Lord, the same for ever.
To you, O God our prize,
the church of Christ shall rise
beyond all measured height
to that eternal light,
where Christ shall reign all–holy.
Christopher Idle

827

1 Glorious things of you are spoken,
Sion, city of our God:
he whose word cannot be broken
formed you for his own abode.
On the Rock of Ages founded,
what can shake your sure repose?
With salvation's walls surrounded,
you may smile at all your foes.

2 See, the streams of living waters,
springing from eternal love,
well supply your sons and daughters
and all fear of want remove:
who can faint, while such a river
ever flows their thirst to assuage –
grace, which like the Lord, the giver,
never fails from age to age?

3 Blest inhabitants of Sion,
washed in their Redeemer's blood:
Jesus, whom their souls rely on,
makes them Kings and priests to God.
'Tis his love his people raises
over self to reign as kings,
and, as priests, his solemn praises
each for a thank–offering brings.

4 Saviour, since of Sion's city
I, through grace, a member am,
let the world deride or pity,
I will glory in your name:
fading is the wordling's pleasure,
all his boasted pomp and show;
solid joys and lasting treasure
none but Sion's children know.
John Newton (1725–1807)

828

1 As a fire is meant for burning
with a bright and warming flame,
so the church is meant for mission,
giving glory to God's name.
Not to preach our creeds or customs,
but to build a bridge of care,
we join hands across the nations,
finding neighbours ev'rywhere.

2 We are learners; we are teachers;
we are pilgrims on the way.
We are seekers; we are givers;
we are vessels made of clay.
By our gentle, loving actions,
we would show that Christ is light.
In a humble, list'ning Spirit,
we would live to God's delight.

3 As a green bud in the springtime
is a sign of life renewed,
so may we be signs of oneness
'mid earth's peoples, many hued.
As a rainbow lights the heavens
when a storm is past and gone,
may our lives reflect the radiance
of God's new and glorious dawn.
Ruth Duck

829

1 O Christ, the great foundation
on which your people stand
to preach your true salvation
in every age and land:
pour out your Holy Spirit
to make us strong and pure,
to keep the faith unbroken
as long as worlds endure.

2 Baptized in one confession,
one church in all the earth,
we bear our Lord's impression,
the sign of second birth:
one holy people gathered
in love beyond our own,
by grace we were invited,
by grace we make you known.

3 Where tyrants' hold is tightened,
where strong devour the weak,
where innocents are frightened
the righteous fear to speak,
there let your church awaking
attack the powers of sin
and, all their ramparts breaking,
with you the victory win.

4 This is the moment glorious
when he who once was dead
shall lead his church victorious,
their champion and their head.
The Lord of all creation
his heavenly kingdom brings
the final consummation,
the glory of all things.
Timothy T'infang Lew (1891-1947), alt.

830

1 The Church's one foundation,
is Jesus Christ, her Lord;
she is his new creation,
by water and the Word;
from heav'n he came and sought her
to be his holy bride,
with his own blood he bought her,
and for her life he died.

2 Elect from every nation,
yet one o'er all the earth,
her charter of salvation
one Lord, one faith, one birth;
one holy name she blesses,
partakes one holy food,
and to one hope she presses,
with every grace endued.

3 'Mid toil, and tribulation,
and tumult of her war,
she waits the consummation
of peace for evermore;
till with the vision glorious
her longing eyes are blest,
and the great Church victorious
shall be the Church at rest.

4 Yet she on earth hath union
with God the Three in One,
and mystic sweet communion
with those whose rest is won:
O happy ones and holy!
Lord, give us grace that we
like them, the meek and lowly
on high may dwell with thee.
S. J. Stone (1830–1900)

831

1 In Christ there is no east or west,
in him no south or north,
but one great fellowship of love
throughout the whole wide earth.

2 In him shall true hearts ev'rywhere
their high communion find.
His service is the golden cord
close-binding humankind.

3 Join hands, disciples in the faith
whate'er your race may be.
Who serve each other in Christ's love
are surely kin to me.

4 In Christ now meet both east and west,
in him meet south and north.
All Christly souls are one in him
throughout the whole wide earth.
John Oxenham (1852–1941)

832

*One bread, one body, one Lord of all,
one cup of blessing which we bless.
And we, though many, throughout the earth,
we are one body in this one Lord.*

1 Gentile or Jew, servant or free,
woman or man, no more.

2 Many the gifts, many the works,
  one in the Lord of all.

3 Grain for the fields,
  scattered and grown, gathered to one, for all.
  John B. Foley, S.J.

833

1 O thou, who at thy Eucharist didst pray
  that all thy Church might be for ever one,
  grant us at every Eucharist to say,
  with longing heart and soul, 'Thy will be
    done'.
  O may we all one bread, one body be,
  one through this sacrament of unity.

2 For all thy Church O Lord, we intercede;
  make thou our sad divisions soon to cease;
  draw us the nearer each to each, we plead,
  by drawing all to thee, O Prince of peace;
  thus may we all one bread, one body be,
  one through this sacrament of unity.

3 We pray thee too for wanderers from thy
    fold,
  O bring them back, good shepherd of the
    sheep,
  back to the faith which saints believed of
    old,
  back to the Church which still that faith
    doth keep;
  soon may we all one bread, one body be,
  one through this sacrament of unity.

4 So, Lord, at length when sacraments shall
    cease,
  may we be one with all thy Church above,
  one with thy saints in one unbroken peace,
  one with thy saints in one unbounded love:
  more blessed still, in peace and love to be
  one with the Trinity in unity.
  W.H. Turton (1856–1938)

834

Refrain: Fa-ther God, bless this fa-mi-ly; Bro-ther Christ, re-main with

us; Ho-ly Love, Spi-rit of u-ni-ty, make us one fa-mi-ly, God's Ho-ly

Verses
Fa - mi - ly.
1. For the Word of God pro-claimed, for the
2. For the help to those in need, for the
3. For the wel-come that we feel, for the
4. For the bles-sings of the past, for the

signs we ce-le-brate, Word and sa-cra-ment gi-ving life:
hea-ling of our pain, lo-ving ser-vice we give to all:
friends who share our days, watch-ing, wait-ing in hope and joy:
hope of days to come, young and old joi-ning hands and hearts:

This is our fa-mi-ly, God's ho-ly fa-mi-ly, God's ho-ly fa - mi - ly.

John Schiavone

➤ *See also: Dedication of a Church (454-457)*

835

Out of darkness God has called us, claimed by Christ as God's own people.

Ho-ly na-tion, roy-al priest-hood, walk-ing in God's marv'-lous light.—

1 Let us take the words you give,
   strong and faithful words to live.
   Words that in our hearts are sown;
   words that bind us as your own.

2 Let us take the Christ you give.
   Broken Body, Christ we live.
   Christ the risen from the tomb;
   Christ who calls us as your own.

3 Let us take the love you give,
   that the way of love we live.
   Love to bring your people home;
   love to make us all your own.

Verses for Easter

1 Sing a joyful Alleluia,
   sing to Christ the Risen Saviour,
   'He is not among the dead!
   He is risen, as he said.'

2 We have died to sin with Christ.
   We will rise with him at last.
   Now the second Adam lives.
   Now eternal life he gives!

3 Let your sadness be no more,
   Christ has opened heaven's door.
   Death has no more power to slay.
   This is Resurrection Day!

Christopher Walker

836

1. Summoned by the God who made us rich in our di-ver-si-ty,
   Ga-thered in the name of Je-sus, rich-er still in u-ni-ty.

Let us— bring the gifts that dif-fer and, in— splen-did, va-ried ways,

sing a new Church in-to be-ing, one in faith and love and praise.

2 Radiant risen from the water,
   robed in holiness and light,
   male and female in God's image,
   male and female, God's delight:

3 Trust the goodness of creation;
   trust the Spirit strong within.
   Dare to dream the vision promised
   sprung from seed of what has been.

4 Bring the hopes of ev'ry nation;
   bring the art of ev'ry race.
   Weave a song of peace and justice;
   let it sound through time and space.

5 Draw together at one table
   all the human family;
   shape a circle ever wider
   and a people ever free.

Delores Dufner, O.S.B.

837

1 Faith of our fathers! Living still
   in spite of dungeon, fire and sword;
   oh, how our hearts beat high with joy
   whene'er we hear that glorious word!
   Faith of our fathers! Holy Faith!
   We will be true to thee till death,
   we will be true to thee till death.

2 Our fathers, chained in prisons dark,
   were still in heart and conscience free;
   how sweet would be their children's fate,
   if they, like them, could die for thee!

3 Faith of our fathers, Mary's prayers
   shall win our country back to thee.
   And through the truth that comes from God
   our land shall then indeed be free.

4 Faith of our fathers, we will love
   both friend and foe in all our strife,
   and preach thee too, as love knows how,
   by kindly words and virtuous life.
   F.W. Faber (1814–63)

Forgiveness, Penance & Reconciliation

838

O Lord, be not mind-ful of our guilt and our sins;
O Lord, do not judge us for our faults and of-fen-ces. May your
mer-ci-ful love be u-pon us.

Lucien Deiss

1 Help your people, Lord, O God our Saviour,
   deliver us for the glory of your name!

2 Pardon us, O Lord, all our sins, ...

3 Praise to you, O Lord,
   through all the ages without end...

839

Ostende nobis   *Canon*

O-sten-de no-bis, Do-mi-ne, mi-se-ri-cor-di-am tu-
am. A-men! A-men! Ma-ra-na-tha! Ma-ra-na-tha! O-sten-de tha.

Show us, O Lord, your mercy: Taizé chant by Jacques Berthier

840

1 God of mercy and compassion,
   Lord of life and blinding light,
   truth whom creatures would refashion,
   place on us the gift of sight.
   Truth insistent and demanding
   Love resented and ignored,
   Life beyond all understanding,
   give us peace and pardon, Lord.

2 God most holy and forgiving,
   penetrate our pride and sloth;
   on a people partly living,
   place the gift of life and growth.

3 Lord, who out of love consented
   to the worst that we could do;
   Lord, abandoned and tormented,
   let us love and suffer too.
   Michael Hodgetts, alt.

841

1 Diverse in culture, nation, race,
   we come together by your grace.
   God, let us be a meeting ground
   where hope and healing love are found.

2 God, let us be a bridge of care
   connecting people everywhere.
   Help us confront all fear and hate
   and lust for power that separate.

3 When chasms widen, storms arise,
   O Holy Spirit, make us wise.
   Let us resolve, like steel, be strong
   to stand with those who suffer wrong.

4 God, let us be a table spread
   with gifts of love and broken bread,
   where all find welcome, grace attends
   and enemies arise as friends.
   Ruth Duck

842

1 Come back to me with all your heart.
   Don't let fear keep us apart.
   Trees do bend, though straight and tall;
   so must we to others' call.
   Long have I waited
   for your coming home to me
   and living deeply our new life.

2 The wilderness will lead you
   to your heart, where I will speak.
   Integrity and justice
   with tenderness you shall know.

3 You shall sleep secure with peace;
   faithfulness will be your joy.

4 Come back to me with all your heart.
   Don't let fear keep us apart.
   Trees do bend, though straight and tall;
   so must we to others' call.
   Gregory Norbet, based on Hosea

843

Re - mem-ber, re - mem-ber your mer - cy, Lord.— Re - mem-ber, re-mem-ber your mer- cy, Lord.— Hear your peo-ple's prayer as they call to you: re - mem- ber, re-mem-ber your mer - cy, Lord.—

1 Lord, make me know your ways.
   Lord, teach me your paths.
   Make me walk in your truth, and teach me:
   for you are God my Saviour.

2 Remember your mercy, Lord,
   and the love you have shown from of old.
   Do not remember the sins of my youth.
   In your love, remember me,

   in your love remember me,
   because of your goodness, O Lord.

3 The Lord is good and upright.
   He shows the path to all who stray,
   he guides the humble in the right path;
   he teaches his way to the poor.
   Response: Paul Inwood,
   Verses: Psalm 25:4-9 Grail version

844

1 How can we sing with joy to God,
   how can we pray to him,
   when we are far away from God
   in selfishness and sin?

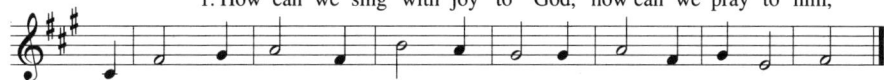

2 How can we claim to do God's will
   when we have turned away
   from things of God to things of earth,
   and willed to disobey?

3 How can we praise the love of God
   which all his works make known,
   when all our works turn from his love
   to choices of our own?

4 God knows the sinful things we do,
   the godless life we live,
   yet in his love he calls to us
   so ready to forgive.

5 So we will turn again to God -
   his ways will be our ways,
   his will our will, his love our love,
   and he himself our praise!

Brian Foley

Melody by
Stephen Dean

1. How can we sing with joy to God, how can we pray to him, when we are far a - way from God in sel - fish - ness and sin?

845

1 'Forgive our sins as we forgive,'
   you taught us, Lord, to pray,
   but you alone can grant us grace
   to live the words we say.

2 How can your pardon reach and bless
   the unforgiving heart
   that broods on wrongs and will not let
   old bitterness depart?

3 In blazing light your Cross reveals
   the truth we dimly knew:
   what trivial debts are owed to us,
   how great our debt to you!

4 Lord, cleanse the depths within our souls
   and bid resentment cease.
   Then, bound to all in bonds of love,
   our lives will spread your peace.

Rosamond Herklots

19th C. American
melody

1. 'For - give our sins as we— for - give,' you taught us, Lord, to pray, but you a - lone can grant— us— grace to live the words we say.

846

1 Amazing grace! How sweet the sound
   that saved a wretch like me.
   I once was lost but now I'm found,
   was blind, but now I see.

2 'Twas grace that taught my heart to fear,
   and grace my fears relieved.
   How precious did that grace appear
   the hour I first believed.

3 Through many dangers, toils and snares
   I have already come.
   'Tis grace hath brought me safe thus far,
   and grace will lead me home.

4 The Lord has promised good to me;
   his word my hope secures.
   He will my shield and portion be
   as long as life endures.

John Newton (1725–1807)

847

1 Oh Lord, all the world belongs to you,
and you are always making all things new.
What is wrong you forgive,
and the new life you give
is what's turning the world upside down.

2 The world's only loving to its friends,
but you have brought us love that never
ends;
loving enemies too,
and this loving with you
is what's turning the world upside down.

3 This world lives divided and apart.
You draw us together and we start
in your body to see
that in fellowship we
can be turning the world upside down.

4 The world wants the wealth to live in state,
but you show us a new way to be great;
like a servant you came,
and if we do the same,
we'll be turning the world upside down.

5 Oh Lord, all the world belongs to you,
and you are always making all things new.
Send your Spirit on all
in your Church whom you call
to be turning the world upside down.
Patrick Appleford

848

1 The Master came to bring good news,
the news of love and freedom,
to heal the sick and seek the poor,
to build the peaceful kingdom.
Father, forgive us! Through Jesus hear us!
As we forgive one another!

2 The Law's fulfilled through Jesus Christ,
the man who lived for others,
the law of Christ is: Serve in love
our sisters and our brothers.

3 To seek the sinners Jesus came,
to live among the friendless,
to show them love that they might share
the kingdom that is endless.

4 Forgive us, Lord, as we forgive
and seek to help each other.
Forgive us, Lord, and we shall live
to pray and work together.
Ralph Finn

849

1 God forgave my sin in Jesus' name;
I've been born again in Jesus' name;
and in Jesus' name I come to you
to share his love as he told me to.
He said: 'Freely, freely, you have received;
freely, freely give.
Go, in my name, and because you believe,
others will know that I live.'

2 All pow'r is giv'n in Jesus' name,
in earth and heav'n in Jesus' name;
and in Jesus' name I come to you
to share his pow'r as he told me to.

3 God gives us life in Jesus' name,
he lives in us in Jesus' name;
and in Jesus' name I come to you
to share his peace as he told me to.
Carol Owens

850

1 Take this moment, sign and space;
take my friends around;
here among us make the place
where your love is found.

2 Take the time to call my name,
take the time to mend
who I am and what I've been,
all I've failed to tend.

3 Take the tiredness of my days,
take my past regret,
letting your forgiveness touch
all I can't forget.

4 Take the little child in me,
scared of growing old;
help him/her here to find his/her worth
made in Christ's own mould.

5 Take my talents, take my skills,
   take what's yet to be;
   let my life be yours, and yet,
   let it still be me.
                    John L. Bell and Graham Maule

851

1 Awake, awake: fling off the night!
   For God has sent his glorious light;
   and we who live in Christ's new day
   must works of darkness put away.

2 Awake and rise, in Christ renewed,
   and with the Spirit's power endued,
   the light of life in us will glow,
   and fruits of truth and goodness show.

3 Let in the light; all sin expose
   to Christ, whose life no darkness knows.
   Before his cross for guidance kneel;
   his light will judge and, judging heal.

4 Awake, and rise up from the dead,
   and Christ his light on you will shed.
   Its power will wrong desires destroy,
   and your whole nature fill with joy.

5 Then sing for joy, and use each day;
   give thanks for everything alway.
   Lift up your hearts; with one accord
   praise God through Jesus Christ our Lord.
                    J.R. Peacey (1896–1971) from Eph. 5:6-20

Commitment, Discipleship, Mission

852

1 We have a gospel to proclaim,
   good news for all throughout the earth;
   the gospel of a saviour's name:
   we sing his glory, tell his worth.

2 Tell of his birth at Bethlehem,
   not in a royal house or hall
   but in a stable dark and dim:
   the Word made flesh, a light for all.

3 Tell of his death at Calvary,
   hated by those he came to save;
   in lonely suffering on the cross
   for all he loved, his life he gave.

4 Tell of that glorious Easter morn:
   empty the tomb, for he was free;
   he broke the power of death and hell
   that we might share his victory.

5 Tell of his reign at God's right hand,
   by all creation glorified;
   he sends his Spirit on his church
   to live for him, the lamb who died.

6 Now we rejoice to name him king;
   Jesus is Lord of all the earth;
   the gospel–message we proclaim:
   we sing his glory, tell his worth.
                    Edward J. Burns

853

1 Forth in the peace of Christ we go;
   Christ to the world with joy we bring;
   Christ in our minds, Christ on our lips,
   Christ in our hearts, the world's true King.

2 King of our hearts, Christ makes us kings;
   kingship with him his servants gain;
   with Christ, the Servant–Lord of all,
   Christ's world we serve to share Christ's
        reign.

3 Priests of the world, Christ sends us forth
   the world of time to consecrate,
   the world of sin by grace to heal,
   Christ's world in Christ to recreate.

4 Prophets of Christ, we hear his word:
   he claims our minds, to search his ways,
   he claims our lips, to speak his truth,
   he claims our hearts, to sing his praise.

5 We are the Church; he makes us one:
   here is one hearth for all to find,
   here is one flock, one Shepherd–King,
   here is one faith, one heart, one mind.
                    James Quinn, S.J.

854

Marty Haugen

Cantor: / *All:*

1. You are salt for the earth, O peo-ple: Salt for the King-dom of God!
2. You are a light on the hill, O peo-ple: Light for the Ci-ty of God!
3. You are a seed of the Word, O peo-ple: Bring forth the King-dom of God!
4. We are a blest and a pil-grim peo-ple: Bound for the King-dom of God!

Cantor: / *All:*

Share the fla-vour of life, O peo-ple: Life in the King-dom of God!
Shine so ho-ly and bright, O peo-ple: Shine for the King-dom of God!
Seeds of mer-cy and seeds of jus-tice, Grow in the King-dom of God!
Love our journey and love our home-land: Love is the King-dom of God!

Refrain

Bring forth the King-dom of mer-cy, bring forth the King-dom of peace;

bring forth the King-dom of jus-tice, bring forth the Ci-ty of God!

855

Sent by the Lord am I; my hands are rea-dy now to

Repeat.

make the earth the place in which the king-dom comes.

The ang-els can-not change a world of hurt and pain in-to a world of

love, of jus-tice and of peace. The task is mine to do, to

set it real-ly free. Oh, help me to o-bey; help me to do your will.

Nicaraguan traditional, tr. Jorge Maldonado

856

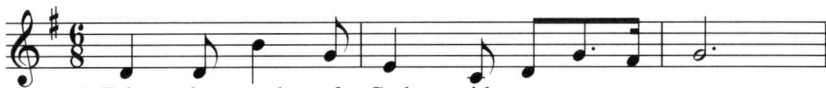

1. Take the word of God with you as you go.
2. Take the peace of God with you as you go.

1. Take the seeds of God's word and make them grow.
2. Take the seeds of God's peace and make them grow.

Refrain

Go in peace to serve the world, in peace to serve the world. Take the love of God, the love of God with you as you go.

3 Take the joy of God with you as you go.
Take the seeds of God's joy and
make them grow.

4 Take the love* of God with you as you go.
Take the seeds of God's love and
make them grow.

Add other words if needed, such as 'faith', 'hope' ...

James Harrison

857

1. Sing to the world of Christ our sov' - reign Lord;
tell of his birth which brought new life to all. Speak of his
life, his love, his ho-ly word; let ev'-ry na-tion hear and know his
call. Sing to the world of Christ our Sov' - reign Lord.

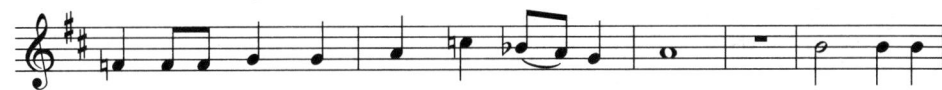

2 Sing to the world of Christ the Prince of peace,
showing to us the Father's loving care,
pleading that love should reign and wars might cease,
teaching we need the love of God to share.
Sing to the world of Christ the Prince of peace.

3 Sing to the world of Christ our steadfast friend,
off'ring himself to live the constant sign;
food for our souls until we meet life's end,
gives us his flesh for bread, his blood for wine.
Sing to the world of Christ our steadfast friend.

4 Sing to the world of Christ our Saviour King,
    born that his death the world's release should win;
    hung from a cross, forgiveness he could bring;
    buried, he rose to conquer death and sin.
    Sing to the world of Christ our Saviour King.

5 Sing to the world of Christ at God's right hand,
    praise to the Spirit both have sent from heav'n.
    living in us till earth shall reach its span,
    time be no more, and Christ shall come again.
    Sing to the world of Christ at God's right hand.

Patrick Lee

858

Bernadette Farrell

1. God has cho-sen me, _ God has cho-sen me _ to bring good news _ to the poor.
2. God has cho-sen me, _ God has cho-sen me _ to set a-light _ a new fire.
3. God is call-ing me, _ God is call-ing me _ in all whose cry _ is un-heard.

God has cho-sen me, _ God has cho-sen me _ to bring _ new sight _ to those
God has cho-sen me, _ God has cho-sen me _ to bring _ to birth _ a new
God is call-ing me, _ God is call-ing me _ to raise up the voice _ with no

search-ing for light: _ God has cho-sen me, _ cho-sen me. _ And to tell the world _
king-dom on earth: _ God has cho-sen me, _ cho-sen me. _
pow-er or choice: _ God is call-ing me, _ call-ing me. _

that God's king-dom is near, _ to re-move op-pres-sion and break down _ fear.

Yes, God's time is near, God's time is near, _ God's time is near, God's time is near. _

859

Refrain

We have been told, we've seen his face, and heard his voice _ a-live in our

hearts; 'Live in my love with all your heart, _ as the Fa-ther has

Verse 1

loved me, so I have loved you.' __ 1. 'I am the vine,

D.C.

you are the bran-ches, and all who live in me will bear great fruit.'

Verses 2, 3

2. 'You are my friends, if you keep my com - mands, _ no long - er slaves,
3. 'No grea- ter love _____ is there than this: to lay down one's life,

D.C.

David Haas

I call you friends.' _____
for _ a friend.' _____

860

1 Fight the good fight with all thy might,
Christ is thy strength, and Christ thy
right;
lay hold on life and it shall be
thy joy and crown eternally.

2 Run the straight race through God's good
grace,
lift up thine eyes and seek his face;
life with its way before us lies,
Christ is the path, and Christ the prize.

3 Cast care aside, lean on thy Guide
his boundless mercy will provide;
trust, and the trusting soul shall prove
Christ is its life, and Christ its love.

4 Faint not nor fear, his arms are near,
he changeth not, and thou art dear;
only believe, and thou shalt see
that Christ is all in all to thee.
J. S. B. Monsell (1811–75)

861

1 Forth in thy name, O Lord, I go,
my daily labour to pursue;
thee, only thee, resolved to know,
in all I think or speak or do.

2 The task thy wisdom hath assigned
O let me cheerfully fulfil;
in all my works thy presence find,
and prove thy good and perfect will.

3 Thee may I set at my right hand,
whose eyes my inmost substance see,
and labour on at thy command,
and offer all my works to thee.

4 Give me to bear thy easy yoke,
and every moment watch and pray,
and still to things eternal look,
and hasten to thy glorious day;

5 For thee delightfully employ
whate'er thy bounteous grace hath given,
and run my course with even joy,
and closely walk with thee to heaven.
Charles Wesley (1707–88)

862

1 He who would valiant be
'gainst all disaster,
let him in constancy
follow the Master
There's no discouragement
shall make him once relent
his first avowed intent
to be a pilgrim.

2 Who so beset him round
with dismal stories,
do but themselves confound:
his strength the more is.
No foes shall stay his might
though he with giants fight;
he will make good his right
to be a pilgrim.

3 Since, Lord, thou dost defend
us with thy Spirit,
we know we at the end
shall life inherit.
Then fancies flee away!
I'll fear not what they say,
I'll labour night and day
to be a pilgrim.
Percy Dearmer (1867–1936),
after John Bunyan (1628–88)

863

Follow me, follow me,
leave your home and family,
leave your fishing nets and boats upon
the shore.
Leave the seed that you have sown,
leave the crops that you've grown,
leave the people you have known and
follow me.

1 The foxes have their holes
and the swallows have their nests,
but the Son of man has no place to lay
down.
I do not offer comfort, I do not offer
wealth,
but in me will all happiness be found.

2 If you would follow me,
you must leave old ways behind.
You must take my cross and follow on
my path.
You may be far from loved ones,
you may be far from home
but my Father will welcome you at last.

3 Although I go away
you will never be alone,

for the Spirit will be there to comfort you.
Though all of you may scatter,
each follow his own path,
still the Spirit of love will lead you home.
Michael Cockett

864

1 God's Spirit is in my heart,
who has called me and set me apart.
This is what I have to do,
what I have to do.

He sent me to give the Good News to
the poor,
tell prisoners that they are prisoners
no more,
tell blind people that they can see,
and set the downtrodden free,
and go tell ev'ryone
the news that the Kingdom of God has
come,
and go tell ev'ryone
the news that God's kingdom has come.

2 Just as the Father sent me,
so I'm sending you out to be
my witnesses throughout the world,
the whole of the world.

3 Don't carry a load in your pack,
you don't need two shirts on your back.
A workman can earn his own keep,
can earn his own keep.

4 Don't worry what you have to say,
don't worry because on that day
God's spirit will speak in your heart,
will speak in your heart.
Alan Dale & Hubert Richards

865

1 I, the Lord of sea and sky,
I have heard my people cry.
All who dwell in dark and sin
my hand will save.
I who made the stars of night,
I will make their darkness bright.
Who will bear my light to them?
Whom shall I send?

Here I am, Lord. Is it I, Lord?
I have heard you calling in the night.
I will go, Lord, if you lead me.
I will hold your people in my heart.

2 I, the Lord of snow and rain,
I have borne my people's pain.
I have wept for love of them.
They turn away.
I will break their hearts of stone,
give them hearts for love alone.
I will speak my word to them.
Whom shall I send?

3 I, the Lord of wind and flame,
I will tend the poor and lame.
I will set a feast for them.
My hand will save.
Finest bread I will provide
till their hearts be satisfied.
I will give my life to them.
Whom shall I send?
Daniel L. Schutte

866

I will be with you wherever you go.
Go now throughout the world!
I will be with you in all that you say.
Go now and spread my word!

1 Come, walk with me on stormy waters.
Why fear? Reach out, and I'll be there.

2 And you, my friend, will you now leave me,
or do you know me as your Lord?

3 Your life will be transformed with power
by living truly in my name.

4 And if you say: 'Yes, Lord I love you,'
then feed my lambs and feed my sheep.
Gerald Markland

867

Leave your country and your people,
leave your fam'ly and your friends.
Travel to the land I'll show you;
God will bless the ones he sends.

1 Go like Abraham before you,
when he heard the Father's call,
walking forth in faith and trusting;
God is master of us all.

2 Sometimes God's Word is demanding,
leave security you know,
breaking ties and bonds that hold you,
when the voice of God says: 'Go'.

3 Take the path into the desert,
barren seems the rock and sand.
God will lead you through the desert
when you follow his command.

4 Go with courage up the mountain,
climb the narrow, rocky ledge,
leave behind all things that hinder,
go with only God as pledge.
Willard F. Jabusch

868

1 'Moses I know you're the man,'
    the Lord said.
'You're going to work out my plan,'
    the Lord said.
'Lead all the Israelites out of slavery.
And I shall make them a wandering race
called the people of God.'
So ev'ry day we're on our way,
for we're a travelling, wandering race
called the people of God.

2 'Don't get too set in your ways,'
    the Lord said.
Each step is only a phase,' the Lord said.
I'll go before you and I shall be a sign
to guide my travelling, wandering race.
You're the people of God.

3 'No matter what you may do,'
    the Lord said,
I shall be faithful and true,' the Lord said.
'My love will strengthen you as you go
    along,
for you're my travelling, wandering race.
You're the people of God.

4 'Look at the birds in the air,'
      the Lord said,
   They fly unhampered by care,'
      the Lord said.
   You will move easier if you're travelling
      light,
   for you're a wandering vagabond race.
   You're the people of God.'

5 Foxes have places to go,'
      the Lord said.
   But I've no home here below,'
      the Lord said.
   So if you want to be with me all your days,
   keep up the moving and travelling on.
   You're the people of God.'
      Estelle White

869

1 Lord of Creation, to you be all praise!
   Most mighty your working, most
      wondrous your ways.
   Your glory and might are beyond us to
      tell,
   and yet in the heart of the humble you
      dwell.

2 Lord of all power, I give you my will,
   in joyful obedience your tasks to fulfil.
   Your bondage is freedom, your service
      is song,
   and, held in your keeping, my weakness
      is strong.

3 Lord of all wisdom, I give you my mind,
   rich truth that surpasses our knowledge
      to find.
   What eye has not seen and what ear has
      not heard
   is taught by your Spirit and shines from
      your Word.

4 Lord of all bounty, I give you my heart;
   I praise and adore you for all you impart:
   your love to inspire me, your counsel to
      guide,
   your presence to cheer me, whatever
      betide.

5 Lord of all being, I give you my all;
   if e'er I disown you I stumble and fall;
   but, sworn in glad service your word to
      obey,
   I walk in your freedom to the end of the
      way.
      Jack C. Winslow

      This hymn may also start at Verse 2

870

1 Lord, you give the great commission:
   'Heal the sick and preach the word.'
   Lest the Church neglect its mission,
   and the Gospel go unheard,
   help us witness to your purpose
   with renewed integrity;

   With the Spirit's gifts empower us
   for the work of ministry.

2 Lord, you call us to your service:
   'In my name baptise and teach.'
   That the world may trust your promise,
   life abundant meant for each,
   give us all new fervour, draw us
   closer in community;

3 Lord, you make the common holy:
   'This my body, this my blood.'
   Let us all, for earth's true glory,
   daily lift life heavenward,
   asking that the world around us
   share your children's liberty;

4 Lord, you show us love's true measure;
   'Father, what they do, forgive.'
   Yet we hoard as private treasure
   all that you so freely give.
   May your care and mercy lead us
   to a just society;

5 Lord, you bless with words assuring:
   'I am with you to the end.'
   Faith and hope and love restoring,
   may we serve as you intend,
   and, amid the cares that claim us,
   hold in mind eternity;
      Jeffrey Rowthorn

871

1. Lord, _____ you have come to the sea-shore, _____ nei-ther searching for _____
2. Lord, _____ see my goods, my pos-ses-sions; _____ in my boat you find _____

_____ the rich nor the wise, _____ de-sir-ing on-ly _____ that I should
_____ no po-wer, no wealth. _____ Will you ac-cept then, _____ my nets and

Refrain

fol-low. _____ O Lord, _____ with your eyes set up-on me, _____ gent-ly
la-bour? _____

f

smil-ing, _____ you have spo-ken my name, _____ all I longed for _____ I have

mp

found by the wa-ter, _____ at your side, _____ I will seek oth-er shores. _____

3 Lord, take my hands and direct them,
   help me spend myself in seeking the lost.
   Returning love for the love you gave me.

4 Lord, as I drift on the waters,
   be the resting place of my restless heart.
   My life's companion, my friend
      and refuge.

Cesareo Gabarain (1936-91), tr. Robert C. Trupia

872

1 My God, accept my heart this day,
   and make it wholly thine,
   that I from thee no more may stray,
   no more from thee decline.

2 Before the cross of him who died,
   behold, I prostrate fall;
   let every sin be crucified,
   and Christ be all in all.

3 Anoint me with thy heavenly grace,
   and seal me for thine own,
   that I may see thy glorious face,
   and worship at thy throne.

4 Let every thought, and work and word
   to thee be ever given,
   then life shall be thy service, Lord,
   and Death the gate of heaven.

5 All glory to the Father be,
   all glory to the Son,
   all glory, Holy Ghost, to thee,
   while endless ages run.
      Matthew Bridges (1800–94)

873

1 Come, Lord Jesus, come.
   Come, take my hands, take them for
      your work.
   Take them for your service Lord.
   Take them for your glory, Lord,
   Come, Lord Jesus, come.
   Come, Lord Jesus, take my hands.

2 Come, Lord Jesus, come.
   Come, take my eyes, may they shine
      with joy.

Take them for your service, Lord.
Take them for your glory, Lord.
Come, Lord Jesus, come.
Come, Lord Jesus, take my eyes.

3 Come, Lord Jesus, come.
Come, take my lips, may they speak
   your truth.
Take them for your service, Lord.
Take them for your glory, Lord.
Come, Lord Jesus, come.
Come, Lord Jesus, take my lips.

4 Come, Lord Jesus, come.
Come take my feet, may they walk
   your path.
Take them for your service, Lord.
Take them for your glory, Lord.
Come, Lord Jesus, come.
Come, Lord Jesus, take my feet.

5 Come, Lord Jesus, come.
Come, take my heart, fill it with
   your love.
Take it for your service, Lord.
Take it for your glory, Lord.
Come, Lord Jesus, come.
Come, Lord Jesus, take my heart.

6 Come, Lord Jesus, come.
Come, take my life, take it for your own.
Take it for your service, Lord.
Take it for your glory, Lord.
Come, Lord Jesus, come.
Come, Lord Jesus, take my life.
                    Kevin Mayhew

874

1 Take my life, and let it be
consecrated, Lord, to thee;
take my moments and my days,
let them flow in ceaseless praise.

2 Take my hands, and let them move
at the impulse of thy love.
Take my feet, and let them be
swift and purposeful for thee.

3 Take my voice, and let me sing
always, only, for my King.
Take my intellect, and use
every power as thou shalt choose.

4 Take my will, and make it thine:
it shall be no longer mine.
Take my heart; it is thine own:
it shall be thy royal throne.

5 Take my love; my Lord, I pour
at thy feet its treasure–store.
Take myself, and I will be
ever, only, all for thee.
              Frances R. Havergal (1836–79)

875

1 O Jesus, I have promised
to serve thee to the end;
be thou for ever near me,
my Master and my Friend;
I shall not fear the battle
if thou art by my side,
nor wander from the pathway
if thou wilt be my guide.

2 O let me feel thee near me:
the world is ever near;
I see the sights that dazzle,
the tempting sounds I hear;
my foes are ever near me,
around me and within;
but, Jesus, draw thou nearer,
and shield my soul from sin.

3 O let me hear thee speaking
in accents clear and still,
above the storms of passion,
the murmurs of self-will;
O speak to reassure me,
to hasten or control;
O speak, and make me listen,
thou guardian of my soul.

4 O Jesus, thou hast promised
to all who follow thee,
that where thou art in glory
there shall thy servant be;
and, Jesus, I have promised

to serve thee to the end:
O give me grace to follow,
my Master and my Friend.

5 O let me see thy foot–marks,
and in them plant mine own;
my hope to follow duly
is in thy strength alone:
O guide me, call me, draw me,
uphold me to the end;
and then in heaven receive me,
my Saviour and my Friend.
J.E. Bode (1816-1874)

876

1 Thy hand, O God, has guided
thy flock from age to age;
the wondrous tale is written,
full clear, on ev'ry page;
our fathers owned thy goodness,
and we their deeds record;
and both of this bear witness:
one Church, one Faith, one Lord.

2 Thy heralds brought glad tidings
to greatest, as to least;
they bade them rise, and hasten
to share the great king's feast;
and this was all their teaching,
in every deed and word,
to all alike proclaiming
one Church, one Faith, one Lord.

3 When shadows thick were falling,
and all seemed sunk in night,
thou, Lord, didst send thy servants,
thy chosen ones of light.
On them and on thy people
thy plenteous grace was poured,
and this was still their message:
one Church, one Faith, one Lord.

4 Through many a day of darkness,
through many a scene of strife,
the faithful few fought bravely,
to guard the nation's life.
Their gospel of redemption,
sin pardoned, hope restored,

was all in this enfolded:
one Church, one Faith, one Lord.

5 And we, shall we be faithless?
Shall hearts fail, hands hang down?
Shall we evade the conflict,
and cast away our crown?
Not so: in God's deep counsels
some better thing is stored;
we will maintain, unflinching,
one Church, one Faith, one Lord.

6 Thy mercy will not fail us,
nor leave thy work undone;
with thy right hand to help us
the vict'ry shall be won;
and then, by earth and heaven
thy name shall be adored.
And this shall be their anthem:
one Church, one Faith, one Lord.
E.H. Plumptre (1821–91)

877

1 Will you come and follow me
if I but call your name?
Will you go where you don't know
and never be the same?
Will you let my love be shown,
will you let my name be known,
will you let my life be grown
in you and you in me?

2 Will you leave yourself behind
if I but call your name?
Will you care for cruel and kind
and never be the same?
Will you risk the hostile stare
should your life attract or scare?
Will you let me answer prayer
in you and you in me?

3 Will you let the blinded see
if I but call your name?
Will you set the prisoners free
and never be the same?
Will you kiss the leper clean,
and do such as this unseen,
and admit to what I mean
in you and you in me?

4 Will you love the 'you' you hide
   if I but call your name?
   Will you quell the fear inside
   and never be the same?
   Will you use the faith you've found
   to reshape the world around,
   through my sight and touch and sound
   in you and you in me?

5 Lord, your summons echoes true
   when you but call my name.
   Let me turn and follow you
   and never be the same.
   In your company I'll go
   where your love and footsteps show.
   Thus I'll move and live and grow
   in you and you in me.

John Bell & Graham Maule

878

1 You shall go out with joy
   and be led forth with peace.
   The mountains and the hills will
   break forth before you;
   there'll be shouts of joy,
   and all the trees of the field
   will clap, will clap their hands.

2 And all the trees of the field
   will clap their hands,
   the trees of the field
   will clap their hands.
   The trees of the field
   will clap their hands
   while you go out with joy.

Repeat You shall go out ...

Stuart Dauermann

879

Refrain Take Christ to the world, ce-le-brate our faith, ma-ni-fest his love to all: take Christ to the world, show that we are his in the way we live.

1 We are the body of Christ made
      incarnate
   in this time and place.
   Let us open ourselves to be truly
   pathways of his grace.

2 When we gather together to pray
   in his holy name,
   he is our strength and the song on our lips,
   he is present in our midst.

3 We are called to be hearers and bearers
   of the word of Christ;
   may it flourish and grow in our hearts,
   bringing others to his light.

4 When we offer ourselves to join
   more completely in his life,
   we are the altar, we are the meal,
   we become his sacrifice.

5 Going forth, we can be for the world
   living witnesses of love
   in our service all those we meet
   as we journey on in faith.

After verse 5, Final Refrain:

Take Christ to the world,
celebrate our faith,
manifest his love to all;
Take Christ to the world,
show that we are his in the way we live.

Take Christ to the world,
celebrate our faith,
dedicate our lives to him;
Take Christ to the world,
show that we are his in the way we live.

Paul Inwood

➤ See also: Blessing and dismissal (652-54)

Justice & Peace

880

1 Tell out, my soul, the greatness of the Lord!
   Unnumbered blessings, give my spirit voice;
   tender to me the promise of his word;
   in God my Saviour shall my heart rejoice.

2 Tell out, my soul, the greatness of his name!
   Make known his might, the deeds his arm has done;
   his mercy sure, from age to age the same;
   his holy name – the Lord, the Mighty One.

3 Tell out, my soul, the greatness of his might!
   Powers and dominions lay their glory by.
   Proud hearts and stubborn wills are put to flight,
   the hungry fed, the humble lifted high.

4 Tell out, my soul, the glories of his word!
   Firm is his promise, and his mercy sure.
   Tell out, my soul, the greatness of the Lord
   to children's children and for evermore!

Timothy Dudley–Smith
(from the Magnificat)

881

1. God of day and God of darkness, now we stand before the night,
   as the shadows stretch and deepen, come and make our darkness bright.
   All creation still is groaning for the dawning of your might,
   when the Sun of peace and justice fills the earth with radiant light.

2. Still the nations curse the darkness, still the rich oppress the poor;
   still the earth is bruised and broken by the ones who still want more.
   Come and wake us from our sleeping, so our hearts cannot ignore,
   all your people lost and broken, all your children at our door.

3. Show us Christ in one another, make us servants strong and true;
   give us all your love of justice, so we do what you would do.
   Let us call all people holy, let us pledge our lives anew,
   make us one with all the lowly, let us all be one in you.

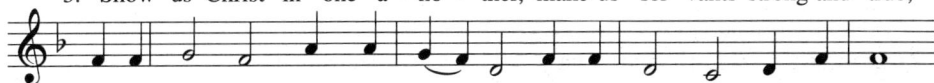

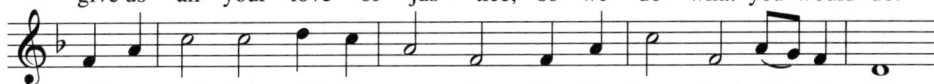

4 You shall be the path that guides us,
   you the light that in us burns;
   shining deep within all people,
   yours the love that we must learn
   for our hearts shall wander restless
   'til they safe to you return;
   finding you in one another,
   we shall all your face discern.

5 Praise to you in day and darkness,
   you our source and you our end:
   praise to you who love and nurture us,
   like a father, mother, friend.
   Grant us all a peaceful resting,
   let each mind and body mend,
   so we rise refreshed tomorrow,
   hearts renewed to kingdom tend.

Marty Haugen. Music: 19th C. American

882

1. Christ's is the world in which we move, Christ's are the
folk we're summoned to love, Christ's is the voice which calls us to
care, and Christ is the one who meets us here.

2. Feel for the people we most avoid, strange or bereaved or never employed; feel for the women, and feel for the men who fear that their living is all in vain.

Refrain

To the lost Christ shows his face; to the un-loved he gives his embrace; to those who cry in pain or dis-grace, Christ makes, with his friends, a touching place.

3 Feel for the parents who've lost their child,
feel for the women whom men have defiled,
feel for the baby for whom there's no breast,
and feel for the weary who find no rest.

4 Feel for the lives by life confused,
riddled with doubt, in loving abused;
feel for the lonely heart, conscious of sin,
which longs to be pure but fears to begin.

John L. Bell and Graham Maule

883

1. Long-ing for light, we wait in dark-ness. Long-ing for truth, we turn to you. Make us your own, your ho-ly peo-ple, light for the world to see.

2. Long-ing for peace, our world is trou-bled. Long-ing for hope, man-y de-spair. Your word a-lone has pow'r to save us. Make us your liv-ing voice.

3. Long-ing for food, man-y are hun-gry. Long-ing for wa-ter, man-y still thirst. Make us your bread, bro-ken for oth-ers, shared un-til all are fed.

Christ, be our light! Shine in our hearts. Shine through the dark - ness.

Christ, be our light! Shine in your church gath-ered to - day. _____

4 Longing for shelter, many are homeless.
   Longing for warmth, many are cold.
   Make us your building, sheltering others,
   walls made of living stones.

5 Many the gifts, many the people,
   many the hearts that yearn to belong.
   Let us be servants to one another,
   Making your kingdom come.

                              Bernadette Farrell

884

1 God, whose purpose is to kindle:
   now ignite us with your fire;
   while the earth awaits your burning,
   with your passion us inspire.
   Overcome our sinful calmness,
   stir in us your saving name;
   baptise with your fiery Spirit,
   crown our lives with tongues of flame.

2 God, who in your holy gospel
   wills that all should truly live,
   make us sense our share of failure,
   our tranquillity forgive.
   Teach us courage as we struggle
   in all liberating strife;
   lift the smallness of our vision
   by your own abundant life.

3 God, who still a sword delivers
   rather than a placid peace,
   with your sharpened word disturb us,
   from complacency release!

Save us now from satisfaction,
when we privately are free,
yet are undisturbed in spirit
by our neighbour's misery.

                              David E. Trueblood

885

1 Lord, whose love in humble service
   bore the weight of human need,
   who upon the Cross forsaken,
   offered mercy's perfect deed;
   we, your servants, bring the worship
   not of voice alone, but heart:
   consecrating to your purpose
   ev'ry gift which you impart.

2 Still your children wander homeless;
   still the hungry cry for bread;
   still the captives long for freedom;
   still in grief we mourn our dead.
   As, O Lord, your deep compassion
   healed the sick and freed the soul,
   use the love your Spirit kindles
   still to save and make us whole.

Melody: 19th C. American (hymns 884 & 885)

3 As we worship, grant us vision,
till your love's revealing light,
till the height and depth and greatness
dawns upon our human sight:
making known the needs and burdens
your compassion bids us bear,
stirring us to tireless striving,
your abundant life to share.

4 Called from worship into service
forth in your great name we go,
to the child, the youth, the aged,
love in living deeds to show;
hope and health, goodwill and comfort,
counsel, aid, and peace we give
that your children, Lord, in freedom,
may your mercy know and live.
Albert F. Bayly (1901-84)

886

1 For the healing of the nations,
Lord, we pray with one accord,
for a just and equal sharing
of the things that earth affords.
To a life of love in action
help us rise and pledge our word.

2 Lead us forward into freedom,
from despair your world release,
that, redeemed from war and hatred,
all may come and go in peace.
Show us how through care and goodness
fear will die and hope increase.

3 All that kills abundant living,
let it from the earth be banned;
pride of status, race or schooling,
dogmas that obscure your plan.
In our common quest for justice
may we hallow life's brief span.

4 You, creator–God, have written
your great name on humankind;
for our growing in your likeness
bring the life of Christ to mind;
that by our response and service
earth its destiny may find.
Fred Kaan

887

1 God, whose almighty Word
chaos and darkness heard,
and took their flight;
hear us, we humbly pray,
and where the Gospel–day
sheds not its glorious ray
let there be light!

2 Saviour, who came to bring
on your redeeming wing
healing and sight,
health to the sick in mind,
sight to the inly blind,
ah! Now to all mankind
let there be light.

3 Spirit of truth and love,
life–giving, holy dove,
speed forth your flight!
Move on the water's face,
bearing the lamp of grace,
and in earth's darkest place
let there be light!

4 Blessed and holy Three,
glorious Trinity,
wisdom, love, might;
boundless as ocean tide
rolling in fullest pride,
through the world far and wide
let there be light!
J Marriott (1780–1825)

888

1 When I needed a neighbour
were you there, were you there?
When I needed a neighbour
were you there?
And the creed and the colour
and the name won't matter,
were you there?

2 I was hungry and thirsty, ...

3 I was cold, I was naked, ...

4 When I needed a shelter, …

5 When I needed a healer, …

6 Wherever you travel, I'll be there,
　I'll be there.
Wherever you travel, I'll be there.
And the creed and the colour
and the name won't matter, I'll be there.
Sydney Carter

889

1 Jesus Christ is waiting, waiting in the
　streets;
no-one is his neighbour, all alone he eats.
Listen, Lord Jesus, I am lonely too.
Make me, friend or stranger, fit to wait
　on you.

2 Jesus Christ is raging, raging in the
　streets,
where injustice spirals and real hope
　retreats.
Listen, Lord Jesus, I am angry too.

In the Kingdom's causes let me rage with
　you.

3 Jesus Christ is healing, healing in the
　streets;
curing those who suffer, touching those
　he greets.
Listen, Lord Jesus, I have pity too.
Let my care be active, healing just like you.

4 Jesus Christ is dancing, dancing in the
　streets,
where each sign of hatred he, with love,
　defeats.
Listen, Lord Jesus, I should triumph too.
On suspicion's graveyard let me dance
　with you.

5 Jesus Christ is calling, calling in the
　streets,
'Who will join my journey? I will guide
　their feet.'
Listen, Lord Jesus, let my fears be few.
Walk one step before me; I will follow
　you.
John L. Bell and Graham Maule

890

1. The God of li - be - ra - tion has chal - lenged us to fight in - jus - tice, ex - ploi-
ta - tion and sins a - gainst the light by state or cor - po - ra - tion or a - ny seeking
gain from hu - man de - gre - da - tion or pro - fit wrought from pain.

2 The God of re-creation
has called us to proclaim
the work of reparation,
of rescue from our shame;
the city's restoration,
repair for homes and ways,
a time for jubilation,
fresh hope, new faith and praise.

3 The God of our salvation
has sent us Christ to be
our source of inspiration,
the truth which sets us free;
a reconciliation,
the pathway to release,
and healing for the nation,
where justice leads to peace.
Patrick Lee. Music by Stephen Dean

891

1. Poor folk won't al-ways be for-got-ten, nor will the hope-less hope in vain. Rise, God, re-strain the cruel ex-ploi-ters, strike them with fear.

2 God has prepared a throne for judgement;
nations will know who reigns supreme.
God will judge all the earth with justice
and equity.

3 May God indeed empower the weary,
and for the troubled be their tower.
Lord, do not turn from those who seek you,
trusting your name.

4 Sing, sing to God among the nations,
proclaim our great avenger's name.
God keeps in mind all the afflicted;
God hears their cry.

5 So, with a full heart, Lord, I praise you,
grateful for all you are and do.
I shall sing out for you, the highest;
I shall rejoice.

John Bell and Graham Maule

892

The Lord hears the cry of the poor,
blessed be the Lord.

1 I will bless the Lord at all times,
with praise ever in my mouth.
Let my soul glory in the Lord,
who will hear the cry of the poor.

2 Let the lowly hear and be glad:
the Lord listens to their pleas;
and to hearts broken God is near,
who will hear the cry of the poor.

3 Ev'ry spirit crushed God will save;
will be ransom for their lives;
will be safe shelter for their fears,
and will hear the cry of the poor.

4 We proclaim your greatness, O God,
your praise ever in our mouth;
ev'ry face brightened in your light,
for you hear the cry of the poor.

John B. Foley, SJ, based on Psalm 34

893

1 What does the Lord require
for praise and offering?
What sacrifice, desire
or tribute bid you bring?

Do justly; love mercy;
walk humbly with your God.

2 Rulers of earth, give ear!
should you not justice know?
Will God your pleading hear,
while crime and cruelty grow?
Do justly; love mercy;
walk humbly with your God.

3 All who gain wealth by trade,
for whom the worker toils,
think not to win God's aid
if greed your commerce soils.
Do justly; love mercy;
walk humbly with your God.

4 Still down the ages ring
the prophet's stern commands:
to merchant, worker, king,
he brings God's high demands:
Do justly; love mercy;
walk humbly with your God.

5 How shall our life fulfil
God's law so hard and high?
Let Christ endue our will
with grace to fortify.
Then justly, in mercy;
we'll humbly walk with God.

Albert F. Bayly (1901–84)

894

1. The gift of the Ho-ly Spi-rit is the gift of God's great love.
To us comes the touch of hea-ling from the God of heav'n a-bove;
joy and strength for our dai-ly li-ving, trust and love for the work of gi-ving, and the spi-rit of true for-gi-ving each one.

2 Anointed, we are Christ's witness
in the walk of life each day,
a comfort and light to others
whom we meet along the way.
We will cherish your life within us,
show the mercy you show to sinners,
by your suffering, you chose to win us
from death.

3 Thanksgiving we bring, and honour,
to the Father and the Son
and, with them, the Holy Spirit,
God for ever, Three in One.
Praise and glory we give and blessing,
one faith, one in truth confessing,
one in love in your all–embracing design.

Sr. Katherine Boschetti, M.S.C.

895

Let jus-tice roll like a ri-ver,_____ and wash all op-pres-sion__ a-way;__ Come, O God and take us, move and shake us, Come now, and make us a-new,__ that we might live just-ly like you.__

1 Take from me your holy feasts, all your
offerings and your music;
let justice flow like waters,
and integrity like an ever-flowing stream.

2 How long shall we wait, O God, for the
day of your mercy to dawn,
the day we beat our swords into
ploughs, when your peace reigns over
the earth?

3 Hear this, all of you who use the poor
in your thirst of power and riches;
the Lord will turn your laughter to
tears, on the wondrous Day of our God.

4 Even now return to me, let your heart
be broken and humble,
for I am gracious, generous and kind;
come and seek the mercies of God.

5 You have been told the way of life, the
way of justice and peace;
to act justly, to love gently, and walk
humbly with God.

Amos 5:21-24, 8:4; Micah 4:3-4.6:8;
Joel 2:12-14, arr. by Marty Haugen

896

1 The Church of Christ, in every age
beset by change but Spirit-led,
must claim and test its heritage
and keep on rising from the dead.

2 Across the world, across the street,
the victims of injustice cry
for shelter and for bread to eat,
and never live until they die.

3 Then let the servant Church arise,
a caring Church that longs to be
a partner in Christ's sacrifice,
and clothed in Christ's humanity.

4 For he alone, whose blood was shed,
can cure the fever in our blood,
and teach us how to share our bread
and feed the starving multitude.

5 We have no mission but to serve
in full obedience to our Lord:
to care for all, without reserve,
and spread his liberating Word.

F. Pratt Green

897

1. Like a migh-ty ri-ver flo-wing, like a flower in beau-ty gro-wing, far be-yond all hu-man kno-wing is the per-fect peace of God.

2 Like the hills serene and even,
like the coursing clouds of heaven,
like the heart that's been forgiven
is the perfect peace of God.

3 Like the summer breezes playing,
like the tall trees softly swaying,
like the lips of silent praying
is the perfect peace of God.

4 Like the morning sun ascended,
like the scents of evening blended,
like a friendship never ended
is the perfect peace of God.

5 Like the azure ocean swelling,
like the jewel all-excelling,
far beyond our human telling
is the perfect peace of God.

Michael Perry (1942-96)

898

1 Make me a channel of your peace.
Where there is hatred, let me bring your
love.
Where there is injury your pardon, Lord.
And where there's doubt true faith in you.

2 Make me a channel of your peace.
Where there's despair in life, let me
bring hope.
Where there is darkness only light,
and where there's sadness ever joy.

3 Oh, Master, grant that I may never seek
so much to be consoled as to console,
to be understood as to understand,
to be loved, as to love with all my soul.

4 Make me a channel of your peace.
It is in pardoning that we are pardoned,
in giving of ourselves that we receive,
and in dying that we're born to
eternal life.

Sebastian Temple (1928-97)
from the 'Prayer of St Francis'

899

1 Lord, make me a means of your peace.
   Where there's hatred grown, let me sow
      your love.
   Where there's injury, Lord, let forgive
      ness be my sword.
   Lord, make me a means of your peace.

2 Lord, make me a means of your peace.
   Where there's doubt and fear, let me
      sow your faith.
   In this world's despair, give me hope in
      you to share.

3 Lord, make me a means of your peace.
   Where there's sadness here, let me sow
      your joy.
   When the darkness nears, may your
      light dispel our fears.

4 Lord, grant me to seek and to share:
   less to be consoled than to help console,
   less be understood than to understand
      your good.

5 Lord, grant me to seek and to share:
   to receive love less than to give love free,
   just to give in thee, just receiving from
      your tree.

6 Lord, grant me to seek and to share:
   to forgive in thee, you've forgiven me:
   for to die in thee is eternal life to me.
   John Foley, S.J. from the 'Prayer of St Francis'

900

1 O day of peace that dimly shines
   through all our hopes and prayers and
      dreams,
   guide us to justice, truth and love,
   delivered from our selfish schemes.
   May swords of hate fall from our hands,
   our hearts from envy find release,
   till by God's grace our warring world
   shall see Christ's promised reign of peace.

2 Then shall the wolf dwell with the lamb
   nor shall the fierce devour the small;
   as beasts and cattle calmly graze,
   a little child shall lead them all.
   Then enemies shall learn to love,
   all creatures find their true accord;
   the hope of peace shall be fulfilled,
   for all the earth shall know the Lord.
   Carl P. Daw, Jr.

901

The peace of the earth— be with you, the peace of the hea-vens too; The
the peace of the ri - vers be with you, the peace of the o - ceans

too. Deep   peace   fal - ling o - ver you;
God's   peace   grow - ing in   you.

Deep— peace, deep peace fal - ling o - ver you;
God's— peace, God's peace grow - ing in   you.

Music on previous page.

The peace of the earth be with you,
the peace of the heavens too;
the peace of the rivers be with you,
the peace of the oceans too.
Deep peace falling over you;
God's peace growing in you.
Guatemalan, tr. Christine Carson

902

1 Peace is flowing like a river,
flowing out through you and me,
spreading out into the desert,
setting all the captives free.

2 Love is flowing like a river …

3 Joy is flowing like a river …

4 Hope is flowing like a river …
Carey Landry

903

With our wor-king hands, we care for and nur-ture
E Na Li-ma Ha-na, E Ma-la-ma Ai-na;
the land, the bo-dy, and the heart.
Me-ke Ki-no, Me-ka Pu-u'-wai.

1 With our hands, we press onward to
the plough.
Never turning back, we face the
mystery far beyond.
With our hands, we will shape each
other's stories.
We'll write the vision down, never
tire until it's done.

2 With our hands, we will put our
weapons down.
We will care for the earth; we will
speak a word of peace.

With our hands, we will wash each
others' feet.
We will break the bread of justice.
We will share the cup of dreams.

3 With our hands, we'll reach out to one
another.
We will touch and heal each other;
we will dry each other's tears.
With our hands, we will work
to build the promise;
for our God will be our strength,
and like the eagle we will fly.
David Haas and Joe Camacho

Dona nobis pacem cordium

904

Do-na no-bis pa-cem cor-di-um.

Give us peace of heart. Taizé chant by Jacques Berthier

Love for God; God in us

905

1. All that I coun-ted as gain now I con-si-der as loss,
2. Rich-es and ho-nours will fade, earth-ly de-lights dis-ap-pear,
3. Sil-ver and gold have I none, no land to count as my home, yet
4. Faith is the wealth I pos-sess fin-ding its source in my God:

emp-ty and worth-less to me_____ in the light of the love of the Lord._____
fade like the grass of the field_____ in the light of the love of the Lord.__ *Ref.*
wealth be-yond mea-sure I own_____ in the light of the love of the Lord._____
faith in the pro-mise of Christ is my life and my love of the Lord.__ *Ref.*

REFRAIN *after vv 2, 4*

What more could bring us hope than to know the power of his life?__ What

more could bring us peace than to share in his suff-'ring and death?__ What

more could be our fi-nal wish than to live in the love of the Lord?__

Philippians 3:7-11, adapted by Michael Joncas

906

1. If we are liv-ing we are in the Lord, and if we
2. Through-out our lives____ we have fruit to bear. All of our
3. When there is sad-ness, when__ there is pain in Christ the
4. And in this world____ we will al-ways find those who are

die____ we are in the Lord, for if we live____
good works are for us to share. Whe-ther we give,__
Lord,__ we have love to gain. Whe-ther we suf-fer
weep-ing, sick in heart and mind. They need our help,__

or if we die we be-long to God, we be-long to God.
or we re-ceive
or we re-joice,
they need our care.

v.1: Romans 14:8; vv2-4, traditional
Spanish. tr. Deborah L. Schmitz

907

1 Abide with me, fast falls the eventide;
the darkness deepens, Lord, with me abide!
When other helpers fail, and comforts flee,
help of the helpless, O abide with me.

2 Swift to its close ebbs out life's little day;
earth's joys grow dim, its glories pass away;
change and decay in all around I see;
O thou who changest not, abide with me.

3 I need thy presence every passing hour;
what but thy grace can foil the tempter's
power?
Who like thyself my guide and stay can be?
Through cloud and sunshine, O abide
with me.

4 I fear no foe with thee at hand to bless;
ills have no weight and tears no bitterness.
Where is death's sting? Where, grave,
thy victory?
I triumph still, if thou abide with me.

5 Hold thou thy Cross before my closing
eyes;
shine through the gloom, and point me
to the skies;
heaven's morning breaks, and earth's
vain shadows flee:
in life, in death, O Lord, abide with me!
H.F. Lyte (1793–1847)

908

1 Blest are the pure in heart,
for they shall see our God;
the secret of the Lord is theirs,
their soul is Christ's abode.

2 The Lord who left the heavens
our life and peace to bring,
to dwell in lowliness with us,
their pattern and their king.

3 Still to the lowly soul
he doth himself impart
and for his dwelling and his throne
chooseth the pure in heart.

4 Lord, we thy presence seek;
may ours this blessing be:
give us a pure and lowly heart,
a temple meet for thee.
Vv 1, 3: John Keble (1792–1866), vv 2, 4
from W. J. Hall's Psalms and Hymns (1836)

909

1 Be still and know that I am God,
be still and know that I am God,
be still and know that I am God.

2 I am the Lord that healeth thee...

3 In thee, O Lord, I put my trust..
Anonymous

910

1 Christ be beside me, Christ be before me,
Christ be behind me, King of my heart.
Christ be within me, Christ be below me,
Christ be above me, never to part.

2 Christ on my right hand, Christ on my
left hand,
Christ all around me, shield in the strife.
Christ in my sleeping, Christ in my sitting,
Christ in my rising, light of my life.

3 Christ be in all hearts thinking about me,
Christ be in all tongues telling of me.
Christ be the vision in eyes that see me,
in ears that hear me, Christ ever be.
Adapted from 'St Patrick's Breastplate'
by James Quinn, S.J.

911

1 Come, my Way, my Truth, my Life:
such a Way, as gives us breath;
such a Truth, as ends all strife;
such a Life, as killeth death.

2 Come, my Light, my Feast, my Strength:
such a Light, as shows a feast;
such a Feast, as mends in length;
such a Strength, as makes his guest.

3 Come, my Joy, my Love, my Heart:
   such a Joy, as none can move;
   such a Love, as none can part;
   such a Heart, as joys in love.
   George Herbert (1593-1633)

912

1 God is my great desire,
   his face I seek the first;
   to him my heart and soul aspire,
   for him I thirst.
   As one in desert lands,
   whose very flesh is flame,
   in burning love I lift my hands
   and bless his name.

2 God is my true delight,
   my richest feast his praise,
   through silent watches of the night,
   through all my days.
   To him my spirit clings,
   on him my soul is cast;
   beneath the shadow of his wings
   he holds me fast.

3 God is my strong defence
   in ev'ry evil hour;
   in him I face with confidence
   the tempter's power.
   I trust his mercy sure,
   with truth and triumph crowned:
   my hope and joy for evermore
   in him are found.
   Timothy Dudley–Smith

913

1 Jesus, my Lord, my God, my all,
   how can I love thee as I ought?
   And how revere this wondrous gift
   so far surpassing hope or thought?
   Sweet Sacrament, we thee adore;
   Oh, make us love thee more and more.

2 Had I but Mary's sinless heart
   to love thee with, my dearest King,
   O, with what bursts of fervent praise
   thy goodness, Jesus, would I sing!

3 Ah, see! Within a creature's hand
   the vast Creator deigns to be,
   reposing, infant–like, as though
   on Joseph's arm, or Mary's knee.

4 Thy body, soul, and Godhead, all;
   O mystery of love divine!
   I cannot compass all I have,
   for all thou hast and art are mine;

5 Come now ye angels to our aid,
   sound, sound God's praises higher still;
   'tis God, whose power created us,
   and in whose praise creation thrills.
   F.W. Faber (1814–63), alt.

914

1 God be in my head, and in my
      understanding;
   God be in mine eyes, and in my looking;
   God be in my mouth, and in my
      speaking;
   God be in my heart, and in my thinking;
   God be at mine end, and at my departing.
   Anon. from a Book of Hours of the
   Blessed Virgin Mary (1514)

915

We hold a treasure, not made of gold,
in earthen vessels, wealth untold;
one treasure only: the Lord, the Christ,
in earthen vessels.

1 Light has shone in our darkness;
   God has shone in our heart,
   with the light of the glory of Jesus,
      the Lord.

2 He has chosen the lowly,
   who are small in this world;
   in this weakness is glory, in Jesus, the Lord.
   John B. Foley, S.J. (2 Cor 4:6-7; I Cor 1:27-29)

916

1 Lord, it belongs not to my care
   whether I die or live;
   to love and serve thee is my share,
   and this thy grace must give.

2 If life be long, I will be glad
  that I may long obey;
  if short, yet why should I be sad
  to end my little day?

3 Christ leads me through no darker rooms
  than he went through before;
  he that into God's kingdom comes
  must enter by this door.

4 Come, Lord, when grace hath made
    me meet
  thy blessèd face to see:
  for if thy work on earth be sweet,
  what will thy glory be!

5 My knowledge of that life is small,
  the eye of faith is dim;
  but 'tis enough that Christ knows all,
  and I shall be with him

Richard Baxter (1615-91), alt.

Jésus le Christ/Lord Jesus Christ

917

Lord Jesus Christ, your light shines within us. Let not my doubts and my darkness speak to me. Lord Jesus Christ, your light shines within us. Let my heart always welcome your love.

*Taizé chant by
Jacques Berthier*

Love for one another

918

David Haas, from 1 Jn 4:16; 1 Cor 13:4-7.10.13

Where there is love, there is God. The love of God has gathered us together; Alleluia.

1 Love is patient, love is kind,
  never jealous, never proud,
  never seeking for one's self,
  Love never leads to anger.

2 Love is gracious and forgiving,
  taking no delight in wrong;

  love rejoices in the truth;
  love will endure.

3 Many things will pass away,
  there are but three things that last;
  Faith, Hope and Love;
  the greatest of these is Love.

919

1 Not for tongues of heaven's angels,
  not for wisdom to discern,
  not for faith that masters mountains,
  for this better gift we yearn:
    *May love be ours, O Lord.**

2 Love is humble, love is gentle,
  love is tender, true and kind;
  love is gracious, ever patient,
  generous of heart and mind.

3 Never jealous, never selfish,
  love will not rejoice in wrong;
  never boastful nor resentful,
  love believes and suffers long.

4 In the day this world is fading,
  faith and hope will play their part:
  but when Christ is seen in glory,
  love shall reign in every heart.
    Timothy Dudley-Smith, from I Cor 13

* this line may be repeated

1. Not for tongues of hea-ven's an-gels, not for wis-dom to dis-cern,
not for faith that mas-ters moun-tains, for this bet-ter gift we yearn:
May love be ours, O Lord; may love be ours.

*Melody by
Stephen Dean*

920

*A new Commandment I give unto you,
that you love one another as I have loved
  you,
that you love one another as I have loved
  you.*

By this shall all mankind know you are
  my disciples,
if you have love one for another.
By this shall all mankind know you are
  my disciples,
if you have love one for another.
    Anonymous, based on John 13:34–35

2 No greater love can be than this:
  to choose to die to save one's friends.
  You are my friends if you obey
  what I command that you should do.

3 I call you now no longer slaves;
  no slave knows all his master does.
  I call you friends, for all I hear
  my Father say you hear from me.

4 You chose not me, but I chose you,
  that you should go and bear much fruit.
  I chose you out that you in me
  should bear much fruit that will abide.

921

1 This is my will, my one command,
  that love should dwell among you all.
  This is my will, that you should love
  as I have shown that I love you.

5 All that you ask my Father dear
  for my name's sake you shall receive.
  This is my will, my one command,
  that love should dwell in each, in all.
    James Quinn, S.J., from John 15:12-17

922

Bind us together, Lord,
bind us together with cords
that cannot be broken.
Bind us together, Lord,
bind us together, Lord
Bind us together with love.

1 There is only one God.
   there is only one King.
   there is only one Body.
   that is why we sing:

2 Made for the glory of God,
   purchased by his precious Son,
   born with the right to be free,
   Jesus the victory has won.

3 We are the family of God,
   we are the promise divine,
   we are God's chosen desire,
   we are the glorious new wine.
   Bob Gillman

923

1. Our Fa-ther, by whose name all pa-rent-hood is known, in love di-vine you claim each fam'-ly as your own. Bless mothers, fa-thers, guar-ding well, with cons-tant love as sen-ti-nel, the homes in which your peo-ple dwell.

2 O Christ, yourself a child
   within an earthly home,
   with heart still undefiled,
   to full adulthood come;
   our children bless in every place
   that they may all behold your face
   and knowing you may grow in grace.

3 O Holy Spirit, bind
   our hearts in unity
   and teach us how to find
   the love from self set free,
   in all our hearts such less increase
   that every home, by this release,
   may be the dwelling-place of peace.
   F. Bland Tucker (1895-1984)

924

1 Brother, sister, let me serve you,
   let me be as Christ to you;
   pray that I may have the grace to
   let you be my servant too.

2 We are pilgrims on a journey,
   we are trav'llers on the road;
   we are here to help each other
   walk the mile and bear the load.

3 I will hold the Christ–light for you
   in the night–time of your fear;
   I will hold my hand out to you,
   speak the peace you long to hear.

4 I will weep when you are weeping;
   when you laugh I'll laugh with you.
   I will share your joy and sorrow
   till we've seen the journey through.

5 When we sing to God in heaven
   we shall find such harmony,
   born of all we've known together
   of Christ's love and agony.

6 Brother, sister, let me serve you,
   let me be as Christ to you;
   pray that I may have the grace to
   let you be my servant too.
   Richard Gillard

925

Shalom, my friend,
   shalom my friend, shalom, shalom.
May peace and joy be with you today,
   shalom, shalom.
     Traditional Israeli song

926

Whatsoever you do
to the least of my people,*
that you do unto me.

1 When I was hungry you gave me to eat.
   When I was thirsty you gave me to
    drink.
   Now enter into the home of my Father.

* or 'brothers' or 'sisters'

2 When I was homeless you opened your
    door.
   When I was naked you gave me your coat.
   Now enter into the home of my Father.

3 When I was weary you helped me find
    rest.
   When I was anxious you calmed all my
    fears.
   Now enter into the home of my Father.

4 When in a prison you came to my cell.
   When on a sick bed you cared for my needs.
   Now enter into the home of my Father.

5 When I was aged you bothered to smile.
   When I was restless you listened and
    cared.
   Now enter into the home of my Father.

6 When I was laughed at you stood by my
    side.
   When I was happy you shared in my joy.
   Now enter into the home of my Father.
     W. F. Jabusch

927

1 Where charity and love prevail
   there God is ever found;
   brought here together by Christ's love
   by love are we thus bound.

2 With grateful joy and holy fear
   his charity we learn;
   let us with heart and mind and soul
   now love him in return.

3 Forgive we now each other's faults
   as we our faults confess;
   and let us love each other well
   in Christian holiness.

4 Let strife among us be unknown,
   let all contention cease;
   be his the glory that we seek,
   be ours his holy peace.

5 Let us recall that in our midst
   dwells God's begotten Son;
   as members of his body joined
   we are in him made one.

6 No race nor creed can love exclude
   if honoured be God's name;
   our common life embraces all
   whose Father is the same.
     Omer Westendorf (1916-97)

Melody by
Paul Benoit,
O.S.B

1. Where cha - ri - ty and love pre - vail   there God is e - ver found;

brought here to - ge - ther by Christ's love   by love are we thus bound.

Petition

➤ See also nos 9, 26-28, 221, 547-52, 740

928

Lord, to whom shall we go? Yours are the words of e-ter-nal life.

John L.Bell & Graham Maule

929 **O Lord, hear my prayer**

Taizé chant. music by Jacques Berthier

O Lord. hear my prayer, O Lord, hear my prayer. When I call an-swer me.
The Lord is my song, the Lord is my praise: all my hope comes from God.

O Lord. hear my prayer, O Lord, hear my prayer. Come and lis-ten to me. O
The Lord is my song, the Lord is my praise: God, the well-spring of life. The

930

John Bell and Graham Maule

Lis-ten, Lord, Lis-ten, Lord, not to our words but to our prayer. You a-lone,

you a-lone un-der-stand and care.

1. Where the voice that once was wel-come
2. Where the faith that once was firm is
3. Where the wis-dom meant to heal is

sounds no more, send your love to homes turned si-lent, hearts turned sore.
bruised and torn, place a man-ger where heav'n's stran-ger may be born.
spent to harm, rouse the smothered cons-cience, soun-ding heav'n's a-larm.

4 Where the withered hands and hopes
    stretch out in vain,
  burst the storehouse of your grace and
    of our grain.

5 Turn the world and spurn the spite of
    human greed,
  train our adult eyes on where a child
    may lead.

931

O living water, refresh my soul.
O living water, refresh my soul.
Spirit of joy, Lord of creation.
Spirit of hope, Spirit of peace.

1   Spirit of God. Spirit of God.

2   O set us free. O set us free.

3   Come, pray in us. Come, pray in us.
Sr Virginia Vissing, S.S.M.N.

932

Abba, Abba, Father, you are the potter,
we are the clay, the work of your hands.

1   Mould us, mould us and fashion us
into the image
of Jesus, your Son,
of Jesus, your Son.

2   Father, may we be one in you
as he is in you,
and you are in him,
and you are in him.

3   Glory, glory and praise to you,
glory and praise to you
for ever. Amen.
For ever. Amen.
Carey Landry

933

1   Father, hear the prayer we offer:
not for ease that prayer shall be,
but for strength that we may ever
live our lives courageously.

2   Not for ever in green pastures
do we ask our way to be;
but the steep and rugged pathway
may we tread rejoicingly.

3   Not for ever by still waters
would we idly rest and stay;
but would smite the living fountains
from the rocks along the way.

4   Be our strength in hours of weakness,
in our wanderings be our guide;
through endeavour, failure, danger,
Father, be there at our side.
Love Maria Willis (1824–1908), and others

934

1   Dear Lord and Father of mankind,
forgive our foolish ways!
Re–clothe us in our rightful mind,
in purer lives thy service find,
in deeper reverence praise.   *(repeat)*

2   In simple trust like theirs who heard,
beside the Syrian sea,
the gracious calling of the Lord,
let us, like them, without a word,
rise up and follow thee.

3   O Sabbath rest by Galilee!
O calm of hills above,
where Jesus knelt to share with thee
the silence of eternity,
interpreted by love!

4   Drop thy still dews of quietness,
till all our strivings cease;
take from our souls the strain and stress,
and let our ordered lives confess
the beauty of thy peace.

5   Breathe through the heats of our desire
thy coolness and thy balm;
let sense be dumb, let flesh retire;
speak through the earthquake, wind
and fire,
O still small voice of calm!
J.G Whittier (1807–92)

935

1   O God of earth and altar,
bow down and hear our cry,
our earthly rulers falter,
our people drift and die;
the walls of gold entomb us,
the swords of scorn divide,
take not thy thunder from us,
but take away our pride.

2 From all that terror teaches,
from lies of tongue and pen,
from all the easy speeches
that comfort cruel men,
from sale and profanation
of honour and the sword,
from sleep and from damnation,
deliver us, good Lord!

3 Tie in a living tether
the prince and priest and thrall,
bind all our lives together,
smite us and save us all;
in ire and exultation
aflame with faith, and free,
lift up a living nation,
a single sword to thee.

G. K. Chesterton (1874–1936)

936

1 'Look around you, can you see?
Times are troubled, people grieve.
See the violence, feel the hardness;
all my people, weep with me.'
Kyrie eleison, Christe eleison,
Kyrie eleison.

2 'Walk among them, I'll go with you.
Reach out to them with my hands.
Suffer with me, and together we will
serve them,
help them stand.'

3 Forgive us, Father; hear our prayer.
We would walk with you anywhere,
through your suff'ring, with forgiveness;
take your life into the world.

Jodi Page Clark

937

1 Lord Jesus, we must know you
if we would make you known;
for how can we proclaim you
but by your grace alone?
We long to know your fullness,
your life of risen power,
for you alone can answer
the challenge of this hour.

2 Our broken world is seeking
what only you can give;
our words may go unheeded,
but not the way we live.
O Saviour, live within us
your life so strong, so true,
that others, touched with wonder,
may seek and worship you!

3 Lord Jesus, by your Spirit
renew your Church, we pray,
till what we are makes valid
the truth of what we say.
So truly may we know you,
so make your life our own,
that we become so like you
our lives must make you known.

Margaret Clarkson

938

1 Soul of my Saviour, sanctify my breast;
Body of Christ, be thou my saving guest;
Blood of my Saviour, bathe me in thy tide,
wash me with water flowing from thy side.

2 Strength and protection may thy Passion be;
O Blessed Jesus, hear and answer me;
deep in thy wounds, Lord, hide and
shelter me;
so shall I never, never part from thee.

3 Guard and defend me from the foe malign;
in death's dread moments make me only
thine;
call me, and bid me come to thee on high,
when I may praise thee with thy saints
for aye.

Ascribed to John XXII (1249–1334), tr. anon.

939

1 Spirit of truth and grace,
come to us in this place
as now in Jesus's name God's people
gather.
Open our eyes to see
truths that will ever be,
and in communion draw us close
together.

2 Spirit of joy and peace
   make all anxieties cease
   with knowledge of the Father's perfect
      caring.
   Then may God's children know
   love that won't let us go
   and joy that fills each day, beyond
      comparing.

3 Spirit of life and power,
   revive us in this hour
   and stir our hearts to praise with true
      devotion.
   Fill us with heavenly fire,
   and every heart inspire,
   that we may serve the world with your
      compassion.
   Iain D. Cunningham

940

1 Lord, for tomorrow and its needs
   I do not pray;
   keep me, my God, from stain of sin,
   just for today.

2 Let me both diligently work
   and duly pray;
   let me be kind in word and deed,
   just for today.

3 Let me be slow to do my will,
   prompt to obey;
   help me to mortify my flesh,
   just for today.

4 Let me no wrong or idle word
   unthinking say;
   set thou a seal upon my lips,
   just for today.

5 And if today my tide of life
   should ebb away,
   give me thy sacraments divine,
   sweet Lord, today.

6 So, for tomorrow and its needs
   I do not pray;
   but keep me, guide me, love me, Lord,
   just for today.
   Sister M. Xavier

941

There is a long-ing in our hearts, O Lord, for
you to re-veal your-self to us._ There is a long-ing in our
hearts for love we on-ly find in you, our God.

Verses

1. For jus-tice, for free-dom, for mer-cy: *hear our prayer._*
2. For wis-dom, for cour-age, for com-fort:
3. For heal-ing, for whole-ness, for new life:
4. Lord save us, take pi-ty, light in our dark-ness._

In sor-row, in grief:_ *be near, hear our prayer, O God.*
In weak-ness, in fear:_
In sick-ness, in death:_
We call you, we wait:_

Anne Quigley

1   Lord, for the years your love has kept and guided,
    urged and inspired us, cheered us on our way,
    sought us and saved us, pardoned and provided:
    Lord of the years, we bring our thanks today.

2   Lord, for that word, the word of life that fires us,
    speaks to our hearts and sets our souls ablaze,
    teaches and trains, rebukes us and inspires us:
    Lord of the word, receive your people's praise.

3   Lord, for our land in this our generation,
    spirits oppressed by pleasure, wealth and care:
    for young and old, for commonwealth and nation,
    Lord of our land, be pleased to hear our prayer.

4   Lord, for our world: when we disown and doubt him,
    loveless in strength, and comfortless in pain,
    hungry and helpless, lost indeed without him:
    Lord of the world, we pray that Christ may reign.

5   Lord, for ourselves; in living power remake us -
    self on the cross and Christ upon the throne,
    Past put behind us, for the future take us,
    Lord of our lives, to live for Christ alone.

Timothy Dudley-Smith

943

1. Give thanks to the Lord— who does wondrous deeds,—
2. Give thanks to the Lord— who has blessed our land,—
4. Give thanks to the God— of the sum-mer rains,—
5. Give thanks to the Lord— who is mer-ci-ful,—
7. Give thanks to the Lord— for the bla-zing sun,—
8. Give thanks to the Lord— for the crim-son skies,—
10. Give thanks to the God— who has set us free,—

who mas-ters the winds— and the ra-ging seas,— whose love is for
who guards ev-'ry step— with a migh-ty hand,—
who spreads out the hills— and the gol-den plains,—
whose kind-ness is wide,— and love boun-ti-ful,—
for great, rol-ling waves— where the dol-phins run,—
for wild win-dy heights where the ea-gle flies,—
who raised us to life— on a bles-sed tree,—

Fine

e-ver, whose love is for e-ver, whose love is for e-ver-more!

3. O bless the Lord for ev - 'ry gift that comes to grace our way, and
6. O bless the Lord with mu - sic, ev - 'ry crea - ture great and small, and
9. O bless the Lord all peo - ple, for the mu - sic of the skies, and

D.C.

praise the God_ of faith - ful - ness who comes to light our day.__
sing through all_ the a - ges of God's fav - our to us all.__
tell the wond - rous sto - ry of a love that ne - ver dies.__

Daniel L. Schutte

944

In the Lord I'll be ev - er thank-ful, in the Lord I will re-

joice! Look to God, do not be a - fraid; lift up your voi-ces, the Lord is

near; lift up your voi-ces, the Lord is near.

In the Lord
Taizé chant by
Jacques Berthier

945

1 Now thank we all our God,
with heart and hands and voices,
who wondrous things hath done,
in whom his world rejoices;
who from our mother's arms
hath blessed us on our way
with countless gifts of love,
and still is ours today.

2 O may this bounteous God
through all our life be near us,
with ever joyful hearts
and blessed peace to cheer us;

and keep us in his grace,
and guide us when perplexed,
and free us from all ills
in this world and the next.

3 All praise and thanks to God
the Father now be given,
the Son, and him who reigns
with them in highest heaven,
the one Eternal God,
whom earth and heaven adore;
for thus it was, is now,
and shall be evermore.

Martin Rinkart (1586–1649),
tr. Catherine Winkworth (1827-78)

946

Stephen Dean

1. Thanks be to God whose love has gathered us this day. Thanks be to God who helps and guides us on our way. Thanks be to God who gives us voice, that we may thank him: *De - o gra-ti-as, De - o gra-ti-as, thanks be to God most high.*

2 Thanks be to God for all the gifts of life and light;
   thanks be to God whose care protects us, day and night;
   thanks be to God who keeps in mind us who forget him:

3 Thanks be to God who knows our secret joys and fears;
   thanks be to God who when we call him, always hears;
   thanks be to God our rock and strength, ever sustaining:

4 Thanks be to God who never turns his face away;
   thanks be to God who heals and pardons all who stray;
   thanks be to God who welcomes us into the Kingdom:

5 Thanks be to God who made our world and all we see;
   thanks be to God who gave his Son to set us free;
   thanks be to God whose Spirit brings warmth and rejoicing:

Trust, Hope Guidance

Nada te turbe/Nothing can trouble

St Teresa of Avila.
Music: Taizé chant by Jacques Berthier

947

Na - da te tur - be, na - da te es-pan-te, Quien a Dios tie - ne
No-thing can trou-ble, no-thing can frigh-ten. Those who seek God shall

na-da le fal - ta. Na-da te tur - be, na - da te es-pan-te, so - lo Dios bas-ta.
ne-ver go wan-ting. Nothing can trou-ble, no-thing can frigh-ten. God al-one fills us.

948

1 Because the Lord is my shepherd,
I have ev'rything I need.
He lets me rest in the meadow
and leads me to the quiet streams.
He restores my soul and he leads me
in the paths that are right:

Lord, you are my shepherd, you are my
friend.
I want to follow you always, just to
follow my friend.

2 And when the road leads to darkness,
I shall walk there unafraid.
Even when death is close
I have courage for your help is there.

You are close beside me with comfort,
you are guiding my way:

3 In love you make me a banquet
for my enemies to see.
You make me welcome, pouring down
honour from your mighty hand;
and this joy fills me with gladness,
it is too much to bear:

4 Your goodness always is with me
and your mercy I know.
Your loving kindness strengthens me
always as I go through life.
I shall dwell in your presence forever,
giving praise to your name:

Psalm 23. Christopher Walker (b.1947)

949

God a-lone may lead my spi-rit far a-way from want and fear,

for the Lord is my true shep herd___ and I know the Lord is near.

1 I am led beside God's peaceful water
and I sleep in the arms of the earth.
Who guides me along paths of honour?
Who refreshes my life from my birth?

2 Though I wander the valley of dying,
I shall know that I walk in your sight,
with your staff that is ever before me
and your rod to guard at my right.

3 You have spread your banquet before me
in the unbroken sight of my foes,
while my head is anointed with kindness
and the cup of my life overflows.

4 Only mercy and goodness pursue me
while that breath and that justice endure.
And I'll dwell in the house of God's
keeping
who has opened the mouths of the poor.

Tom Conry, based on Psalm 23

950

My soul is longing for your peace,
near to you, my God.

1 Lord, you know that my heart is not proud,
and my eyes are not lifted from earth.

2 Lofty thoughts have never filled my mind,
far beyond my sight all ambitious deeds.

3 In your peace I have maintained my soul,
I have kept my heart in your quiet peace.

4 As a child rests on a mother's knee,
so I place my soul in your loving care.

5 Israel, put all your hope in God,
place your trust in God, now and
evermore. *Ps 131 (132). Lucien Deiss*

➤ See also: Like a child rests (453)

951

Shep-herd me, O God, be-yond my wants, be-yond my fears, from death in-to life.

Psalm 23, Marty Haugen

1 God is my shepherd, so nothing shall I
    want,
  I rest in the meadows of faithfulness
    and love,
  I walk by the quiet waters of peace.

2 Gently you raise me and heal my weary
    soul,
  you lead me by pathways of righteous
    ness and truth,
  my spirit shall sing the music of your name.

3 Though I should wander the valley of death,

I fear no evil, for you are at my side,
your rod and your staff, my comfort and
  my hope.

4 You have set me a banquet of love
  in the face of hatred,
  crowning me with love beyond my pow'
    to hold.

5 Surely your kindness and mercy follow m
  all the days of my life;
  I will dwell in the house of my God for
    evermore.

952

1 You who dwell in the shelter of the Lord,
    who abide in his shadow for life,
    say to the Lord:'My refuge,
    my Rock in whom I trust!'

Michael Joncas,
from Psalm 91

And he will raise you up on ea-gle's wings, bear you on the breath of dawn, make you to shine like the sun, and hold you in the palm of his hand.

Last time to Coda

2 The snare of the fowler will never
    capture you,
  and famine will bring you no fear:
  under his wings your refuge
  his faithfulness your shield.

3 You need not fear the terror of the night,
  nor the arrow that flies by day;

though thousands fall about you,
near you it shall not come.

4 For to his angels he's given a command
  to guard you in all of your ways;
  upon their hands they will bear you up,
  lest you dash your foot against a stone.
Refrain, ending with Coda:

Last time: Coda

And hold you, hold you in the palm of his hand.

953

1 Safe in the shadow of the Lord,
 beneath his hand and power,
 I trust in him, I trust in him,
 my fortress and my tower.

2 My hope is set on God alone
 though Satan spreads his snare;
 I trust in him, I trust in him
 to keep me in his care.

3 From fears and phantoms of the night,
 from foes about my way,
 I trust in him, I trust in him
 by darkness as by day.

4 His holy angels keep my feet
 secure from every stone;
 I trust in him, I trust in him
 and unafraid go on.

5 Strong in the everlasting name,
 and in my Father's care,
 I trust in him, I trust in him
 who hears and answers prayer.

6 Safe in the shadow of the Lord,
 possessed by love divine,
 I trust in him, I trust in him
 and meet his love with mine.
 Timothy Dudley–Smith, from Psalm 91

954

Blest be the Lord; blest be the Lord,
the God of mercy, the God who saves.
I shall not fear the dark of night,
nor the arrow that flies by day.

1 He will release me from the nets
  of all my foes.
 He will protect me from their
  wicked hands.
 Beneath the shadow of His wings
  I will rejoice
 to find a dwelling place secure.

2 I need not shrink before the terrors
  of the night,
 nor stand alone before the light of day.
 No harm shall come to me,

no arrow strike me down,
no evil settle in my soul.

3 Although a thousand strong have
  fallen at my side,
 I'll not be shaken with the Lord at hand.
 His faithful love is all the armour
  that I need
 to wage my battle with the foe.
 Daniel L. Schutte, from Psalm 91

955

1 O God, our help in ages past,
 our hope for years to come,
 our shelter from the stormy blast,
 and our eternal home;

2 Beneath the shadow of thy throne,
 thy saints have dwelt secure;
 sufficient is thine arm alone,
 and our defence is sure.

3 Before the hills in order stood,
 or earth received her frame,
 from everlasting thou art God,
 to endless years the same.

4 A thousand ages in thy sight,
 are like an evening gone;
 short as the watch that ends the night
 before the rising sun.

5 Time, like an ever–rolling stream,
 bears all its sons away;
 they fly forgotten, as a dream
 dies at the opening day.

6 O God, our help in ages past,
 our hope for years to come,
 be thou our guard while troubles last,
 and our eternal home.
 Isaac Watts (1674–1748) from Ps 90

956

1 I watch the sunrise
 lighting the sky,
 casting its shadows near.
 And on this morning
 bright though it be,
 I feel those shadows near me.

But you are always close to me
following all my ways.
May I be always close to you
following all your ways, Lord.

2 I watch the sunlight
   shine through the clouds,
   warming the earth below.
   And at the mid–day life seems to say:
   'I feel your brightness near me.'
   For you are always ...

3 I watch the sunset
   fading away,
   lighting the clouds with sleep.
   And as the evening closes its eyes
   I feel your presence near me.
   For you are always ...

4 I watch the moonlight
   guarding the night,
   waiting till morning comes.
   The air is silent, earth is at rest -
   only your peace is near me.
   Yes, you are always ...
                          John Glynn

957

1 As if you were not there,
   the skies ignite and thunder,
   rivers tear their banks asunder,
   thieves and nature storm and plunder:
       all beware,
   as if you were not there.

2 As if you were not there,
   famine and flood together
       usher death, disease and terror;
   stricken mothers wonder whether
       God heeds prayer,
   as if you were not there.

3 As if you were not there,
   we televise the dying,
   watch the helpless victims crying,
   salve our consciences by sighing
       'Life's unfair!'
   as if you were not there.

4 As if you were not there,
   your Son, when faith defied him,
   faced a crowd which crucified him,
   leaving friends who had denied him
       in despair,
   as if you were not there.

5 Because he rose again
   and showed God's love is vaster
       than the ultimate disaster,
   we entreat you now to master
       strife and pain,
   because he rose again.
                John L. Bell and Graham Maule

958

1 God is our fortress and our rock,
   our mighty help in danger;
   he shields us from the battle's shock
   and thwarts the devil's anger:
   for still the prince of night
   prolongs his evil fight;
   he uses every skill
   to work his wicked will –
   no earthly force is like him.

2 Our hope is fixed on Christ alone,
   the Man, of God's own choosing;
   without him nothing can be won
   and fighting must be losing:
   so let the powers accursed
   come on and do their worst,
   the Son of God shall ride
   to battle at our side,
   and he shall have the victory.

3 The word of God will not be slow
   while demon hordes surround us,
   though evil strike its cruellest blow
   and death and hell confound us:
   for even if distress
   should take all we possess,
   and those who mean us ill
   should ravage, wreck, or kill,
   God's kingdom is immortal!
                after M. Luther (1483-1546) by
                Michael Perry (1942-96)

959

1 All my hope on God is founded;
he doth still my trust renew.
Me through change and chance he
    guideth,
only good and only true.
God unknown, he alone
calls my heart to be his own.

2 Human pride and earthly glory,
sword and crown betray God's trust;
what with lavish care man buildeth,
tower and temple, fall to dust.
But God's power, hour by hour,
is my temple and my tower.

3 God's great goodness ay endureth,
deep his wisdom, passing thought:
splendour, light and life attend him,
beauty springeth out of nought.
Evermore, from his store
new–born worlds rise and adore.

4 Daily doth the almighty giver
bounteous gifts on us bestow;
his desire our soul delighteth
pleasure leads us where we go.
Love doth stand at his hand,
joy doth wait at his command.

5 Still from earth to God eternal
sacrifice of praise be done,
high above all praises praising
for the gift of Christ his Son.
Christ doth call one and all;
ye who follow shall not fall.

Robert S. Bridges (1844–1930)
based on a hymn by J. Neander (1650–80)

960

1 Guide me, O thou great Redeemer,
pilgrim through this barren land;
I am weak, but thou art mighty,
hold me with thy pow'rful hand:
    bread of heaven,
feed me till I want no more.

2 Open now the crystal fountain,
whence the healing stream doth flow;
let the fire and cloudy pillar
lead me all my journey through;
    strong Deliverer,
be thou still my strength and shield.

3 When I tread the verge of Jordan,
bid my anxious fears subside,
death of death, and hell's destruction,
land me safe on Canaan's side;
    songs of praises
I will ever give to thee.

W. Williams (1717–91),
tr. P. and W. Williams

ORIGINAL VERSION

1 Arglywdd, arwain drwy'r anialwch
fi, bererin gwael ei wedd,
nad oes ynof nerth na bywyd,
fel yn gorwedd yn y bedd:
    hollalluog,
ydyw'r un a'm cwyd i'r lan.

2 Colofn dân rho'r nos i'm harwain,
 a rho golofn niwl y dydd;
dal fi pan fwy'n teithio'r mannau
geirwon yn fy ffordd y sydd;
    rho i mi fanna,
fel na bwyf yn llwfwrhau.

3 Agor y ffynhonnau melys
sydd yn tarddu o'r graig i maes;
r hyd yr anial mawr canlyned
afon iachawdwriaeth gras:
    rho i mi hynny;
dim i mi ond dy fwynhau.

William Williams (1717-91)

961

1 Lead, kindly light amid th' encircling
    gloom,
lead thou me on;
the night is dark, and I am far from home,
lead thou me on.
Keep thou my feet; I do not ask to see
the distant scene; one step enough for me.

2 I was not ever thus, nor prayed that thou
    shouldst lead me on;
  I loved to choose and see my path; but now
  lead thou me on.
  I loved the garish day, and, spite of fears,
  pride ruled my will; remember not past
    years.

3 So long thy power hath blest me, sure it
    still
  will lead me on
  o'er moor and fen, o'er crag and torrent,
    till
  the night is gone,
  and with the morn those angel faces smile
  which I have loved long since, and lost
    awhile.

J.H. Newman (1801–90)

962

1 Firmly I believe and truly
  God is three, and God is one,
  and I next acknowledge duly
  manhood taken by the Son.

2 And I trust and hope most fully
  in that manhood crucified;
  and each thought and deed unruly
  do to death, as he has died.

3 Simply to his grace and wholly
  light and life and strength belong;
  and I love supremely, solely,
  him the holy, him the strong.

4 And I hold in veneration,
  for the love of him alone,
  Holy Church, as his creation,
  and her teachings, as his own.

5 Adoration aye be given,
  with and through th' angelic host,
  to the God of earth and heaven,
  Father, Son and Holy Ghost.

J.H. Newman (1801–90)

963

1 Eternal Father, strong to save,
  whose arm doth bind the restless wave,
  who bidd'st the mighty ocean deep,
  its own appointed limits keep:
  O hear us when we cry to thee
  for those in peril on the sea.

2 O Saviour, whose almighty word
  the winds and waves submissive heard,
  who walkedst on the foaming deep
  and calm amid its rage didst sleep:
  O hear us when we cry to thee
  for those in peril on the sea.

3 O sacred Spirit, who didst brood
  upon the waters dark and rude,
  and bid their angry tumult cease,
  and give, for wild confusion, peace:
  O hear us when we cry to thee
  for those in peril on the sea.

4 O Trinity of love and power,
  our brethren shield in danger's hour.
  From rock and tempest, fire and foe,
  protect them wheresoe'er they go,
  and ever let there rise to thee
  glad hymns of praise from land and sea.

W. Whiting (1825–78)

964

1 You shall cross the barren desert,
  but you shall not die of thirst.
  You shall wander far in safety
  though you do not know the way.
  You shall speak your words in foreign lands
  and they will understand.
  You shall see the face of God and live.
  Be not afraid, I go before you always.
  Come, follow me, and I will give you rest.

2 If you pass through raging waters in the
    sea,
  you shall not drown.
  If you walk amid the burning flames,
  you shall not be harmed.
  If you stand before the pow'r of hell

and death is at your side,
know that I am with you through it all.

3 Blessed are your poor,
for the kingdom shall be theirs.
Blest are you that weep and mourn,
for one day you shall laugh.
And if wicked tongues insult and hate you
all because of me,
blessed, blessed are you!

Robert J. Dufford, S.J.

965

1 As the deer pants for the water,
so my soul longs after you.
You alone are my heart's desire
and I long to worship you.
You alone are my strength, my shield,
to you alone may my spirit yield.
You alone are my heart's desire
and I long to worship you.

2 I want you more than gold or silver,
only you can satisfy.
You alone are the real joy–giver
and the apple of my eye.

3 You're my Friend and you're my Brother,
even though you are a king.
I love you more than any other,
so much more than anything.

Martin Nystrom
© Copyright 1983 Restoration Music Ltd,
admin. by Sovereign Music UK

966

Walk with me, oh my Lord,
through the darkest night and brightest day.
Be at my side, oh Lord,
hold my hand and guide me on my way.

1 Sometimes the road seems long,
my energy is spent.
Then, Lord, I think of you
and I am given strength.

2 Stones often bar my path
and there are times I fall,
but you are always there
to help me when I call.

3 Just as you calmed the wind
and walked upon the sea,
conquer, my living Lord,
the storms that threaten me.

4 Help me to pierce the mists
that cloud my heart and mind
so that I shall not fear
the steepest mountain–side.

5 As once you helped the lame
and gave sight to the blind,
help me when I'm downcast
to hold my head up high.

Estelle White

967

1 O, the love of my Lord is the essence
of all that I love here on earth.
All the beauty I see
he has given to me
and his giving is gentle as silence.

2 Every day, every hour, every moment
have been blessed by the strength of his
love.
At the turn of each tide
he is there at my side,
and his touch is as gentle as silence.

3 There've been times when I've turned
from his presence,
and I've walked other paths, other ways.
But I've called on his name
in the dark of my shame,
and his mercy was gentle as silence.

Estelle White

968

1 Be still, and know I am with you,
be still, I am the Lord.
I will not leave you orphans.
I leave with you my world. Be one.

2 You fear the light may be fading,
you fear to lose your way.
Be still, and know I am near you.
I'll lead you to the day and the sun.

3 Be glad the day you have sorrow,
be glad, for then you live.
The stars shine only in darkness,
and in your need I give my peace.
Anne Conway

969

1 Lord of all hopefulness, Lord of all joy,
whose trust, ever child–like, no cares
could destroy,
be there at our waking, and give us, we
pray,
your bliss in our hearts, Lord, at the
break of the day.

2 Lord of all eagerness, Lord of all faith,
whose strong hands were skilled
at the plane and the lathe,
be there at our labours and give us, we
pray,
your strength in our hearts, Lord,
at the noon of the day.

3 Lord of all kindliness, Lord of all grace,
your hands swift to welcome, your
arms to embrace,
be there at our homing and give us, we
pray,
your love in our hearts, Lord, at the
eve of the day.

4 Lord of all gentleness, Lord of all calm,
whose voice is contentment, whose
presence is balm,
be there at our sleeping and give us, we
pray,
your peace in our hearts, Lord, at the
end of the day.
Jan Struther (1901–53)

970

1 Be thou my vision, O Lord of my heart,
naught be all else to me save that thou art;
thou my best thought in the day and the
night,
waking or sleeping, thy presence my light.

2 Be thou my wisdom, be thou my true
Word;
I ever with thee, and thou with me, Lord;
thou my great Father, and I thy true son;
thou in me dwelling, and I with thee one.

3 Be thou my breast–plate, my sword for
the fight;
be thou my armour, and be thou my might,
thou my soul's shelter, and thou my high
tower,
raise thou me heavenward, O Power of
my power.

4 Riches I heed not, nor man's empty
praise,
thou mine inheritance through all my
days;
thou, and thou only, the first in my heart,
high King of heaven, my treasure thou art!

5 High King of heaven, when battle is done,
grant heaven's joy to me, O bright
heaven's sun;
Christ of my own heart, whatever befall,
still be my vision, O Ruler of all.
*Irish, c.8th C, tr. Mary Byrne (1881–1931),
versified by Eleanor Hull (1860–1935)*

971

1 Father, I place into your hands
the things I cannot do.
Father, I place into your hands
the things that I've been through.
Father, I place into your hands
the way that I should go,
for I know I always can trust you.

2 Father, I place into your hands
my friends and family.
Father, I place into your hands
the things that trouble me.
Father, I place into your hands
the person I would be,
for I know I always can trust you.

3 Father, we love to see your face,
we love to hear your voice.
Father, we love to sing your praise
and in your name rejoice.
Father, we love to walk with you
and in your presence rest,
for we know we always can trust you.

4 Father, I want to be with you
and do the things you do.
Father, I want to speak the words
that you are speaking too.
Father, I want to love the ones
that you will draw to you,
for I know that I am one with you.
Jenny Hewer

972

Do not be afraid,
for I have redeemed you.
I have called you by your name;
you are mine.

1 When you walk through the waters I'll
be with you.
You will never sink beneath the waves.

2 When the fire is burning all around you,
you will never be consumed by the flames.

3 When the fear of loneliness is looming,
then remember I am at your side.

4 When you dwell in the exile of the
stranger,
remember you are precious in my eyes.

5 You are mine, O my child, I am your
Father,
and I love you with a perfect love.
Gerald Markland

973

1 He's got the whole world in his hand,
he's got the whole world in his hand,
he's got the whole world in his hand,
he's got the whole world in his hand.

2 He's got you and me, brother, in his hand...
he's got the whole world in his hand.

3 He's got you and me, sister, in his hand...
he's got the whole world in his hand.

4 He's got everybody here in his hand...
he's got the whole world in his hand.

5 He's got the little tiny baby in his hand...
he's got the whole world in his hand.

repeat verse 1
Traditional

The Word of God

974

We do not live by bread— a - lone, but by ev' - ry
word that comes— from the mouth of— God.—

1 Lead our hearts away from worldly gain,
turn our eyes from seeing what is vain,
teach us your wisdom.
Give us knowledge;
in your word we hope and trust.

2 A lamp to our feet, a light to our path,
sweeter than honey, precious as gold,

your word is our delight;
it brings eternal life.

3 When the snares of evil hem us in,
and oppression weighs us down,
liberation and salvation
come as promised through your word.
Matthew 4:4:, Ps 119: Donald J. Reagan

975

In the land,— in the land— is a hun - ger, in the land — is a hun - ger for more than bread.— In our hearts, in our hearts is a hun - ger, in our hearts is a hun - ger for the Word of God.—

1 Listen, all who fear, listen all who search,
to the voice that speaks of peace:
one who knows your name, one who calls
you home,
one who waits to hear your cry.

2 Listen, all who mourn, listen, all who
weep,
to the hope you fear is gone:

One who shared our fate, one who died
our death,
one who lives to set us free.

3 Listen, all who hope, listen all who dream,
to the promise we have heard:
One who routs the proud, sets the
captive free,
one whose world is upside down.

Bernadette Farrell

976

In the land there is a hun - ger, in the land there is a need not for the taste of wa - ter, not for the taste of bread. In the land there is a hun - ger, in the land there is a need for the sound of the word of God u - pon ev' - ry word we feed.

1 Hear, O Lord my cry,
day and night I call.
My soul is thirsting
for you, my God.

2 Your word, O Lord
is spirit and life
You have the words, Lord,
of everlasting life.

3 Only in God
is my soul at rest.
He is my rock
and my salvation.

Mike Lynch

977

1 Lord, thy word abideth,
  and our footsteps guideth;
  who its truth believeth
  light and joy receiveth.

2 When our foes are near us,
  then thy word doth cheer us,
  word of consolation,
  message of salvation.

3 When the storms are o'er us,
  and dark clouds before us,
  then its light directeth,
  and our way protecteth.

4 Who can tell the pleasure,
  who recount the treasure,
  by thy word imparted
  to the simple-hearted?

5 Word of mercy, giving
  courage to the living;
  word of life, supplying
  comfort to the dying!

6 O that we discerning
  its most holy learning,
  Lord, may love and fear thee,
  evermore be near thee.
        H.W. Baker (1821-1877)

978

1 Lord, your word shall guide us,
  and with truth provide us:
  teach us to receive it
  and with joy believe it.

2 When our foes are near us,
  then your word shall cheer us,
  word of consolation,
  message of salvation.

3 When the storms distress us,
  and dark clouds oppress us,
  then your word protects us,
  and its light directs us.

4 Who can tell the pleasure,
  who recount the treasure,
  by your word imparted
  to the simple-hearted?

5 Word of mercy, giving
  courage to the living;
  word of life, supplying
  comfort to the dying!

6 O that we discerning
  its most holy learning,
  Lord, may love and fear you,
  evermore be near you.
        H.W. Baker (1821-1877)
        altered by Michael Perry (1944-97)

979

Oh the word of my Lord, deep within my
    being,
oh the word of my Lord, you have filled
    my mind.

1 Before I formed you in the womb
  I knew you through and through,
  I chose you to be mine.
  Before you left your mother's side
  I called to you, my child, to be my sign.

2 I know that you are very young,
  but I will make you strong
  – I'll fill you with my word;
  and you will travel through the land,
  fulfilling my command which you have
      heard.

3 And ev'rywhere you are to go
  my hand will follow you;
  you will not be alone.
  In all the danger that you fear
  you'll find me very near, your words my
      own.

4 With all my strength you will be filled:
  you will destroy and build,
  for that is my design.
  You will create and overthrow,
  reap harvests I will sow – your word is
      mine.
        Damian Lundy (1942-97)

980

Your words are spi-rit and life, O Lord: rich-er than gold, stron-ger than death. Your words are spi-rit and life, O Lord; live e-ver-las-ting.

1 God's Law is perfect, refreshing the soul,
   reviving the weary spirit.
   God's rule can be trusted: bringing us wisdom,
   bringing God's wisdom to birth.

2 God's precepts keep us, their purpose is right,
   They gladden the hearts of people.
   God's command is so clear, it brings us new vision;
   bringing God's light to our eyes.

3. Living by God's truth is holy and sure;
   God's presence is everlasting.
   God's truth is eternal, bringing us justice,
   bringing God's justice to earth.

4. God's word is precious, desired more than gold;
   worth more than we dare imagine
   and, sweeter than honey, this word will feed us,
   bringing fulfilment and joy.

   Bernadette Farrell, from Ps 18(19):8-11

981

Refrain

1- 4. To ev'-ry-thing there is a sea-son; a time to be born and a time to die.

1 4. A time to plant, and a time for har-vest;
2. A time to speak, and a time for si-lence;
3. A time for joy, and a time for grie-ving;

a time to meet and a time to part.
a time to wound and a time to heal.
a time to seek and a time to lose.

Fine Verses

1. A so-wer went
2. Noth-ing can
3. God's word is

out to sow the seed. Some of it fell up-on the path, some fell on
grow in bar-ren soil; bri-ars and ra-vens take their toil; still there is
like the far-mer's seed, roo-ted in joy-ful, lo-ving hearts, grow-ing like

shal - low, roc - ky soil; and some am - ong cho-king thorns.
grain a hun-dred - fold, from seed that took root and grew.
grain in fer - tile ground, a har - vest that o - ver- flows.

M.D.Ridge, based on Eccl.3:1-9; Mt 13:4-8.

The Lord's Coming

982

1 O Jesus Christ, remember,
  when thou shalt come again,
  upon the clouds of heaven,
  with all thy shining train;
  when every eye shall see thee
  in deity revealed,
  who now upon this altar
  in silence art concealed.

2 Remember then, O Saviour,
  I supplicate of thee,
  that here I bowed before thee
  upon my bended knee;
  that here I owned thy presence,
  and did not thee deny,
  and glorified thy greatness
  though hid from human eye.

3 Accept, divine Redeemer,
  the homage of my praise;
  be thou the light and honour
  and glory of my days.
  Be thou my consolation
  when death is drawing nigh:
  be thou my only treasure
  through all eternity.
  Edward Caswall (1814–78)

983

1 Hills of the north, rejoice;
  river and mountain–spring,
  hark to the advent voice;
  valley and lowland, sing:
  though absent long, your Lord is nigh;
  he judgement brings and victory.

2 Isles of the southern seas,
  deep in your coral caves
  pent be each warring breeze,
  lulled be your restless waves:
  he comes to reign with boundless sway,
  and makes your wastes his great highway.

3 Lands of the east, awake,
  soon shall your sons be free;
  the sleep of ages break, and rise to liberty.
  On your far hills, long cold and grey,
  has dawned the everlasting day.

4 Shores of the utmost west,
  ye that have waited long, unvisited,
      unblest,
  break forth to swelling song;
  high raise the note, that Jesus died,
  yet lives and reigns, the Crucified.

5 Shout, while ye journey home;
  songs be in every mouth;
  lo, from the north we come,
  from east and west and south.
  City of God, the bonds are free,
  we come to live and reign in thee!
  C.E. Oakley (1832–65)

984

1 All over the world the Spirit is moving,
  all over the world
  as the prophets said it would be.
  All over the world there's a mighty
      revelation
  of the glory of the Lord
  as the waters cover the sea.

2 All over this land..

3 All over the church...

4 All over us all..

5 Deep down in my heart...   *Roy Turner*

985

1. In— God's good time our eyes will o-pen, we'll see great signs and mar-vels, and know the day has come: Yes, in God's good time we will hear glad mu-sic, and an-gels and arch-an-gels will call us home. *Who can tell when these won-ders will hap-pen? We know not the se-cond, the mi-nute, the hour, but the day will come when our chains will break and our (v.3 a great ho-san-na will a-tears will dry a-way in God's good time.* God's good time. *rise)*

2 In God's good time, the poor will prosper,
   the hungry will be sated, the sick will be made whole,
   yes, in God's good time things we dare not dream of
   will fill our deepest longings of heart and soul.
   None can tell when such marvels will happen;
   it may be tomorrow, it may be today
   but the day will come when the clouds will burst
   and the night will turn to day in God's good time

3 In God's good time all war will vanish
   old hates will be forgotten, old enemies forgive:
   and all hearts will stir, and all swords will shatter,
   what's hidden will be open, what's dead will live.
   Come, Lord Jesus, and change us for ever,
   we're getting impatient, so hasten the day
   when the world will sing and a great hosanna
   will arise from earth to heaven in God's good time.

Stephen Dean

986

M.D.Ridge

In the day of the Lord,—the sun will shine like the dawn of e-ter - nal day.

All cre-a-tion will rise— to dance and sing the glo-ry of the Lord!

Verses

1. And on that day will jus - tice tri-umph, on that day will all be
2. Then shall the na - tions throng to - ge - ther to the moun-tain of the

free: free from want, free from fear,— free to live!_____
Lord: they shall walk in the light— of the Lord!_____

3 And they shall beat their swords to
  ploughshares;
  there will be an end to war:
  one in peace, one in love, one in God!

4 For Israel shall be delivered,
  and the desert lands will bloom.
  Say to all, 'Do not fear. Here is your God!'

5 And on that day of Christ in glory,
  God will wipe away our tears,
  and the dead shall rise up from their
    graves!

6 O, give us eyes to see your glory,
  give us hearts to understand.
  Let our ears hear your voice till you
    come!

987

1 Mine eyes have seen the glory of the
    coming of the Lord.
  He is trampling out the vintage
    where the grapes of wrath are stored.
  He has loosed the fateful lightning of his
    terrible swift sword.
  His truth is marching on.
    Glory, glory hallelujah!
    Glory, glory hallelujah!
    Glory, glory hallelujah!
  His truth is marching on.

2 I have seen him in the watchfires of a
    hundred circling camps.
  They have gilded him an altar in the
    evening dews and damps.

I can read his righteous sentence by the
    dim and flaring lamps.
His day is marching on.

3 He has sounded forth the trumpet that
  shall never sound retreat.
  He is sifting out the hearts of all before
    his judgement seat.
  O, be swift my soul to answer him, be
    jubilant my feet!
  Our God is marching on.

4 In the beauty of the lilies Christ was born
    across the sea
  with a glory in his bosom that
    transfigures you and me.
  As he died to make us holy, let us make
    all people free,
  whilst God is marching on.
    Julia Ward Howe (1819–1910)

988

Sha-rers in the pro-mise, hea-rers of the Word, may we work for one same King-dom, may we serve one Lord.

Stephen Dean

989

1　Word made flesh, Son of God.
Come, Lord Jesus, come again;
Come, Lord Jesus, come again;

2　Lord and Saviour, Son of God:

3　Prince of Peace, Son of God:

4　Alleluia, Son of God:

5　Bread of life, Son of God:

6　Light of the World, Son of God:

7　Jesus Christ, Son of God;
Sister Virginia Vissing, SS.M.N.

The Heavenly City

990

One thing I ask of the Lord, for this— I long, to live in the house of the Lord, all the days of my life.

1　The Lord is my light and my help.
Whom shall I fear?
The Lord is the stronghold of my life,
before whom shall I shrink?

2　Though armies do battle against me
my heart will not fear.
Though war and destruction break forth,
even then would I trust.

3　For there in his house I am safe
in evil's dark hour.
He hides me and shelters my soul,
my defender, my rock.

4　There is one thing I ask of the Lord,
for this I long:
to live in the house of the Lord
all the days of my life,
to save the sweetness of the Lord,
to behold his temple.

5　I know I shall see the Lord's goodness
in his promised land.
Take heart and stand firm, O my soul,
put your hope in the Lord!

Verses from Ps 26 (27). Music by Stephen Dean

991

1 Jerusalem the golden,
  with milk and honey blest,
  beneath thy contemplation
  sink heart and voice oppressed.
  I know not, ah, I know not
  what joys await us there,
  what radiancy of glory,
  what bliss beyond compare.

2 They stand, those halls of Sion,
  all jubilant with song,
  and bright with many an angel,
  and all the martyr throng;
  the Prince is ever with them,
  the daylight is serene;
  the pastures of the blessed
  are decked in glorious sheen.

3 There is the throne of David;
  and there, from care released,
  the shout of them that triumph,
  the song of them that feast;
  and they, who with their leader
  have conquered in the fight,
  for ever and for ever
  are clad in robes of white.

4 O sweet and blessed country,
  the home of God's elect!
  O sweet and blessed country
  that eager hearts expect!
  Jesus, in mercy bring us
  to that dear land of rest;
  who art, with God the Father
  and Spirit, ever blest.

St Bernard of Cluny (12th century),
tr. J. M. Neale (1818–66)

992

1. I rejoiced when I heard them say: 'Let us
2. Like a temple of u - ni - ty is the
3. It is faith - ful to Is - rael's law, there to
4. For the peace of all na - tions, pray: for God's
5. For the love of my friends and kin I will

go to the house of God.' And now our feet are
cit - y, Je - ru - sa - lem. It is there all tribes will
praise the name of God. All the judge- ment seats of
peace with - in your homes. May God's last - ing peace sur -
bless you with signs of peace. For the love of God's own

stand-ing in your gates, O Je - ru - sa - lem! Sha - lom, sha- lom, the
gath - er, all the tribes of the house of God.
Da - vid were set down in Je - ru - sa - lem.
round us; may it dwell in Je - ru - sa - lem.
peo - ple I will la - bour and pray for you.

peace of God be here. Sha- lom, sha- lom, God's jus- tice be ev - er near.

Bernadette Farrell, from Psalm 122

993

Ho-ly Ci-ty, new Je-ru-sa-lem, heaven's bright-ness to us bring.

By the shi-ning of his glo-ry, light the com-ing of our King!

1. Sure-ly shel-ter-ing God's peo-ple, Mo-ther Church, you watch and pray,
2. And I saw a new cre-a-tion (for the first had passed from sight)

feed-ing us with heaven's grac-es: now look up to see God's Day.
and the sea of tears and mourn-ing driv-en back be-fore God's might.

3 And I heard a Voice declaring,
   'Soon I come to be with you:
   soon to dwell with all my people,
   I, the Lord, make all things new!'

4 Bride in beauty for your Husband,
   waiting long till he appear:
   ready coming with your children,
   run to greet the Voice you hear!
            Mark Woodruff

I am with you always

Stephen Dean

994

REFRAIN

May you walk with Christ be-side you, Saints and an-gels share your

way. May the Ho-ly Spi-rit guide you to the dawn of end-less day.

Verses

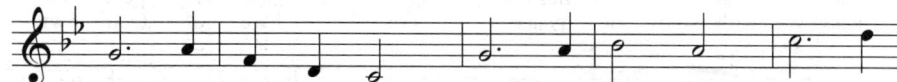

1. Peace in hearth and home, peace sur-round you; peace of
2. Light to bless your eyes, light to lead you, light of

Christ our God in hearts of those a-round you.
Christ to shine and on your jour-ney speed you.

3 Christ to hold and heal,
   Christ to welcome,
   Christ to bring the wanderer
   home to fold and shelter.

4 Three to guard and shield,
   Three unsleeping
   Father, Son and Spirit,
   rest you in their keeping.

995

There is a time for pray-ing,_____ and a
place in our hearts for e-v'ry-one.

Sing in four part canon.

Julie McCann

996

Stand,__ O__ stand firm; stand,__ O__stand firm; stand,__O__
stand firm and see what the Lord can do. *O my sis-ters, stand ve-ry firm!*

O my brothers, stand very firm..   All you elders, stand very firm..

All you children, stand very firm..   Let God's people stand very firm..

From Cameroon

997

Cantor (1My sisters,)   (my sisters,)   (my sisters,)

Joyfully   Bless the Lord,   bless the Lord,

(2. My brothers),

bless the Lord: there is no o - ther God.

My sisters...   You children..   Together..

My brothers..   You elders..   *From Kenya (source unknown)*

998

Go out to the whole world; pro-claim the Good News.—
Al – le – lu – ia, al – le – lu – ia.—

Mark 16:15. Music: Bill Tamblyn

999

Ba ba ba ba bam, ba ba ba ba bam. ba ba ba ba bam ba ba ba bam ba ba ba ba

Last time

A – me – ni, a – me – ni, a – men, a-men, a-men, a – me – ni. men.

bam.

from South Africa, arranged by David Dargie

1000

Je-sus Christ, Je-sus Christ, yes-ter-day,— to-day and for – e-ver.

Suzanne Toolan, RSM

LET everything that lives and that breathes
give praise to the Lord. Alleluia!

Psalm 150:6

Acknowledgements

3   © James Quinn, S.J., administered by The Continuum International Publishing Group Ltd
4   Verses © The Grail; Music & refrain text: © 1998 S. Dean
5   Text and music © The Grail (England)
6   © James Quinn, S.J., administered by Continuum plc
7   Text: © The Grail. Music: © 1998 Stephen Dean
8   © 1992 G.I.A. Publications Inc.
9   © 1998 Stephen Dean
11, 29   Text: Bishops' Conference of England & Wales; Music: © 1998 Stephen Dean
12   Text: © 1987 Patrick Lee; Music: © 1988 Worth Abbey Music, Crawley, W. Sussex RH10 4SB
14   © Church Pension Fund, 445 Fifth Avenue, New York, NY 10016, USA
15   © 1983 Paul Inwood, published by OCP Publications
17   Text: © The Grail. Music: © 1994 Stephen Dean
18   © 1997 G.I.A. Publications, Inc.
19   Text: © The Grail. Music: © 1989 Stephen Dean
20   Music: © Margaret Daly-Denton
21   Text © 1989, National Council of Churches of Christ. Response, music: © Martin Foster. Verses: © Ampleforth Abbey Trustees
22   Text as no 21. Music: © Stephen Dean
23   Text & Music: © The Grail (England)
24   The Grail (England); Music: © Ampleforth Abbey Trustees
25   © 1986 Paul Inwood, published by OCP Publications
26   © 1989 Stephen Dean
27   © 1990 Stephen Dean
28   © 1991 Stephen Dean
29   see 11
30   Music: © Philip Duffy
32   © 1995 Saint Mary's Abbey, West Malling, Kent, ME19 6JX
33   Words: © The Grail (England); Music: © M. Daly-Denton
34   Words: © The Grail (England); Music: © M. Daly-Denton
35   Words: © The Grail (England); Music: © Stephen Dean
36   Words: © The Grail (England); Music: © StephenDean
37   Words: © Bishops' Conference of England & Wales. Music: © 1988 Stephen Dean
38   Words: © The Grail (England); Music: © 1988 S. Dean
39   © The Grail (England)
40   Words: © The Grail (England); Music: © 1985, 1992 P. Inwood
41   Words: © The Grail (England); Music: © 1985 P. Inwood
41   Words: © The Grail (England); Music: © 1987 S. Dean
42   © The Grail (England)
43   Text: The © Grail (England); Response 1: © Stephen Dean. Psalmtone: © Ampleforth Abbey Trustees. Second setting: © 1996 Peter Jones
44   Text: The Grail (England); Music: © 1987 S.Dean
45   Text: The Grail (England). Music: Resp. 1: © Anne Ward. Psalmtone: © Stephen Dean. Second setting: © 1984, 1992 Paul Inwood, published by OCP Publications
46   Words: © The Grail (England). Music: Response: © Francis Duffy. Psalmtone: © S. Dean.
47   Words, Response. 2 & Psalmtone 2: © The Grail. Response 1 & Psalmtone: © 1982 Irish Church Music Association (ICMA).
48   Words & Psalmtone: © The Grail (England). Responses 1 & 2: © Stephen Dean
49   © 1987 G.I.A. Publications, Inc.
50   Words: The Grail (England); Music: © 1987 Alan Smith
51   Words: The Grail (England); Music: Resp. 1 & Psalmtone: © 1972 Bill Tamblyn. Alt Psalmtone: © Stephen Dean. Response 2 and Psalmtone: Notre Dame
52   Words and Psalmtone 2: © The Grail (England); Music: Resp. 1 & Psalmtone: © ICMA. Response 2: © Stephen Dean.
53   Words: The Grail (England); Music: © 1993 S. Dean.
54   Words: © The Grail (England); Music: © ICMA
55   Words: © The Grail; Music: Resp. 1 & Psalmtone: © S. Dean.

Setting 2: © Bob Hurd, published by OCP Publications
55   © 1988 Bob Hurd, published by OCP Publications
56   Words: © The Grail (England); Music: © ICMA
57   Words: © The Grail (England); Music: © S. Dean
58   Words: © The Grail (England); Music: © 1981 P. Inwood
59   Words: © The Grail (England); Music: © ICMA
60   Words and music © 1959 The Grail (England)
61   Words and music © 1959 The Grail (England)
62   Words and music © 1989 G.I.A. Publications, Inc.
63   Words: © The Grail (England). Resp. 1 & Psalm: © McCrimmon Publishing Co. Ltd. Resp. 2 & Psalm: © S. Dean
64   © 1987 B. Farrell, published by OCP Publications
65   © 1988 John Schiavone, published by OCP Publications
66   © 1991 G.I.A. Publications Inc.
67   © 1994 Stephen Dean
68   © 1994 Ken Simmons
69   © 1988 G.I.A. Publications, Inc.
70   © 1994 Stephen Dean
71   © 1978 Christopher Walker
72   © 1988, 1989, 1990 C. Walker, published by OCP Pubs.
73   © 1996 C. Walker, published by OCP Publications
74   © 1991 G.I.A. Publications Inc
75/6 © 1991 G.I.A. Publications Inc
77   © 1991 G.I.A. Publications Inc
78   © 1982 B. Farrell, published by OCP Publications.
79   © 1995 Stephen Dean
80   © 1986 G.I.A. Publications, Inc
81   © 1982 B. Farrell, published by OCP Publications
82   © 1990, 1991 Peter McGrail
83   © 1993 Owen Alstott, published by OCP Publications
84   © 1976 Kevin Mayhew Ltd, from Hymns Old & New
85   © Revd. Herbert O'Driscoll, Christ Church, 3602 8th Street, Calgary, Alberta T2T 3A7 Canada
87   © 1959 The Order of St Benedict, Inc. Collegeville, MN 56321
88   © 1984 Ateliers et Presses de Taizé
89   © 1987 Wild Goose Resource Group
90   © Christopher Idle/Jubilate Hymns
93   © 1992 Wild Goose Resource Group
95   translation: © McCrimmon Publishing Co Ltd
96   © 1981, 1982 Michael Joncas. Published by Cooperative Ministries, Inc. Exclusive agent: OCP Pubs
97   © Panel on Worship of the Church of Scotland
98   © 1984 S. Dean, published by OCP Publications
99   © Chrysogonus Waddell, O.C.S.O., Gethsemani Abbey, Trappist, Kentucky 40073
101   © Willard F. Jabusch, exclusive agent OCP Pubs.
103   © Roger Ruston
104   Words: © Mrs B. Perry/Jubilate Hymns. Music: © Hymns Ancient & Modern Ltd
107   Words © Willard F. Jabusch, exclusive agent OCP Pubs.
108   Words © McCrimmon Publishing Co Ltd
111   © 1982 G.I.A. Publications, Inc
114   Words © Mrs B. Perry/Jubilate Hymns
116   Words © Stainer & Bell Ltd.
118   Verse text © 1996 Bob Hurd, published by OCP Pubs.
119   © 1996 Bob Hurd, published by OCP Publications
120   Words © Paul Inwood
121   © 1983 G.I.A. Publications, Inc
122   © 1980 S.Dean, published by OCP Publications
123   © 1982 Bernadette Farrell, published by OCP Pubs.
124   © 1989 Wild Goose Resource Group
125   © 1980 I.C.E.L., Inc. From A Resource Collection of hymns and music for the liturgy
126   © Faber Music Ltd, from the New Catholic Hymnal
132   © 1927 Frederick Harris Music Co. Ltd.Unit 1, 5865 McLaughlin Road, Chris Luce, Mississauga, Ontario, Canada L5R 1B8
134   © Oxford University Press

138 Words from *The Kingsway Carol Book* published by Evans Bros. London
142 © Mrs B. Perry/Jubilate Hymns
143 © 1987 Wild Goose Resource Group
146 © James Quinn S.J., administered by Continuum
147 © 1994 S. Dean, published by OCP Publications
148 © 1987 G.I.A. Publications, Inc.
149 Words © 1984, 1993 Christopher Walker, published by OCP Publications
152 © A.R. Mowbray & Co. Ltd, a division of Continuum
153 © Society for the Promotion of Christian Knowledge
157 © 1983 G.I.A Publications, Inc.
158 © 1967 Gooi en Sticht, bv. Exclusive agent for English-language countries: OCP Publications
161 © 1976 Joint Board of Christian Education and Youth, 2nd floor, 10 Queen St, Melbourne, Victoria 3000, Australia
162 © 1934 G. Schirmer Inc., by permission of Music Sales Ltd, 8-9 Frith Street, London W1V 5TZ
163 Text © 1984 Brian Moore. Music © 1984 Christopher Willcock. Published by OCP Publications
165 © 1989 Wild Goose Resource Group
171 © Stanbrook Abbey
173 © 1979, 1982 Timothy Dudley-Smith
176 Text: *A Liturgical Psalter: A text for study and comment* © 1994 ICEL. Music © 1995 P. McGrail
177 Words © 1992 G.I.A. Publications Inc
179 © 1994 G.I.A. Publications, Inc.
180 © 1996 Bob Hurd, published by OCP Publications
181 © 1996 Bob Hurd, published by OCP Publications
182 © World Library Publications, Inc.
183 © 1993 G.I.A. Publications, Inc
184 © James Walsh
185 © Martin Foster
186 © Chris O'Hara & McCrimmon Publishing Co Ltd
187 © Stephen Dean
188-90 ©1982, 1983, 1993 The Sisters of St Benedict, S Joseph, MN. Published by OCP Publications
191 © 1996 Stephen Dean
192 © 1986 G.I.A. Publications, Inc
193 © 1990, 1991 G.I.A. Publications, Inc
194 © 1986 Stephen Dean, administered by OCP
195 © 1988, 1989 Christopher Walker, published by OCP Pubs.
196 ©1980 ICEL, Inc. From *A Resource Collection of Hymns and Service Music for the Liturgy*
197 English text by Owen Alstott © 1973 OCP Publications
198 © 1978 New Dawn Music
199 © Peter J.Scagnelli
200 © 1986 B. Farrell, published by OCP Publications
201 © 1996 Wild Goose Resource Group
202 © 1980 ICEL, Inc. From *A Resource Collection of hymns and music for the liturgy*
203 © 1984 Kevin Mayhew Ltd, from Hymns Old & New.
207 © 1993 Wild Goose Resource Group
208 © 1989 G.I.A. Publications, Inc
209 © Hymns Ancient & Modern
210 © 1976 NALR
211 © 1980 ICEL, Inc. From *A Resource Collection of hymns and music for the liturgy*
213 © 1982 G.I.A. Publications Inc
214 © 1988 Bob Hurd, published by OCP Publications
215 Text and music: © 1987 American Catholic Press, 16160 South Seton Drive, South Holland, IL 60473, USA
217 © 1980 Robert C. Trupia. Published by OCP Pubs.
218 © 1987 G.I.A. Publications Inc.
219 Refrain: © Charles Watson, O.S.B./Abbey of Tamie Verses:The Grail Music: Abbey of Tamié, by permission of SEFIM
220 © 1965, 1966, 1968, 1973 World Library Publications
221 © 1987 Wild Goose Resource Group
222 © 1991 Ateliers et Presses de Taizé
224 © 1995 Suzanne Toolan, R.S.M. published by OCP Pubs.
227 © Ateliers et Presses de Taizé
228 © 1988 Christopher Walker, published by OCP Pubs.

231 © 1992 Stephen Dean
232 © Oxford University Press
233 © 1984 Ateliers et Presses de Taizé
234 © 1993 S. Dean, published by OCP Publications
235 © 1994 P. Jones, administered by OCP Publications
236 © Faber Music Ltd
237 © Burns & Oates Ltd., a division of Continuum
238 © 1992 John Ainslie
240 © 1989 John Schiavone, published by OCP Publications
241 © 1982 Hope Publishing Co., administered by Copycare
242 © James Quinn, S.J., administered by Cassells plc
243 © McCrimmon Publishing Co. Ltd
245 © 1979 Ateliers et Presses de Taizé
248 © 1974 Stainer & Bell Ltd.
249 © Ateliers et Presses de Taizé
251 © 1992 P. Jones, published by OCP Publications
253 © Ateliers et Presses de Taizé
254 Music © 1992 Stephen Dean
255 © Oxford University Press, taken from *The English Hymnal*
256 © 1992 S.Dean, administered by OCP Publications
257 © 1981, 1982 Michael Joncas. Published by Cooperative Ministries, Inc. Exclusive agent: OCP Pubs.
258 Verses: © The Grail (England). Refrain text and music © 1990 Bernadette Farrell, published by OCP Publications
259 © James Quinn, S.J., administered by Continuum
260 English text © Peter J. Scagnelli
262 © 1988, 1990 Bernadette Farrell, published by OCP Pubs.
263 © 1989 S.Dean, published by OCP Publications
265 © Ateliers et Presses de Taizé
266 © 1984 Ateliers et Presses de Taizé
268 © 1973 The Word of God. Administered by CopyCare
270 © 1978 Pamela Stotter
271 © Burns & Oates Ltd., a division of Continuum
272 © 1969, 1995 Stainer & Bell Ltd.
274 © 1988 Wild Goose Resource Group
276 © Willard F. Jabusch, published by OCP Pubs.
277 © James Quinn, S.J., administered by Cassells plc
278 © Oxford University Press, taken from *The Oxford Book of Carols*
281 © 1986 G.I.A. Publications, Inc.
282 © 1975 Robert J. Dufford, S.J. & New Dawn Music
284 Melody © 1984 G.I.A. Publications, Inc
285 © 1989 G.I.A. Publications, Inc.
286 © A.R. Mowbray & Co. Ltd, a division of Continuum
287 Words © World Student Christian Federation, 5 Route des Morillons, 1218 Grand-Saconex, Geneva, Switzerland
288 Words © 1995 G.I.A.Publications, Inc.
289 © James Quinn, S.J., administered by Continuum
292 © Burns & Oates Ltd., a division of Continuum
293 © 1974, 1993 Sisters of St Mary of Namur
294 © 1982 James Walsh. Published by OCP Publications
295 Words © 1977, 1978 Michael Shaw & Paul Inwood. Music: © 1977 Paul Inwood. Published by OCP Publications
298 © Ateliers et Presses de Taizé
299 Melody: © 1984, 1985 C. Walker, published by OCP Publs.
304 © 1995 Wild Goose Resource Group
305 © 1988 Wild Goose Resource Group
306 © 1963 Birdwing Music/Universal Songs. Administered by CopyCare
307 © 1982 Christopher Walker, published by OCP Pubs.
308 Words © 1967 Gooi en Sticht, bv. Exclusive agent for English-language countries: OCP Publications
309 © Bernadette Farrell, published by OCP Publications
310 Words: © 1968 Timothy Dudley-Smith. Melody: © 1985, 1988 G.I.A. Publications, Inc
311 © Faber Music Ltd. From the *New Catholic Hymnal*
313 © Christian Conference of Asia
314 © James Quinn, S.J., administered by Continuum
317 Chevalier Press, P.O. Box 13, Kensington, New South Wales 2033, Australia
317 © Oxford University Press
318 © James Quinn, S.J., administered by Continuum
319 © Burns & Oates Ltd., a division of Continuum

Choosing Music for the Liturgy

Singing is at the heart of all worship. It is a gift of God, a part of being human, a natural response to an impulse of joy, gratitude or grief. It is a vital part of the proper celebration of Mass.

Music in liturgy must fulfill certain conditions. It must allow the community to express the praise, thanksgiving and repentance that we owe to God. To do this, it must form a bond of unity between the people taking part, so that they can sing with one heart and voice.

The Christian message is always the same, but there is a variety of seasons and rites in the liturgy so it is always heard in a different way. In every liturgy there are parts that never vary and others that change from week to week. The invariable parts of the Mass, especially the acclamations of the Eucharistic Prayer, should provide a strong framework for the assembly's prayer week by week, while the choice of variable pieces - hymns and songs - should be guided by the scripture of the day, especially the Gospel. The task of choosing the music is a service to the community, giving people words in which to express the faith of the Church. It should be done with great consideration to the people of that particular community.

By singing hymns we express sentiments such as love for other people and love for God and commit ourselves to meaning them. Both those who choose the hymns and those who sing them must strive to make their lives conform to the words they utter.

LAUDATE is arranged in liturgical order. However, the categories cannot reflect all the possible ways the hymns can be used. The following pages offer some help in finding suitable hymns for the seasons of the year, using the whole book.

Choosing Hymns for the Liturgical Year

Advent 64-117

Sunday 1: Day of the Lord: esp. 81-92, 109. ➤ *Also* The Lord's coming (982-989); I rejoiced (992)
Sunday 2: John the Baptist cries in the desert. See especially 83, 92, 94, 96, 97, 108
Sunday 3: John the Baptist foretells Jesus. See especially 96-108. 'Gaudete' Sunday: 851
Sunday 4: 'O' antiphons (111-112); hymns 113-117; ➤ *Also* Our Lady (Annunciation, 330-334; The Magnificat: 23-25, 335-340, 880)

Christmas seasonal music 118-123
➤Also: Lamb of God, with Christmas verses: 590

Christmas hymns 124-164
➤ Word of God (Christmas Day, 2nd Sunday): 85, 158, 160, 161, 738-742
➤The Holy Family: 131, 143. 144, 147-149; Into one we all are gathered (243), Sing of Mary (341), God's Holy Family (834); Like a child rests (453); Sections: Love of God in us (906-927, esp. 923) Psalm: 58, 409

New Year, Epiphany 165-170
Baptism of the Lord 171-173 ➤ *See also Advent section*
Candlemas 174-178
Ordinary Time before Lent
➤ Sunday 2 always uses the Gospel of John. Yrs A, B: Behold the Lamb of God (98, 598). Year C tells of the marriage feast of Cana: use songs about the Banquet (613-635).

From then on the Calling of the Disciples (Sundays 3A, 3B) and Jesus's first preaching of the Kingdom are the subject of the Gospels. See sections: Jesus ministering (738-47); Kingdom (814-821); Justice and Peace (887-904); Sending out/Discipleship.Commitment (852-875, esp. 871).

In *Year A,* the Year of Matthew, the Sermon on the Mount dominates the season (Sundays 4-7). Settings of the Beatitudes (read on Sunday 4) are: 370, 814-816, 615 (for Communion)

In *Year B* Sundays 4-6 Jesus's miracles are proclaimed; see the section on Healing (427-437)

In *Year C* Sunday 3: Jesus Word of God, Ps 18 (19); Sunday 5: 'Holy, Holy'; Sunday 6: the Beatitudes; Sunday 7: see sections: Love of God in us (906-927), God's love and mercy (774-813)

Lent   179-226

➤ *See also* Forgiveness/Penance/Reconciliation (838-851); God's love and mercy (774-813); Petition (928-941); Trust etc (947-74) For the RCIA: nos 391-395. Even if the Scrutinies are not celebrated in your parish, every Christian should pray for all in the Church preparing for baptism.

For each Sunday there is a Gospel Response (188-190) which could be sung straight after the gospel or at the Prep. of Gifts. Consult the Psalms index (p.409) to see if the Lectionary psalm for the day is there. A second setting of the day's psalm could be sung, for instance, at Communion.

➤ **Ash Wednesday**: Psalm 50(51), no 48 (also for Sunday 1A.) For the Ashes rite: Come back to the Lord (193), Turn to me (786). The sections God's love and mercy (774-813) and Forgiveness, penance, reconciliation (838-851) should be consulted.

➤ **Sunday 1**: Psalm for year A 50(51)no 48; year B 24(25) no 43; Year C 90 (91) no 51. In choosing hymns, look for those referring to Christ's temptation, or the desert (e.g. 201, 315, 964).

➤ **Sunday 2:** Transfiguration (208-209); Christ is the world's Light (744); Be thou my vision (969)

➤ **Year A,** Sunday 3: Thirst (203, settings of Ps 41/42: 213-5, 219, 450). Covenant: 664
Sunday 4: He healed the darkness (435). Psalm 22 (23) as Communion Song: 42, 757
Sunday 5: Out of the depths (see Psalm Index, p.409). Deep within (218); Grant to us (220).

➤ **Year B,** Sunday 3: Psalm 18(19); Not on bread alone (191).
Sunday 4: The waters of Babylon (216); Awake, awake (851). See also Jesus suffering (748-57)
Sunday 5: Unless a grain (748); Deep within (218); Grant to us (220); Jesus suffering (748-57)

➤ **Year C,** Sunday 3: Ps 102(103) - see Psalm index (p.409); also God's love and mercy (774-813)
Sunday 4: The Prodigal Son. Our Father we have wandered (211); Praise we our God with joy (784); God forgave my sin (849). Communion song: Taste and see (617-8).
Sunday 5: See section Forgiveness/Penance (838-851).

Palm Sunday:

➤ See Lent section (nos. 227-237); Jesus Suffering (748-757).

The Paschal Triduum 227-253

The Three Days (Maundy Thursday evening to Easter evening) are the centre of the Church's year, when the death and resurrection of the Lord are made present and all Christians relive their symbolic dying and rising in baptism. LAUDATE contains a basic repertoire of music for the three days.

Maundy Thursday

➤ See nos. 238-249. No 238 is an entry hymn for the whole Triduum. For the Washing of Feet and the Procession of Gifts, see also: Love of others (906-927), esp. 920, 921, 927. Psalm: 55, setting 2. Eucharist: Communion songs (613-651) esp. 613, 616, 628, 638; also no. 833.

Good Friday
See nos 250-253. Also: When I survey (756), Praise to the holiest (788).

Easter Vigil
Psalms for Liturgy of the Word: 1st: nos. 299 or 45. 2nd: no.40. 3rd: no.254. 5th: no 692. 7th: no 48 or a version of Ps 41(42): nos. 47, 213-5, 219.

Baptismal liturgy: see nos 396-408; also 369 (Litany), 517-519; Out of darkness (835).

Easter Day
From the Easter section these are particularly suitable: 255-257; 260, 267, 265-66, 269.

Eastertide   254-288
➤ *See also* Jesus in glory (758-773); Christ the King (319-327)

➤ **Sunday 2,** all years: Versions of Ps 117(118). The doubting Thomas story: We walk by faith (284); O sons and daughters (264, 280)

➤ **Sunday 3,** Year A: The Emmaus Road. Nos 263, 288; also Communion Processional songs, especially 624, 634.

Year B: the end of the Emmaus story; meeting Jesus in the breaking of bread.

Year C: Meeting Jesus in a meal: see Communion sections. The Gospel also emphasises Jesus's command 'Feed my sheep', see Sending Out section (852-879), esp. 852, 871, 878-9

➤ **Sunday 4,** 'Good Shepherd' Sunday. Year A: see versions of Ps 22(23) p.409. Look in sections God's love and mercy (774-813); Trust/Hope Guidance (947-973)

Year B: Psalm 117(118) esp. no 258, and as last year

Year C: Psalm 99(100) esp. no 53, and as other years

➤ **Sunday 5,** Year A: Way Truth and Life. Jesus you are Lord (766), and section Trust/Hope/ Guidance (947-973), especially Nada te turbe (947).

Year B: The Vine. Shepherd of souls (665); Unless a grain (748)

Year C: Love of others. See section Love of God in us (906-917) esp. 920

➤ **Sunday 6,** Year A: Love of God (906-917); God's love and mercy (774-813)

Year B: as above, and also: Unless a grain (748); This is my will (921)

Year C: as above, A & B.. See also This is my body (627).

Ascension   289-294
➤ *see also* Jesus in Glory (758-73); Christ the King

➤ **Sunday 7:** A 'between' Sunday, both post - Ascension, see sections listed above, also nos.290, 293, 644; and pre-Pentecost, 304, 627. Year A has psalm 26(27), see Psalm Index (p.409).

Pentecost   295-311
The day of Pentecost is the end of the Fifty Days of Eastertide. No.299 is today's Psalm, and 294 may be used as the Gospel acclamation.

Trinity Sunday   312-317
➤ Many hymns are Trinitarian in structure (e.g. 887, 315). God beyond all names (686) is an expression of the mystery of God and the limitations of all words and titles applied to God.

Corpus Christi   318
➤ *see also* Communion sections (613-651). If it occurs on a weekday (like the Ascension) possibilities may be limited by the number of people present, so use music which is well-known.

	Year A	Year B	Year C
9	*A house built on rock.* Love Divine; Trust/hope /guidance	*Master of the Sabbath.* Gathering, Praise. 464, 765, 992	*Faith of a foreigner* Ps 116 (117) Praise. 698, 700, 852
10	*Not the virtuous, but sinners* Sending out; Forgiveness	*The end of Satan.* Psalm 129(130) Forgiveness etc. Kingdom. 201, 834	*The widow's daughter raised to life* Jesus ministering; Healing
11	*We belong to him.* Psalm 99(100) Sending out. 743, 825, 852	*The Kingdom is like a seed.* God the creator. Kingsom. 2r: 906	*Your sins are forgiven* Forgiveness etc. Petition 221, 632, 844
12	*Be not afraid.* Sending out. 794, 883, 894	*Calming the Sea.* Love of God in us; Trust/Hope. 745, 934/58/63/66	*You are the Christ.* Ps 62(63) Trust/hope; Jesus suffering. 679, 962
13	*Welcoming the Lord's disciples.* Sending out. 743; 400 (2nd R.)	*Restored to life.* Jesus' ministry; Healing; Praise. 427, 431, 433	*Following Christ.* Ps 15(16) Sending out. Kingdom. 824, 877
14	*Gentle and humble of heart.* Love divine; Sending out; Trust etc.	*Our eyes are on the Lord.* Praise; Trust/Hope; Love divine 854, 969	*Rejoice in the Lord.* As last week; also Justice/Peace. 828, 856 2R:756
15	*Word, seed, harvest.* Harvest. 637, 737, 748, 887. 1R: 203/612	*Go; prophesy.* Psalm 84(85) Sending out. 851, 858, 870,871	*Who is my neighbour?* Ps 18(19) Love of God in us/Love of others 609, 831
16	*Slow to Anger.* Psalm 102(103) Forgiveness. Harvest. Kingdom. 821/54	*Sheep without a shepherd.* Ps 22(23) Love divine. Word of God. 975,976	*God among us* Trust/Hope; Love of God in us; Petition 650, 912, 941
17	*The real treasure.* Trust/hope/guidance. 821/48, 969/78	17-21. JOHN 6: the eucharistic Gospel. Ps 144(5). Gathering; Love Div.; Comm.	*Ask and you shall receive* Ps 137(138) Petition; Trust/hope/guidance 61, 313
18	*A God who feeds us.* 1R: 203/612 Communion sections. 477, 684, 692	*I am the bread of life.* Trust/hope/guidance. 203, 629/40, 960	*Look for the things of heaven* Ps 94(95) Trust/hope etc; Love of God in us 737, 811
19	*Calming the sea.* 745, 934, 963/6 Love of God in us/Trust. hope etc.	*Taste and see.* Ps 33(34) Communion 473, 615, 636, 748	*Stay awake.* Ps 32(33) Sending out; Church; Gathering 469,855
20	*God loves all peoples.* Praise; Gathering; Sending out. 857	*My flesh is real food.* Versions of Ps 115(116) 664,748	*Fire on the earth* Kingdom; Church; Sending out 828, 884, 972
21	*On this rock...* 284, 958 Kingdom; Trust/hope; Love divine	*Lord, to whom shall we go?* Hope/trust/guidance 41, 928	*Gathering the people* Ps 116(117) Kingdom; Church; Gathering 458,775,831
22	*If you would follow me...* Ps 62(63) Jesus suffering; Love of God 222,727	*God's word in your heart.* 195, 370 Word of God in Scripture. Just/Peace.	*The banquet* Communion; Gathering 623, 632
23	*Helping, forgiving each other* Ps 94(95) Jus/Peace; Forgiveness; Love of God 827	*The deaf hear, the dumb speak.* 471, Healing; Jesus' ministry; Kingdom 821	*God's mysterious ways* Sending out; Hope/trust 743,877,916,955
24	*Slow to anger, rich in mercy.* Ps 102(3) Jus/Peace; Love of God in us; 621, 810	*You are the Christ.* Ps115(116) Trust/hope. Jesus suffering. 679, 962	*The Prodigal Son.* cf Lent 4C. Forgiveness. 211, 646, 672
25	*God's Ways.* Ps 144(145) Harvest, Praise, Thanksgiving. 203, 612	*Be the servant of all.* Love of God in us/L. of others 743, 924	*You cannot serve two masters* Justice & Peace. 625; 883,891/2/4
26	*The path to those who stray.* Ps 24(25) Forgiveness etc. 843, 124. 2nd R: 754/5	*For Jesus or against him?* Ps18(19) Sending out. Forgiveness. 41, 926	*The Lord loves the just* Justice & Peace. 688, 882, 883, 890
27	*The Vineyard of the Lord.* Jesus Suffering/risen. 22, 222, 734, 852	*God's holy family.* Ps127(128) Marriage; love of God in us 834, 923	*Increase our faith.* Ps 94(95) Petition; Trust/Hope 284, 708
28	*The Wedding Feast.* Ps 22(23) Gathering.Communion. 475, 623, 830	*Wisdom to know what is God's* Gathering, Kingdom, Healing 435, 955	*The Ten Lepers.* Healing; Thanksgiving; Praise 713, 745, 945
29	*No other God beside me.* Praise. 857; 882	*The Son of God came to give his life.* Ps 32(33). Jesus suffering; Lent; Praise	*Never lose heart.* Trust; Petition. 892, 930, 995
30	*The greatest commandment.* 811,882 Love divine; Love of God in us; Just/P	*Your faith has healed you.* Ps125(126) Healing; Jesus' ministry. 475	*The Pharisee and the Publican.* Petition; Forgiveness. 882,892
31	*Being a servant.* Ps 130(131) Love of God in us. 908, 924	*Love of God, our strength.* Trust/hope/guidance; Love of God in us	*Zacchaeus.* Ps 144(145) Forgiveness; Love of God; Sending out
32	*Watch and Wait.* Ps 62(63) Advent; Coming of the Lord. 88, 839	*The welcoming community.* Gathering. Justice and peace. 625	*The Resurrection* Jesus in glory; Heaven; Easter 748, 761,990
33	*Well done, faithful servant* Ps 127(128) Coming of the Lord. 600, 896	*The day of the Lord.* Advent. The Lord's coming. 985, 990	*The Lord comes to rule* The Lord's coming; Advent. 475,985, 90
Christ the King	Jesus's paschal mystery; Justice & Peace; Praise	*The King of All* 89, 327, 857, 942, 998	*A Suffering King.* Jesus suffering. Jesus in glory. 253

Settings (complete or partial) of the psalm text in the Grail version are in **bold** type. The other settings listed are categorised thus: **PsS** indicates a verse/response song.   **H** is a hymn (metrical) version.   **A**: contains a slight allusion (e.g. one verse)

Index of First Lines